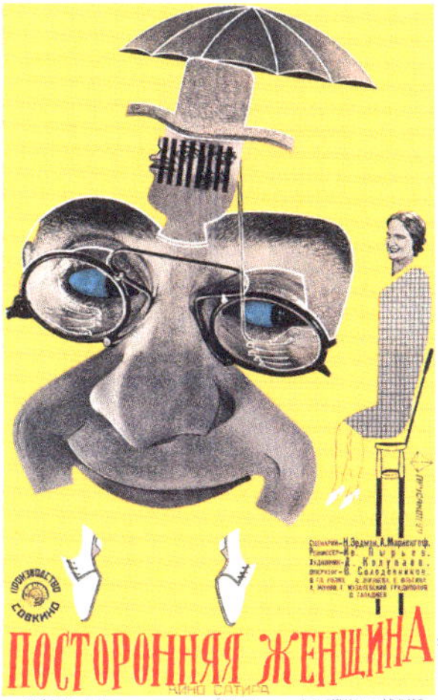

1929 · Anonymous · RU · Poster

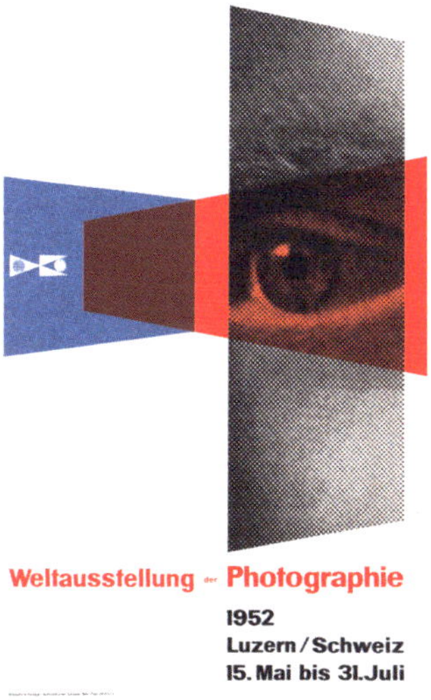

1952 · Ernst A. Heininger · CH · Poster

1930 · Willy Petzold · DE · Poster

1950 · Anonymous · UK · Poster

1938 · Paul Rand · US · Logo · Esquire magazine

2013 · Edel Rodriguez · CU/US · Magazine cover

1970 · Georges Beaupré · CA · Logo · National Film Board of Canada

1950 · Tom Eckersley · UK · Magazine cover

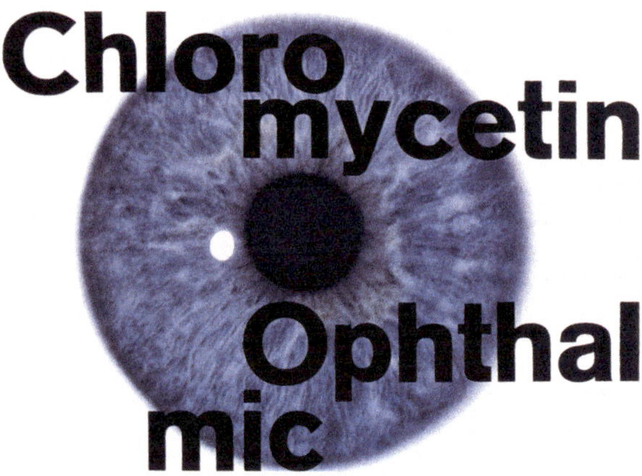

1960 · Michael Engelmann · DE/CH · Leaflet

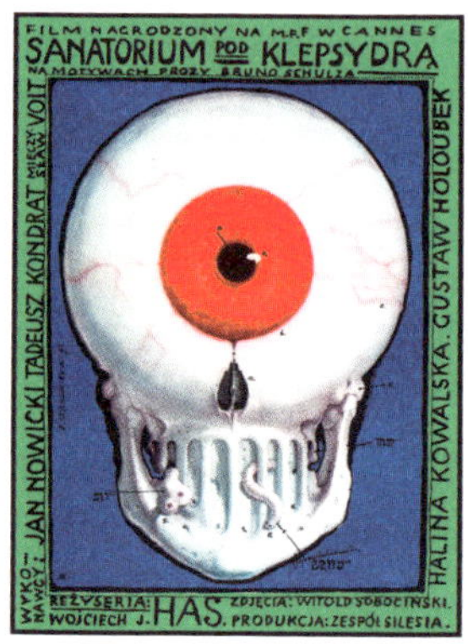

1973 · Franciszek Starowieyski · PL · Poster

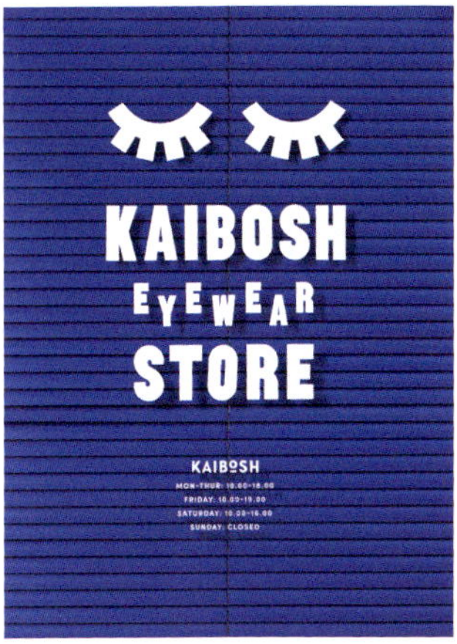

2016 · Snask · SE · Poster/Identity

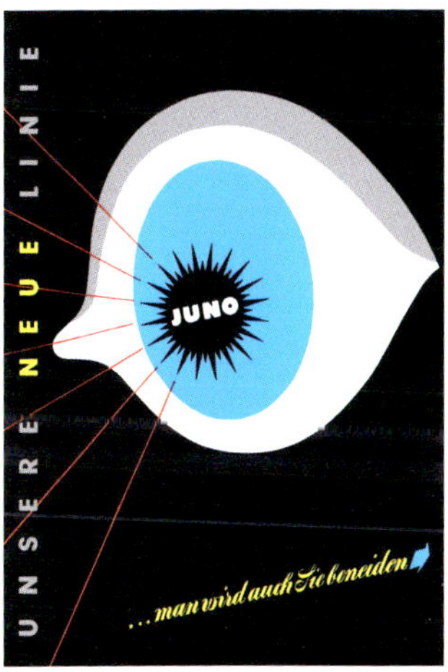

1950s · Heinz Schwabe · DE · Brochure cover

1968 · Tadahito Nadamoto · JP · Poster

1990 · Steff Geissbuhler · US · Logo · Time Warner Cable

1960 · Anonymous · US · Record cover

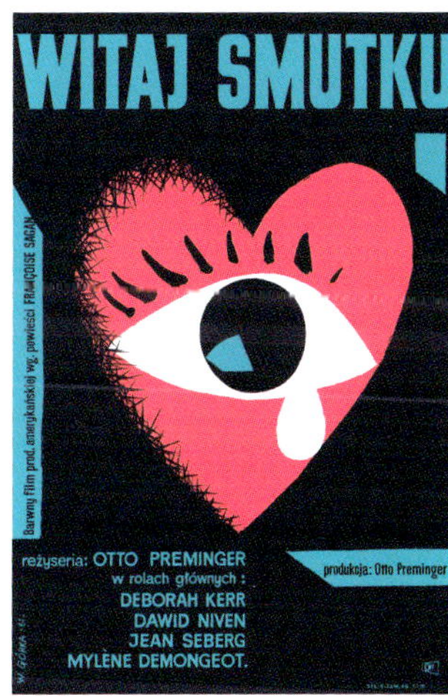

1961 · Wiktor Górka · PL · Poster

THE HISTORY OF

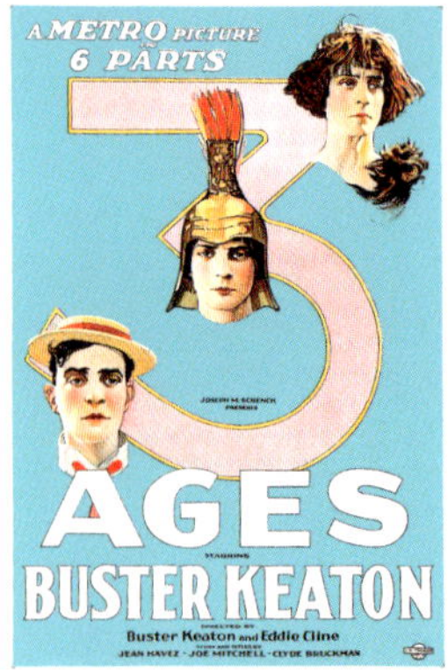

1923 · Anonymous · US · Poster

1900s · "Edw. A." · FR · Poster

1928 · Niklaus Stoecklin · CH · Poster

Jens Müller
Julius Wiedemann (Ed.)

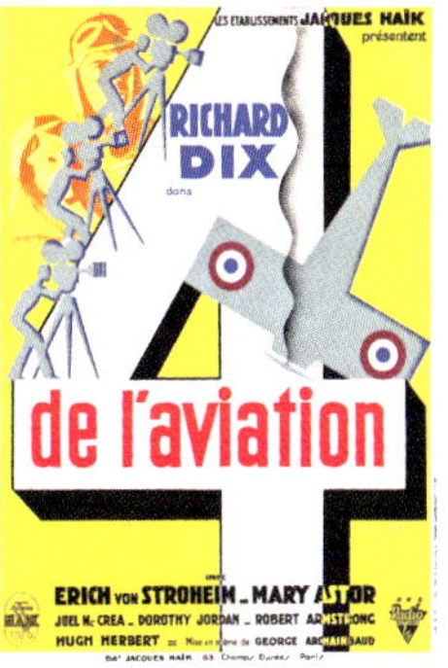

1932 · Abel Brunyer · FR · Poster

GRAPHIC DESIGN

1890—TODAY

TASCHEN

CONTENTS

1929 · Walter Dexel · DE · Poster

1938 · Gino Boccasile · IT · Poster

1952 · Richard Roth · DE · Poster

1954 · Kenji Itoh · JP · Poster

1957 · Hans Fabigan · AT · Poster

1925 · Anonymous · FR · Poster

VOL. 29 NO. 721 AUGUST 10 1895 PRICE 10 CENTS

Judge

ENTERED AT THE POST OFFICE AT NEW YORK AS SECOND CLASS MATTER. COPYRIGHT 1895 BY THE JUDGE PUBLISHING CO. TITLE REGISTERED AS A TRADE MARK

THE TROUBLE IN CUBA.

UNCLE SAM—"I've had my eye on that morsel for a long time; guess I'll have to take it in!"

1895 · Bernhard Gillam · US · Magazine cover

A VISUAL HISTORY

Introduction by Jens Müller

The roadside billboard advertising an event, the hotel booking app, the news magazine bought at the kiosk, the arrivals and departures boards at the airport, the traffic signs on the freeway—or even this book—are but a few specific examples of the countless millions of things that have had to be created. They all belong in the world of graphic design, which for the past 150 years or so has had a dramatic impact on the way our world looks. Of course, methods of communication had been around long before this, for instance, we only have to think of Johannes Gutenberg and the printing revolution he started in the 15th century, however, the customized marketing of products and services only came into being with the industrialization of graphic design.

The transition to the digital age once again increased the importance of visual communication. The worlds of business, science, culture, and politics could not function without professionally created design solutions, and the same is true of the public sector. Over the past 100 years, the range of available media formats has expanded considerably, and an even greater leap forward came with the breakthrough of digital media in the 1990s. Even so, the basics remained largely unchanged, whether the work of a graphic designer was to create an advertisement, such as a billboard, or a distinguishing mark, such as a logo. Other works might give directions, as in a signposting system, or provide information, as with an infographic, or again arrange texts and illustrations in proper order, such as for a magazine layout.

Whilst the basic functions of graphic design have not changed over the years, the actual designs themselves are in a state of constant development and alteration. The reason for this may simply be that, unlike a piece of architecture, many graphic works are designed to be used within a relatively short time frame. Like fashion, graphic design is constantly and instinctively redefining itself, always reassessing what looks up-to-the-minute and what seems outmoded. On the one hand, newly created forms, colors, or visual styles are a product of the prevailing zeitgeist, which in turn is a distillation of the influences of art, architecture, pop culture, and technology. On the other hand though, the look of graphic design is, to a significant extent, molded by social, economic, and political developments.

An example of this can be seen in the apparently uninspired designs from the early 1940s, which can only be correctly categorized if seen in the context of the Second World War. The same applies in different ways to the neutral, down-to-earth Swiss Style or the experimental graphics of the hippie era. All of these are inextricably linked to the place, time, and circumstances in which they were created, and the exciting correlation between design history and contemporary events will be a major focus of attention in this book. Each decade is introduced by a timeline, which presents a year-by-year selection of different historical events across the world. Here, the reader can also see an assortment of different types of packaging, logos, record sleeves, and election posters relating to specific moments in history. Over the years, many of these have become veritable icons, images which, in some cases, are more deeply ingrained in our memory than the events themselves.

The illustrated sections of the book can be interpreted from at least two different angles. The images themselves can be considered from a purely stylistic and design-historic point of view, and in this way the reader can discover various visual trends and counter-trends, recognize developments that lead to permanent changes in graphic design or identify the design tools used in the process, and, last but not least, appreciate the virtuosity of individual designers. However, each piece of work can also be seen as a historical document, a kind of relic of momentous events in human history. Cultural, political, economic, and technological landmarks are directly or indirectly referred to in many different kinds of visual material, from election posters through cover designs for novels, to the logo for a technology company. A look at 20th-century graphic design not only presents us with the aesthetic aspects of the developmental history of design but also offers us a particularly vivid picture of the economic, cultural, and social history of the recent past.

This book includes internationally recognized works, as well as several which have either largely been consigned to oblivion or are known only to experts in the field. The fact that award-winning posters and examples of poster art in museums appear alongside everyday graphic designs distributed in their millions is just one of the peculiarities of the profession, the nature of which has, from the very beginning, straddled the boundaries between art, commerce, craftsmanship, and service provision. Perhaps it is precisely the continuing and complex demands made on graphic design (which are the meat and drink of its practitioners) that account for why it has been harder for the profession to gain acceptance. Although practically all of us come into daily contact with graphic design, and many of us delight in the qualities of particular works, such as the opening credits of a TV series, comparatively few people beyond the confines of the design world know what the job actually entails.

Above all, public attention is most often drawn to graphic design when individual designers produce remarkable creations that stand out from the rest. This volume, which covers the years between 1890 and 2019, introduces more than 40 of these extraordinary people from all around the world who have made a particular impact across the various decades. As is the case with many other disciplines, certain ground rules have been established over time, and these affect individual designers as well as single works or groups of works. It would have been all too easy to tell the history of design, based solely on iconic images, but through an intensive analysis of historic publications and working with the cooperation of several international practitioners it has been possible to bring together a multitude of lesser-known works to give the reader a much broader appreciation. Despite the abundance of illustrations though, each one selected is no more than a snippet—yet large enough all the same to exemplify particular styles and show how they have developed.

The worldwide spread of graphic trends, whether passing crazes or lasting developments, is a phenomenon the literature on the subject has so far failed to tackle. All too often, the history of design has been approached in the same way as the history of aesthetics and treated as purely a history of style, with specific periods being strung together, usually according to geographic location. Those adopting this approach have generally omitted to mention that many developments in design have spread from their place of origin to the four corners of the Earth. There is plenty of evidence to show that one effect of this, which seems logical in the age of portfolio websites, design blogs, and social media, was already being felt in the early days of graphic design, with Bauhaus graphics being found in China, and Art Deco posters in Japan. By taking examples from different parts of the world and classifying them chronologically, this book provides an impressive overview of visual developments which transcend international boundaries.

Complex developments such as these were not always logical or consistent and sometimes caused conflicting ideas to appear simultaneously. One example is the chronological parallel between cool, understated avant-garde graphics in red and black and multicolored Art Deco with its luxurious and opulent visual vocabulary—this type of opposing development also reached a high point in the 1920s. Time after time, individual designers emerged with completely new ways of working, and in the process changed the very spirit of the age. Some designs, for example, modern, minimalist logos, proved to be so timeless that it's hard to gauge in retrospect exactly when they were created. Even so, apart from a few exceptions, every age has a look all its own, determined by technological possibilities as well as by the trends, use of color, photographic imagery, and typography prevalent at the time. If we compare works using similar motifs, this constantly changing aesthetic becomes particularly clear.

For students of architecture, music, and cinema, a knowledge of the past is an essential and relevant part of their education. After all, it is important to know what already exists and how new works can be based on that. However, looking back through design history is a lengthy business, and in fact it was not until the early 1970s that design history books began to appear which undertook a comprehensive examination of graphic works. By the 1980s, universities were beginning to establish the first design history departments and degree courses. In a profession where innovation has always counted most, it is noteworthy that for many years knowledge of the past was dismissed as somewhat irrelevant.

The most recent chapter of the graphic design story is not always easy to evaluate, often because a certain interval has to be allowed to pass before a fair or neutral assessment can be made of the relevance of a design's various aspects. At the same time, it would have been illogical to record the history of design up to any other point than the present. We invited about 150 design studios from around the globe—from one-person businesses to international organizations with large design teams—to submit their best and most relevant projects from recent years, an editing decision which on its own presented problems as regards how to preselect which studios to contact. Never before in history have so many designs been produced at the rate they are today, and even in countries without any long tradition in design, studios and single designers are busy creating huge numbers of top-quality works.

From the very beginnings of design history, graphic designers have taken decidedly different approaches. Even now, the profession embraces a huge spectrum of people working in their own way, from uncompromising avant-gardists to design contractors driven purely by commercial interests. In the course of history, members of both camps have been eager to innovate, as in the 1940s, for example, when leading U.S. publishers introduced state-of-the-art design to mass-market magazines, which in turn had an effect on periodicals put out by independent publishers. Then, in the 1970s, came an era of experimentation, set against the backdrop of the British punk scene, where new visual trends emerged which in their turn reappeared in far less radical and far more commercial contexts. Accordingly, this book examines works created for the mainstream culture industry just as much as solutions intended to target small audiences in different subcultures.

Alongside the commercially and culturally motivated fields of application, graphic design has time and again served as a driving force, giving a face to political and social issues and playing a role that should not be undervalued, especially so during turbulent times in world politics. However, the past has shown that visual communications can be used in the cause of both good and evil. The designer Helmut Schmid's claim that "design is attitude" and the statements in Ken Garland's famous *First Things First* manifesto, published in 1964, are no less important today than they were at the time when they first appeared. It is hard to predict the direction graphic design will take from here, in terms of both content and aesthetics. With intelligent software making massive progress in every type of computer application, individual creativity, inventiveness, and the exploration of visual possibilities are likely to gain ever-increasing importance. Looking back can be both invigorating and inspiring.

1925 · Werner Graul · DE · Magazine cover

1932 · Leonetto Cappiello · IT/FR · Poster

EINE VISUELLE GESCHICHTE

Einleitung von Jens Müller

Das Veranstaltungsplakat am Straßenrand, die App zur Hotelbuchung, das Nachrichtenmagazin am Kiosk, die Anzeigetafel am Flughafen, das Verkehrsschild an der Autobahn oder auch dieses Buch sind nur einige wenige Beispiele für Abermillionen gestalteter Dinge. Sie alle gehören in den Bereich des Grafikdesigns, das seit etwa 150 Jahren das Aussehen unserer Welt maßgeblich mitbestimmt. Zwar gab es auch schon lange vor diesem Zeitraum gestaltete Kommunikationsmedien – man denke nur an Johannes Gutenberg und seine Revolution des Buchdrucks im 15. Jahrhundert –, jedoch ließ erst die individualisierte Vermarktung von Produkten und Dienstleistungen im Zeitalter der Industrialisierung modernes Grafikdesign entstehen.

Der Übergang zum Informationszeitalter ließ die Bedeutung visueller Kommunikation noch einmal wachsen. Neben der kommerziellen Welt sind auch die Wissenschaft, die Kultur, die Politik und der öffentliche Raum nicht mehr ohne professionell gestaltete Lösungen denkbar. Die dazu genutzten Medienformate wurden in den vergangenen 100 Jahren immer weiter ergänzt – zuletzt ganz massiv nach dem Durchbruch digitaler Medien in den 1990er-Jahren. Die generelle Aufgabe blieb dabei jedoch im Wesentlichen unverändert. Arbeiten aus dem Bereich des Grafikdesigns können werbend (Veranstaltungsplakat), kennzeichnend (Logo), anleitend (Wegeleitsystem), vermittelnd (Infografik) oder ordnend (Magazinlayout) sein.

Permanenten Veränderungen ist vor allem die äußere Erscheinungsform unterworfen. Dies mag vielleicht besonders daran liegen, dass viele Arbeiten aus dem Bereich des Grafikdesigns – im Gegensatz etwa zur Architektur – für die Nutzung in einem verhältnismäßig kurzen Zeitraum entwickelt werden. Vergleichbar mit der Mode wird unbewusst und immerwährend neu definiert, was zeitgemäß ist und was aus der Zeit gefallen erscheint. Als aktuell empfundene Formen, Farben oder Bildstile ergeben sich zum einen aus dem gerade vorherrschenden Zeitgeist, der wiederum eine Essenz von Einflüssen aus Kunst, Architektur, Design, Popkultur und Technik ist. Zum anderen wird das Aussehen grafischer Arbeiten auch in hohem Maße durch gesellschaftliche, wirtschaftliche und politische Entwicklung geprägt.

Wenig innovative Arbeiten der frühen 1940er-Jahre können beispielsweise nur im Kontext des Zweiten Weltkriegs richtig eingeordnet werden, ebenso wie der sachlich-neutrale „Swiss Style" oder experimentelle Grafik aus der Zeit der Hippiebewegung: Sie alle sind untrennbar mit Ort, Zeit und Umständen ihres Entstehens verbunden. Der spannungsreichen Korrelation zwischen Zeit- und Designgeschichte wird in diesem Buch ein besonderes Augenmerk zuteil. Jede Dekade wird zunächst mit Timelines eingeleitet, die Jahr für Jahr eine Auswahl unterschiedlicher gesellschaftlicher Ereignisse aus aller Welt darstellen. Schon hier sind ausgewählte Verpackungen, Logos, Plattencover oder Wahlplakate zu sehen, die gewisse geschichtliche Begebenheiten visualisieren. Viele dieser Objekte sind über die Jahre zu regelrechten Ikonen geworden, die als Bilder in unserem Gedächtnis manchmal sogar stärker verwurzelt sind als die eigentlichen Ereignisse.

Die Lesart der Bildteile in diesem Buch lässt mindestens zwei Perspektiven zu: Man kann die gezeigten Exponate unter rein stilistischen und designhistorischen Aspekten betrachten. Hierbei lassen sich visuelle Trends und Gegentrends entdecken, nachhaltige Weiterentwicklungen erkennen, handwerkliche Mittel identifizieren, und nicht zuletzt zeigt sich natürlich auch individuelle Meisterschaft. Man kann jede Arbeit jedoch auch als Zeitzeugnis betrachten, als eine Art Relikt historischer Ereignisse der Menschheit. Kulturelle, politische, wirtschaftliche und technische Momente zeigen sich direkt oder indirekt in den zahlreichen verschiedenartigen visuellen Lösungen – vom Wahlplakat über den Coverentwurf eines Romans bis hin zum Branding eines Technologiekonzerns. Der Blick auf das Grafikdesign des 20. Jahrhunderts bietet also neben ästhetischen Aspekten zur Entwicklungsgeschichte von Gestaltung eine besonders anschauliche Wirtschafts-, Kultur- und Sozialgeschichte der jüngeren Vergangenheit.

Dieses Buch verknüpft weltweit bekannte Arbeiten mit in Vergessenheit geratenen oder nur in Fachkreisen bekannten Beispielen. Dass dabei prämierte und in Museen ausgestellte Plakatkunst neben millionenfach verbreiteter Alltagsgrafik gezeigt wird, gehört zu den Eigentümlichkeiten der Profession, die sich seit ihren Anfängen im Grenzbereich von Kunst, Kommerz, Handwerk und Dienstleistung bewegt. Vielleicht sind es diese bis heute sehr vielschichtigen Ansprüche an das Grafikdesign, die einerseits die Basis des Berufs bilden, gleichzeitig aber auch dessen Rezeption erschweren. Obwohl praktisch jeder Mensch ständig mit Arbeiten aus dem Bereich des Grafikdesigns in Berührung kommt und sich viele Menschen für die Qualitäten einzelner Arbeiten, etwa des Vorspanns einer Fernsehserie, begeistern können, ist die Kenntnis über das Metier außerhalb der Szene nicht besonders ausgeprägt.

Es sind vor allem einzelne Persönlichkeiten, die sich mit herausragenden Arbeiten aus der Masse hervorheben und die Öffentlichkeit immer wieder einmal auf das Grafikdesign aufmerksam machen. Der vorliegende Band, der sich mit den Jahren 1890 bis 2019 beschäftigt, stellt mehr als 40 dieser besonderen Persönlichkeiten aus aller Welt vor, die in unterschiedlichen Dekaden besonders wichtige Impulse lieferten. Wie in vielen anderen Disziplinen hat sich über die Jahre auch im Grafikdesign ein gewisser Kanon etabliert, der einzelne Personen, Arbeiten und Werkgruppen umfasst. Allzu einfach wäre es gewesen, die Designgeschichte ein weiteres Mal ausschließlich am Beispiel dieser Ikonen zu erzählen. Durch eine intensive Analyse historischer Publikationen und unter Mitwirkung von Praktikern und Theoretikern aus unterschiedlichen Teilen der Welt ist es gelungen, auch zahlreiche weniger bekannte Arbeiten zusammenzutragen, die eine breiter gefasste Wahrnehmung erlauben. Trotz der großen Menge an Abbildungen ist jede Auswahl naturgemäß nur ein Ausschnitt. Ein Ausschnitt, der jedoch groß genug ist, um Stile und Entwicklungen sichtbar werden zu lassen.

Die weltweite Verbreitung grafischer Strömungen – seien es kurzzeitige Trends oder nachhaltige Entwicklungen – ist ein Phänomen, das in der bisherigen Literatur zum Thema noch nicht ausreichend berücksichtigt worden ist. Allzu oft wurde Designgeschichte als reine Stilgeschichte nach dem Vorbild der Kunsttheorie erzählt, indem man einzelne, meist geografisch verortete Epochen aneinanderreihte. Bei dieser Betrachtung blieb unerwähnt, dass sich viele Designentwicklungen ausgehend von ihrem Entstehungsort weltweit ausbreiteten. Ein Effekt, der in Zeiten von Portfoliowebsites, Designblogs oder Social Media logisch erscheint, der sich jedoch auch schon in den Anfangstagen des Grafikdesigns vor über 100 Jahren nachweisen lässt – so gibt es Bauhaus-Grafik in China oder japanische Art-déco-Plakate. Die Berücksichtigung von Beispielen aus vielen verschiedenen Teilen der Welt gibt, im Zusammenspiel mit der chronologischen Sortierung, den Blick auf grenzüberschreitende visuelle Entwicklungen eindrucksvoll frei.

Diese komplexen Entwicklungen waren nicht immer logisch und stringent – manchmal brachten sie sogar zur gleichen Zeit gegensätzliche Konzepte hervor. Ein Beispiel ist die zeitliche Parallele von kühl reduzierter Avantgarde-Grafik in Rot und Schwarz und dem farbenfrohen Grafikdesign des Art déco mit seiner luxuriös-opulenten Bildsprache – diese gegensätzlichen Entwicklungen erlebten gleichermaßen in den 1920er-Jahren ihren Höhepunkt. Auch gab es immer wieder einzelne Gestalterinnen und Gestalter, die völlig neuartige Arbeiten hervorbrachten und damit den Zeitgeist überwanden. Oder aber das Gestaltete fiel bei seiner Entstehung so zeitlos aus, dass sich im Nachhinein nur schwer eine Entstehungszeit festmachen ließ – wie beispielsweise im Fall der reduzierten modernistischen Logos. Unabhängig von wenigen Ausnahmen hat jede Zeit dennoch ihre ganz eigene Optik, bestimmt durch technische Möglichkeiten und gerade vorherrschende Tendenzen in Bereichen wie Farbe, Fotografie oder Typografie. Der Vergleich von Arbeiten mit ähnlichen Motiven zeigt diese sich ständig verändernde Ästhetik besonders deutlich.

In der Architektur, der Musik- oder der Filmbranche ist das Wissen um die Vergangenheit ein selbstverständlicher und relevanter Teil der Ausbildung. Es ist schließlich wichtig zu wissen, was es bereits gab und worauf man sich in neuen Arbeiten beziehen kann. Im Grafikdesign setzte sich der Blick zurück jedoch erst langsam durch. Erst in den 1970er-Jahren erschienen erste umfassende

Geschichtsbücher der Grafik. In den 1980er-Jahren hielten eigenständige Seminare und Studiengänge zur Historie erstmals Einzug in die Hochschulen. In einem Metier, in dem schon immer vor allem das Neue zählte, haftete dem Alten lange Zeit der Makel einer gewissen Irrelevanz an.

Besonders die jüngsten Kapitel der Geschichte zu bewerten ist nicht immer ganz einfach, ermöglicht doch erst eine gewisse Distanz zur Vergangenheit den neutralen Blick auf die Relevanz der Dinge. Es wäre gleichzeitig inkonsequent gewesen, die Designgeschichte an einem anderen Punkt als in der Gegenwart enden zu lassen. Wir baten daher rund 150 Designstudios aus aller Welt – von Büros einzelner Gestalterinnen und Gestalter bis zu international agierenden Unternehmen mit vielen Mitarbeitern –, ihre besten und relevantesten Projekte aus den vergangenen Jahren einzusenden. Schon die Vorauswahl der Studios war nicht einfach. Wohl nie zuvor in der Geschichte wurde so viel Grafikdesign produziert wie heute. Selbst in Ländern ohne langjährige Tradition in diesem Metier sind Studios und Einzelpersönlichkeiten mit extrem hohem und hochqualitativem Output aktiv.

Bereits die Anfänge der Designgeschichte waren durch unterschiedliche Herangehensweisen an den Beruf geprägt. Bis heute umfasst die Profession eine große Bandbreite, die von kompromisslos arbeitenden Avantgardisten bis hin zu rein kommerziell getriebenen Kreativdienstleistern reicht. Beide Lager sorgten im Laufe der Geschichte gleichermaßen für wechselseitige Innovation. In den 1940er-Jahren wurde beispielsweise neuartige Zeitschriftengestaltung von den großen US-Verlagen für den Massenmarkt entwickelt, deren Wirkung sich bald auch in unabhängigen Magazinen zeigte. In den 1970er-Jahren entwickelten sich aus dem experimentellen Umfeld der britischen Punkszene neue visuelle Tendenzen, die wiederum nach einiger Zeit in weniger radikaler Ausprägung Einzug in hochkommerzielle Anwendungsbereiche fanden. Entsprechend berücksichtigt dieses Buch weltweit verbreitete Arbeiten aus dem Sektor der Massenkultur genauso wie Lösungen, die sich im Kontext der Subkultur nur an ein kleines Publikum richteten.

Neben kommerziell und kulturell motivierten Einsatzbereichen manifestiert sich Grafikdesign aber auch immer wieder als Triebkraft, die politischen und gesellschaftlichen Anliegen ein Gesicht gibt. Gerade in unruhigen Zeiten der Weltpolitik ist diese Rolle nicht zu unterschätzen. Die Vergangenheit zeigt jedoch auch, dass visuelle Kommunikation gleichermaßen für die gute wie für die schlechte Sache genutzt werden kann. „Gestaltung mit Haltung", wie vom Designer Helmut Schmid einmal gefordert oder 1964 von Ken Garland im viel beachteten *First-Things-First*-Manifest formuliert, ist heute nicht weniger wichtig als damals. Wohin sich die Profession inhaltlich und ästhetisch in Zukunft bewegen wird, ist kaum vorherzusagen. Vor dem Hintergrund, dass intelligente Software in sämtlichen Anwendungsformen riesige Fortschritte macht, werden individuelle Kreativität, Autorenschaft und das Ausloten visueller Möglichkeiten vermutlich noch stärker an Bedeutung gewinnen. Die Rückschau kann dabei Impuls und Anregung sein.

1950 · Will Burtin · US · Magazine cover

1951 · Sena de Silva · PT · Poster

UNE HISTOIRE VISUELLE

Introduction par Jens Müller

L'affiche d'un événement au bord de la route, l'application pour réserver une chambre d'hôtel, le magazine d'actualité vendu en kiosque, les tableaux d'affichage dans un aéroport, le panneau de signalisation sur l'autoroute, ou encore ce livre, ne sont que quelques exemples parmi les millions d'objets qui ont fait l'objet d'un processus créatif. Tous relèvent du graphisme qui, depuis quelque 150 ans, contribue largement à définir l'apparence de notre monde. S'il est vrai que des moyens de communication ont existé avant cette période – il suffit de penser à Gutenberg et sa révolution de l'imprimerie au XVe siècle –, c'est seulement avec la commercialisation individualisée des produits et services à l'ère industrielle moderne qu'est apparu le graphisme moderne.

Avec le passage à l'ère de l'information, l'importance de la communication visuelle s'est encore fortement accrue. À côté du monde commercial, d'autres domaines comme la science, la culture, la politique et l'espace public sont devenus inconcevables sans solutions graphiques professionnelles. Les formats médiatiques utilisés à cet effet n'ont cessé de se parfaire au cours des cent dernières années – et de façon tout à fait massive après l'émergence des médias numériques dans les années 1990. L'objet général du graphisme est toutefois resté fondamentalement inchangé. Le travail d'un graphiste peut être d'ordre publicitaire (affiche événementielle), identificateur (logo), directif (signalisation), instructif (graphique) ou organisateur (mise en page de magazine).

Les aspects qui sont en revanche soumis à des changements perpétuels concernent surtout les propres créations. En effet, nombre de productions graphiques – contrairement à l'architecture, par exemple –, sont développées pour une utilisation relativement éphémère. Tout comme la mode, le graphisme redéfinit sans cesse inconsciemment ce qui est dans l'air du temps et ce qui est perçu comme désuet. Les formes, les couleurs ou les styles esthétiques ressentis comme actuels résultent d'une part du Zeitgeist, qui concentre des influences émanant de l'art, de l'architecture, du design, de la culture populaire et de la technologie. D'autre part, l'aspect des productions graphiques est aussi influencé dans une très large mesure par les évolutions sociales, économiques et politiques.

Certains travaux peu innovants du début des années 1940, par exemple, ne peuvent se comprendre qu'en tenant compte du contexte de la Seconde Guerre mondiale. De même, le style objectif et neutre dit «suisse» ou le graphisme expérimental du mouvement hippie ne peuvent être dissociés du lieu, de l'époque et des circonstances de leur apparition. Dans ce livre, le lien passionnant entre histoire d'une époque et histoire du graphisme occupe une place privilégiée. Chaque décennie est introduite par une frise chronologique qui reprend et présente année par année une sélection de différents faits historiques du monde entier. On pourra y voir une sélection d'emballages, de logos, de pochettes d'albums ou d'affiches électorales liés à des moments historiques. Au fil des années, nombre de ces objets sont devenus de véritables icônes dont l'image s'est parfois imprimée plus profondément dans notre mémoire que les événements mêmes.

Les sections illustrées du livre dénotent au moins deux approches. Les travaux présentés peuvent être abordés d'un point de vue purement stylistique en ayant à l'esprit l'histoire du graphisme. Cette lecture permet de découvrir des tendances et des contre-courants visuels, de reconnaître des développements à l'origine de changements radicaux, d'identifier des techniques de travail, mais aussi, point non négligeable, de mettre en lumière le talent des graphistes. Mais chaque œuvre peut aussi être abordée comme un témoin de son époque, en quelque sorte comme le reliquat de certaines configurations historiques de l'humanité. Les aspects culturels, politiques, économiques et technologiques se manifestent directement ou indirectement à travers les solutions visuelles nombreuses et variées – de l'affiche électorale à l'identité visuelle d'une entreprise de technologie, en passant par la couverture d'un roman. À côté des aspects esthétiques liés à l'évolution historique de la création graphique, un retour sur le graphisme du XXe siècle offre donc une illustration visuelle de l'histoire économique, culturelle et sociale de notre passé récent.

Ce livre réunit des réalisations mondialement célèbres et des exemples oubliés ou seulement connus des cercles spécialisés. Le fait que des affiches primées et exposées dans des musées côtoient des créations ordinaires diffusées à des millions d'exemplaires renvoie aux spécificités de la profession, qui a toujours évolué aux confins de l'art, du commerce, de l'artisanat et des services. Si cette diversité des exigences posées au graphisme est une base essentielle du métier, elle rend aussi sa reconnaissance plus complexe. Bien que tout le monde ou presque soit constamment en contact avec des productions graphiques, et bien que beaucoup de gens puissent se passionner pour la qualité de certaines d'entre elles, comme les génériques des séries télévisées, on ne peut pas affirmer que la connaissance du métier soit très répandue en dehors de la scène professionnelle.

Ce sont surtout des créateurs individuels qui émergent de la masse grâce à des réalisations exceptionnelles et qui attirent régulièrement l'attention du public sur le graphisme. Le présent volume traite des années 1890 à 2019 et présente une quarantaine de personnalités du monde entier qui ont marqué ces décennies. Comme dans beaucoup d'autres disciplines, au fil des années, un certain canon historique s'est établi dans le graphisme, englobant différents créateurs, travaux et groupes d'œuvres. Il aurait été trop simple de raconter une fois de plus l'histoire du graphisme en s'appuyant uniquement sur ces icônes. Une analyse intensive des publications historiques et la collaboration de praticiens et de théoriciens des différentes parties du monde ont aussi permis de réunir nombre de travaux moins connus, et d'avoir ainsi un regard plus étendu sur le sujet. Malgré la grande quantité de reproductions publiées dans ce livre, une sélection ne peut offrir par nature qu'un aperçu certes partiel, mais suffisant pour illustrer des styles et des évolutions.

La diffusion globale des tendances en vigueur dans le domaine du graphisme – qu'il s'agisse de courants éphémères ou d'évolutions durables –, est un phénomène qui n'a été qu'insuffisamment pris en compte dans les ouvrages consacrés au graphisme. L'histoire du graphisme est trop souvent racontée comme une évolution purement stylistique calquée sur le modèle de la théorie de l'art: on égrène des époques, généralement en les classant géographiquement. Cette approche occulte le fait que beaucoup d'évolutions graphiques se sont diffusées mondialement à partir de leur lieu d'apparition. S'il s'agit là d'un effet très logique à l'ère des sites portfolios, des blogs de graphisme et des médias sociaux, le phénomène peut être retracé jusqu'aux débuts du graphisme, il y a plus de cent ans: on trouve ainsi un graphisme chinois de style Bauhaus ou des affiches Art déco au Japon. Combinée au classement chronologique, la prise en compte d'exemples provenant de différentes parties du monde élargit le regard de façon impressionnante sur des évolutions visuelles qui se jouent des frontières géographiques.

Ces évolutions complexes n'ont pas toujours été cohérentes et judicieuses – elles ont parfois produit des concepts antagonistes à une même époque. Un exemple en est la concomitance chronologique entre un graphisme avant-gardiste caractérisé par une sobre réduction en rouge et noir d'une part, et d'autre part le graphisme haut en couleur de l'Art déco avec son langage visuel luxuriant. Ces deux évolutions antagonistes ont connu leur apogée dans les années 1920. Il y a toujours eu aussi des créatrices et créateurs qui ont produit des œuvres entièrement nouvelles et qui ont ainsi transcendé l'air du temps. Ou encore, certaines réalisations ont été tellement intemporelles dès leur apparition qu'il est difficile de les attribuer rétrospectivement à une époque – ceci vaut notamment pour les logos modernistes sous leur forme la plus réduite. Exception faite de quelques cas isolés, chaque époque possède toutefois son propre style visuel déterminé par les possibilités technologiques et les tendances du moment concernant la couleur, la photographie ou la typographie. La comparaison de travaux présentant des motifs similaires illustre très clairement ce changement esthétique incessant.

En architecture ou dans les domaines de la musique et du cinéma, la connaissance du passé est une composante incontournable de la formation. De fait, il est important de savoir ce qui a existé avant et à quoi peuvent se référer de nouvelles œuvres. Dans le graphisme en revanche, le regard rétrospectif ne s'est imposé que lentement: dans les années 1970 seulement ont été publiés les premiers ouvrages sur ce thème, et dans les années 1980 que les séminaires et cursus d'études consacrés à l'histoire du graphisme se sont imposés dans les écoles supérieures. Dans une profession qui privilégie depuis toujours la nouveauté, l'ancien a longtemps été affecté de la tare d'une certaine inutilité.

Il n'est pas toujours facile d'apprécier les chapitres de l'histoire récente, et seul un certain recul permet de porter un regard neutre sur la valeur des réalisations passées. Il aurait cependant été inconséquent de vouloir arrêter le cours de l'histoire à un autre moment qu'à l'époque contemporaine. Nous avons donc demandé à quelque 150 studios de graphisme du monde entier – bureaux de graphistes individuels ou entreprises internationales employant de nombreux collaborateurs – de nous adresser leurs réalisations phares des dernières années. Cette présélection n'a déjà pas été facile. Jamais par le passé on n'a produit autant de graphisme qu'aujourd'hui, et même dans des pays qui ne peuvent s'appuyer sur une longue tradition professionnelle, les studios de graphisme et les graphistes individuels génèrent de nos jours des volumes d'activité très élevés et du meilleur niveau.

L'histoire du graphisme a été marquée dès ses débuts par différentes approches du métier. Jusqu'à ce jour, la profession couvre un vaste éventail qui va de l'avant-gardisme inconditionnel à la prestation de service motivée par des considérations purement commerciales. Tout au long de l'histoire, les deux camps ont été une source d'innovation. Dans les années 1940 par exemple, les éditeurs de magazines américains ont développé un nouveau graphisme éditorial à destination du marché de masse, graphisme qui allait bientôt aussi faire sentir ses effets dans des publications indépendantes. Dans les années 1970, le champ expérimental de la scène punk britannique a produit des tendances visuelles inédites qui sont à leur tour entrées un peu plus tard, sous une forme moins radicale, dans des cas d'application foncièrement commerciaux. Conformément à ces phénomènes, le présent livre tient compte des œuvres issues de la culture de masse diffusées dans le monde entier aussi bien que des solutions qui ne s'adressent qu'à un public restreint dans le contexte de sous-cultures.

En marge des domaines d'application aux motivations commerciales ou culturelles, le graphisme se manifeste toutefois aussi et toujours comme une force dynamique qui donne un visage à des sujets politiques et sociaux. Particulièrement aux périodes agitées de la politique mondiale, ce rôle ne doit pas être sous-estimé. Le passé montre toutefois aussi que la communication visuelle peut servir la bonne aussi bien que la mauvaise cause. «Design is attitude», comme le déclarait le graphiste Helmut Schmid, et les arguments que Ken Garland a formulés en 1964 dans son manifeste très remarqué *First Things First* n'ont rien perdu de leur pertinence. Quant à savoir dans quelle direction la profession va évoluer en termes d'esthétique et de contenu, il n'est guère possible de le prédire. Avec les immenses progrès de l'intelligence artificielle sous toutes ses formes d'utilisation, la créativité individuelle, les réalisations d'auteur et l'exploration des possibilités visuelles prendront sans doute encore davantage d'importance. Un regard rétrospectif peut alors s'avérer riche de stimuli et d'inspirations.

1901 · Anonymous · PT · Magazine cover

1899 · Leopoldo Metlicovitz · IT · Poster

1890s · Auguste Roubille · FR · Poster

1890

1895 · Aubrey Beardsley · UK · Poster

1890s · Anonymous · RU · Poster

—1899

VOL. XLVII. APRIL, 1894. No. 6.

THE CENTURY ILLUSTRATED MONTHLY MAGAZINE

MDCCCXCIV

THE CENTURY CO·UNION SQUARE·NEW YORK

T·FISHER UNWIN·PATERNOSTER SQ·LONDON

Copyright, 1894, by The Century Co.] [Trade-Mark Registered Oct. 18th, 1881.] [Entered at N. Y. Post Office as Second Class Mail Matter.

1894 · Anonymous · US · Magazine cover

1890s · Anonymous · US · Logo · Levi Strauss & Co.

In the field of technology, it is often not the major successes but the minor advances that enable inventions to make a breakthrough and change whole industries overnight. So it was in the case of lithography, a groundbreaking planographic printing process invented in Germany by Alois Senefelder in 1799, which proved to be a cheap and rapid means of duplicating images etched onto stone plates. During the 1880s, the French printer and designer Jules Chéret discovered that it was technically possible to produce multicolored posters in only a few printings, instead of having to use a single printing for each tone. These seemingly insignificant advances led to the development of color posters in which the two design elements—text and image—could be interwoven into a coherent whole. Today's graphic design industry regards that discovery as its "big bang" moment, and it was in 1890s Paris that the modern artistic poster first came into being. It fitted perfectly into a new visual age that saw not only the first magazines illustrated with photographic reproductions but also the new medium of film.

The lithography workshop of the Schwann printing works in Düsseldorf, for the production of color posters.

Blick in die lithografische Abteilung der Druckerei Schwann in Düsseldorf, in der mehrfarbige Plakate hergestellt wurden.

Vue de l'atelier lithographique de l'imprimerie Schwann à Düsseldorf, dans lequel étaient produites des affiches en couleur.

Im Bereich der Technik sind es oft nicht die ganz großen Würfe, sondern kleine Weiterentwicklungen, die Erfindungen zum Durchbruch verhelfen und in kürzester Zeit ganze Branchen verändern. So auch im Falle der Lithografie, einem bereits 1799 von Alois Senefelder in Deutschland entwickelten neuartigen Flachdruckverfahren. Auf Steinplatten gezeichnete Motive konnten damit kostengünstig und schnell vervielfältigt werden. Für jede verwendete Farbe war jedoch eine eigene Steinplatte nötig. Im Laufe der 1880er-Jahre entdeckte der französische Drucker und Gestalter Jules Chéret eine technische Möglichkeit, vielfarbige Plakate mit nur wenigen Druckgängen herzustellen. Diese scheinbar marginale Weiterentwicklung führte zum Durchbruch farbiger Plakate, bei denen Schrift und Bild als untrennbare Gestaltungselemente ineinander verwoben waren. Heute gilt dieser Moment als eine Art Urknall des Grafikdesigns. Ausgehend von Paris, entstand in den 1890er-Jahren das moderne Bildplakat. Es passte perfekt in ein neues Bildzeitalter, das in weiterer Folge nicht nur erste Zeitschriften mit reproduzierten Fotografien hervorbrachte, sondern auch das neue Medium Film.

Souvent, dans le domaine technologique, ce ne sont pas les grandes réussites, mais les petites évolutions secondaires qui permettent à certaines inventions de s'imposer et de transformer des secteurs entiers en un tournemain. La lithographie, nouveau procédé d'impression à plat mis au point par Alois Senefelder dès 1799 en Allemagne, en est une illustration exemplaire. Des motifs dessinés sur des plaques de pierre pouvaient ainsi être reproduits en nombre, rapidement et à prix réduit. Le procédé obligeait toutefois à utiliser une plaque par couleur. Au cours des années 1880, l'imprimeur et graphiste Jules Chéret découvrit une technique pour produire des affiches polychromes réduisant le nombre d'étapes d'impression. Ce progrès apparemment insignifiant conduisit à la percée de l'affiche en couleur, dans laquelle le texte et l'image sont liés comme des éléments visuels inséparables. Aujourd'hui, ce moment est considéré comme une sorte de Big Bang du graphisme. L'affiche moderne voit le jour dans les années 1890 à Paris et correspond parfaitement à la nouvelle ère de l'image, qui produira dans son sillage non seulement les premières revues illustrées et leurs reproductions photographiques, mais aussi les débuts du cinéma.

1890

The Mergenthaler **Linotype** Company is established in Brooklyn, to distribute the first automatic typesetting machine developed by German-born Ottmar Mergenthaler

The **Typographische Gesellschaft München** (Munich Typographic Society) is founded

1890 · F. H. Tensi · IT · Poster

1890 · Anonymous · US · Poster

1890s · Jules Chéret · FR · Poster

1890 · Christian Bettels · DE · Poster

1890 · Anonymous · US · Book cover

1890s · Giovanni Mataloni · IT · Poster

1891

George Batten founds an advertising agency in New York City that later evolves into **BBDO**

1891 · Fritz Rehm · DE · Poster

1891 · Anonymous · CA · Magazine cover

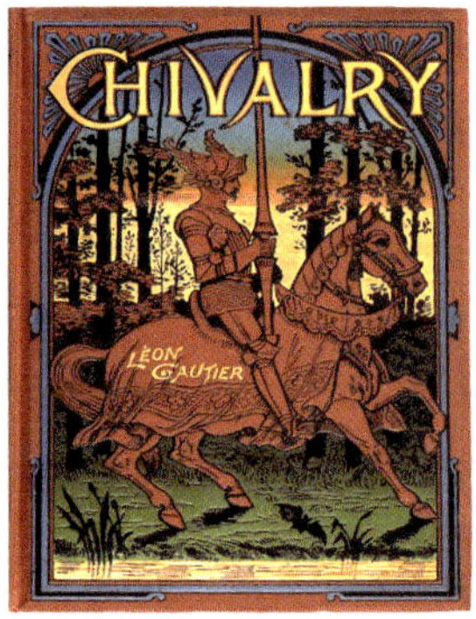

1891 · Anonymous · UK · Book cover

1891 · Anonymous · IT · Poster

1891 · Anonymous · US · Book cover

1891 · Anonymous · US · Poster

1891 · Anonymous · US · Magazine cover

1891 · Anonymous · UK · Book cover

1899 · Henri de Toulouse-Lautrec · FR · Poster

Henri de Toulouse-Lautrec
(1864, Albi – 1901, Saint-André-du-Bois, France), who died at the age of only 36, was nevertheless among the most representative Post-Impressionist artists of his generation. Coming from a noble family, in his short life Lautrec created some 30 posters and 700 canvases—his work defined the image of Paris in the late 19th century, notably through his fascination with the city's bohemian nightlife, and the so-called urban underclass. His 1891 poster for the Moulin Rouge (*La Goulue*) has remained an iconic piece of early graphic design.

Henri de Toulouse-Lautrec
(1864, Albi – 1901, Saint-André-du-Bois, Frankreich) war bei seinem Tod erst 36 Jahre alt, zählt aber dennoch zu den repräsentativsten postimpressionistischen Künstlern seiner Generation. Er stammte aus einer Adelsfamilie. Im Laufe seines kurzen Lebens schuf er gut dreißig Plakate und 700 Ölgemälde, in denen er das Paris im ausgehenden 19. Jahrhundert einfing, insbesondere das bohemehafte Nachtleben der Stadt und die sogenannte urbane Unterschicht, die beide eine besondere Faszination auf ihn ausübten. Das Plakat, das er 1891 für das Moulin Rouge entwarf *(La Goulue)*, gilt bis heute als ein Meisterwerk der frühen Grafik.

Henri de Toulouse-Lautrec
(1864, Albi – 1901, Saint-André-du-Bois), mort prématurément à l'âge de 36 ans, n'en est pas moins un des artistes post-impressionnistes les plus représentatifs de sa génération. Issu d'une famille noble, pendant sa courte vie, Lautrec a créé quelque 30 affiches et 700 peintures: son œuvre a défini l'image de Paris à la fin du XIXe siècle, particulièrement du fait de sa fascination pour la vie nocturne de la bohème et ce qu'il est convenu d'appeler le quart-monde. L'affiche qu'il réalise en 1891 pour le Moulin Rouge (*La Goulue*) est restée une icône des débuts du graphisme.

»The eye-catching arrangements of bright colors and arresting blacks were some of the properties of Lautrec's posters. [...] A few public controversies about his radically concise representations of personalities [...] only served to increase the growing interest in his popular work.«

Riva Castleman, *Henri de Toulouse-Lautrec: Images of the 1890s*, 1985

1893 · Henri de Toulouse-Lautrec · FR · Poster

1895 · Henri de Toulouse-Lautrec · FR · Poster

1894 · Henri de Toulouse-Lautrec · FR · Poster

1892 · Henri de Toulouse-Lautrec · FR · Poster

1892

The **Gebrüder Klingspor type foundry** is set up in Offenbach am Main, Germany

23 U.S. type foundries merge to become the **American Type Founders** (ATF)

1892 · Eugène Grasset · CH/FR · Poster

1892 · Ernst Klimt · AT · Poster

1892 · Eugène Grasset · CH/FR · Poster

1892 · Strobridge Lithographing Co. · US · Poster

1892 · Leopoldo Metlicovitz · IT · Poster

1892 · Thomas Worth · US · Magazine cover

1893

1893 · Eugène Grasset · CH/FR · Poster

1893 · Anonymous · UK · Book cover

1893 · Alfred Choubrac · FR · Poster

1893 · Enquirer Job Printing Co. · US · Poster

1893 · Frédéric Rouge · CH · Poster

1890s · Ferdinand Bac · FR · Poster

1890s · Anonymous · US · Poster

1890s · "Diane" · UK · Poster

1894

The St. Bride Foundation Institute's Printing School opened, which later evolved to become the **London College of Communication**

1894 · Anonymous · UK · Book cover

1894 · Georges Meunier · FR · Poster

1894 · Alphonse Mucha · CZ/FR · Poster

1894 · Aubrey Beardsley · UK · Poster

1894 · Anonymous · UK · Book cover

1894 · Edward Penfield · US · Poster

1894 · Jan Toorop · NL · Poster

1895

The **D. Stempel** type foundry is established in Frankfurt am Main, Germany

1895 · E. Pickert · US · Poster

1895 · Dudley Hardy · UK · Poster

1895 · Dudley Hardy · UK · Poster

1895 · Dudley Hardy · UK · Poster

1895 · Anonymous · US · Poster

1895 · "Pal" (Jean de Paléologue) · RO/FR · Poster

1895 · D. Whitelaw · UK · Poster

1895 · Dudley Hardy · UK · Poster

1895 · "Ener" · FR · Poster

1896

The sanserif typeface **Akzidenz-Grotesk** is created by an anonymous designer for the Berthold type foundry in Germany

The **Wolfsonian Museum**, library and research center for art and design, opens in Miami Beach, Florida

1896 · Jean Ubaghs · FR · Poster

1896 · Julius Diez · DE · Poster

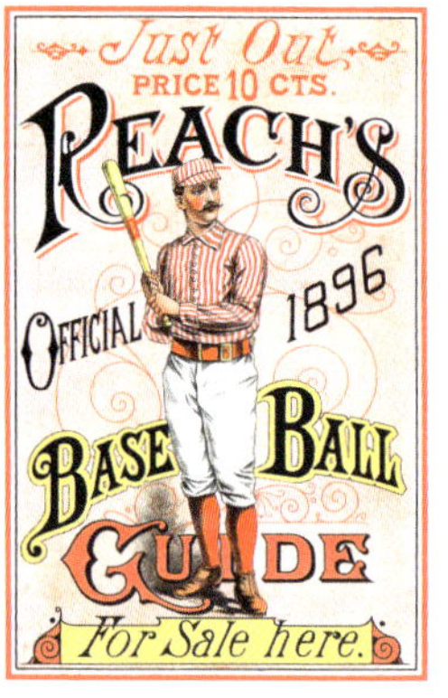

1896 · Anonymous · US · Poster

1896 · Anonymous · US · Poster

1896 · Ludwig Sütterlin · DE · Poster

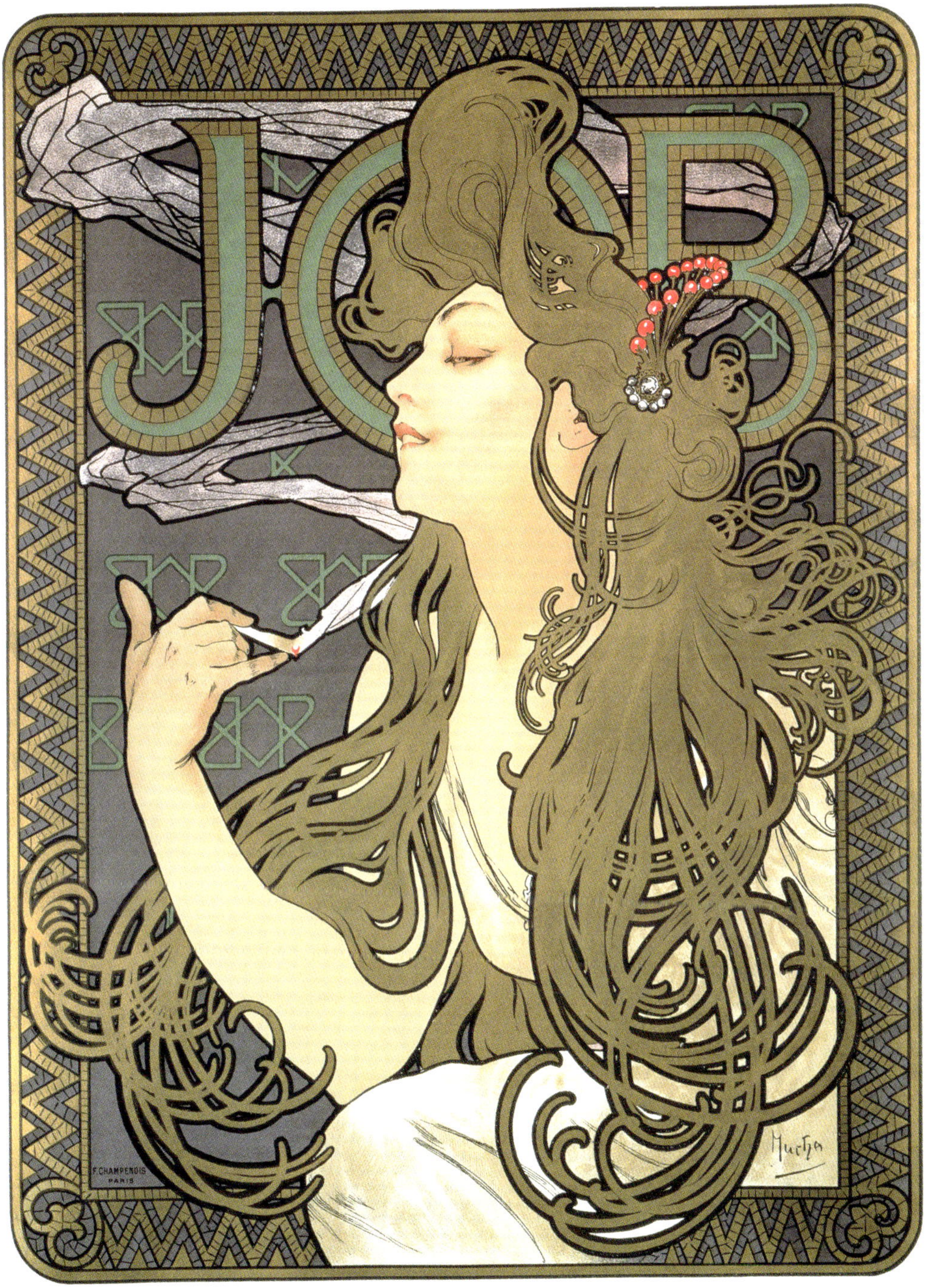

1896 · Alphonse Mucha · CZ/FR · Poster

In 1896, Georg Hirth and Fritz von Ostini founded the Munich-based artistic and literary magazine *Jugend*, an innovative journal which succeeded in publishing texts by such famous authors as Hermann Hesse, Kurt Tucholsky, and Maxim Gorky. It also attached special importance to layout and several leading contemporary German artists and graphic designers contributed images, while the aesthetic of the magazine was sufficiently distinct that it gave its name to Jugendstil—the "*Jugend* style," which was the equivalent of Art Nouveau in Germany. This playful, floral style, which also found its way into the architecture and product design of the period, was clearly visible on the magazine's colorful covers. *Jugend*'s characteristic brand of visuals and content met with an enthusiastic response internationally and set the pattern for several other publications that were similar in appearance.

Im Jahr 1896 gründeten Georg Hirth und Fritz von Ostini die Münchner Kunst- und Literaturzeitschrift *Jugend*. Das innovative Heft zeichnete sich nicht nur durch Texte berühmter Autoren wie Hermann Hesse, Kurt Tucholsky oder Maxim Gorki aus, sondern legte besonderen Wert auf die visuelle Ausstattung. Führende zeitgenössische deutsche Künstler und Grafikdesigner lieferten dafür Beiträge. Die Ästhetik der Zeitschrift war so prägend, dass sie dem Jugendstil ihren Namen gab. Die farbigen Umschläge zeigten erstmals besonders deutlich jene floral-verspielte Stilistik, die parallel auch in der Architektur und im Produktdesign Einzug hielt. Das visuelle und inhaltliche Konzept der *Jugend* fand internationale Resonanz und führte vielfach zu vergleichbaren Publikationen.

La revue d'art et de littérature *Jugend* fut fondée en 1896 à Munich par Georg Hirth et Fritz von Ostini. Cette revue innovatrice ne se distinguait pas seulement par la publication de textes d'auteurs célèbres comme Hermann Hesse, Kurt Tucholsky ou Maxime Gorki, mais accordait aussi une importance particulière à la présentation visuelle, à laquelle contribuèrent de grands artistes et graphistes allemands contemporains. L'esthétique de la revue fut si marquante qu'elle donna son nom au «Jugendstil», la version allemande de l'Art nouveau. Les couvertures imprimées en couleurs présentaient pour la première fois et très clairement le style floral et enjoué qui fit aussi son entrée dans les mondes de l'architecture et du design de produits. La conception de la revue *Jugend* en matière de contenu et d'image eut un retentissement international et suscita l'apparition de nombreuses publications similaires.

1896 · Otto Eckmann · DE · Magazine cover

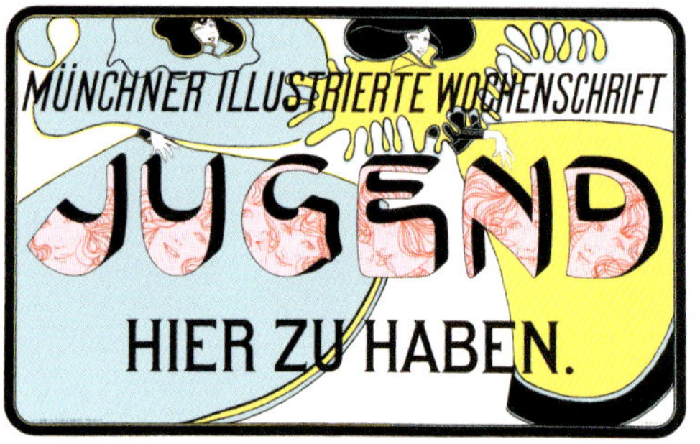

1896 · Josef Rudolf Witzel · DE · Poster

»Poster or wallpaper, type design or scenography, […] architecture or painting and drawing—all these forms of artistic expression were, without class distinction or inferiority complexes, recognized as a new art that added beauty to life and was a laudable interpretation and expression of the age.«

Hellmut Rademacher, *Deutsche Plakatkunst und ihre Meister*, 1965

1896 · Anonymous · DE · Magazine cover

1897 · August von Meissl · DE · Magazine cover

1897 · Hans Christiansen · DE · Magazine cover

1896 · "PB" · DE · Magazine cover

1898 · Fritz Erler · DE · Magazine cover

1898 · "Halmi" · DE · Magazine cover

1898 · Hans Christiansen · DE · Magazine cover

1899 · Josef Rudolf Witzel · DE · Magazine cover

1897

The **Cooper Hewitt Museum** is founded in Manhattan

The first general book on graphic design, **Das moderne Plakat,** is published in Dresden, Germany, by Jean Louis Sponsel

1897 · Miquel Utrillo · ES · Poster

1897 · Louis Rhead · UK/US · Poster

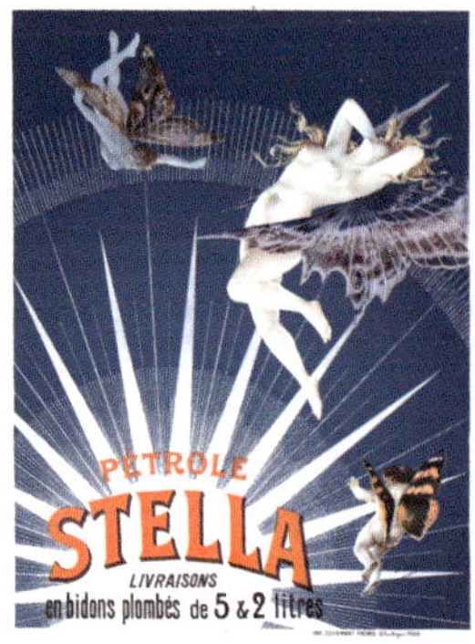

1897 · Henri Gray · FR · Poster

1897 · Fernand Toussaint · BE · Poster

1897 · Fritz Rehm · DE · Poster

The **Monotype machine** is developed by engineer Tolbert Lanston in the United States

1897 · Manuel Robbe · FR · Poster

1897 · Henri Privat-Livemont · BE · Poster

1897 · Henri Meunier · FR · Poster

1898

The first issue of the magazine **The Poster** is published in London

1898 · "Pal" (Jean de Paléologue) · RO/FR · Poster

1898 · Ferdinand Hart Nibbrig · NL · Poster

1898 · Ramon Casas · ES · Poster

1898 · Henri-Gustave Jossot · FR · Poster

1898 · Anonymous · US · Logo · Pepsi-Cola

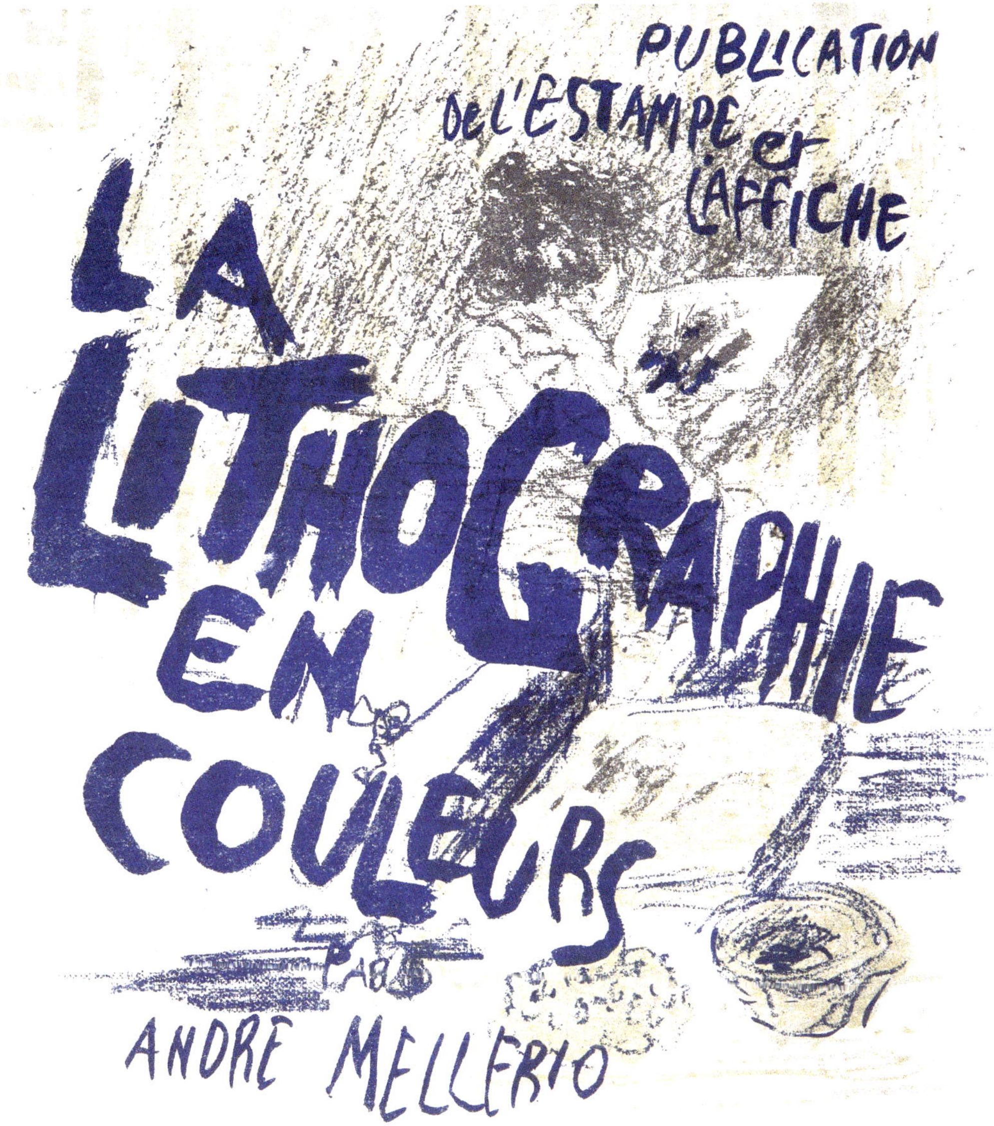

1898 · Pierre Bonnard · FR · Book cover

The French conglomerate which produces everything from tires to travel guides has long had the consistent support of its mascot, the Michelin Man, officially known as Bibendum. Instantly recognizable, the character was introduced in 1894 at the Lyon International Exhibition, where the Michelin brothers had a stand. The character was further developed by the cartoonist Marius Rossillon four years later, under the guidance of André Michelin, and over the decades has been used in countless pieces in both 2D and 3D.

Der französische Konzern, dessen Ursprünge in der Reifenherstellung liegen und der mit seinen Reiseführern zu einer Ikone der Freizeit wurde, arbeitet seit langen Jahren mit der Unterstützung seines Maskottchens, des Michelin-Männchens, das offiziell „Bibendum" heißt. Die unverkennbare Figur wurde bei der Industrieausstellung in Lyon 1894 auf dem Stand der Brüder Michelin präsentiert. Vier Jahre später wurde das Männchen von dem Cartoonisten Marius Rossillon unter Anleitung von André Michelin weiter ausgearbeitet und wird seitdem in zahllosen zwei- und dreidimensionalen Inkarnationen verwendet.

Le groupe industriel français qui, de simple fabricant de pneumatiques, devint un symbole de loisirs avec ses guides de voyages, a toujours bénéficié du soutien de sa mascotte, le Bonhomme Michelin, officiellement baptisé Bibendum. Instantanément reconnaissable, ce personnage a fait sa première apparition en 1894 à l'Exposition universelle de Lyon, où les frères Michelin tenaient un stand. Quatre ans plus tard, il allait être créé graphiquement par le dessinateur humoristique Marius Rossillon d'après les directives d'André Michelin. Au fil des décennies, il a été utilisé sur d'innombrables supports, en 2D comme en 3D.

1898 · "O'Galop" (Marius Rossillon) · FR · Poster

1911 · Anonymous · US · Campaign

»The Michelin Man exemplifies the traits that have contributed to the appeal of advertising characters in general. [...] His anthropomorphic design, a stack of automobile tires with human features, demonstrates the power of iconography.«

Warren Dotz and Masud Husain, *Meet Mr. Product*, 2003

1912 · H. L. Roowy · UK/FR · Poster

1912 · "O'Galop" (Marius Rossillon) · FR · Poster

1913 · "O'Galop" (Marius Rossillon) · FR · Poster

1913 · Anonymous · US · Magazine cover

1899

1890s · Morikawa Chikashige · JP · Poster

1899 · "Pal" (Jean de Paléologue) · RO/FR · Poster

1899 · A. L. Rich · US · Logo · General Electric

1890s · Alick P. F. Ritchie · UK · Poster

1899 · Peter Behrens · DE · Logo · Insel Verlag

1899 · Anonymous · US · Poster

1899 · Henry-Claudius Forestier · FR · Poster

1899 · Koloman Moser · AT · Magazine cover

1899 · Anonymous · UK · Poster

1899 · Emil Rudolf Weiss · DE · Poster

1890s · Ateliers Choubrac · FR · Poster

1905 · Albert Levering · US · Magazine cover

1900

1907 · Thomas Theodor Heine · DE · Poster

1902 · Anonymous · ES · Logo · Real Madrid

1905 · Anonymous · RU · Poster

1909

1908 · Berthold Löffler · AT · Poster

With the advent of a period of social and economic change, a new class of consumer began to emerge in several countries, namely the working class. In conjunction with this development, innovative posters with eye-catching imagery—initially regarded as being "too modern" by the conventional brand industry—slowly became established as the foremost advertising medium. Targeted poster campaigns were now able to reach a mass audience, especially in the rapidly expanding major cities. However, industry as a whole increasingly recognized the further possibilities offered by professionally produced graphic design, and at the turn of the century it was economically successful Germany that led the way in the advancement of this area. For the first time corporate identity began to appear across different types of media, whilst the systematic use of the Sachplakat, or "object poster," which had the advantage of transmitting information clearly and directly through minimalist design, also originated in Germany at this period.

Durch die gesellschaftlich-wirtschaftlichen Veränderungen der Zeit stiegen in vielen Ländern die Arbeiter zu einer neuen Konsumentenschicht auf. Neuartige Plakate in expressiver Bildsprache, die bei der konventionellen Markenindustrie zunächst noch als zu modern gegolten hatte, setzten sich auch hier langsam als wichtigstes Werbemedium durch. Vor allem in den wachsenden Großstädten konnte man nun mit gezieltem Plakataushang die Massen erreichen. Die Industrie erkannte jedoch zunehmend die weiteren Möglichkeiten, die eine professionelle visuelle Gestaltung für sie bereithielt. Vor allem das wirtschaftlich erfolgreiche Deutschland war Anfang des Jahrhunderts federführend in der Weiterentwicklung des modernen Grafikdesigns. Hier wurde erstmals gezielt mit medienübergreifenden Firmenidentitäten gearbeitet. Auch das sogenannte Sachplakat, bei dem die kommunikativen Vorteile einer aufs Minimum reduzierten Gestaltung systematisch genutzt wurden, hat seinen Ursprung im damaligen Deutschland.

Avec les évolutions socio-économiques de l'époque, dans beaucoup de pays la classe ouvrière devient une nouvelle couche sociale de consommateurs. Des affiches d'un genre nouveau, dont le langage visuel expressif avait été jugé trop moderne par l'industrie conventionnelle, s'imposent lentement aussi dans ce domaine et deviennent peu à peu le support publicitaire dominant. C'est principalement dans les grandes métropoles en pleine croissance que les masses peuvent être atteintes par un affichage ciblé. Qui plus est, l'industrie prend peu à peu conscience des possibilités qu'offre une création visuelle professionnelle. Au début du siècle, c'est surtout l'Allemagne, avec son économie florissante, qui prend la tête de cette évolution en développant le graphisme moderne. C'est aussi en Allemagne que l'on travaille pour la première fois de manière ciblée sur des identités de marque qui ne se cantonnent plus à un support unique. Et c'est encore en Allemagne que voit aussi le jour à la même époque l'« affiche objet », dans laquelle les avantages communicatifs d'un graphisme réduit au minimum sont exploités de manière systématique.

Large-format posters on an American street in the first years of the 20th century.

Großplakate an einer Straße in den USA aus den Jahren kurz nach der Jahrhundertwende.

Affiches grand format dans une rue aux États-Unis, peu après le tournant du XXe siècle.

1900

Steglitzer Werkstatt, a prototype of the modern design studio, is established in Berlin

Otto Eckmann creates his **Eckmann-Schrift,** which quickly becomes the most popular typeface of the German Jugendstil

1900 · Anonymous · FR · Poster

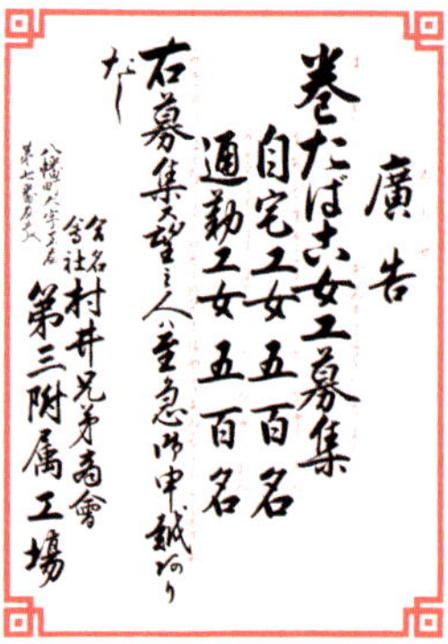

1900 · Anonymous · JP · Poster

1900 · Anonymous · US · Poster

1900 · Daniel de Losques · FR · Poster

1900 · Charles E. Dawson · UK · Poster

1900 · Charles E. Dawson · UK · Poster

1900 · Jules Chéret · FR · Poster

1900 · Anonymous · US/DE · Poster

1900 · Anonymous · DE · Brochure cover

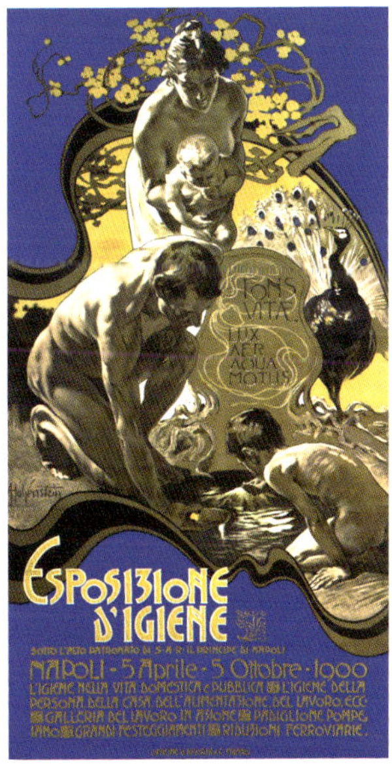

1900 · Adolf Hohenstein · DE/IT · Poster

Alfred Roller (1864, Brno, Czech Republic – 1935, Vienna) was a painter and leading graphic and stage designer. Abandoning traditionalism, Roller went on to design posters and sets for the composer Gustav Mahler, eventually becoming chief stage designer for the Vienna State Opera. From 1898 to 1903 he was editor-in-chief of the periodical *Ver Sacrum* (the official publication of the Austrian creative scene), which aimed to foster engagement amongst the artistic class. Through its promotion of Jugendstil art, it became the seminal document expressing the aspirations of the Viennese Secession movement, co-founded by Roller in 1897.

Alfred Roller (1864, Brünn, heute Tschechische Republik – 1935, Wien) war ein Maler und führender Grafikdesigner und Bühnenbildner. Er löste sich vom Traditionalismus, gestaltete in der Folge Plakate und Bühnenbilder für den Komponisten Gustav Mahler und wurde schließlich Chefbühnenbildner der Wiener Staatsoper. Von 1898 bis 1903 war er Herausgeber von *Ver Sacrum*, der offiziellen Zeitschrift der kreativen Szene in Österreich, die sich für ein verstärktes Engagement der Künstler einsetzte. Sie bekannte sich zum Jugendstil und vertrat maßgeblich die Gedanken der Wiener Secession, die Roller 1897 mit ins Leben gerufen hatte.

Alfred Roller (1864, Brno, République tchèque – 1935, Vienne) fut un peintre, graphiste et décorateur de théâtre de première importance. Après avoir renoncé au traditionalisme, Roller poursuivit sa carrière en concevant des affiches et des décors pour le compositeur Gustav Mahler et devint finalement décorateur en chef de l'Opéra national de Vienne. De 1898 à 1903, il fut rédacteur en chef de la revue *Ver Sacrum*, publication officielle de la scène créative autrichienne qui visait à favoriser l'engagement au sein du monde de l'art. Par sa promotion du Jugendstil, l'Art nouveau autrichien, la revue devint un document majeur des visées de la Sécession viennoise, que Roller avait cofondée en 1897.

1898 · Alfred Roller · AT · Magazine cover

1902 · Alfred Roller · AT · Poster

1899 · Alfred Roller · AT · Poster

»The particular impact of Viennese artists on the creation of posters at the turn of the century is clear to see in the realm of posters designed for exhibitions and events. Most worthy of mention are advertisements for art exhibitions.«

Werner J. Schweiger, *Aufbruch und Erfüllung*, 1988

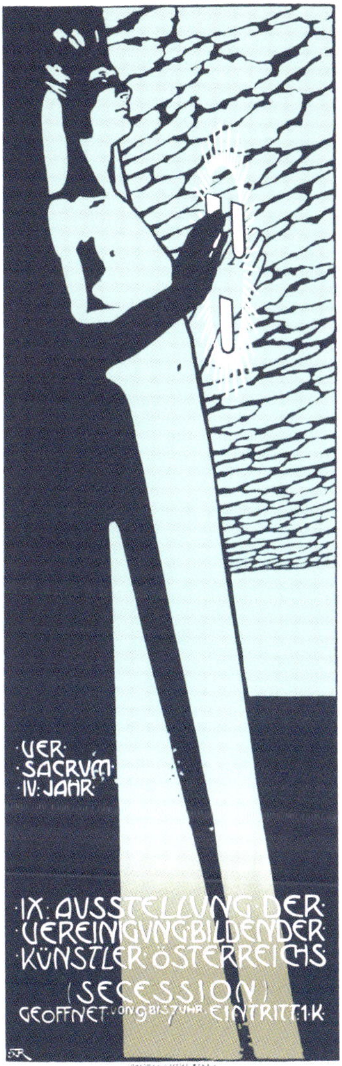

1901 · Alfred Roller · AT · Poster

1902 · Alfred Roller · AT · Poster

1901

METROPOLITAIN

1901 · Hector Guimard · FR · Logo · Paris Métro

1901 · Anonymous · CH · Logo · Electrolux

1901 · Francis Barraud · UK · Logo · Gramophone Co.

The **Behrens Schrift** typeface is created by Peter Behrens

1901 · Eugène Grasset · CH/FR · Poster

1901 · Anonymous · UK · Magazine cover

The **Japan Advertising Corporation** is founded, which later evolves to become Dentsu, the largest such company in Japan

1901 · Frank Xavier Leyendecker · US · Magazine cover

1901 · Nikolai Vasilyev · RU · Poster

The **Society of Illustrators** is founded in New York City

U.S. designer Frederic W. Goudy creates the **Copperplate Gothic** typeface

LA DOMENICA DEL CORRIERE

	Nel Regno	Estero
Anno	L. 5 —	L. 8 —
Semestre	» 2 50	» 4 —

SI PUBBLICA A MILANO OGNI DOMENICA

Dono agli Abbonati del "Corriere della Sera,,

Uffici del giornale:
Via Pietro Verri, 14
MILANO

Anno III. — N. 29. 21 Luglio 1901. Centesimi 10 il Numero.

IL DRAMMATICO NAUFRAGIO DEL VAPORE "LUSITANIA,, - SULLA SPIAGGIA DI FERRYLAND (AMERICA DEL NORD) - NEL QUALE VIAGGIAVANO MOLTI ITALIANI.

(Disegno di A. Beltrame, da schizzi).

1901 · Achille Beltrame · IT · Magazine cover

1902

Alfred Erickson establishes his own advertising agency in New York City

Morris Fuller Benton creates the first version of the **Franklin Gothic** typeface

1902 · Edmund Edel · DE · Poster

1902 · Félix Vallotton · FR · Magazine cover

1902 · Francisco de Cidón · ES · Poster

1902 · Eugène Ogé · FR · Poster

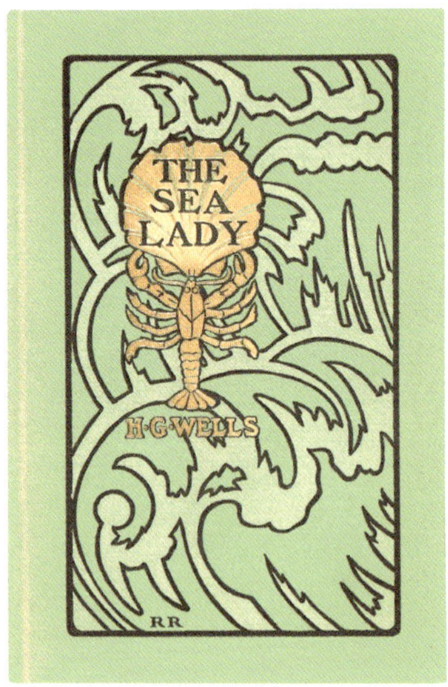

1902 · Rome Richardson · US · Book cover

1902 · George Ford Morris · US · Poster

1902 · Henry Raleigh · US · Poster

1902 · Leonardo Bistolfi · IT · Poster

1903

Ira Washington Rubel develops the first commercial **offset printing system** in New Jersey

The **Wiener Werkstätte**, a working community of visual artists, is established by Koloman Moser and Josef Hoffmann in Vienna

1903 · Louis Galice · FR · Poster

1903 · Ivan Bilibin · RU · Poster

1903 · H. Malaguti · BR · Brochure cover

1903 · Anonymous · UK · Brochure cover

1903 · Koloman Moser · AT · Poster

1903 · Raul Pederneiras · BR · Magazine cover

1903 · Jan Thorn Prikker · NL/DE · Poster

1904

More than 10.000 **Linotype machines** are in use around the world

1904 · Carlo Biscaretti · IT · Logo · Fiat

1904 · Hans Schneider · DE · Logo · Bayer

1904 · Anonymous · NZ · Brochure cover

1904 · Thorvald Bindesbøll · DK · Logo · Carlsberg

1904 · Anonymous · BR · Logo · Kósmos magazine

1904 · Margaret Armstrong · US · Book cover

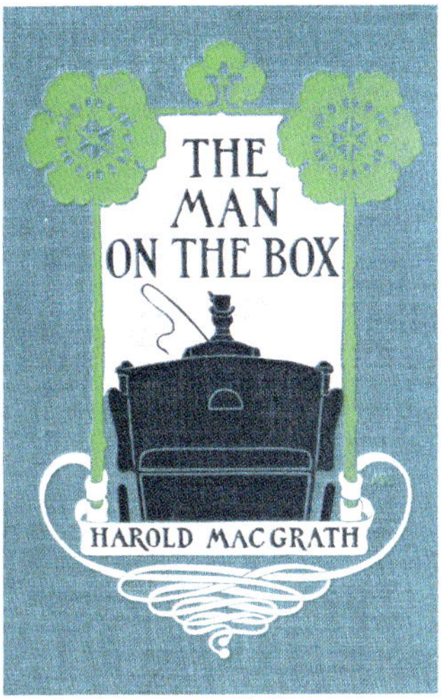

1904 · Anonymous · US · Book cover

1904 · Joseph Adolph Lang · DE · Poster

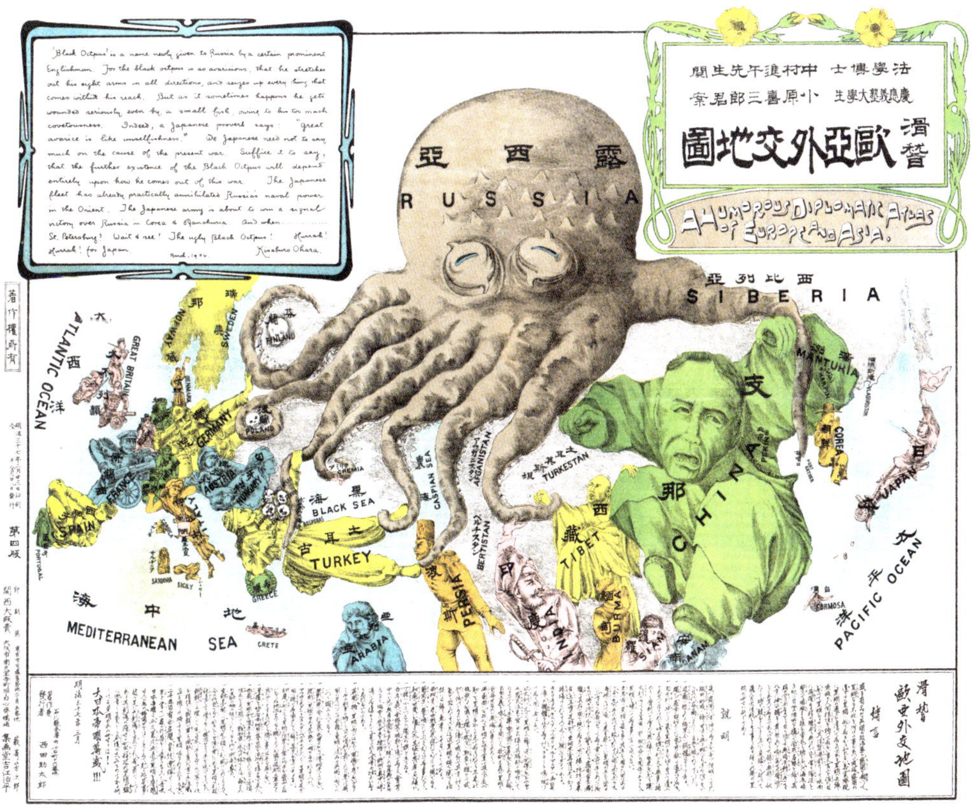

1904 · Kisaburo Ohara · JP · Infographic

1905

The **Society of Printers** is founded in Boston

1905 · Anonymous · DE · Poster

1905 · Anonymous · FR · Poster

1905 · Jan Thorn Prikker · NL/DE · Poster

1905 · Jules Abel Faivre · FR · Poster

1905 · Anonymous · RU · Magazine cover

1905 · Jakob Friedrich Bollschweiler · CH · Poster

1905 · Paul Scheurich · DE · Poster

1906

The four-color wet printing process (**CMYK**) is incorporated for the first time

1906 · Moraes · PT · Magazine cover

1906 · Anonymous · US · Book cover

1906 · Anonymous · FR · Poster

1906 · Anonymous · FR · Poster

1906 · Leonetto Cappiello · IT/FR · Poster

1906 · Anonymous · IT · Magazine cover

1906 · Henrique Alvim Corrêa · BR/FR · Poster

1907

The **Deutscher Werkbund** is established in Germany

1900s · Anonymous · RU · Poster

1907 · Edward Penfield · US · Poster

1907 · Burkhard Mangold · CH · Poster

1907 · Hans Rudi Erdt · DE · Poster

1900s · "Mich" (Michel Liebeaux) · FR · Poster

1907 · Udo J. Keppler · US · Magazine cover

Founded in Berlin in 1883 as the Deutsche Edison-Gesellschaft für angewandte Elektricität and later renamed Allgemeine Elektricitäts-Gesellschaft (General Electrical Company), AEG grew to become the leading German manufacturer of electronic products for domestic and industrial use. Between 1907 and 1914, the artist, graphic designer, and architect Peter Behrens was the corporation's chief artistic consultant. With his multidisciplinary background, Behrens designed advertising posters, as well as consumer products and industrial buildings for AEG. Although his various early projects did not achieve the visual precision of his later designs, Behrens's work for AEG was the first example of a fully fledged corporate identity, embracing for the first time such innovations as a company typeface. In the changing forms of the different AEG logos there can also be seen a gradual move away from Jugendstil art to a neutral and modernist style of graphic design.

Als Deutsche Edison-Gesellschaft für angewandte Elektricität 1883 in Berlin gegründet, wurde das Unternehmen unter dem neuen Namen Allgemeine Elektricitäts-Gesellschaft (kurz: AEG) zum führenden deutschen Hersteller von elektronischen Produkten für Endverbraucher und die Industrie. Zwischen 1907 und 1914 war der Künstler, Grafikdesigner und Architekt Peter Behrens künstlerischer Berater des Unternehmens. Mit seiner interdisziplinären Vorprägung gestaltete Behrens Werbegrafik, Firmenarchitektur und Produkte der AEG. Auch wenn die unterschiedlichen Entwürfe noch nicht die visuelle Stringenz späterer Projekte aufwiesen, ist seine Arbeit für die AEG das erste Beispiel einer umfassenden Corporate Identity in der sich Innovationen wie der Entwurf einer eigenen Hausschrift erstmals zeigten. Die unterschiedlichen Logos der AEG dokumentieren gleichzeitig die Loslösung vom künstlerisch geprägten Jugendstil hin zu einer neutralmodernistischen Grafik.

Fondée en 1883 sous le nom de Deutsche Edison-Gesellschaft für angewandte Elektricität (Société allemande Edison pour l'électricité appliquée), l'entreprise devint le premier fabricant allemand de produits électroniques pour les consommateurs finals comme pour les acteurs de l'industrie sous son nouveau nom Allgemeine Elektricitäts-Gesellschaft (AEG, Société générale électrique). L'artiste, graphiste et architecte Peter Behrens en fut le conseiller artistique de 1907 à 1914. Grâce à un profil interdisciplinaire, il créa pour AEG du graphisme publicitaire, des produits et des bâtiments industriels. Même si ses différents projets pour AEG ne présentent pas encore la cohérence visuelle de ses réalisations ultérieures, son travail est le premier exemple d'une identité de marque de grande envergure dans laquelle apparaissent des solutions inédites comme la conception d'une typographie maison. Les différents logos d'AEG illustrent en même temps l'abandon du Jugendstil au profit d'un graphisme moderniste de tendance plus sobre et plus neutre.

1912 · Louis Oppenheim, Peter Behrens · DE · Poster

1909 · Peter Behrens · DE · Brochure cover

Peter Behrens (1868, Hamburg – 1940, Berlin) was a German designer and architect. After studying in Karlsruhe, Düsseldorf, and Munich, he became a member of the Art Nouveau movement—and in 1893 a co-founder of the Munich Secession—before playing a key role by embracing Modernism and promoting reform in design and architecture. In 1907 he co-founded the German Werkbund and the same year became house artistic consultant for AEG. Working as both a professional and an academic professor, his students and assistants included Ludwig Mies van der Rohe, Le Corbusier, and Walter Gropius.

Peter Behrens (1868, Hamburg – 1940, Berlin) war ein deutscher Grafikdesigner und Architekt. Nach Studienjahren in Karlsruhe, Düsseldorf und München schloss er sich der Jugendstilbewegung an und war 1893 ein Mitbegründer der Münchener Secession. Zur Schlüsselfigur wurde er, als er sich der Moderne zuwandte und eine Reform im Design und in der Architektur propagierte. 1907 beteiligte er sich an der Gründung des Deutschen Werkbunds und wurde im selben Jahr künstlerischer Berater der AEG. Neben seiner praktischen Tätigkeit hatte er auch eine akademische Lehrstelle inne, zu seinen Studenten und Assistenten gehörten Ludwig Mies van der Rohe, Le Corbusier und Walter Gropius.

Peter Behrens (1868, Hambourg – 1940, Berlin) fut un designer et architecte allemand. Après des études à Karlsruhe, Düsseldorf et Munich, il rejoignit le mouvement Art nouveau – il fut un des fondateurs de la Sécession munichoise en 1893 – avant de jouer un rôle clé en embrassant le modernisme et comme ardent promoteur d'une réforme du design et de l'architecture. En 1907, il cofonda le Deutscher Werkbund, et la même année, devint consultant artistique permanent d'AEG. Travaillant à la fois comme professionnel et professeur universitaire, il compta notamment parmi ses élèves et assistants Mies van der Rohe, Le Corbusier et Walter Gropius.

»I tried to show that by their very nature art and technology are two very different intellectual expressions and that it is an aesthetic fallacy for us to believe that only through applying technological principles, namely out of the most extreme and most concise fulfillment of a purpose, can a thing of beauty be created.« Peter Behrens, *Elektrotechnische Zeitschrift*, 1910

1910 · Peter Behrens · DE · Brochure cover

1910 · Peter Behrens · DE · Poster

1907 · Peter Behrens · DE · Logo

1907 · Peter Behrens · DE · Logo

1908 · Peter Behrens · DE · Logo

1912 · Peter Behrens · DE · Logo

1908

The **News Gothic** typeface is created by Morris Fuller Benton

1908 · Emil Cardinaux · CH · Poster

1908 · Anonymous · US · Logo · Chicago Cubs

1908 · Anonymous · IT · Logo · Inter Milan

1908 · Anonymous · CH · Packaging

1908 · Ludwig Hohlwein · DE · Poster

1908 · Konstanty Kietlicz-Rayski · PL · Poster

1908 · Anonymous · FR · Poster

1908 · Daan Hoeksema · NL · Poster

In 1890, Vienna, then one of the two capitals of the Austro-Hungarian Empire, ushered in an incomparable golden age for culture in which every intellectual discipline flourished. The visual arts were strongly influenced firstly by the Vienna Secession, a group of groundbreaking artists which included Gustav Klimt, Koloman Moser, and Joseph Maria Olbrich, and then by the Wiener Werkstätte, a production collective that focused on decorative items, jewelry, and furniture designed by artists. The latter was a highly creative organization whose field of activity also included the production of captivating posters and other printed matter, which had a unique charm that lent them wider international appeal.

Das Kulturleben Wiens als eine der beiden Hauptstädte der k. u. k. Doppelmonarchie erfuhr ab 1890 eine unvergleichliche Blütezeit in sämtlichen Disziplinen. Im Bereich der visuellen Künste waren gleichermaßen die Wiener Secession, eine Vereinigung stilprägender Künstler wie Gustav Klimt, Koloman Moser oder Joseph Maria Olbrich, und die Wiener Werkstätte prägend, die als Produktionsgemeinschaft von Künstlern entworfene Alltagsgegenstände, Schmuck und Möbel vertrieb. Im Umfeld dieser hochkreativen Organisationen entstanden faszinierende Plakate und andere Drucksachen ganz eigenen Ausdrucks von internationaler Strahlkraft.

À partir de 1890, la vie culturelle de Vienne, en tant qu'une des deux capitales de la Double monarchie austro-hongroise, connut un épanouissement sans précédent dans toutes les disciplines. Dans le domaine des arts visuels, la Sécession viennoise, association d'artistes stylistiquement marquants comme Gustav Klimt, Koloman Moser ou Joseph Maria Olbrich, joua à cet égard un rôle aussi déterminant que la Wiener Werkstätte, un atelier de production qui diffusait des objets quotidiens, des bijoux et des meubles créés par des artistes. Dans le cadre de ces structures hautement créatives virent le jour des affiches fascinantes et des imprimés caractérisés par un style tout à fait unique, dont le retentissement fut mondial.

1905 · Josef Hoffmann · AT · Poster

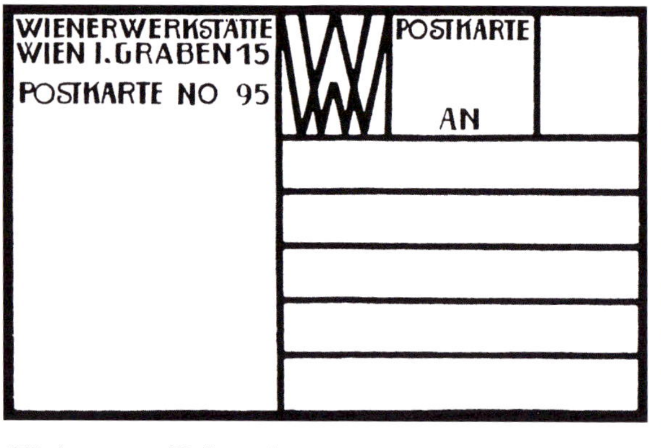

1907 · Anonymous · AT · Postcard

»Nowhere in Europe was aesthetic culture so intensely associated with personal standing as in Viennese middle-class society. Art offered the members of the Viennese bourgeoisie the opportunity to place themselves on a par with the politically all-powerful aristocracy.«

Gabriele Fahr-Becker, *Wiener Werkstätte*, 1995

1906 · Ferdinand Andri · AT · Poster

1909 · Koloman Moser · AT · Brochure cover

1908 · Rudolf Kalvach · AT · Poster

1908 · Oskar Kokoschka · AT · Poster

1902 · Koloman Moser · AT · Poster

1909

F. T. Marinetti publishes his
Manifesto of Futurism

1909 · Alfred Nathaniel Oppenheim · DE · Poster

1909 · Anonymous · HU · Poster

1909 · Ernest Montaut · FR · Poster

1909 · Hisui Sugiura · JP · Book cover

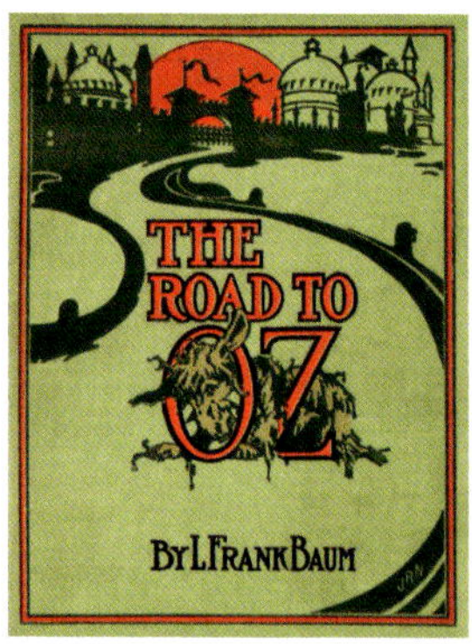

1909 · John R. Neill · US · Book cover

1909 · Anonymous · DE · Logo · Daimler

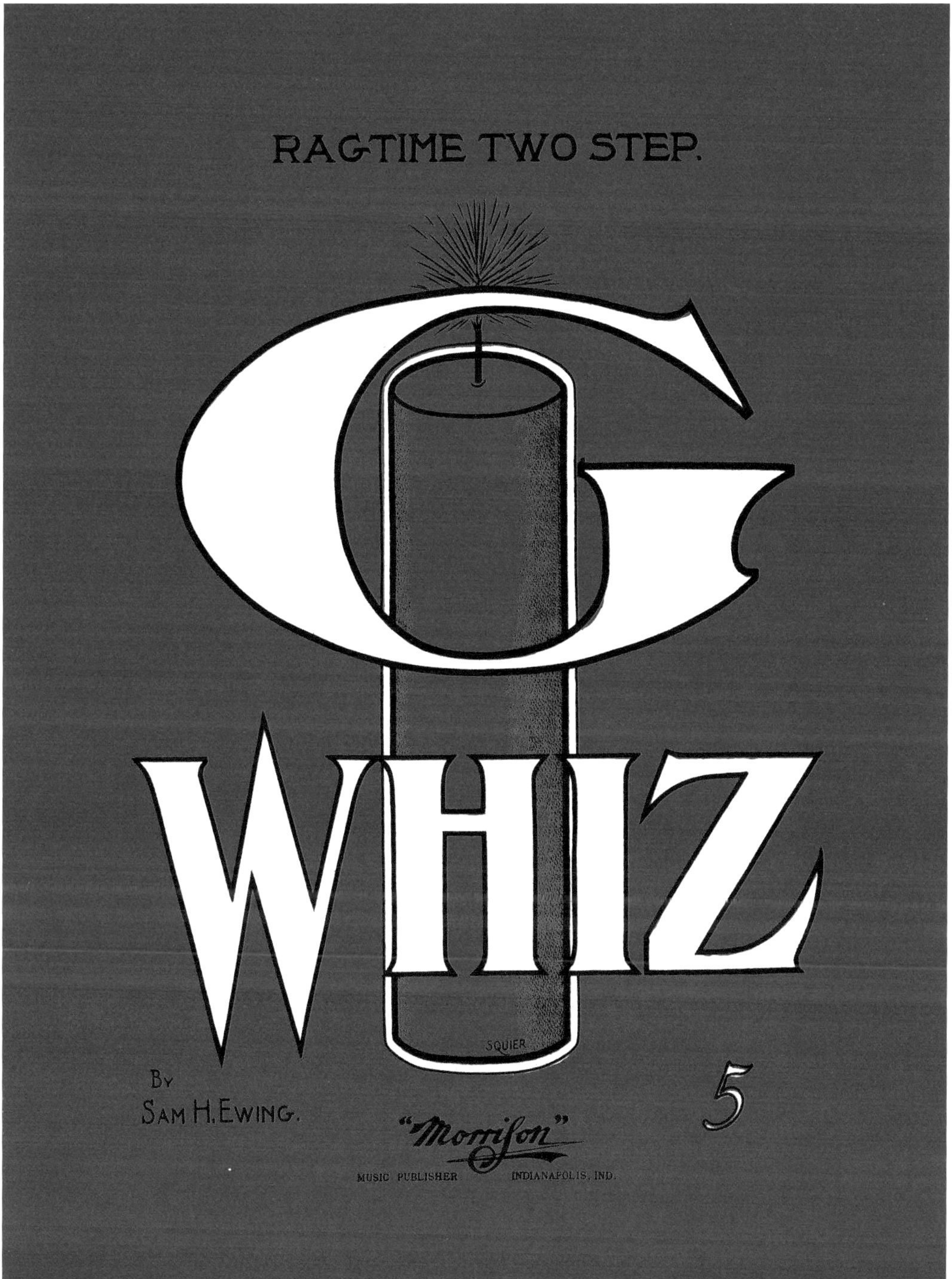

1909 · "Squier" · US · Brochure cover

1912 · Anonymous · US · Logo · Ford

1917 · Anonymous · UK/NL · Magazine cover

1910

1911 · Hans Rudi Erdt · DE · Poster

1917 · Anonymous · US · Poster

1919

1911 · Anonymous · US · Ad

UNITED
ARTISTS

1919 · Anonymous · US · Logo · United Artists

By the 1910s it had become a matter of course for companies to hire design and advertising specialists, and in many countries these areas of expertise became properly recognized professions, as seen in the founding of several trade associations and journals. During the years of the First World War, graphic design was the obvious and most expressive choice for the numerous propaganda posters put out by the various warring countries. At the same time, avant-garde movements of different persuasions were appearing in countries across Europe and in Russia, whose leading lights eagerly pushed the boundaries of art and design. New forms of expression took hold which would have a lasting impact on the development of the visual arts in the following decades.

Für Unternehmen wurde es zunehmend selbstverständlich, Fachleute für Gestaltung und Werbung zu engagieren. In den 1910er-Jahren professionalisierte sich die Branche in vielen Ländern, Berufsverbände und Fachzeitschriften entstanden. Während des Ersten Weltkriegs zeigt sich die selbstverständliche Durchsetzung von Grafikdesign als visuelles Kommunikationsmittel in den zahlreichen Propagandaplakaten der unterschiedlichen Kriegsteilnehmer besonders eindrucksvoll. Gleichzeitig entwickelten sich in einigen europäischen Ländern und in Russland erste Avantgardebewegungen verschiedener Ausprägungen. Deren Protagonisten bewegten sich teils nahtlos an der Grenze von Kunst und Design. Neue Ausdrucksformen etablierten sich, die die visuelle Entwicklung des folgenden Jahrzehnts nachhaltig beeinflussen sollten.

Les entreprises considèrent de plus en plus comme une évidence la nécessité d'engager des spécialistes du graphisme et de la publicité. Dans les années 1910, le secteur se professionnalise dans bien des pays, et des associations professionnelles et revues spécialisées voient le jour. Durant les années de la Première Guerre mondiale, l'évidence avec laquelle le graphisme s'impose en tant que moyen de communication visuelle se manifeste de manière particulièrement frappante à travers les nombreuses affiches de propagande des belligérants. En même temps naissent en Russie et en Europe des mouvements avant-gardistes de différentes tendances dont les protagonistes repoussent les limites de l'art comme du graphisme. De nouvelles formes d'expression acquièrent droit de cité et vont influencer le développement des arts visuels des décennies suivantes.

The retail outlet of a printer and signwriter's workshop in Italy, with one of its advertising bikes.

Das Ladengeschäft einer Schrift- und Schilderwerkstatt in Italien samt Werbefahrrad.

La boutique d'un atelier de typographie et d'enseignes en Italie – avec sa bicyclette publicitaire.

1910

The first issue of **Das Plakat**, a forerunner of modern design magazines, is published in Berlin

1910 · Emil Flohri · US · Magazine cover

1910 · Lucien Lopes Silva · FR · Poster

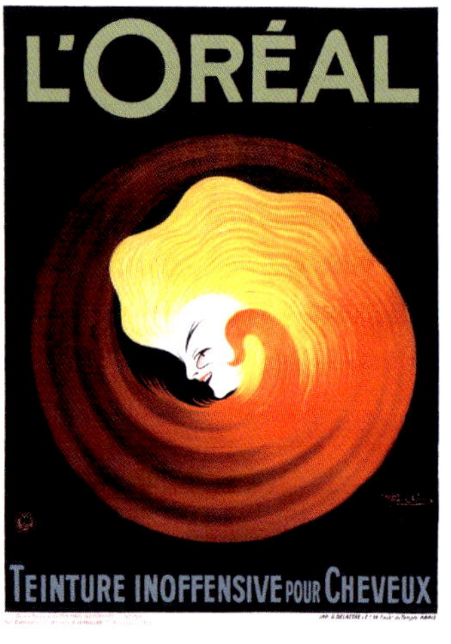

1910 · Raoul Vion · FR · Poster

1910 · Mariusz Zaruski · PL · Poster

1910 · Gordon Ross · US · Magazine cover

1910 · Anonymous · FR · Poster

1910 · Anonymous · FR · Poster

1910 · Anonymous · IT · Magazine cover

1910 · Anonymous · US · Poster

1910 · Albert Knab · DE · Poster

1911

For the first time **Arabic text** is set on a Linotype machine

1911 · Anonymous · US · Logo · Buick

1911 · Anonymous · DE · Logo · Verlag für Sozialpolitik

1911 · Anonymous · US · Logo · St. Louis Giants

1911 · Franz von Stuck · DE · Poster

1911 · "Sem" (Georges Goursat) · FR · Poster

1911 · Anonymous · DE · Magazine cover

1911 · Alois Hugonnet · FR · Poster

1911 · Anonymous · FR · Poster

1911 · Anonymous · RU · Brochure cover

1912

Harrison King McCann, along with four partners, launches the **H. K. McCann Co.** advertising agency, which went on to become the world-conquering McCann-Erickson

1912 · Anonymous · UK · Poster

1912 · Anonymous · UK · Poster

1912 · Walter Thomas · US · Poster

The German job description **Gebrauchsgraphiker,** meaning graphic designer, is first used in a publication by Walter von Zur Westen

1912 · Herbert Meyer · US · Magazine cover

1912 · Hans Rudi Erdt · DE · Poster

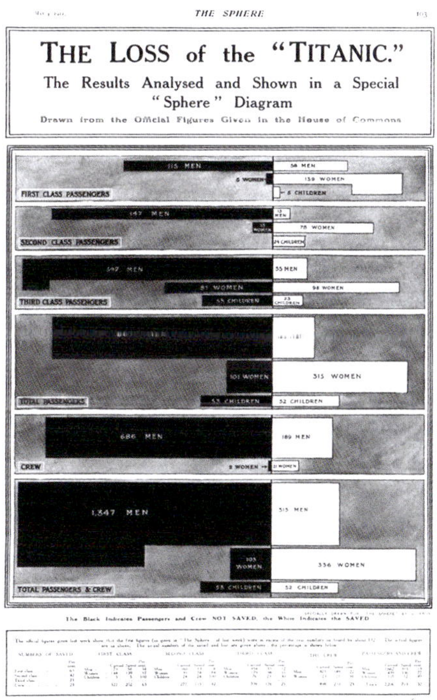

1912 · Anonymous · UK · Infographic

1912 · Leonetto Cappiello · IT/FR · Poster

On February 20, 1909, the French daily newspaper *Le Figaro* published on its front page the Italian writer Filippo Tommaso Marinetti's *Futurist Manifesto*. Its publication marked the beginning of the Futurist avant-garde art movement, whose intention was no less than to create an entirely new culture and civilization. In the years that followed, artists, musicians, writers, and architects, most of them Italian or Russian, signed up to the cause and set about developing a vision of life in the modern world. At the same time, Marinetti's written works presented a pioneering approach to typography, which broke the rules of conventional typesetting by directly integrating type and photography.

Am 20. Februar 1909 druckte die französische Tageszeitung *Le Figaro* das „Futuristische Manifest" des italienischen Schriftstellers Filippo Tommaso Marinetti auf ihrer Titelseite ab. Die Veröffentlichung stellt den Beginn einer avantgardistischen Kunstbewegung dar, die nichts weniger als eine neue Kultur erschaffen wollte. In den folgenden Jahren schlossen sich Künstler, Musiker, Literaten und Architekten vor allem aus Italien und Russland dem Futurismus an und entwickelten Visionen für das moderne Leben. In den Publikationen Marinettis zeigte sich dabei ein neuartiger Umgang mit Typografie, der das Regelwerk des klassischen Buchsatzes ignorierte und Schrift zu Bildern werden ließ.

Le 20 février 1909, *Le Figaro* publiait en première page le «Manifeste du futurisme» de l'écrivain italien Filippo Tommaso Marinetti. Cette publication marque le coup d'envoi d'un mouvement artistique avant-gardiste qui prétendait fonder rien moins qu'une nouvelle culture. Au cours des années suivantes, des artistes, musiciens, écrivains et architectes, la plupart originaires d'Italie et de Russie, rejoignirent le futurisme et développèrent des visions de la vie moderne. Dans les publications de Marinetti se dessine en même temps une pratique typographique qui bouscule les règles de la composition classique et combine pour la première fois textes et images.

1914 · Filippo Tommaso Marinetti · IT · Book cover

»We intend to sing the love of danger, the habit of energy and fearlessness.«

F. T. Marinetti, *The Manifesto of Futurism*, 1909

Filippo Tommaso Marinetti (1876, Alexandria, Egypt – 1944, Ballagio, Italy) was an Italian poet, editor, and art theorist, best known as the founder of the Futurist movement and author of its manifesto, published in 1909. He grew up in Egypt and went to school there before moving to Paris to study at the Sorbonne and later moving to Italy where he also attended the University of Pavia. Marinetti's writings were instrumental in the early development of a different aesthetic in the first years of the 20th century but his later life was marked by controversy after the Futurist Political Party he founded in 1918 merged only a year later with Mussolini's Fascists, and Marinetti became one of the first affiliates of the Italian Fascist Party.

Filippo Tommaso Marinetti (1876, Alexandria, Ägypten – 1944, Ballagio, Italien) war ein italienischer Dichter, Redakteur und Kunsttheoretiker, der vor allem als Begründer der futuristischen Bewegung und als Verfasser ihres 1909 veröffentlichten Manifests bekannt wurde. Er wuchs in Ägypten auf, wo er auch die Schule besuchte. Anschließend ging er nach Paris, um an der Sorbonne zu studieren, und später nach Italien, wo er sein Studium an der Universität Pavia fortsetzte. Marinettis Schriften hatten in den ersten Jahren des 20. Jahrhunderts einen maßgeblichen Einfluss auf die Entwicklung einer neuen Ästhetik, doch sein späteres Leben war von Kontroversen geprägt, nachdem sich die Futuristische Partei, die er 1918 ins Leben gerufen hatte, nur ein Jahr später mit Mussolinis Faschisten zusammenschloss und Marinetti eines der ersten Mitglieder der Faschistischen Partei Italiens wurde.

Filippo Tommaso Marinetti (1876, Alexandrie, Égypte – 1944, Ballagio, Italie) fut un poète, éditeur et artiste théoricien italien connu surtout comme fondateur du mouvement futuriste et auteur du manifeste éponyme publié en 1909. Il grandit et fut scolarisé en Égypte avant de s'installer à Paris pour y suivre des études à la Sorbonne, puis s'établit en Italie, où il fréquenta aussi l'université de Pavie. Les écrits de Marinetti ont joué un rôle clé dans l'apparition de différentes esthétiques au début du XXe siècle. Sa vie ultérieure restera marquée par des controverses : dès 1919, le parti politique futuriste qu'il avait fondé en 1918 fusionna avec les fascistes de Mussolini, et deux ans plus tard, Marinetti devint un des premiers membres du Parti national fasciste.

1919 · Filippo Tommaso Marinetti · IT · Book cover

1922 · Filippo Tommaso Marinetti · IT · Book cover

1919 · Filippo Tommaso Marinetti · IT · Poster

1913

1913 · Pierre de Coubertin · FR · Logo

1913 · Emil Flohri · US · Magazine cover

1913 · Anonymous · US · Poster

1913 · Albrecht Mayer · CH · Poster

1913 · Konstantin Mikhaylovich Kuzginow · RU · Poster

1913 · Anonymous · DE · Brochure cover

1913 · Anonymous · IT · Poster

1913 · Mihály Biró · HU · Poster

1913 · Ludwig Hohlwein · DE · Poster

1914

The **American Institute of Graphic Arts (AIGA)** is founded in New York City

1914 · Anonymous · CH · Brochure cover

1914 · Valentin Zietara · DE · Poster

The **Bugra** World Exhibition of the Book is held in Leipzig, Germany

1914 · Anonymous · US · Book cover

1914 · Anonymous · UK · Brochure cover

1914 · Anonymous · US · Logo · Universal Films

The **Souvenir** typeface is
created by Morris Fuller Benton

1914 · London Recruiting Department · UK · Poster

1914 · Alfred Leete · UK · Magazine cover

1914 · Karl Maria Stadler · DE · Poster

1914 · Constant Duval · FR · Poster

The First World War was without question less technological than the Second, and was fought mostly by armies on foot or horseback. The chief means of communication were either radio or printed material, used both because of the need to explain what was happening but also because of the importance and urgency of being prepared. Apart from recruitment, government propaganda set out various types of information to justify the war, and for this a wide range of infographics was produced, including a number of examples by the German, but London-educated, designer Louis Oppenheim.

Der Erste Weltkrieg war wesentlich weniger technisch als der Zweite, er wurde vorwiegend mit Dragonern und Fußsoldaten geführt. Für die vorrangigen Kommunikationsmedien – Radio und gedrucktes Material – war es von überragender Bedeutung, nicht nur die Ereignisse zu erklären, sondern auch die Notwendigkeit einer guten Vorbereitung. Von Rekrutierungszwecken abgesehen, verbreitete die staatliche Propaganda Informationen, die den Krieg rechtfertigten, und zu dem Zweck wurde eine ganze Reihe von Informationsgrafiken angefertigt, unter anderem von dem in Deutschland geborenen und in London ausgebildeten Grafikdesigner Louis Oppenheim.

La Première Guerre mondiale a été nettement moins technologique que la Seconde. Elle fut en effet livrée en bonne partie par la cavalerie et l'infanterie. Les moyens de communication utilisés étaient principalement la radio et les médias imprimés, et la nécessité d'expliquer non seulement les événements, mais aussi l'importance de la capacité de réaction, étaient les urgences du moment. Au-delà du recrutement, la propagande gouvernementale décidait du type d'information propre à justifier la guerre. À cet effet fut produit un vaste éventail de graphismes d'information conçus notamment par Louis Oppenheim, graphiste allemand d'origine et britannique de formation.

1917 · Norman Tolson · US · Poster

1917 · James Montgomery Flagg · US · Poster

»Unlike product advertising, political propaganda promoted not goods but abstract ideas. These always referred to principles such as support for the state or, in the nationalist sense, the regeneration of the state, and to moral values such as love of and readiness to defend the Fatherland [...] etc.«

Anita Kühnel, *Verführungen, Plakate aus Österreich und Deutschland von 1914–1945*, 1998

1918 · Julius Ussy Engelhard · DE · Poster

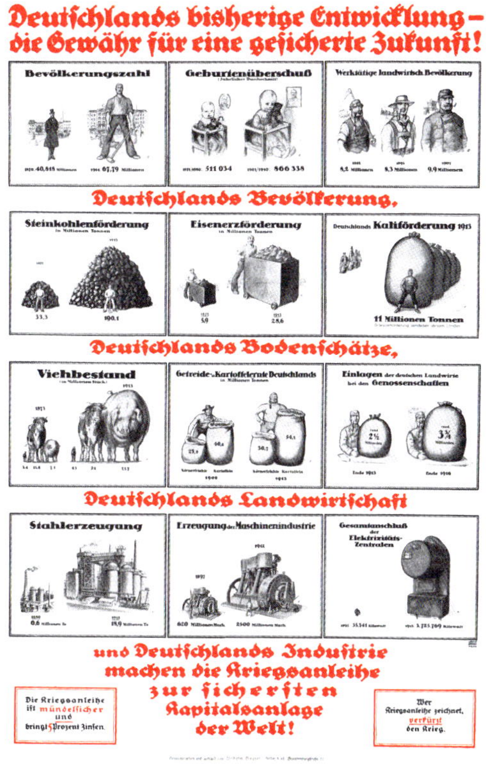

1914 · Louis Oppenheim · DE · Poster

1916 · Louis Oppenheim · DE · Poster

1918 · Louis Oppenheim · DE · Poster

1915

1915 · Lucian Bernhard · DE · Poster

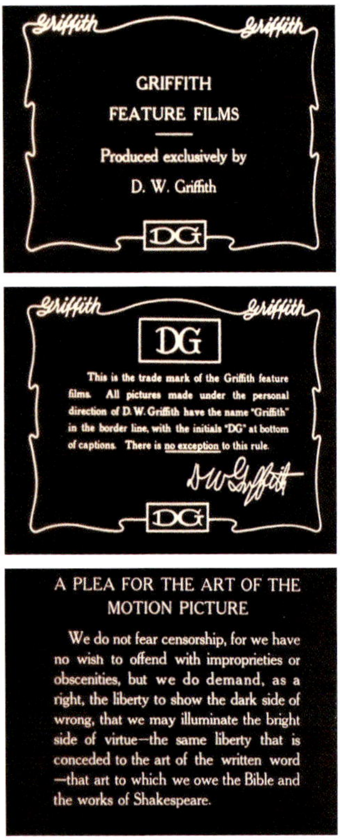

1915 · Anonymous · US · Opening titles

1915 · Anonymous · JP · Magazine cover

1915 · Frédéric Rouge · CH · Poster

1915 · Anonymous · IT · Magazine cover

1915 · Adolf Uzarski · DE · Poster

1915 · Henry Mayer · US · Magazine illustration

1916

Edward Johnston creates a typeface for the London Underground system

The **Dada** movement starts in Zurich

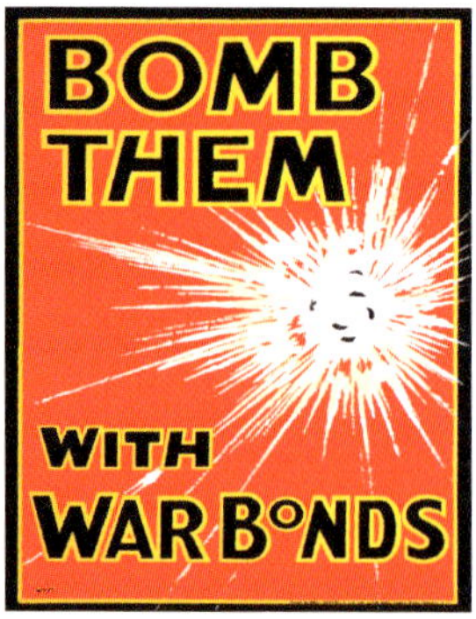

1916 · Anonymous · UK · Poster

1916 · Frank Walts · US · Magazine cover

1916 · Edward Johnston · UK · Logo

1916 · Otto Linnemann · DE · Poster

1916 · Frank Walts · US · Magazine cover

1916 · Paul Scheurich · DE · Poster

1916 · Frank Walts · US · Magazine cover

1916 · Hugo Gellert · HU/US · Magazine cover

1916 · Frank Walts · US · Magazine cover

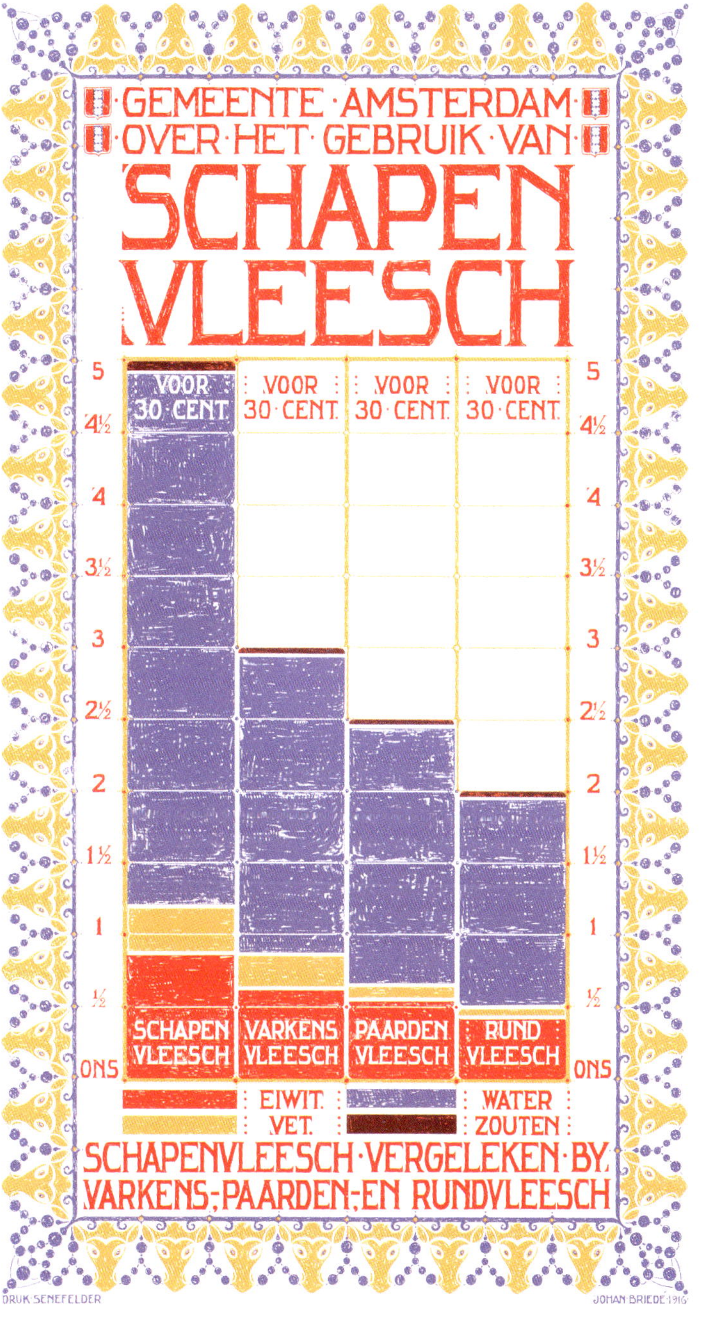

1916 · Johan Briedé · NL · Poster

1917

Larry Valenstein and Arthur Fatt open an advertising agency which later evolves into the global corporation **Grey**

The avant-garde publishing company **Malik Verlag** is founded in Berlin by John Heartfield

1917 · Anonymous · DE · Ad

1917 · "Hahn" · NL · Catalog cover

1917 · W. Gordel · NL · Poster

1917 · H. L. Roowy · UK/IT · Poster

1917 · Daan Hoeksema · NL · Poster

The first issue of **De Stijl** magazine is published by Theo van Doesburg in the Netherlands

1917 · Anonymous · US · Poster

1917 · James Allen St. John · US · Poster

1917 · Anonymous · US · Poster

1917 · Anonymous · US · Poster

1917 · "Sem" (Georges Goursat) · FR · Poster

1917 · Anonymous · US · Poster

In Leiden in 1917 a group of Dutch painters, graphic designers, and architects together founded a new artistic movement which they called simply De Stijl—"The Style." Its members were united by their desire to create and by their shared attempts to find new geometric and abstract solutions to apply in their respective fields of artistic activity. As well as putting their ideas into practice, the group also discussed design-theoretical issues, including topics such as asymmetry and symmetry, color and non-color, objectivity and subjectivity. Their magazine, also called *De Stijl*, was founded in 1917 too and edited by the writer and designer Theo van Doesburg; it became one of the driving forces behind the highly influential group's activities and was for many years its mouthpiece.

Im Jahr 1917 gründete eine Gruppe niederländischer Künstler, Grafikdesigner und Architekten unter dem Namen De Stijl eine neue Künstlervereinigung in Leiden. Die Mitglieder verbanden der Wunsch und die Suche nach neuartigen geometrisch-abstrakten Lösungen in ihren Anwendungsfeldern. Neben der Praxis wurden in der Gruppe Themen der modernen Designtheorie diskutiert, darunter Fragen zu Asymmetrie und Symmetrie, Farbe und Nichtfarbe oder Objektivem und Subjektivem. Unter der Leitung des Autors und Grafikdesigners Theo van Doesburg, eine der treibenden Kräfte der Gruppe, entstand noch im Gründungsjahr die gleichnamige Kunstzeitschrift *De Stijl*, die über viele Jahre das Sprachrohr der einflussreichen Gruppe war.

En 1917, un groupe d'artistes, graphistes et architectes néerlandais fonde à Leyde une nouvelle association d'artistes baptisée De Stijl. Les membres du groupe sont liés par le désir et la recherche de solutions géométriques et abstraites inédites dans leurs champs d'application respectifs. À côté de la pratique, le groupe débat de la théorie moderne du graphisme, notamment de questions portant sur la symétrie et l'asymétrie, la couleur et la non-couleur ou l'objectivité et la subjectivité. L'année même de la fondation de l'association et sous la direction de l'auteur et graphiste Theo van Doesburg, une des grandes forces motrices du groupe, fut aussi créée la revue d'art éponyme *De Stijl*, qui servit pendant de nombreuses années de porte-voix à ce groupe influent.

1927 · Theo van Doesburg · NL · Magazine cover

1924 · Theo van Doesburg · NL · Leaflet

1924 · Theo van Doesburg · NL · Letterhead

1924 · Theo van Doesburg · NL · Letterhead

»The new art has brought forward what the consciousness of time contains: a balance between the universal and the individual.« De Stijl, *Manifesto I*, 1918

Theo van Doesburg (born Christian Emil Marie Küpper, 1883, Utrecht, The Netherlands – 1931, Davos, Switzerland) was a Dutch painter, architect, writer, designer, and a co-founder of the De Stijl movement alongside Piet Mondrian. Arguing for the integration of art, design, and architecture—and making use of simplified and geometric forms—van Doesburg first exhibited his work in 1908. He later dedicated much of his time to writing numerous essays and articles, while also collaborating with El Lissitzky and Kurt Schwitters; he published the Dada magazine *Mécano* under the pseudonym I. K. Bonset.

Theo van Doesburg (1883, geboren als Christian Emil Marie Küpper, Utrecht, Niederlande – 1931, Davos, Schweiz) war ein holländischer Maler, Architekt, Autor, Grafikdesigner und neben Piet Mondrian einer der Mitbegründer der Bewegung De Stijl. Er trat für eine Verbindung von Kunst, Design und Architektur ein, arbeitete mit schlichten geometrischen Formen und stellte sein Werk erstmals 1908 aus. Später schrieb er zahlreiche Essays und Artikel und arbeitete mit El Lissitzky und Kurt Schwitters zusammen. Unter dem Pseudonym I.K. Bonset verlegte er die Dada-Zeitschrift *Mécano*.

Theo van Doesburg (né Christian Emil Marie Küpper, 1883, Utrecht, Pays-Bas – 1931, Davos, Suisse) fut un peintre, architecte, écrivain et designer hollandais et cofondateur du mouvement De Stijl avec Piet Mondrian. Défenseur d'une approche intégrative de l'art, du design et de l'architecture – et se servant de formes simplifiées et géométriques –, van Doesburg exposa pour la première fois son œuvre en 1908. Plus tard, il consacra une grande partie de son temps à écrire de nombreux essais et articles, tout en collaborant avec El Lissitzky et Kurt Schwitters. Il publia la revue dadaïste *Mécano* sous le pseudonyme I. K. Bonset.

1917 · Theo van Doesburg · NL · Magazine cover

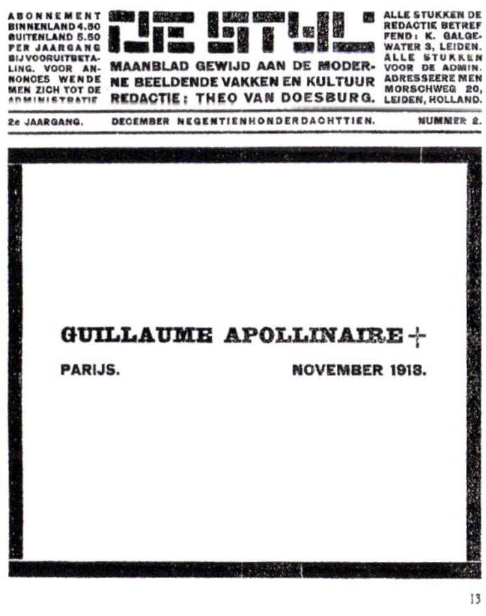

1918 · Theo van Doesburg, Vilmos Huszár · NL/HU · Magazine cover

1927 · Theo van Doesburg · NL · Identity

1917 · Theo van Doesburg · NL · Ad

1918

The **Chinese Central Academy of Fine Arts** is founded, which later establishes a design department

1918 · Anonymous · US · Magazine cover

1918 · Bert Thomas · UK · Poster

1918 · Albert Hahn · NL · Poster

1918 · Otto von Tussenbroek · NL · Packaging

1918 · Anonymous · US · Magazine cover

1918 · Vojtěch Preissig · CZ · Poster

1919

The **Bauhaus** school is founded by Walter Gropius in Weimar, Germany

1919 · Edward McKnight Kauffer · US · Poster

1919 · Anonymous · CH · Logo · Hero

1919 · Sergey Vasilyevich Chekhonin · RU · Poster

1919 · Eric Rohman · SE · Poster

1919 · Machiel Wilmink · NL · Packaging

1919 · Anonymous · US · Poster

1919 · "Danko" · HU · Poster

1927 · Anonymous · US · Identity

1920s · "Mich" (Michel Liebeaux) · FR · Poster

1920

1928 · Anonymous · JP · Ad

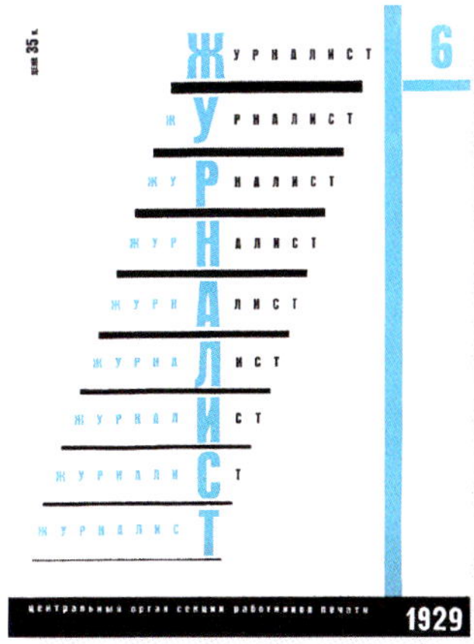

1929 · Anonymous · RU · Magazine cover

1920s · Anonymous · JP · Poster

1929

1925 · Anonymous · BR · Logo · Compania Editoria Nacional

The 1920s were marked, especially in Central Europe, by the parallel influences of commercially operated creative industries and artistically motivated avant-garde movements. Each side had different intentions behind its drive to explore new kinds of graphic work. Photography, for example, found its way into the realm of graphics as a new means of expression, and at the same time the multidisciplinary Bauhaus became one of the principal modernist style-setters, with an influence which extended globally. In France, the new visual language of Art Deco took shape, and, widely used both commercially and artistically, it was soon adopted as an international standard. Set in the positive economic climate that emerged following the horrors of the First World War, the 1920s were a golden age which produced several masterpieces in art, literature, and cinema. But at the end of the decade, the fateful stock market crash of October 1929 foreshadowed the darkening days of the 1930s.

The studio of the Stenberg brothers, whose work revolutionized Russian movie poster design.

Das Atelier der Stenberg-Brüder, die mit ihren Arbeiten das russische Filmplakat revolutionierten.

L'atelier des frères Stenberg, dont les réalisations ont révolutionné l'affiche du cinéma russe.

Die 1920er-Jahre waren vor allem in Mitteleuropa vom Nebeneinander der wirtschaftlich arbeitenden Kreativbranche und der künstlerisch motivierten Avantgarde bestimmt. Beide trieben aus unterschiedlicher Motivation visuelle Entwicklungen voran. Die Fotografie hielt als neues Ausdrucksmittel Einzug in den Bereich der Grafik. Das Bauhaus wurde zur stilprägenden Schule der Moderne mit globalem Einfluss. In Frankreich entwickelte sich mit dem Art déco eine neue Bildsprache, die gleichermaßen kommerziell wie künstlerisch Einsatz fand und bald international adaptiert wurde. Verbunden mit einer positiven globalen Wirtschaftslage, entwickelte sich nach den Schrecken des Ersten Weltkriegs ein oft als „Goldenes Zeitalter" bezeichnetes Jahrzehnt, das auch in Kunst, Literatur und Film zahlreiche Meisterwerke hervorbrachte. Mit einem folgenreichen Börsencrash im Oktober 1929 wurde jedoch noch im ablaufenden Jahrzehnt die düstere Zeit der 1930er-Jahre eingeleitet.

Les années 1920 ont été marquées, en Europe centrale plus qu'ailleurs, par la proximité entre la branche créative commerciale et l'avant-garde artistique. Les deux domaines travaillent aux avancées visuelles pour des motifs différents. La photographie fait son entrée dans le domaine du graphisme en tant que nouveau moyen d'expression. Le Bauhaus devient une école de la modernité qui marque le style de l'époque de son empreinte, dans le cadre d'une influence globale. En France, l'Art déco produit un nouveau langage visuel qui trouve bientôt sa place dans les domaines commercial comme artistique, et qui sera rapidement adapté internationalement. Dans le contexte d'une conjoncture économique mondiale favorable, après les horreurs de la Première Guerre mondiale, s'égrène une décennie que l'on a souvent qualifiée d'« âge d'or », et qui a aussi produit de nombreux chefs-d'œuvre dans les domaines de l'art, de la littérature et du cinéma. En octobre 1929, le terrible krach boursier mit toutefois un terme à cette décennie et introduisit la sombre époque des années 1930.

1920

Czech avant-garde artists group **Devětsil** is founded in Prague

The **Art Directors Club of New York** is established by Louis Pedlar and Earnest Elmo Calkins

1920 · Jorge Barradas · PT · Magazine cover

1920 · Ernst Keller · CH · Poster

1920 · "Toddt" · IT · Magazine cover

1920 · C. De Haas · NL · Leaflet cover

1920 · "Hentschel" · NL · Book cover

"BP"

1920 · A. R. Saunders · UK · Logo · British Petroleum

The first issue of avant-garde magazine **L'Esprit Nouveau** is published by Le Corbusier and Amédée Ozenfant

1920 · Emil Cardinaux · CH · Poster

1920 · Josef Fenneker · DE · Poster

1920 · Theo Ortner · DE · Poster

1920s · Federico Seneca · IT · Poster

1923 · Alexander Rodchenko · RU · Poster

»Photography—the new, rapid, concrete reflector of the world—should surely undertake to show the world from all vantage points, and to develop people's capacity to see from all sides.«
Alexander Rodchenko, 1928

Alexander Rodchenko (1891, St. Petersburg – 1956, Moscow) was an artist, photographer, and designer in the Soviet Union, and the leading voice of the Constructivist movement. After finishing his studies at the Kazan Art School, Rodchenko moved to Moscow, where his 1924 poster for the state publisher Gosizdat, simply titled *Books*, exerted a huge influence on design. Later charged with being a Formalist (and also being part of the Productivist group), Rodchenko taught in the 1920s at the Higher Technical-Artistic Studios, a Bauhaus organization in Moscow. His work and extensive collaborations became intrinsic legacies of the Russian Revolution.

Alexander Rodtschenko (1891, St. Petersburg – 1956, Moskau) war ein sowjetischer Maler, Fotograf und Grafikdesigner und der Wortführer der Konstruktivisten. Nach dem Studium an der Kunstschule von Kasan ging er nach Moskau, wo er 1924 mit seinem Plakat für den Staatsverlag Gosisdat, das den schlichten Schriftzug „Bücher" trägt, einen enormen Einfluss auf die Grafik ausübte. Später wurde gegen Rodtschenko der Vorwurf erhoben, ein Formalist zu sein (und Mitglied der Produktivisten), doch in den 1920er-Jahren unterrichtete er an den Höheren Künstlerisch-Technischen Werkstätten, einer Bauhaus-Einrichtung in Moskau. Seine Arbeit und seine umfangreichen Gemeinschaftsprojekte gehören zu den bleibenden Vermächtnissen der Russischen Revolution.

Alexandre Rodtchenko (1891, Saint-Pétersbourg – 1956, Moscou) fut un artiste, photographe et graphiste de l'Union soviétique, et le chef de file du mouvement constructiviste. Après des études à l'école des beaux-arts de Kazan, Rodtchenko s'installa à Moscou, où son affiche pour la maison d'édition de l'État Gosizdat (1924) – simplement intitulée *Livres* – exerça une immense influence sur le graphisme. Accusé plus tard de formalisme (et aussi à cause de sa participation au groupe productiviste), Rodtchenko enseigna dans les années 1920 aux Ateliers supérieurs d'art et de technique, une organisation moscovite supervisée par le Bauhaus. Son travail et ses nombreuses collaborations sont devenus des héritages intrinsèques de la révolution russe.

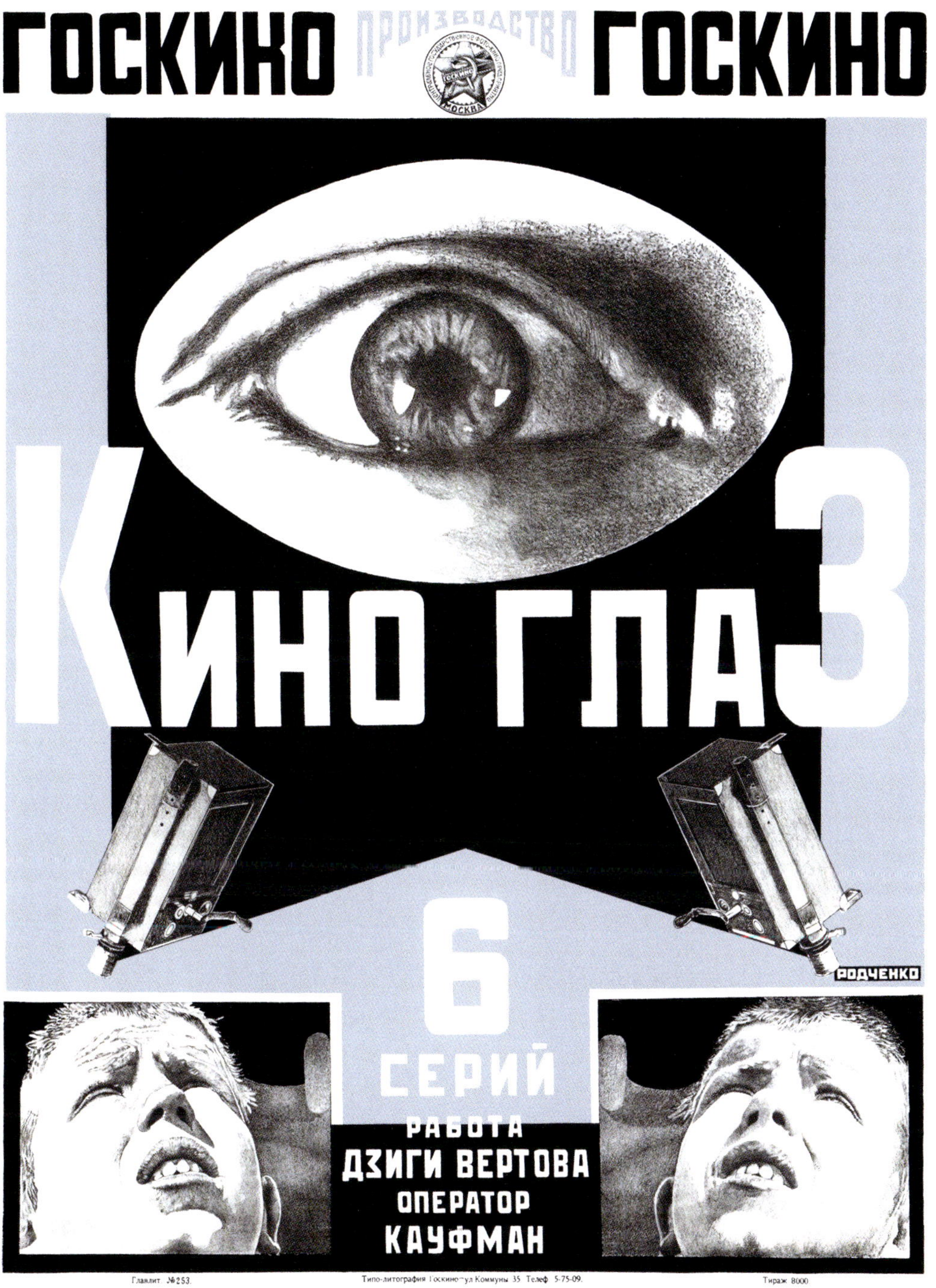

1924 · Alexander Rodchenko · RU · Poster

Having started out in Zurich in 1916 during the First World War as a series of performance-based provocations, Dada evolved into a wider form of expression in the visual and literary arts. Together with the movement's founder Tristan Tzara, artists and writers such as Hans Arp, Hugo Ball, and Marcel Janco were also closely involved, and saw their activities as a revolt against all forms of traditional art and the insanity of nationalism. Throughout Europe and in the United States and also Japan, various Dada groups were established and leading artists such as Man Ray and Marcel Duchamp made important contributions. In what can be seen as a sort of Dadaist spin-off, a number of new artistic journals also sprang up, whose quirky design not only continues to fascinate to this day, but also helped at the time to bring about the transition to modern graphic design.

Ausgehend von Zürich, entwickelte sich während der Zeit des Ersten Weltkriegs ab 1916 Dada zunächst als performancebasierte Ausdrucksform und schlug sich schnell auch in der bildenden Kunst und der Literatur nieder. Dem Begründer der Bewegung, Tristan Tzara, folgten bald Künstler wie Hans Arp, Hugo Ball oder Marcel Janco, die ihre Aktivitäten als Revolte gegen alle Formen der traditionellen Kunstszene und den Irrsinn des Nationalismus verstanden. In ganz Europa, aber auch in den USA und in Japan, bildeten sich Dada-Gruppen und bedeutende Kreative wie Man Ray oder Marcel Duchamp lieferten wichtige Beiträge. Als eine Art Nebenprodukt entstanden zahlreiche Künstlerzeitschriften, die durch ihre unkonventionelle Gestaltung bis heute faszinieren und damals ein Teil des Übergangs hin zum modernen Grafikdesign darstellten.

Pendant la Première Guerre mondiale, partant de son premier foyer zurichois, Dada développe une forme d'expression fondée sur des performances avant d'investir rapidement les domaines des arts plastiques et de la littérature. Aux côtés du fondateur du mouvement Tristan Tzara, des artistes comme Jean Arp, Hugo Ball ou Marcel Janco conçoivent leurs activités comme une révolte contre la scène artistique traditionnelle et la folie nationaliste. Partout en Europe, mais aussi aux États-Unis et au Japon, apparaissent alors divers groupes dada et des artistes comme Man Ray et Marcel Duchamp font d'importantes contributions. Dans ce qui peut être considéré comme un essaimage dadaïste, de nombreuses revues artistiques voient le jour. Leur graphisme anticonformiste fascine encore aujourd'hui comme un des marqueurs forts de la transition vers le graphisme moderne.

1919 · Raoul Hausmann · DE · Magazine cover

1918 · Anonymous · DE · Magazine cover

»Dada's inventive style as well as its rejection of all tradition contributed ingredients to the language of propaganda synthesized during the Twenties. The Dadaist defiance of typographical conventions produced pamphlets and posters on which nearly every word was printed in a different type and size.«

Eckhard Neumann, *Functional Graphic Design in the 20s*, 1967

1923 · Kurt Schwitters, Theo van Doesburg · DE/NL · Poster

1921

The abstract art exhibition **5x5=25** is held in Moscow

The **Cooper Black** typeface is designed by Oswald Cooper

1921 · Frederick Charles Herrick · UK · Poster

1921 · Marcello Dudovich · IT · Poster

1921 · Machiel Wilmink · NL · Magazine cover

1921 · Anonymous · JP · Poster

1921 · Anonymous · US · Poster

1920s · Anonymous · FR · Poster

1921 · Julius Klinger · AT · Poster

1920s · Karü Besnard · HU/DE · Poster

In the second half of the 19th century trademarks began to appear in every branch of commerce and industry, although, with few exceptions, these often over-elaborate and complex early images bore little resemblance to today's logos. It was not until the end of the first decade of the 20th century that German designers, such as Wilhelm Deffke, Karl Schulpig, and F. H. Ehmcke, began to come up with more compact signs. For the first time, these designers concentrated on geometric forms and simpler graphics, thereby laying the foundations for the modern-day logo, which over time has become ubiquitous and led to the development of internationally recognized brand names.

In der zweiten Hälfte des 19. Jahrhunderts setzten sich Markenzeichen in allen Bereichen von Industrie und Handel durch. Mit wenigen Ausnahmen hatten diese meist gegenständlichen und komplexen Zeichen jedoch wenig mit Logos nach heutigem Verständnis zu tun. Die Entwicklung reduzierter Zeichen wurde erst Ende der 1910er-Jahre durch deutsche Gestalter wie Wilhelm Deffke, Karl Schulpig oder F. H. Ehmcke angestoßen. Sie setzten erstmals konsequent auf geometrische Formen und grafische Reduktion; damit begründeten sie nicht weniger als das moderne Logo, das sich im Laufe der Zeit zur allgegenwärtigen und weltweit etablierten Absenderkennzeichnung entwickelt hat.

Pendant la seconde moitié du XIXe siècle, les sigles d'entreprises s'imposent dans tous les domaines de l'industrie et du commerce. Presque toujours figuratifs et complexes, ces premiers sigles n'ont pas grand-chose à voir avec le logo tel que nous le concevons aujourd'hui. La création de signes compacts ne prit son essor qu'à la fin des années 1910, avec des graphistes allemands comme Wilhelm Deffke, Karl Schulpig ou F. H. Ehmcke. Ces graphistes s'appuyèrent pour la première fois sur des formes rigoureusement géométriques et une simplicité graphique, fondant ainsi rien moins que le logo moderne, qui se développera peu à peu jusqu'à devenir une distinction visuelle omniprésente établie aujourd'hui dans le monde entier.

1912 · Julius Gipkens · DE · Logo · W. Wertheim

1920s · Louis Oppenheim · DE · Logo · Own mark

1917 · Wilhelm Deffke · DE · Logo · Gustaf Dorén

1920s · Anonymous · DE · Logo · Telefunken

1919 · Wilhelm Deffke · DE · Logo · Louis Wolf

1921 · Hinrichsen & Reuters · DE · Logo · Own logo

1920 · Anonymous · DE · Logo · A. Molling & Co.

1920 · Wilhelm Deffke · DE · Logo · Vox Records

»Trademarks are intended to protect brand values and at the same time to work as advertisements [...]. Such major tasks can only be fulfilled by trademarks which have their own intrinsic value and, based on public perception and their outward appearance, are seen as well above average.«

Walter F. Schubert, *Die deutsche Werbegraphik*, 1927

1926 · Werner Brand · DE · Logo · Chemische Fabriken Pfeiffer & Dr. Schwandner

1926 · Ernst Böhm · DE · Logo · Horch automobiles

1926 · Johannes Molzahn · DE · Logo · Wilking & Bölts

1926 · Rolf Lange · DE · Logo · Paragummiwerke

1923 · Anonymous · DE · Logo · Voss Werke

1925 · Fritz Rosen · DE · Logo · Berlin Trade Fair

1924 · Otto Arpke · DE · Logo · Autographica

1924 · Max Hertwig · DE · Logo · Dr. Stein & Co.

1924 · Gerhard Marggraff · DE · Logo · Apollo

1924 · Erwin Reusch · DE · Logo · Own logo

1928 · Max Körner · DE · Logo · Pukocid

1922

The term **graphic design** is used for the first time in an article in the *Boston Evening Transcript* by William A. Dwiggins

The first issue of the avant-garde magazine **Mécano** by Theo van Doesburg is published

1922 · Henri Loutan · FR · Poster

1922 · Anonymous · NL · Logo · Verkade's Fabrieken

1922 · Anonymous · BR · Logo · Klaxon

1922 · Anonymous · BR · Logo · Casa Nunes

1922 · Anonymous · NL · Logo · Union

The **DIN-A formats** are established in Germany to regulate paper sizes

The first issue of British design magazine **Commercial Art** is published

Ukrainian-French designer **A. M. Cassandre** immigrates to Paris

Frederic W. Goudy's book **Elements of Lettering** is first published

1922 · Frank Xavier Leyendecker · US · Magazine cover

1922 · Enrico Prampolini · IT · Magazine cover

1922 · "A. R." · FR · Book cover

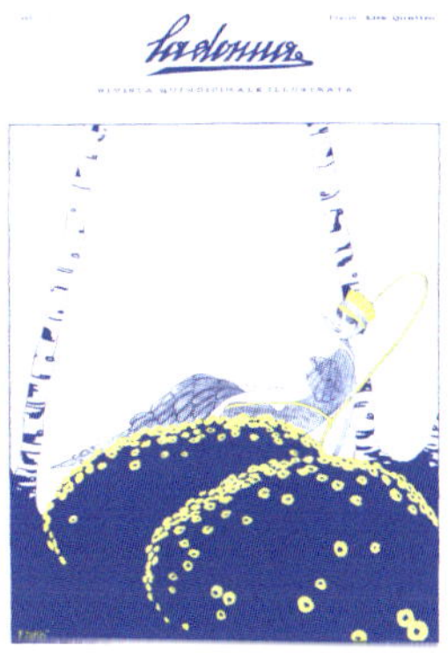

1922 · "Edina" · IT · Magazine cover

1922 · Guy Hoff · US · Magazine cover

1922 · Anonymous · BR · Brochure cover

1922 · El Lissitzky · RU · Magazine cover

1922 · Tom Purvis · UK · Poster

1923

László Moholy-Nagy introduces the term **Neue Typografie** (New Typography)

French type foundry **Deberny & Peignot** is set up in Paris

1923 · "J. A." · NL · Poster

1923 · Kurt Schmidt · DE · Leaflet cover

1923 · László Moholy-Nagy · HU/DE · Book spread

1923 · Hendrik Werkman · NL · Magazine cover

1920s · István Irsai · HU · Poster

1923 · Karl Schulpig · DE · Poster

1920s · Anonymous · RU · Poster

1924

The first issue of German graphic design magazine **Gebrauchsgraphik** is published

1924 · Anonymous · NL · Poster

1924 · Emanuel Josef Margold · AT · Poster

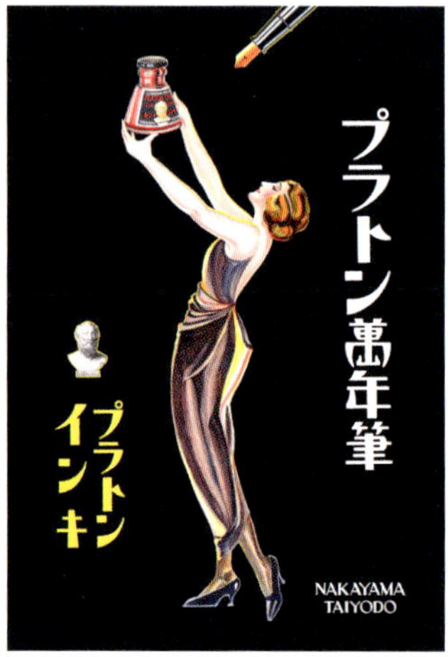

1920s · Anonymous · JP · Poster

1920s · Anonymous · FR · Poster

1924 · "ERS" · SE · Poster

1924 · Anro Jahne · JP · Ad

1924 · Anonymous · JP · Poster

The term "New Typography", as coined by the Bauhaus lecturer László Moholy-Nagy, became synonymous with a form of modern graphic design which made minimal use of type. Starting in 1925, the young designer Jan Tschichold drew up several manifestos for the design movement, which brought together kindred spirits such as El Lissitzky, Otto Baumberger, and Piet Zwart. Mostly laid out in red and white and using the blank page to arrange elements in harmonious combination, the works of the New Typographers broke away from traditional design rules. In its early development, the new style was only put to limited practical use, but had a strong impact on international graphic design and became one of the key elements in its modernization worldwide.

Der Begriff „Neue Typografie" geht auf den Bauhaus-Lehrer László Moholy-Nagy zurück und wurde zum Synonym für modernes Grafikdesign mit den Mitteln reduzierter Typografie. Der junge Gestalter Jan Tschichold verfasste ab 1925 mehrere Manifeste der avantgardistischen Designbewegung, die Gestalter wie El Lissitzky, Otto Baumberger oder Piet Zwart verband. Meist in Rot und Schwarz angelegt, brachen die Arbeiten der Neuen Typografen mit traditionellen Gestaltungsregeln und erzeugten mithilfe von Schrift und Grafikelementen moderne Layoutkompositionen. Die neue Stilistik fand zum Zeitpunkt ihrer Entstehung nur bedingt Anwendung in der Praxis, beeinflusste jedoch das internationale Grafikdesign und trug zu dessen Modernisierung elementar bei.

Le concept de « nouvelle typographie » remonte au professeur du Bauhaus László Moholy-Nagy et devint synonyme de graphisme moderne sous le signe d'une typographie réduite. À partir de 1925, le jeune graphiste Jan Tschichold rédige plusieurs manifestes de l'avant-garde du graphisme, qui regroupe des graphistes comme El Lissitzky, Otto Baumberger ou Piet Zwart. Conçus le plus souvent en rouge et noir, les travaux des nouveaux typographes rompaient avec les règles graphiques traditionnelles et produisirent des compositions modernes d'éléments graphiques. Si cette nouvelle stylistique ne trouva d'abord qu'une application restreinte dans la pratique professionnelle, elle exerça une forte influence sur le graphisme international et apporta une contribution décisive à sa modernisation.

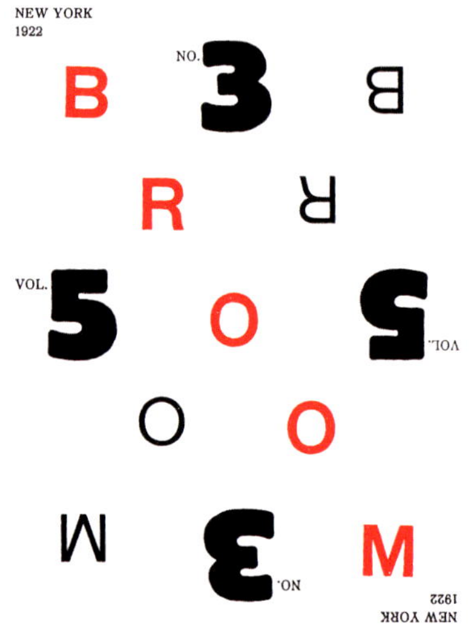

1922 · El Lissitzky · RU · Magazine cover

1923 · El Lissitzky · RU · Magazine cover

»The engineer shapes our age. Distinguishing marks of his work: economy, precision, use of pure constructional forms that correspond to the function of the object.«

Jan Tschichold, *Die neue Typographie*, 1928

1927 · Jan Tschichold · DE · Poster

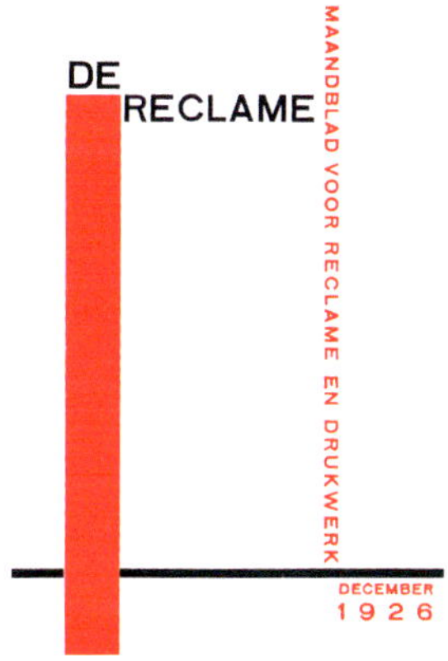

1926 · Machiel Wilmink · NL · Magazine cover

1927 · Karol Labuda · SK · Magazine cover

1924 · Henryk Berlewi · PL · Brochure cover

1925

Edward McKnight Kauffer's book **The Art of the Poster** is published

The **Exposition Internationale des Arts Décoratifs et Industriels Modernes** (International Exhibition of Modern Decorative Arts and Industrial Design) is held in Paris

1925 · Anonymous · UK · Logo · Rolex

1925 · Anonymous · NL · Logo · Sinpo

1925 · Anonymous · RU · Logo · Slowo

1925 · "Gilbas" · FR/IT · Ad

1925 · Anonymous · RU · Poster

1925 · Sven Brasch · DK · Poster

1925 · Oskar Garvens · DE · Book cover

1925 · Louis Kalff · NL · Poster

The **Bauhaus** moves to Dessau

The first issue of the German design magazine **Die Form** is published

1925 · Anonymous · RU · Poster

1925 · "Sonns" · DE · Poster

1925 · El Lissitzky · RU · Book cover

1925 · Fritz Lewy · DE · Brochure cover

1929 · John Heartfield · DE · Book cover

John Heartfield (1891–1968, Berlin) was a graphic artist who worked prolifically in the editorial and performance arts fields. Born Helmut Herzfeld, he changed his name in 1917 to express his protest at the anti-British sentiment sweeping Germany. Heartfield was involved in the Berlin Dada group, but it was his book-jacket designs for Upton Sinclair and stage sets for plays by Bertolt Brecht and Erwin Piscator that really launched his career. His satirical work mocked Hitler and the Nazi regime, often subverting their symbols, and consequently he became a marked man. He escaped assassination by the SS in 1933, and eventually moved to England in 1938.

John Heartfield (1891–1968, Berlin) war ein Grafiker, der im Bereich der Kunst und des Verlagswesens arbeitete. Geboren als Helmut Herzfeld, änderte er 1917 seinen Namen aus Protest gegen die seinerzeit in Deutschland vorherrschenden antibritischen Ressentiments. Heartfield war zunächst in der Berliner Dada-Gruppe aktiv, doch seine eigentliche Karriere begann, als er Schutzumschläge für Bücher von Upton Sinclair und Bühnenbilder für Stücke von Bertolt Brecht und für Inszenierungen von Erwin Piscator entwarf. Seine satirischen Werke machten sich über Hitler und die Nazis lustig, deren Symbole sie oft parodistisch umdeuteten, und damit geriet er automatisch ins Visier des Regimes. 1933 entging Heartfield nur knapp einem Anschlag der SS und ging 1938 schließlich nach England.

John Heartfield (1891–1968, Berlin) fut un graphiste prolifique dans le domaine de l'édition et des arts performatifs. Né Helmut Herzfeld, il change son nom en 1917 pour protester contre la montée de l'anglophobie en Allemagne. Heartfield a fait partie du groupe dada de Berlin, mais ses conceptions de jaquettes de livres pour Upton Sinclair et ses décors pour des pièces de Bertolt Brecht et d'Erwin Piscator vont vraiment lancer sa carrière. Son travail satirique tourne en dérision Hitler et le régime nazi en subvertissant souvent leurs symboles, ce qui fait de lui un homme à abattre. En 1933, Heartfield échappe à un assassinat par les SS et s'installe finalement en Angleterre en 1938.

»The title 'artist' is an insult. The designation 'art' is an annulment of human equality. The deification of the artist is tantamount to self-deification.«

John Heartfield and George Grosz, 1920

1928 · John Heartfield · DE · Poster

1926

Marcel Bleustein-Blanchet founds the **Publicis** advertising agency in Paris at the age of only 20

1926 · Anonymous · NL · Logo · Van Staal & Co.

1926 · Machiel Wilmink · NL · Logo · HI Lichtdruk

1926 · Sándor Bortnyik · HU · Poster

1926 · Anonymous · US · Logo · Topkis Underwear

1926 Roger de Valerio · FR · Poster

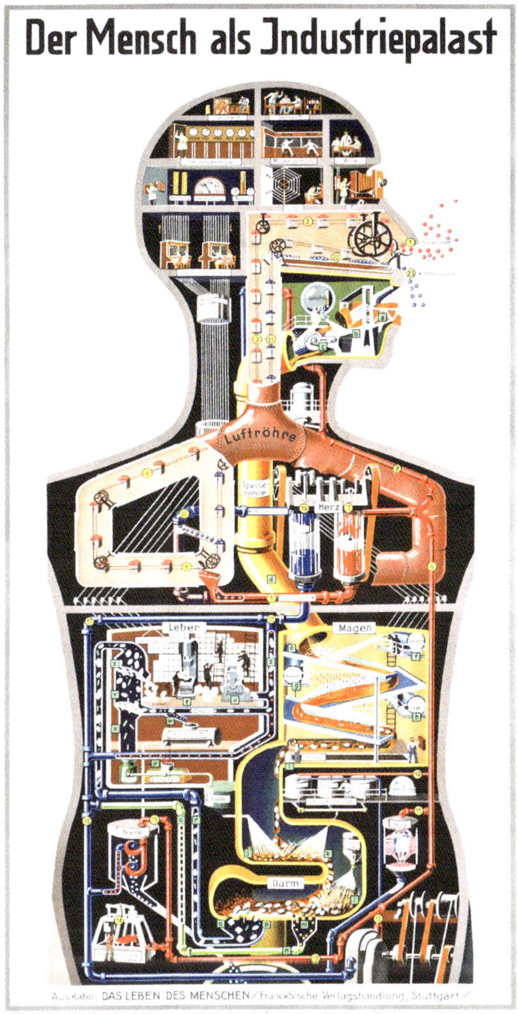

1926 · Fritz Kahn · DE · Poster

1926 · O. K. Gérard · FR · Poster

1926 · M. Wechsler · RU · Poster

1927

German designer Paul Renner creates the **Futura** typeface

The typesetting company **The Composing Room** is established by Sol Cantor and Dr. Robert L. Leslie in the United States

1927 · Machiel Wilmink · NL · Poster

1927 · Ladislas Freiwirth · UK · Poster

1927 · Anonymous · JP · Logo · Yamaha

1927 · Jan Tschichold · DE · Poster

1927 · Willy Petzold · DE · Poster

1927 · Pierre Legrain · FR · Logo · U.S.A.

1927 · Anonymous · FR · Poster

The first issue of Japanese design magazine **Affiches** is published

Rudolf Koch creates the **Kabel** typeface

The first issue of the French design magazine **Arts et Métiers Graphiques** is published

The **Society of Typographic Arts** is established in Chicago

1927 · Leonetto Cappiello · IT/FR · Poster

1927 · Anonymous · FR · Poster

1927 · Atelier Levenstein · RU · Poster

1927 · El Lissitzky · RU · Book cover

1928

Eric Gill creates his first typeface, **Gill San**

Jan Tschichold publishes his manifesto book **Die neue Typographie** (The New Typography)

1928 · Eric Rohman · SE · Poster

1928 · Heinz Schulz-Neudamm · DE · Poster

1928 · Alfred Herrmann · DE · Poster

1928 · Mikhail Dlugach · RU · Poster

The first issue of the Italian design and architecture magazine **Domus** is published

1928 · "Reno" · FR · Poster

1928 · Ernst L. Franke · AT · Poster

1928 · Tom Purvis · UK · Poster

1928 · Slavko Vorkapich · RS/US · Opening titles

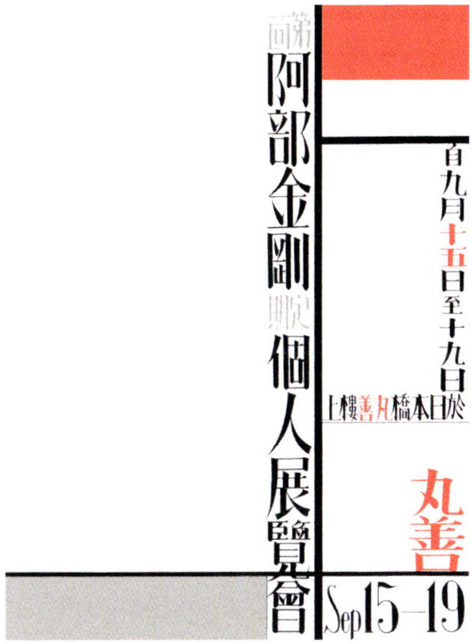

1928 · Anonymous · JP · Poster

1928 · Karel Teige · CZ · Book cover

Only a few years after it was established in 1919, the Bauhaus had already gained an international reputation as the groundbreaking design school of the modern age, and in fact this same towering reputation still resonates to the present day. It was the architect Walter Gropius's vision to find a new way of teaching arts and crafts and he brought together, first in Weimar and later in Dessau and Berlin, a team of pioneering avant-garde artists, including Johannes Itten, Josef Albers, Paul Klee, and Wassily Kandinsky to be teaching staff at the school. In 1923, the Hungarian artist László Moholy-Nagy, who the same year had introduced the concept of "New Typography," was appointed to add graphic design to the Bauhaus curriculum. A few years later, Herbert Bayer became the school's leading designer and his designs were a significant influence on the visual image and creative approach of the Bauhaus, whose relevance still endures today.

Bereits wenige Jahre nach seiner Gründung 1919 hatte das Bauhaus international den Ruf als die wegweisende Designschule der Moderne. Ein Ruf, der bis heute als Mythos nachklingt. Der Architekt Walter Gropius hatte die Vision, Kunst und Handwerk in neuartiger Form zu vermitteln, und versammelte zunächst in Weimar, später auch in Dessau und Berlin wegweisende Künstler der Avantgarde wie Johannes Itten, Josef Albers, Paul Klee oder Wassily Kandinsky als Lehrende. 1923 wurde der ungarische Künstler László Moholy-Nagy berufen, der noch im selben Jahr den Begriff der „Neuen Typografie" einführte und das Grafikdesign am Bauhaus etablierte. Wenige Jahre später wurde Herbert Bayer zum wichtigsten Designer der Schule. Mit seinen Entwürfen prägte er maßgeblich das visuelle Bild des Bauhauses und seiner bis heute relevanten gestalterischen Haltung.

Quelques années seulement après sa fondation en 1919, le Bauhaus jouissait déjà d'une renommée internationale d'école de design et de graphisme résolument innovatrice, une réputation qui s'y attache encore aujourd'hui comme un mythe. À Weimar d'abord, et plus tard à Dessau et à Berlin, l'architecte Walter Gropius, dont la vision était de communiquer l'art et l'artisanat sous une forme nouvelle, réunit un corps d'enseignants comptant des artistes avant-gardistes comme Johannes Itten, Josef Albers, Paul Klee ou Vassily Kandinsky. En 1923, il nomma professeur l'artiste hongrois László Moholy-Nagy, qui établit le graphisme au Bauhaus et inaugura en cette même année le concept de «nouvelle typographie». Quelques années plus tard, Herbert Bayer devint le chef de file de l'école en matière de design : ses projets, qui ont marqué de leur empreinte les critères visuels et l'approche créative du Bauhaus, n'ont rien perdu de leur pertinence jusqu'à nos jours.

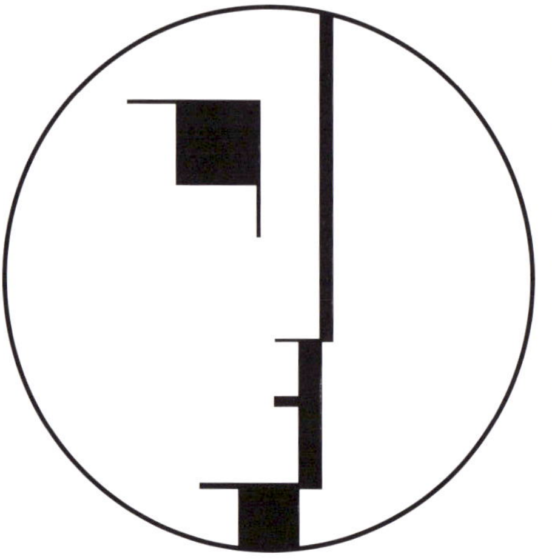

1922 · Oskar Schlemmer · DE · Logo

1929 · Anonymous · DE · Poster

»Essentially, the advances made in typography are not formal but organizational accomplishments. Today, typography is no longer a matter of jigging; it has become a printing technique, in which photomontages are 'models,' created quite separately from the printing process using methods other than jigging.« László Moholy-Nagy, *Gefesselter Blick*, 1930

1923 · Herbert Bayer · DE · Brochure cover

1925 · László Moholy-Nagy · HU/DE · Book cover

1928 · László Moholy-Nagy · HU/DE · Book cover

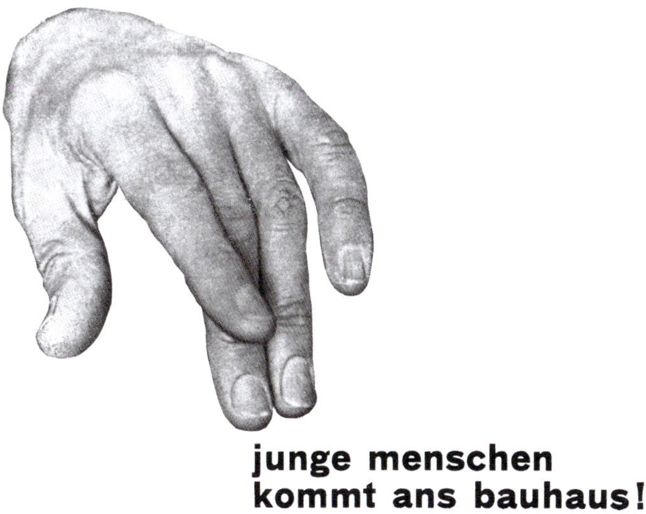

1929 · Hannes Meyer · DE · Postcard

1929 · László Moholy-Nagy · HU/DE · Book cover

1929

The influential **Bifur** typeface is created by Ukrainian-French designer A. M. Cassandre

The Museum of Modern Art is founded in New York City

1929 · Anonymous · FR · Logo · Éd. Berger-Levrault

1929 · Anonymous · IT · Logo · Cinzano

1929 · Anonymous · NL · Logo · Havbank

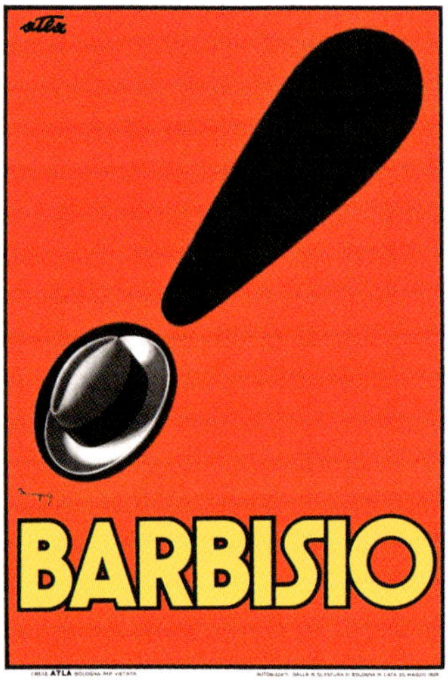

1929 · Giovanni Mingozzi · IT · Poster

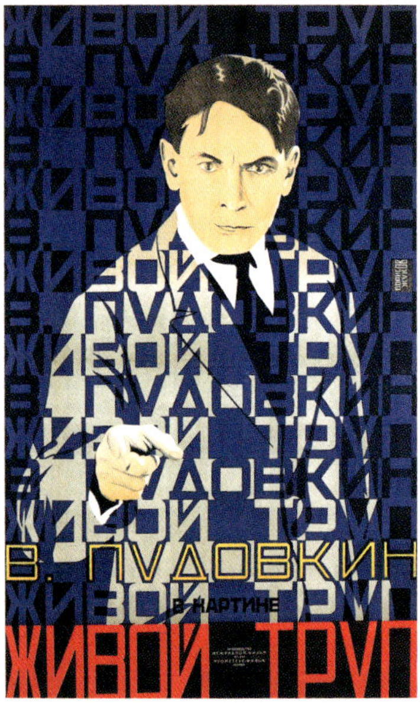

1929 · Grigori Borisov, Pyotr Zhukov · RU · Poster

1929 · Fritz Adolphy · DE · Book cover

1929 · Alfred Mahlau · DE · Poster

1929 · "Moerkerk" · NL · Poster

1929 · "Valkov" · RU · Poster

1929 · Boris Titov, Efim Pernikov · RU · Poster

1929 · Anonymous · JP · Poster

1929 · "Sepo" (Severo Pozzati) · IT · Poster

In the second half of the 1920s, photography began to appear as a more regular presence in graphic design. Avant-garde artists such as John Heartfield were amongst the first to discover the possibilities of this enormously flexible means of expression and deliberately dissociated themselves from the prevailing aesthetic belief in the use of straightforward graphics. By cutting up photographs to construct photomontages, designers were able to create complete and highly effective works of art by combining realistic images with typefaces. Almost immediately, this innovative approach caught on in many parts of the world and was increasingly used in fields of application directed at mass audiences. In France, for example, the popular weekly magazine *VU* made a significant contribution in the 1930s to the introduction of photography into graphic design, a technique that working designers and historians of design now regard as indispensable.

In der zweiten Hälfte der 1920er-Jahre hielt die Fotografie langsam, aber sicher Einzug ins Grafikdesign. Zunächst waren es Vertreter der Avantgarde wie John Heartfield, die das Medium als neuartiges Ausdrucksmittel entdeckten und sich damit ganz bewusst von der vorherrschenden Ästhetik zeichnerischer Lösungen abgrenzten. Mit ausgeschnittenen Bildelementen sowie mit den Mitteln der Fotomontage wurden realistische Abbildungen in Verbindung mit Typografie zu aufmerksamkeitsstarken Gesamtkompositionen. Innerhalb kürzester Zeit fand diese neue Herangehensweise große Verbreitung in vielen Teilen der Welt und wurde zunehmend auch in Einsatzgebieten genutzt, die sich an die breite Masse richteten. So trug in den 1930er-Jahren in Frankreich beispielsweise die populäre Wochenzeitschrift *VU* maßgeblich zur Etablierung der Fotografie in der Grafik bei, einer heute nicht mehr wegzudenkenden Gestaltungstechnik.

Pendant la seconde moitié des années 1920, la photographie fait lentement, mais sûrement, son entrée dans le domaine du graphisme. Ce sont d'abord des représentants de l'avant-garde comme John Heartfield qui découvrent le médium comme moyen d'expression et qui se démarquent ainsi résolument de l'esthétique dominante des solutions réalisées à la main. Par le truchement d'éléments visuels découpés comme pour le photomontage, des représentations réalistes sont associées à la typographie pour former des compositions qui attirent puissamment l'attention. Cette nouvelle approche se répand alors comme une traînée de poudre un peu partout dans le monde et commence à être utilisée dans des champs d'application ciblant les masses. Dans la France des années 1930, la populaire revue hebdomadaire *VU* contribue ainsi de façon déterminante à établir la photographie dans le graphisme. Cette technique de création est aujourd'hui devenue incontournable.

1929 · Anonymous · NL · Ad

1930 · Hans Richter · DE · Magazine cover

»To view an image it is simply a matter of bringing the viewer into a close personal relationship with the object and to focus his or her eye on the critical spot.«

Heinz and Bodo Rasch, *Gefesselter Blick*, 1930

1929 · Hans & Grete Leistikow · DE · Book cover

1930 · György Kepes · HU/US · Book cover

1930 · Walter Cyliax · CH · Ad

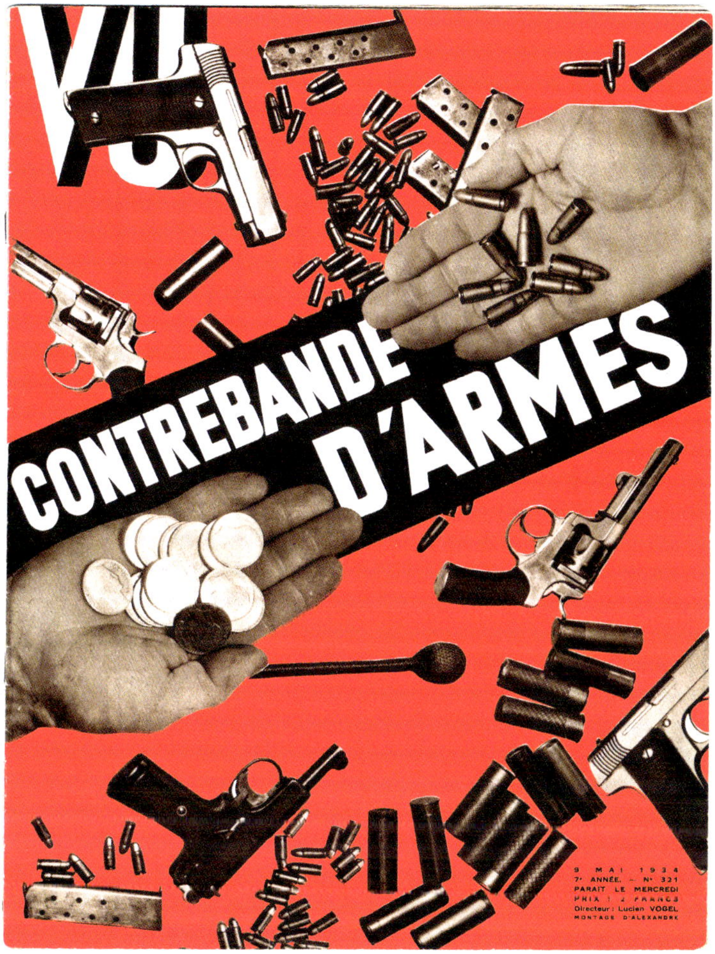

1934 · Anonymous · FR · Magazine cover

1933 · Anonymous · FR · Logo · Air France

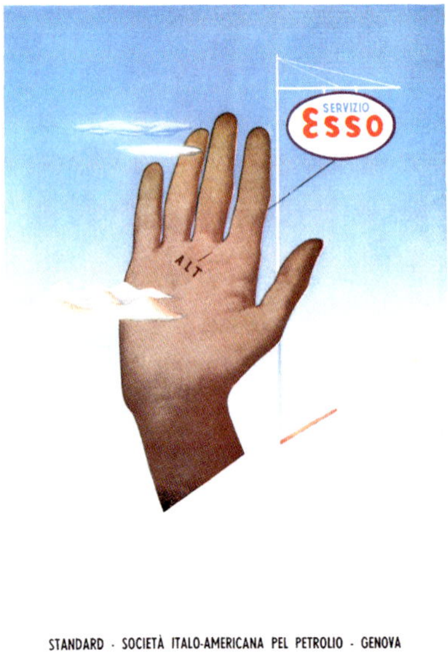

1939 · Dario Bernazzoli · IT · Ad

1930

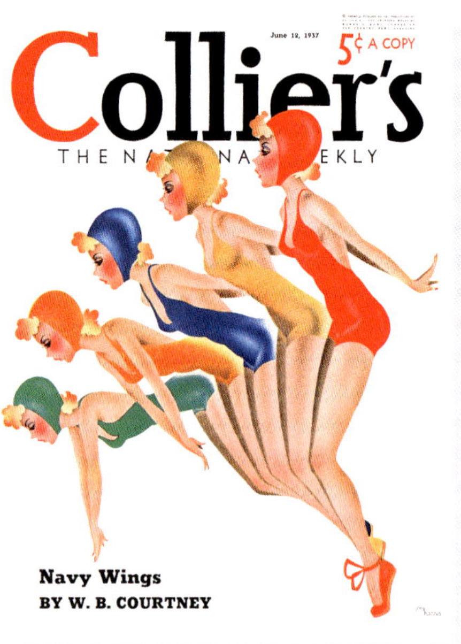

1937 · Benjamin Jorj Harris · US · Magazine cover

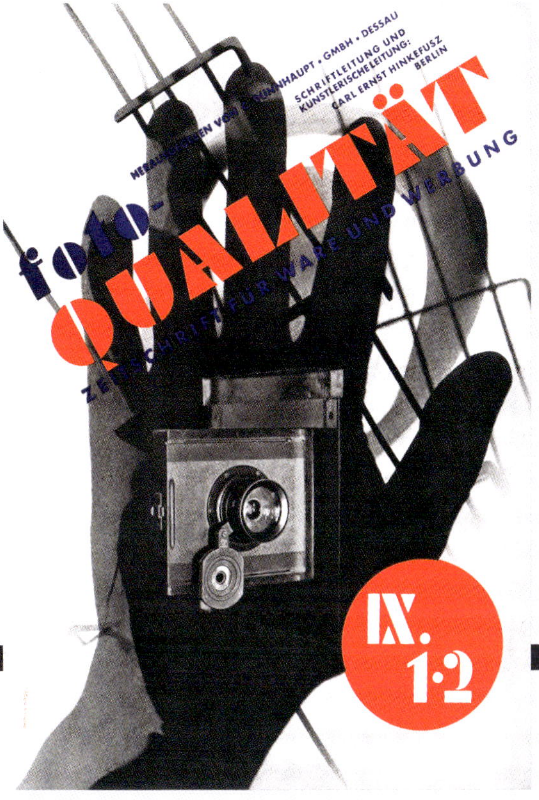

1931 · László Moholy-Nagy · DE · Magazine cover

– 1939

1938 · Hartmund Pfeil · DE · Logo · Fichtel & Sachs

1934 · Hermann Kosel · AT · Poster

At the start of the 1930s, the Great Depression, which had hit the United States, spread across the world. As mass unemployment became a major problem for Western society, Fascist regimes seized power in several European countries, including Germany, where Nazism gained control. At the same time, authoritarian dictatorships took hold in communist Russia, with the result that this was not a good time for the spirit of artistic innovation or creativity. Censorship and state-imposed design policies often proved to be a barrier to progress in these fields, and indeed the decade can be seen as an eloquent example of the correlation between sociopolitical development and visual culture. Many creatives and those in the arts generally immigrated to the United States, and with the outbreak of war in Europe, New York City became the new powerhouse for design and advertising.

Ausgehend von den USA, machte sich Anfang der 1930er-Jahre eine globale Wirtschaftskrise breit. Massenarbeitslosigkeit wurde zum großen Problem westlicher Gesellschaften. In verschiedenen europäischen Ländern kamen in der Folge faschistische Regierungen an die Macht, darunter auch die Nationalsozialisten in Deutschland. Gleichzeitig setzte das kommunistische Russland mit aller Macht ein diktatorisches System durch. Es waren keine guten Zeiten für Innovationsgeist und Kreativität. Zensur und staatliche Gestaltungsdoktrinen behinderten vielfach die visuelle Fortentwicklung. Die Korrelation von politisch-gesellschaftlicher Entwicklung und visueller Kultur zeigte sich am Beispiel dieses Jahrzehnts besonders eindrucksvoll. Ein größerer Teil der Kunstbranche und zahlreiche Kreative emigrierten in die USA. Während in Europa der Zweite Weltkrieg begann, entwickelte sich New York City zum neuen impulsgebenden Zentrum für Design und Werbung.

Partie des États-Unis, une crise économique globale s'étend sur le monde au début des années 1930. Le chômage de masse devient le problème majeur des sociétés occidentales, entraînant dans son sillage l'arrivée au pouvoir de gouvernements fascistes dans différents pays d'Europe, notamment en Allemagne avec les nationaux-socialistes. En même temps, des régimes dictatoriaux s'imposent en Russie et en Chine communistes, ce qui n'est pas favorable à l'innovation artistique et à la créativité. La censure et les doctrines formelles d'État entravent fortement l'évolution des arts visuels. La décennie illustre de manière on ne peut plus flagrante la corrélation entre évolution socio-politique et culture visuelle. De nombreux créatifs émigrent aux États-Unis, et pendant que la Seconde Guerre mondiale fait rage en Europe, la ville de New York devient le nouveau moteur de l'évolution du design et de la publicité.

A German printing works in 1938 showing propaganda posters being prepared for printing.

Blick in eine deutsche Druckerei im Jahr 1938. Propagandaplakate werden für den Druck vorbereitet.

Intérieur d'une imprimerie allemande en 1938, où des affiches de propagande sont préparées pour l'impression.

1930

Morris Fuller Benton creates the **Bank Gothic** typeface

The first issue of the U.S. design magazine **Advertising Arts** is published

1930 · E. Charall · DE · Logo · Berlin Tourist Office

1930 · Marcel Arthaus · FR · Logo · Noir

1930 · Anonymous · FR · Logo · Maison d'Amour

1930 · Noël Fontane · CH · Poster

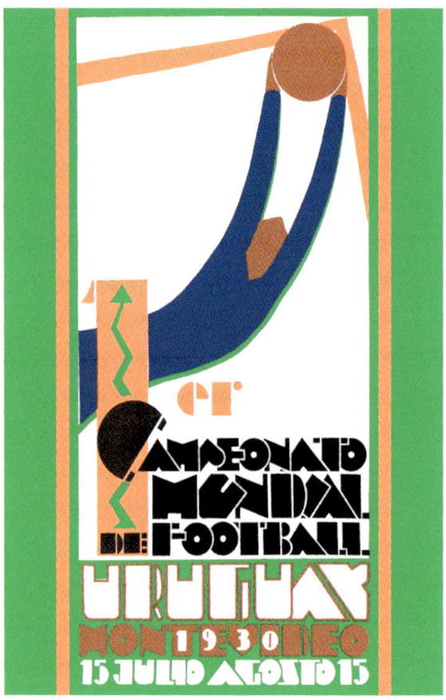

1930 · Guillermo Laborde · UY · Poster

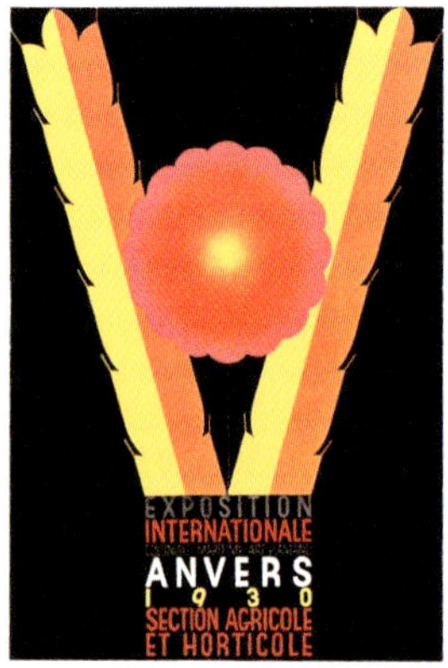

1930 · Les Créations Publicitaires · FR · Poster

1930 · Anonymous · NL · Poster

1930 · Ernst L. Franke · AT · Poster

1930 · Takashi Kono · JP · Ad

1930 · Publivox · CH · Poster

1930 · Anonymous · RU · Poster

1930 · "BK" · YU · Poster

In 1920s Paris a new visual style emerged which, within the space of a few short years, would make its mark on graphic design, product design, and architecture. It was called Art Deco, and this evocative name also came to stand for a new way of seeing the world, as well as being an optimistic vision of a future shaped by technology and the desire for luxury. Iconic posters in this style were duly created by French graphic designers such as A.M. Cassandre, Jean Carlu, and Jean Colin. Having begun in France, the new style quickly spread worldwide and continued to influence the majority of international graphic design until the outbreak of the Second World War.

Im Paris der 1920er-Jahre entwickelte sich ein neuartiger visueller Stil, der sich innerhalb weniger Jahre in Grafikdesign, Produktdesign und Architektur durchsetzte: das Art déco. Der klangvolle Name stand gleichzeitig für ein neues Lebensgefühl und für den optimistischen Blick in eine durch Technik und Luxus geprägte Zukunft. Französische Grafikdesigner wie A. M. Cassandre, Jean Carlu oder Jean Colin schufen ikonografische Plakatwerke. Ausgehend von Frankreich, verbreitete sich der neue Stil rasch weltweit und prägte große Teile des internationalen Grafikdesigns bis zu Beginn des Zweiten Weltkriegs.

Dans le Paris des années 1920, un nouveau style voit le jour et va s'imposer en quelques années dans les domaines du graphisme, du design de produits et de l'architecture: l'Art déco. Ce nom sonore évoque aussi l'air du temps et le regard optimiste que l'époque porte sur un avenir marqué par la technologie et le luxe. Des graphistes français comme A.M. Cassandre, Jean Carlu ou Jean Colin conçoivent alors des affiches emblématiques. Partant de France, le nouveau style se diffuse rapidement dans le monde entier et a grandement marqué de son empreinte le graphisme international jusqu'au début de la Seconde Guerre mondiale.

1927 · A. M. Cassandre · FR · Poster

»In the 1920s, dynamic design became the most effective means of persuading customers to buy a particular product. [...] Reduction was key: saying more with less became the goal. Sharp linear compositions floating on flat areas of background color quickly drew the eye of the passer-by in busy twentieth-century cityscapes.« Alastair Duncan, *The Art Deco Poster*, 2013

1930 · Lajos Marton · HU/FR · Poster

1934 · André Nivault · FR · Poster

1934 · Guo Jian-ying · CN · Magazine cover

1929 · Vladimir Bobri · RU/US · Magazine cover

1930 · Anonymous · JP · Brochure cover

1921 · Theodor Paul Etbauer · DE · Poster

1930 · Jos van Woerkom · NL · Poster

1933 · Anonymous · DE · Poster

1931

Alfred Tolmer's teaching book **Mise en Page – The Theory and Practice of Lay-out** is published

Eric Gill's book **An Essay on Typography** is published

1931 · Anonymous · DE · Poster

1931 · "Kleinschmidt" · DE · Poster

1931 · Anonymous · JP · Poster

1931 · H. Holzinger · DE · Poster

1931 · Anonymous · US · Logo · RKS Advertising

1931 · Sascha A. Maurer · US · Logo · VM cigarettes

The German Institute for Standardization introduces **DIN 1451**, a typeface for use on road signs and other signage

1931 · Gösta Åberg · SE · Poster

One of the most frightening things to realize about fascist regimes is the way they have been able to put different means of communication to such effective use. Through simple language and iconography, followers have consistently been attracted to messages full of nationalism and economic promises. Particularly in Germany and Italy, a large number of artists worked for the fascist parties, many of whom later lost their jobs after the Allied forces freed the European continent. These artists made use of innovative typographic work, illustration, and meticulous composition to produce their propaganda, from book covers to posters, and from products to advertising.

Einer der erschreckendsten Aspekte der faschistischen Herrschaftssysteme war, dass sie Kommunikationsmittel effektiv zu nutzen verstanden. Mithilfe einfachster Sprache und Ikonografie gelang es ihnen, mit einer Botschaft von Nationalismus und wirtschaftlichen Verheißungen zahlreiche Anhänger zu gewinnen. Insbesondere in Deutschland und Italien war eine große Zahl von Künstlern für die faschistischen Parteien tätig; viele dieser Grafikdesigner wurden nach der Befreiung des europäischen Kontinents durch die Alliierten arbeitslos. Sie gestalteten ihre Propaganda mit innovativer Typografie, Illustration und präziser Komposition, von Bucheinbänden bis zu Plakaten, von Waren bis zu Werbung.

Une des choses les plus effrayantes à propos des régimes fascistes a été leur capacité à utiliser des moyens de communication extrêmement efficaces. À travers un langage et une iconographie simples, ils ont invariablement attiré des partisans avec leurs messages nationalistes et leurs promesses économiques. En Allemagne et en Italie particulièrement, beaucoup d'artistes ont travaillé pour des partis fascistes, et beaucoup ont perdu leur emploi quand les forces alliées ont libéré le continent européen. Pour produire leur propagande, ils ont fait preuve d'un esprit novateur dans les domaines de la typographie, de l'illustration et d'une composition soigneusement réfléchie – des couvertures de livres aux affiches et des produits à la publicité.

1932 · Anonymous · DE · Poster

1934 · Xanti Schawinsky, Studio Boggeri · IT · Poster

1937 · "Cimine" · ES · Poster

»Starting in the twentieth century, totalitarian states began using the same graphic identity techniques as modern industries and corporations. Despots and businessmen alike strove to establish branding narratives, supported by visual images […].«
Steven Heller, *Iron Fists*, 2008

1934 · Domenico Chiaudrero · IT · Poster

1936 · Erberto Carboni · IT · Poster

1936 · Klotz & Kienast · DE · Poster

1937 · Sepp Semar · DE · Poster

1935 · Willy Engelhardt · DE · Poster

1933 · Inge Drexler · DE · Poster

1939 · Gottfried Klein · DE · Postcard

1939 · "Dassel" · DE · Poster

1932

Stanley Morison creates the **Times New Roman** typeface for the London newspaper *The Times*

The first **Vogue** cover using color photography is published

1932 · Frederick E. Kliem · US · Logo · National Dairy

1932 · Anonymous · DE · Logo · Audi

1932 · Anonymous · DE · Brochure cover

1932 · Alexey Brodovitch · US · Poster

1932 · "Maga" · IT · Poster

1932 · Equipe da Livraria do Globo · BR · Book cover

1932 · Robert Bartlett · UK · Poster

1932 · "Pina" · PT · Ad

1932 · Paul Schuitema · NL · Magazine covers

1933

Antonio Boggeri sets up the **Studio Boggeri** in Milan

The **Bauhaus** is forced to close under pressure from the Nazis

The first edition of Italian design magazine **Campo Grafico** is published

1933 · Boris Artzybasheff · US · Book cover

1933 · "Sepo" (Severo Pozzati) · IT · Poster

1933 · Nicolay Diulgheroff · BG · Poster

1933 · Anonymous · NL · Brochure cover

1933 · Kenkichi Sugimoto · JP · Poster

1933 · Koos von Stein · NL · Brochure cover

Many creatives, including graphic designers such as **Jan Tschichold** and **John Heartfield,** leave Germany after the Nazis come to power

Grafia, the Association of Visual Communication Designers, is established in Finland

The first issue of the Swiss typography magazine **Typographische Monatsblätter** is published

1933 · Doudow Trapotat · FR · Poster

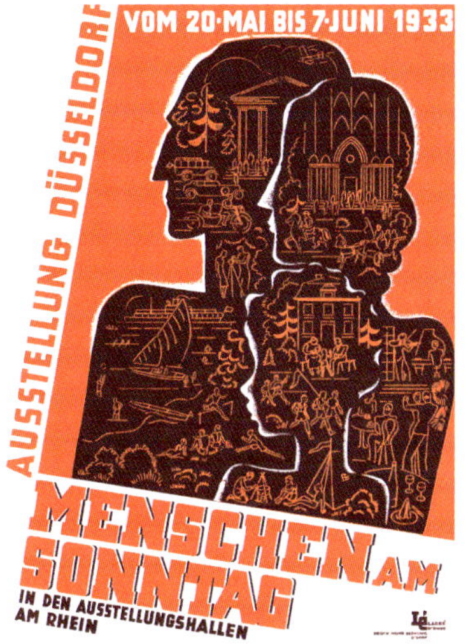

1933 · Werner Labbé · DE · Poster

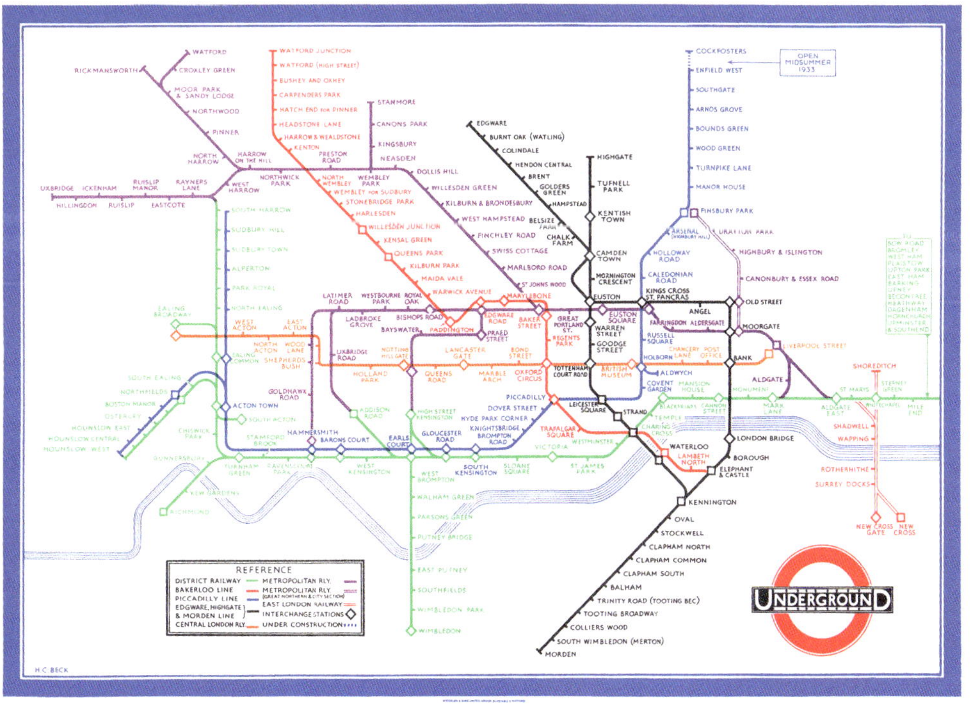

1933 · Harry Beck · UK · Infographic

1934

Alexey Brodovitch does his first work for *Harper's Bazaar* magazine

The first issue of **PM design magazine** is published in the United States

1934 · W. van Andringa de Kempenaer · NL · Poster

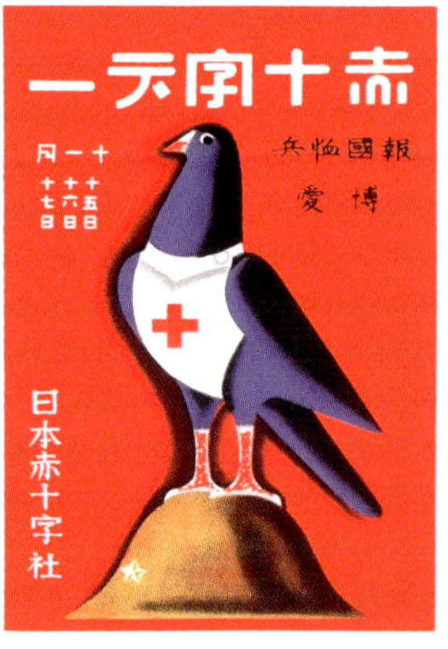

1934 · Anonymous · JP · Poster

1934 · Francisco Rivero Gil · ES · Book cover

1934 · Hugo Noll · AT · Poster

1934 · Will Münch · DE · Logo · Braun

The **Rockwell** typeface is created by an unnamed designer at the Monotype corporation

1934 · Anonymous · US · Magazine cover

1930s · Anonymous · JP/CN · Poster

1934 · Nicolaas P. de Koo · NL · Poster

1934 · Dorothy Waugh · US · Poster

1934 · Viejo Santamarto Acebo · ES · Poster

1934 · Magda Szepes · HU · Poster

1934 · Friedrich Binder · DE · Brochure cover

1935

Leo Burnett opens an advertising agency in Chicago

Allen Lane sets up the publishing company **Penguin Books** in London

1935 · Anonymous · US · Logo · 20th Century Fox

1935 · Anonymous · NL · Logo · Mica

1935 · Hans Schleger · DE/UK · Logo · Bykmyrs

1935 · Eric Rohman · SE · Poster

1935 · Zdeněk Rossmann · CZ · Brochure cover

1935 · K. G. Chapman, Regent Advertising Service · UK · Brochure cover

1935 · Anonymous · BE · Poster

1935 · Jos van Woerkom · NL · Poster

1935 · Rudi Dayan · IL · Ad

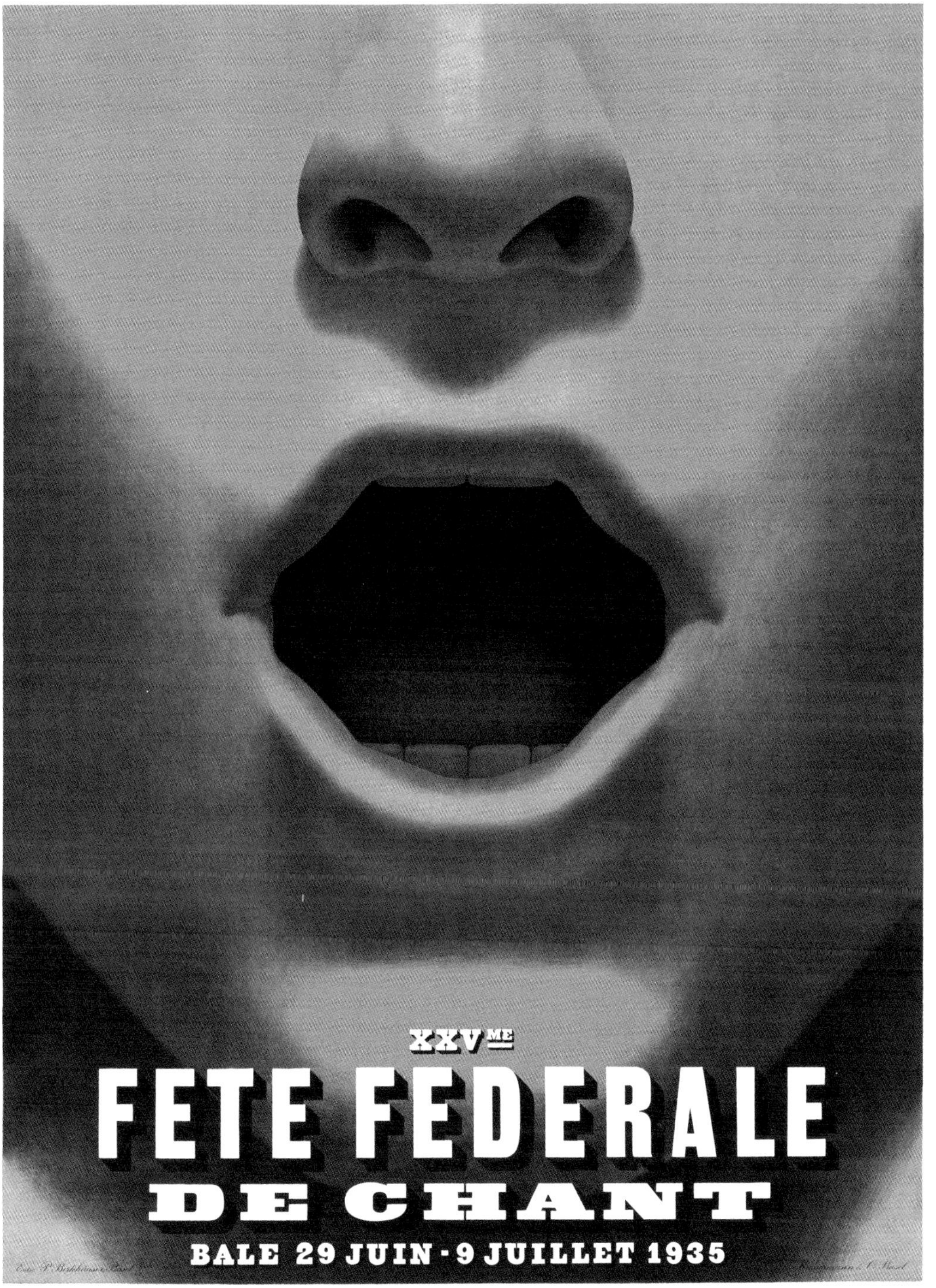

1935 · Peter Birkhäuser · CH · Poster

The photographer and graphic designer Herbert Matter's association with the Swiss Tourist Office began in 1932 and led to the production of numerous posters and brochures. The colorful photomontages he devised introduced a whole new visual language, which quickly came to symbolize the Swiss graphic design industry's commitment to innovation. Even now, the dynamism and precision of Matter's unique pictorial compositions continue to captivate. Long before it became technically feasible to reproduce poster-size color photographs, Matter used the possibilities then available to him by adding black and white photographs to areas of color during the printing process. In the years that followed, this simple but effective method was often copied. It replaced the prevailing pictorial style of illustration of the period and its use spread well beyond the bounds of travel industry advertising.

Die Zusammenarbeit des Fotografen und Grafikdesigners Herbert Matter mit dem Schweizer Verkehrsamt begann 1932. Es entstanden zahlreiche Plakate und Prospekte, die mit colorierten Fotomontagen eine völlig neue Bildsprache etablierten und geradezu sinnbildlich für den Innovationswillen der Schweizer Grafik stehen. Die präzise Dynamik seiner umgewöhnlichen Bildkompositionen ist bis heute bestechend. Lange bevor es technisch machbar wurde, Farbfotografien in Plakatgröße zu reproduzieren, nutzte Matter die vorhandene Möglichkeit, farbige Flächen durch Addition im Druckvorgang mit Schwarz-Weiß-Aufnahmen zu kombinieren. Diese simple wie effektive Methode wurde in den folgenden Jahren oft kopiert und löste nicht nur im Bereich der Tourismuswerbung zunehmend das vorherrschende Mittel der Illustration ab.

La collaboration entre le photographe et graphiste Herbert Matter et l'office du tourisme suisse débute en 1932. Elle a donné lieu à de nombreuses affiches et prospectus dont les photomontages colorés ont établi un langage visuel entièrement nouveau et sont aujourd'hui emblématiques de la volonté d'innovation du graphisme suisse. Avec leur dynamique et leur précision tout à fait uniques, les images composites de Matter n'ont rien perdu de leur pouvoir de fascination. Bien avant que la photographie en couleurs puisse être reproduite au format de l'affiche, Matter a tiré parti des possibilités disponibles à l'époque en insérant des photographies en noir et blanc dans des parties colorées en cours d'impression. Souvent copiée par la suite, sa méthode aussi simple qu'efficace remplacera le style pictural de l'illustration de l'époque, et ses applications déborderont largement le cadre de la publicité touristique.

1935 · Herbert Matter · CH · Poster

Herbert Matter (1907, Engelberg, Switzerland – 1984, Southampton, New York) was a Swiss-American designer and photographer, known for his use of photomontage in commercial art. After attending the École des Beaux-Arts in Geneva and the Académie Moderne in Paris (at the same time as Fernand Léger), he collaborated with A. M. Cassandre and Le Corbusier. Relocating to the United States in 1936, he was hired by Alexey Brodovitch at *Harper's*, before spending two decades as design consultant at Knoll Associates, from 1946. Matter also worked closely with Charles and Ray Eames. His pioneering work in photography gained him a professorship at Yale University from 1952–76.

Herbert Matter (1907, Engelberg, Schweiz – 1984, Southampton, Bundesstaat New York) war ein Schweizer und US-amerikanischer Grafikdesigner und Fotograf, der insbesondere wegen seiner Verwendung von Fotomontagen in der Werbung bekannt wurde. Nach dem Besuch der École des Beaux-Arts in Genf und der Académie Moderne in Paris (gleichzeitig mit Fernand Léger) arbeitete er mit A.M. Cassandre und Le Corbusier. 1936 siedelte er in die USA um, wo Alexei Brodowitsch ihn zu *Harper's* holte, ab 1946 war er dann zwanzig Jahre lang als Berater für Design bei Knoll Associates tätig. Darüber hinaus arbeitete Matter eng mit Charles und Ray Eames zusammen. Wegen seiner bahnbrechenden Arbeiten in der Fotografie berief ihn die Yale University von 1952 bis 1976 zum Professor.

Herbert Matter (1907, Engelberg, Suisse – 1984, Southampton, New York) fut un designer et photographe helvéto-américain connu pour son utilisation du photomontage dans l'art commercial. Après des études à l'École des beaux-arts de Genève et à l'Académie moderne à Paris (en même temps que Fernand Léger), il travailla avec A.M. Cassandre et Le Corbusier. Installé aux États-Unis en 1936, il fut engagé chez *Harper's* par Alexey Brodovitch avant de travailler deux décennies comme consultant en conception chez Knoll Associates à partir de 1946. Matter travailla aussi avec Charles et Ray Eames. Son travail précurseur en photographie lui valut un poste de professeur à l'université Yale, qu'il occupa de 1952 à 1976.

1935 · Herbert Matter · CH · Brochure spread

1935 · Herbert Matter · CH · Poster

1935 · Herbert Matter · CH · Poster

Penguin is one of the rare cases of successful branding for a publisher with a wide audience. One of the reasons for this was the institution of design standards from an early stage, known as the *Penguin Composition Rules*, as well as the logo designed by Edward Young, which is still in use today with hardly any modification. Founded in 1935, Penguin also employed the typographer Jan Tschichold in the late 1940s, who further developed the cover designs and branding standards across all the different book series.

Penguin ist eines der seltenen Beispiele für das erfolgreiche Branding eines Publikumsverlags. Mit ein Grund für den Erfolg war, dass schon sehr früh Designrichtlinien festgelegt wurden – die *Penguin Composition Rules* – sowie das von Edward Young entworfene Logo, das mit sehr geringen Veränderungen bis heute verwendet wird. Penguin, 1935 gegründet, arbeitete Ende der 1940er-Jahre auch mit dem Typografen Jan Tschichold zusammen, der das Cover und die Gestaltungsrichtlinien für alle Buchserien weiterentwickelte.

Penguin est une des rares réussites dans le domaine du branding éditorial à destination du grand public. Une des raisons en furent les Penguin Composition Rules, les standards graphiques établis dès la fondation de la maison d'édition en 1935, mais aussi le logo conçu par Edward Young, et qui est encore utilisé aujourd'hui avec seulement de légères modifications. À partir de la fin des années 1940, les éditions Penguin ont aussi collaboré avec le typographe Jan Tschichold, qui continua de développer les règles graphiques des couvertures et la cohérence de l'identité visuelle à travers l'ensemble des collections.

1935 · Edward Young · UK · Logo

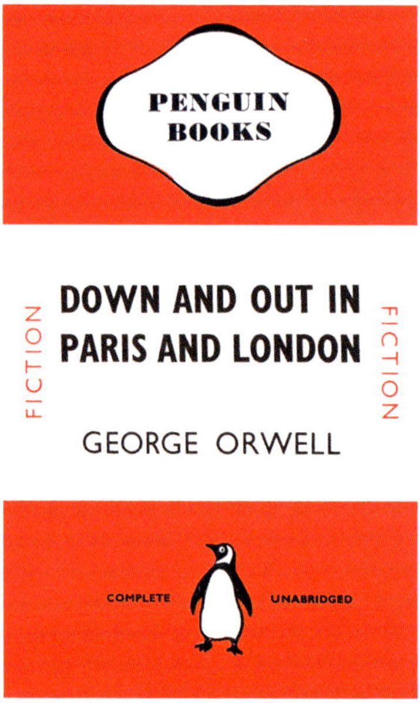

1940 · Edward Young · UK · Book cover

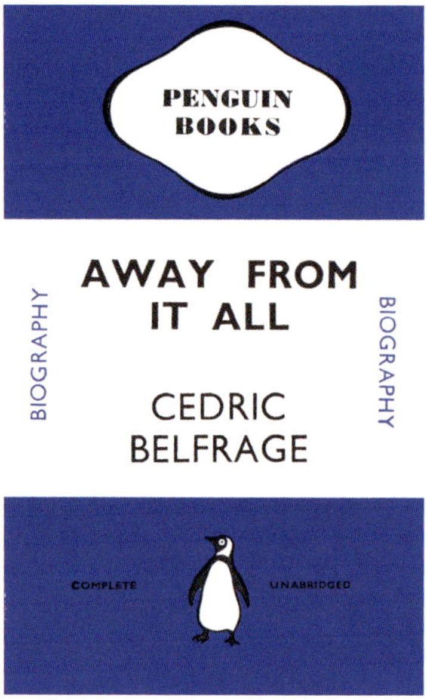

1937 · Edward Young · UK · Book cover

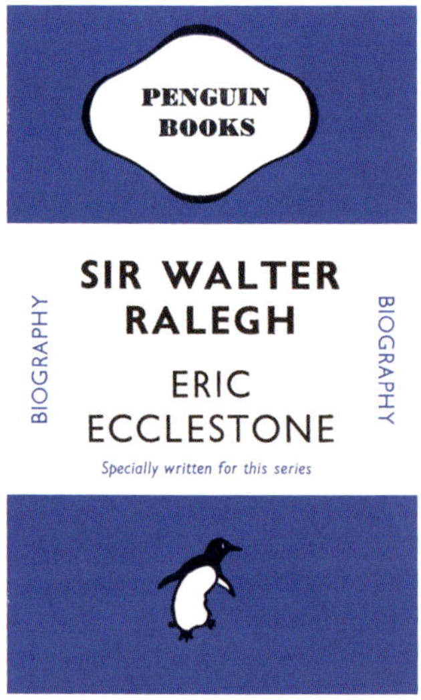

1941 · Edward Young · UK · Book cover

1937 · Edward Young · UK · Book cover

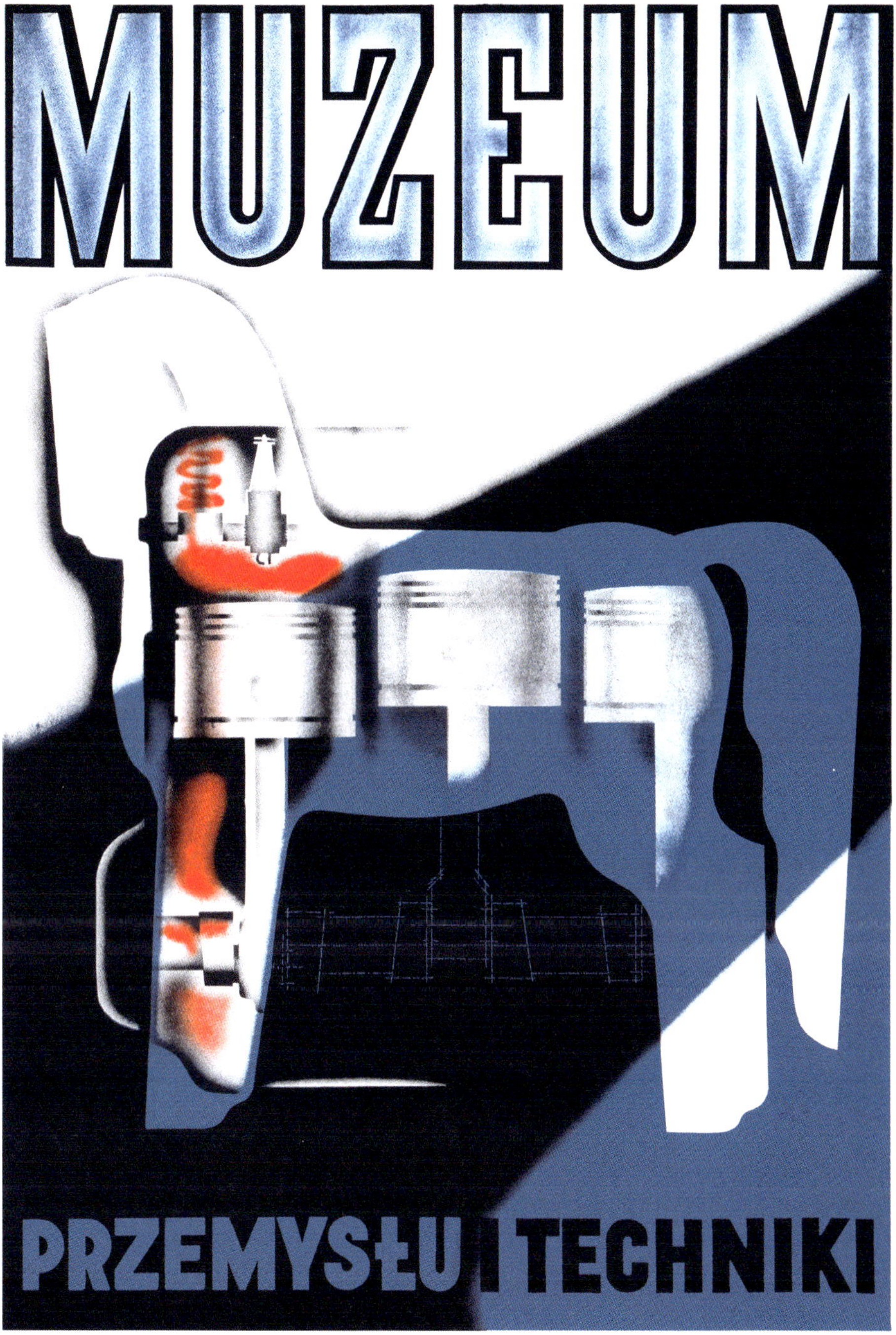

1935 · Andrzej Henryk Rubinrot · PL · Poster

1936

Herbert Matter immigrates to the United States

The **DIN 1451** typeface is introduced as the standard for all German industries, and is still in use today for street signs and license plates

1936 · Max Field-Bush · UK · Logos · Spratt's

1936 · Gert Sellheim · DE/AU · Poster

The first issue of British design magazine **Art & Industry** is published

Paul Rand becomes art director of **Esquire** and **Apparel Arts** magazines

1936 · Anonymous · US · Opening Titles

1936 · Franz Würbel · DE · Poster

1936 · Francesco dal Pozzo · IT · Poster

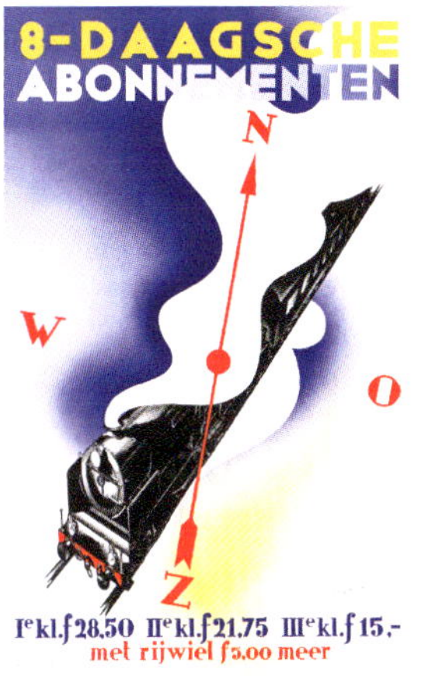

1936 · Fré Drost · NL · Poster

1936 · Renau · ES · Poster

1936 · Tom Purvis · UK · Poster

1937

A. M. Cassandre creates the **Peignot** typeface

László Moholy-Nagy opens the **New Bauhaus** school in Chicago

1937 · Franz X. Reimspieß · DE · Logo · Volkswagen

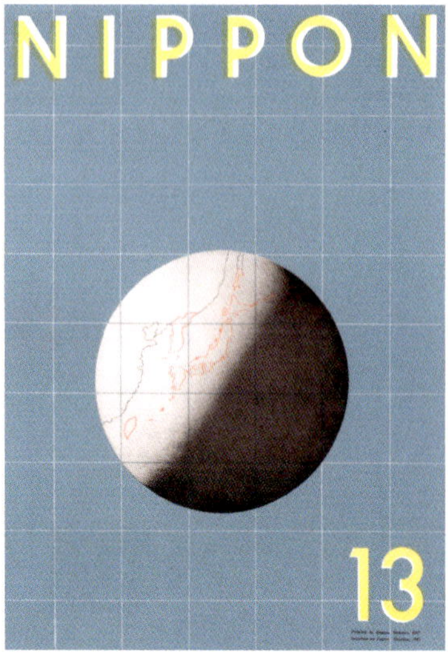

1937 · Ayao Yamana · JP · Magazine

1937 · Wiktor Langner · PL · Poster

1937 · "Dotel" · ES · Poster

1937 · Anonymous · ES · Poster

1937 · "Dotel" · ES · Poster

1937 · Eugène Beaudoin, Marcel Lods · FR · Poster

1937 · Manlio Parrini · IT · Poster

1937 · Munetsugu Satomi · JP · Poster

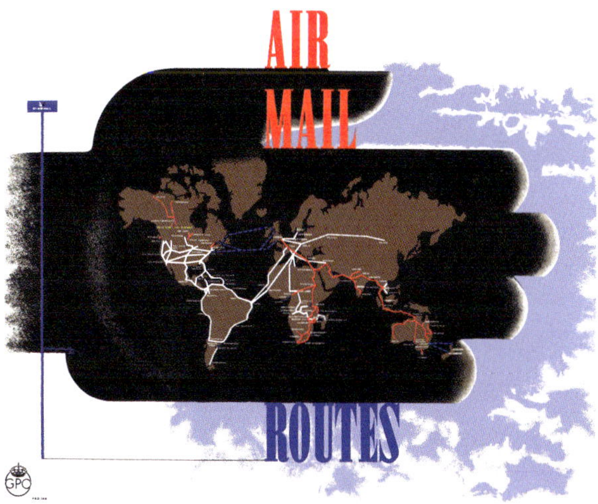

1937 · Edward McKnight Kauffer · US/UK · Poster

1939 · Remo Muratore · IT · Poster

1937 · Paolo Garretto · IT · Poster

1936 · Erberto Carboni · IT · Ad

1934 · Xanti Schawinsky · IT · Poster

1936 · Erberto Carboni · IT · Ad

Antonio Boggeri (1900, Pavia – 1989, Santa Margherita Ligure, Italy) was an Italian graphic designer, photographer, musician, and adman, whose work broke new ground in the use of photography by incorporating ideas from the avant-garde (such as was done by Man Ray and Moholy-Nagy). After studying photography in 1916, Boggeri was hired in 1924 to run the Milanese printers Alfieri & Lacroix, where he developed his own style of photomontage. He established Studio Boggeri in 1933, and many leading Italian graphic designers, including Bruno Munari, Franco Grignani, and Bruno Monguzzi, started their career there, in work for companies such as Pirelli, Roche, and Olivetti.

Antonio Boggeri (1900, Pavia – 1989, Santa Margherita Ligure, Italien) war ein italienischer Grafikdesigner, Fotograf, Musiker und Werbefachmann, dessen Arbeiten bahnbrechend bei der Verwendung von Fotografie waren, denn er griff Ideen der Avantgarde auf (etwa Man Rays und Moholy-Nagys). Nach dem Fotografiestudium 1916 wurde Boggeri 1924 die Leitung der Mailänder Druckerei Alfieri & Lacroix übertragen, wo er seinen eigenen Stil in der Fotomontage entwickelte. 1933 gründete er das Studio Boggeri, und dort nahm die Karriere vieler führender italienischer Grafikdesigner – etwa Bruno Munari, Franco Grignani und Bruno Monguzzi – mit Arbeiten für Firmen wie Pirelli, Roche und Olivetti ihren Anfang.

Antonio Boggeri (1900, Pavie – 1989, Santa Margherita Ligure, Italie) fut un graphiste photographe, musicien et publicitaire italien dont le travail a ouvert des voies nouvelles dans l'utilisation de la photographie et des idées d'avant-garde – notamment de Man Ray et Moholy-Nagy. Après des études de photographie en 1916, Boggeri travailla en 1924 comme directeur de l'imprimerie milanaise Alfieri & Lacroix, où il développa son propre style de photomontage. En 1933, il fonda le Studio Boggeri, où de nombreux grands graphistes italiens, notamment Bruno Munari, Franco Grignani et Bruno Monguzzi, lancèrent leur carrière dans le cadre de commandes d'entreprises comme Pirelli, Roche et Olivetti.

»The consistency of Boggeri's work, of his artistic guidance, springs from the fact that he has always consented to avant-garde trends, while by the exercise of an intellectual discipline conserving his own elegance.« Leonardo Sinisgalli, *Graphis* #38, 1951

1949 · Ezio Bonini · IT · Magazine cover

1947 · Walter Ballmer · CH/IT · Logo · Cedil

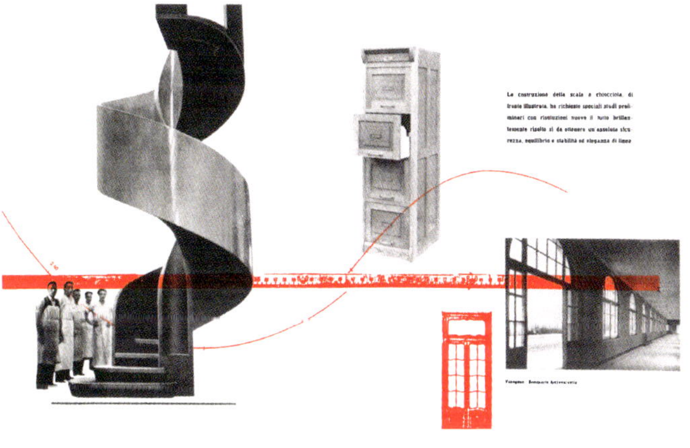

1938 · Remo Muratore · IT · Brochure spread

1947 · Carlo L. Vivarelli · CH/IT · Logo · Tenax

1934 · Xanti Schawinsky · IT · Logo · Olivetti

1952 · M. Schneider · Logo · Silk Quality Mark

1939 · Remo Muratore · IT · Logo · Dalmine Tubes

1938

U.S. designer Chauncey H. Griffith creates the **Bell Gothic** typeface

The **Verband Schweizerischer Grafiker** (Union of Swiss Graphic Designers) is founded

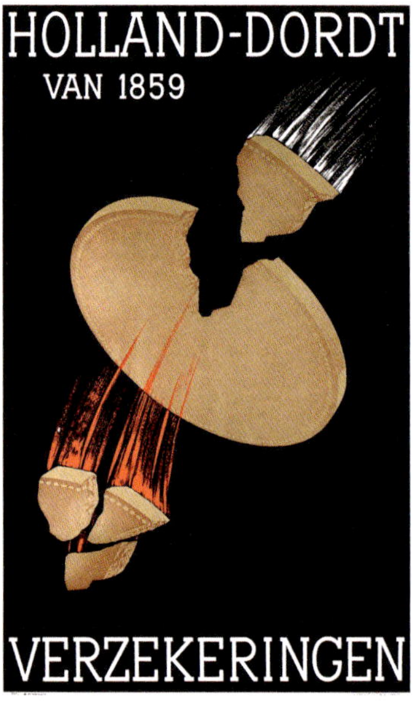

1938 · Wim van Andringa de Kempenaer · NL · Poster

1938 · L. Keizer · BE · Poster

1938 · Theo Matejko · AT · Magazine cover

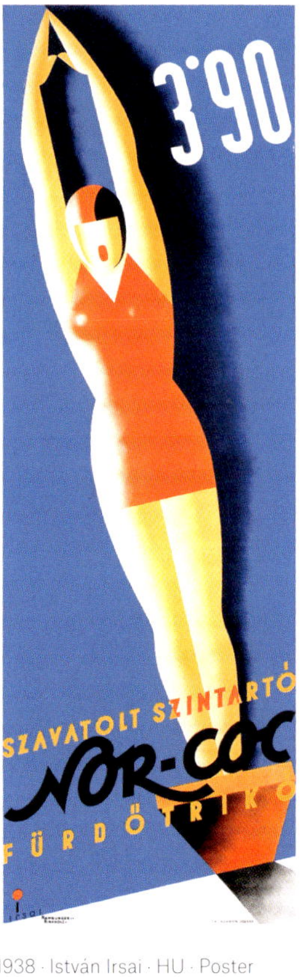

1938 · István Irsai · HU · Poster

1938 · A. Bauer · DE · Poster

1938 · Sanz Miralles · ES · Poster

1938 · Anonymous · US · Magazine cover

1930s · A. Simon · FR · Poster

1938 · Sascha A. Maurer · US · Poster

1938 · Anonymous · US · Menu card

1924 · Herbert Bayer · AT/DE · Magazine store design

Herbert Bayer (1900, Haag am Hausruck, Austria – 1985, Montecito, California) was an Austrian-American artist and designer, who after studying at the Bauhaus was appointed director for printing and advertising by Walter Gropius. In 1928 he left the school for an advertising career in Berlin, transferring many of the Bauhaus ideas to his commercial practice. Moving to New York in 1938, Bayer enjoyed a long career working in all graphic design fields. His relocation to Aspen, Colorado, in 1946 allowed him to work in architecture and interior design for the philanthropist Robert O. Anderson, with whom he curated his art collection.

Herbert Bayer (1900, Haag am Hausruck, Österreich, – 1985 Montecito, Kalifornien) war ein österreichisch-amerikanischer Künstler und Grafikdesigner. Nach seinem Studium am Bauhaus ernannte Walter Gropius ihn zum Leiter der Werkstatt für Druck und Reklame, 1928 jedoch verließ Bayer die Institution und arbeitete in Berlin bei einer Werbeagentur, wobei er viele Gedanken des Bauhauses in seine Entwürfe einfließen ließ. 1938 ging er nach New York, und dort begann seine langjährige Karriere mit Erfolgen in sämtlichen Bereichen des Grafikdesigns. Nach seiner Übersiedlung nach Aspen, Colorado, im Jahr 1946 konnte er für den Philanthropen Robert O. Anderson, mit dem er dessen Kunstsammlung kuratierte, auch auf dem Gebiet der Architektur und Innenarchitektur tätig werden.

Herbert Bayer (1900, Haag am Hausruck, Autriche – 1985, Montecito, Californie) fut un artiste et designer austro-américain qui étudia au Bauhaus avant d'y être nommé directeur de l'atelier d'imprimerie et de graphisme publicitaire par Walter Gropius. En 1928, il quitta l'école pour se lancer dans une carrière publicitaire à Berlin, appliquant nombre d'idées du Bauhaus dans sa pratique commerciale. Après son installation aux États-Unis en 1938, Bayer connut une longue carrière et travailla dans tous les domaines du graphisme. En 1946, son déménagement à Aspen dans le Colorado lui permit de travailler dans l'architecture et le design intérieur pour le philanthrope Robert O. Anderson, qu'il aida aussi à constituer sa collection d'art.

»It is a mistake to believe that design styles could be created as easily and as frequently as the ever-changing fashions of women's clothing. Design style involves more than mere shifts in taste, which have neither substance nor structure and are no more than icing on the cultural cake.«

Herbert Bayer, 1959

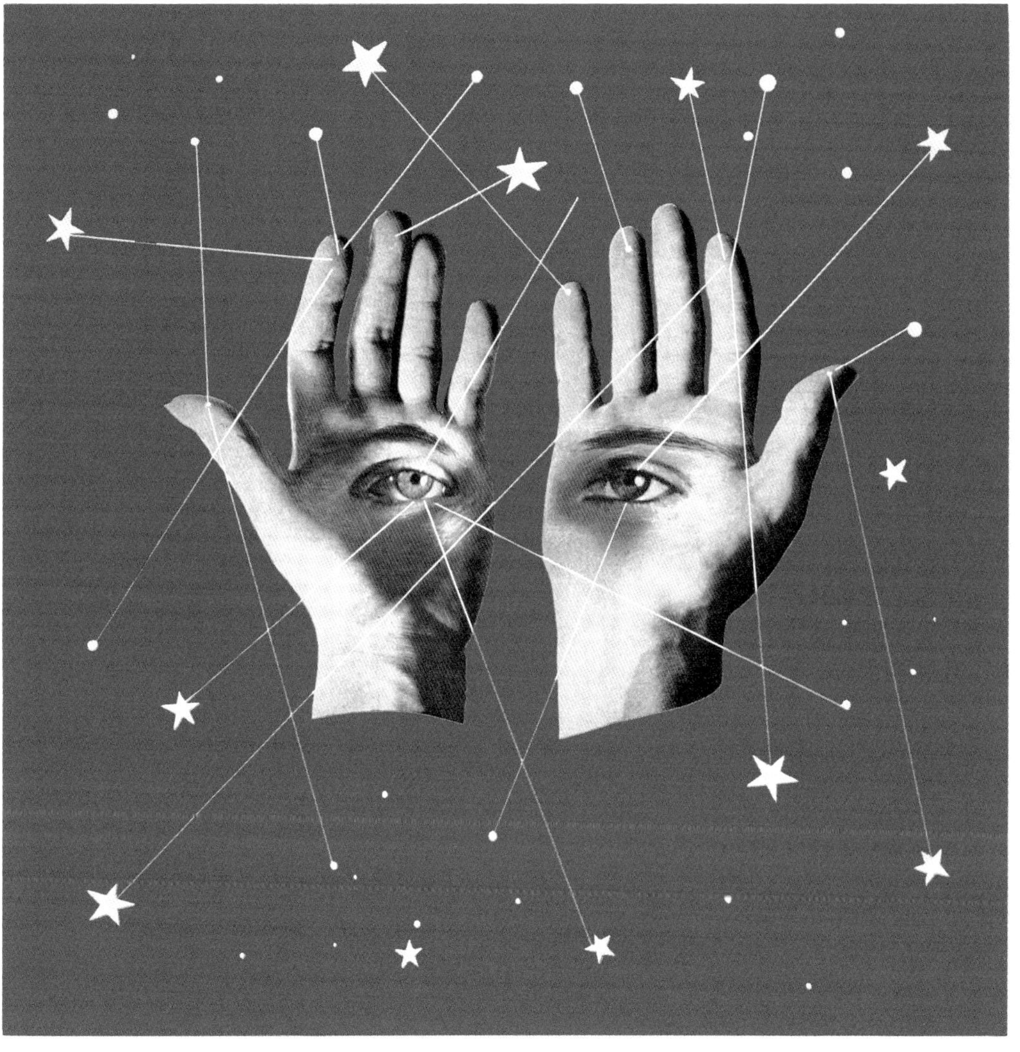

1938 · Herbert Bayer · AT/US · Brochure cover

1939

Bruno Munari becomes art director at **Tempo** magazine in Milan

Ladislav Sutnar moves to New York City

1939 · Anonymous · FR · Logo · Paris Match

1939 · Bernard Rudofsky · CZ/BR · Logo · Fotoptica

1939 · Ferdinand Schott · CH · Logo · Geigy

1939 · Albert Staehle · US · Poster

The British Ministry of Information prints 2.5 million copies of the **Keep Calm and Carry On** motivational poster

1939 · Sophie Täuber-Arp · FR · Magazine cover

1939 · "Karlicek" · AT · Poster

1939 · Anonymous · UK · Poster

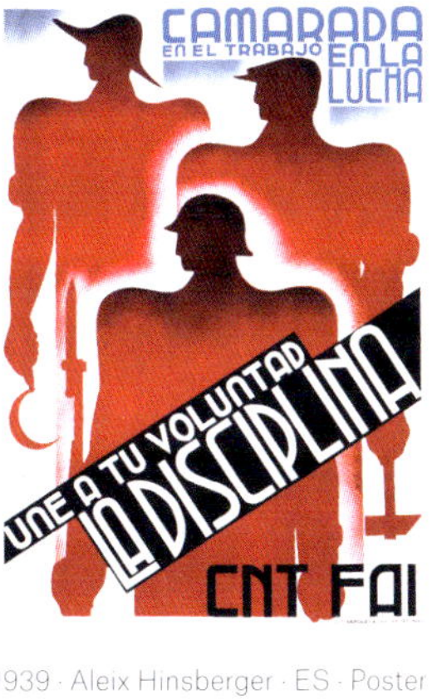

1939 · Aleix Hinsberger · ES · Poster

1939 · René Ravo · FR · Magazine cover

Vogue, the American fashion magazine, was one of a string of publications which set out to make a fresh start after the country's recovery from the Great Depression by devising a new kind of visual language. By 1932, the first cover with color photographs had appeared, and by the end of the decade photographers and graphic designers had found highly inventive ways of applying new techniques, combining images and type to create eye-catching compositions that established a new style in modern graphic design.

Das amerikanische Modemagazin *Vogue* gehörte zu einer Reihe von Zeitschriften, die nach der Überwindung der Großen Depression einen visuellen Neuanfang suchten. Bereits 1932 war das erste Cover mit einer Farbfotografie erschienen, zum Ende des Jahrzehnts nutzten Fotografen und Gestalter die neue Technik in besonders kreativer Art und Weise: Sie kombinierten Bild und Schrift zu faszinierenden Gesamtkompositionen und setzten damit neue Maßstäbe im modernen Grafikdesign.

Le magazine de mode américain *Vogue* fait partie d'une série de publications qui cherchèrent à prendre un nouveau départ en matière de conception visuelle après la Grande Dépression. Dès 1932, la première couverture paraît avec une photographie en couleurs, et à la fin de la décennie, des photographes et graphistes utilisent la nouvelle technique d'une manière particulièrement créative, combinant l'image et l'écriture pour créer de fascinantes compositions et imposant ainsi de nouveaux standards au graphisme moderne.

1940 · Horst P. Horst (PH) · US · Magazine cover

1930s · Anonymous · JP · Poster

1930s · Anonymous · JP · Signage

1930s · Anonymous · RU · Poster

1930s · Gert Sellheim · DE/AU · Poster

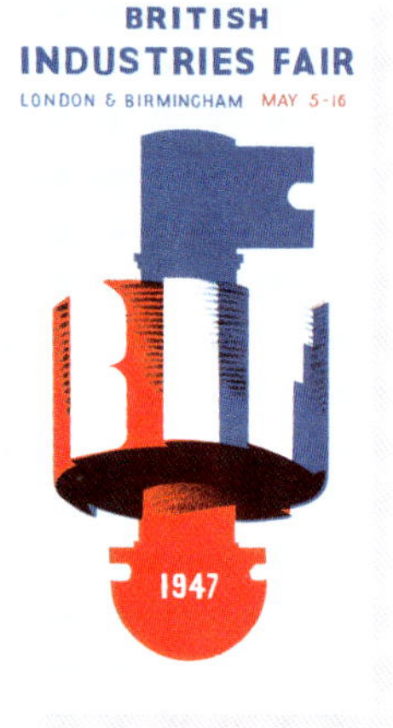

1947 · Anonymous · UK · Brochure cover

1940

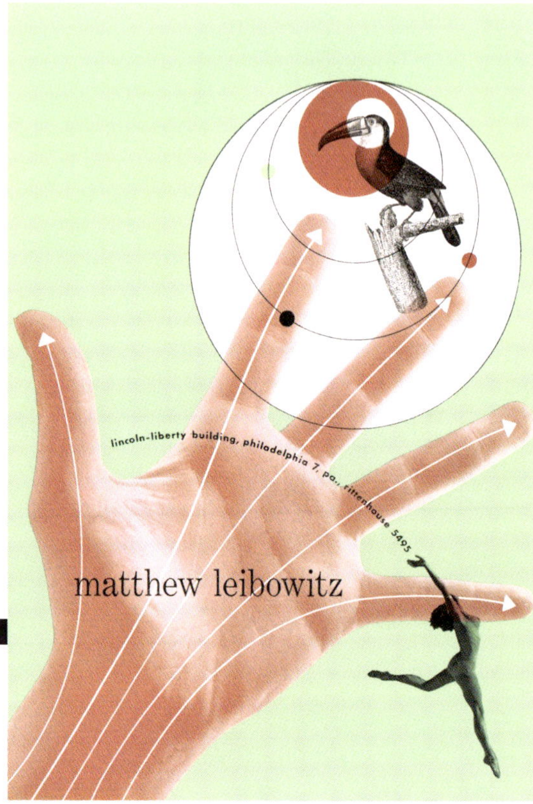

1946 · Matthew Leibowitz · US · Ad

1940s · Walter Herdeg · CH · Logo · Louis Moinat

1943 · Patrick Cokayne Keely · UK · Poster

1941 · Anonymous · US · Poster

1949

1942 · Anonymous · US · Poster

The first half of the decade was defined by the Second World War, with millions of people losing their lives or otherwise being left directly or indirectly affected by the hostilities. The war years made their impact on every aspect of life but also left their mark on graphic design, where even more so than during the First World War, visual communication functioned as an important means of influencing the masses. With the end of the war in 1945 the recovering economies of the different countries restored the creative industry to its role as a driving force, particularly in advertising, and it was largely in the United States that global visual trends began to be set. The many fashion and lifestyle magazines published in New York provided the backdrop for new American graphic design, and although at first illustration was the dominant form used for posters and magazine covers, which suffered from deficiencies in color reproduction technology, photography was fast becoming the stylistic device of the moment.

The graphic designer Alex Steinweiss working on a record sleeve in the New York offices of CBS Records.

Der Grafikdesigner Alex Steinweiss bei der Arbeit an einem Plattencover im New Yorker Büro von CBS Records.

Le graphiste Alex Steinweiss travaille sur une pochette de disque dans les bureaux new-yorkais de CBS Records.

Der Zweite Weltkrieg bestimmte die erste Hälfte dieses Jahrzehnts. Millionen von Menschen verloren ihr Leben und waren direkt oder indirekt von den Kriegshandlungen betroffen. Die Kriegsjahre beeinflussten sämtliche Bereiche des Lebens und hinterließen so auch im Grafikdesign ihre Spuren. Mehr noch als im Ersten Weltkrieg fungierte die visuelle Kommunikation als wichtiges Mittel zur Beeinflussung der Massen. Mit dem Ende des Zweiten Weltkriegs 1945 wurde in den meisten Ländern die wiedererstarkende Wirtschaft erneut zum Treiber der Kreativbranche. Vor allem in den USA entstanden nun globale visuelle Trends. Als Bühne für die neue amerikanische Grafik boten sich unter anderem die zahlreichen in New York publizierten Mode- und Lifestylemagazine an. Auch wenn durch fehlende technische Möglichkeiten der Farbreproduktion auf Plakaten oder Titelseiten zunächst noch die Illustration dominierte, begann sich die Fotografie als das zeitgemäße Stilmittel durchzusetzen.

La Seconde Guerre mondiale occupe la première moitié de cette décennie. Des millions d'hommes et de femmes sont tués et touchés directement ou indirectement par le conflit. Les années de guerre influencent tous les domaines de la vie et laissent aussi leurs traces dans le domaine du graphisme. Plus encore que pendant la Première Guerre mondiale, la communication visuelle est un moyen important pour influencer les masses. À la fin de la Seconde Guerre mondiale en 1945, dans la plupart des pays, l'économie renaissante redevient le moteur de la branche créative. Aux États-Unis surtout apparaissent désormais des tendances visuelles globales. Comme scène du nouveau graphisme américain, elles ont notamment à leur disposition les nombreux magazines new-yorkais de mode et d'art de vivre. Si les affiches ou les couvertures des magazines sont encore dominées par l'illustration – du fait de l'imperfection des moyens techniques de reproduction en couleur –, la photographie commence à s'imposer comme le vecteur stylistique propre à l'époque.

1940

The first issue of the design quarterly **Print** is published in the United States

Walter Landor and his wife Josephine launch a design firm from their small apartment in San Francisco

1940 · Emil Alfred Neukomm · CH · Poster

1940 · Anonymous · JP · Brochure cover

1940 · Gert Sellheim · DE/AU · Magazine cover

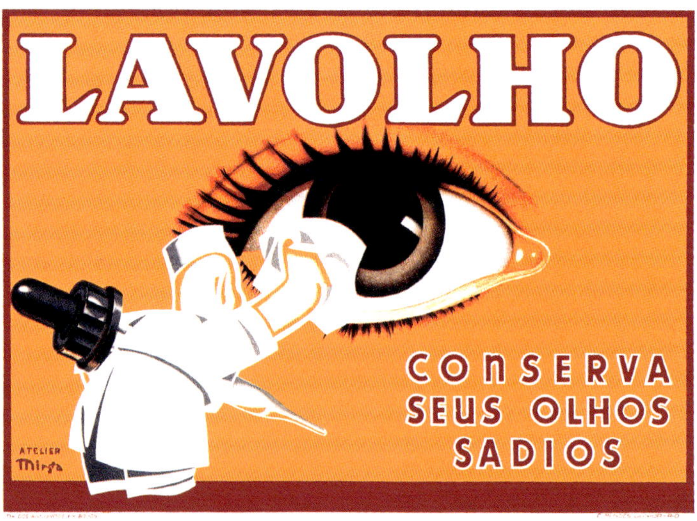

1940 · Henrique Mirgalowski · BR · Poster

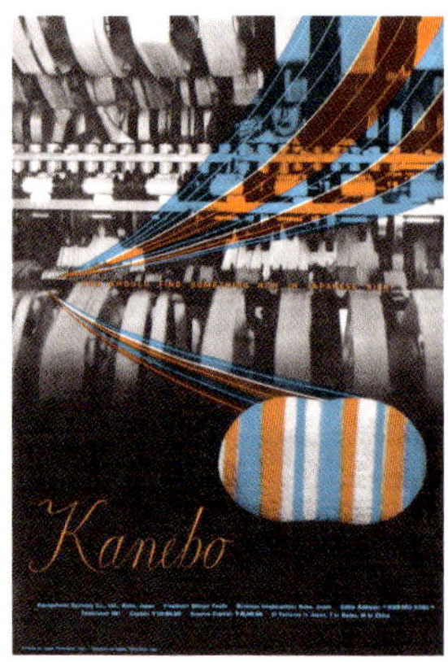

1940 · Anonymous · JP · Ad

1940 · Raymond Loewy · FR/US · Packaging

1940 · Jozef Vlček · SK · Magazine cover

1940 · "Schwarz" · AT · Poster

1940 · Anonymous · RU · Poster

By the beginning of the 1940s, the outbreak of the Second World War had plunged all the great international powers into armed conflict. As in the First World War, governments committed carefully targeted funds to communications design in order to inform people and prepare them for the privations of war. Special departments were set up and posters and other printed material were produced under government or military control. In the United States and Great Britain in particular, leading graphic designers such as Lester Beall and F. H. K. Henrion joined in with the war against Fascism, and alongside numerous run-of-the-mill pieces of propaganda they created a whole range of distinguished works which drew upon the history of the period and the history of design to extraordinarily impressive effect.

Der Zweite Weltkrieg zwang Anfang der 1940er-Jahre alle internationalen Großmächte in den militärischen Konflikt. Wie schon beim Ersten Weltkrieg setzten die Regierungen ganz gezielt Mittel des Kommunikationsdesigns ein, um die Bevölkerung auf den entbehrungsreichen Krieg einzustellen. Spezielle Abteilungen wurden gegründet, und unter staatlicher bzw. militärischer Führung entstanden Plakate und andere Drucksachen. Vor allem in den USA und in Großbritannien stellten sich auch herausragende Grafikdesigner wie Lester Beall oder F.H.K. Henrion dem Kampf gegen die Faschisten zur Verfügung. So entstanden neben zahlreichen grafisch eher unbedeutenden Propagandaerzeugnissen eine ganze Reihe ikonografischer Arbeiten, in denen sich Zeit- und Designgeschichte besonders eindrucksvoll verbinden.

Au début des années 1940, toutes les grandes puissances sont entraînées dans la Seconde Guerre mondiale. Comme pendant la Première Guerre mondiale, les gouvernements font appel de façon tout à fait ciblée aux moyens de communication visuelle pour informer les populations et les préparer aux privations de la guerre. Des départements spécialisés sont créés et produisent des affiches et autres imprimés sous la supervision de l'État ou du commandement militaire. C'est surtout aux États-Unis et en Grande-Bretagne que des graphistes de premier plan comme Lester Beall ou F.H.K. Henrion mettent leurs forces au service de la lutte contre le fascisme. À côté de nombreuses réalisations propagandistes plutôt insignifiantes en termes de graphisme, toute une série de créations exceptionnelles voient le jour, associant de manière particulièrement impressionnante l'histoire de l'époque et celle du graphisme.

1943 · F. H. K. Henrion · UK · Poster

1942 · J. Howard Miller · US · Poster

»The possibilities of the poster in relation to Commerce and Industry were universally recognized before the war years. Designers in this country primarily demonstrated that posters could also service the social interests of the community by designing some of the best educational and instructive work ever produced here.« Abram Games, *Commercial Art*, 1948

1941 · Leo Lionni · US · Poster

1942 · Anonymous · US · Poster

1942 · "Trevor" · CA · Poster

1942 · Robert Muchley · US · Poster

1940s · Julio Prieto Posadas · MX · Poster

1941

Illustrator **Saul Steinberg** emigrates from Romania to the United States and begins his work for *The New Yorker*

1941 · Anonymous · US · Brochure cover

1941 · Jacques Kapralik · US · Brochure cover

1941 · Anonymous · FR · Poster

1941 · Anonymous · RU · Poster

1941 · Herbert Matter · CH/US · Poster

1941 · Anonymous · JP · Magazine cover

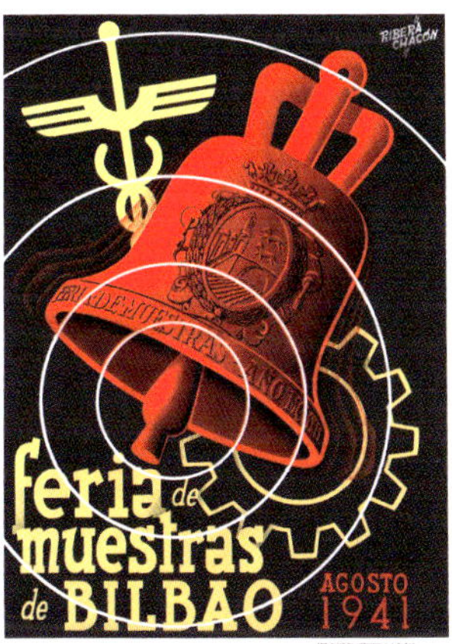

1941 · José Luis Ribera Chacón · ES · Poster

1941 · "Montgomery" · ZA · Poster

1942

Bradbury Thompson is appointed art director of the U.S. Office of War Information

Emil Ruder begins teaching his typography course at the Basel School of Design

1942 · Anonymous · RU · Poster

1942 · U.S. Government Printing Office · US · Poster

1942 · Robert Robinson · US · Magazine cover

1942 · Al Parker · US · Magazine cover

1942 · Anonymous · US · Poster

1942 · Anonymous · US · Poster

1942 · Anonymous · US · Poster

The first issue of the French graphic design magazine **Publimondial** is published

Kodak introduces **Kodacolor,** the first color negative film for making prints

1942 · J. Bonelli · UY · Poster

1942 · "WT" · CH · Poster

1942 · Alex Steinweiss · US · Record cover

1942 · Edward McKnight Kauffer · US · Poster

1943

1943 · Carlo L. Vivarelli · CH/IT · Logo · Drogheria Neri

1943 · Paul Rand · US · Logo · Helibros Watch Co.

The annual contest for the **Most Beautiful Swiss Books** is held for the first time, on the initiative of Jan Tschichold

1943 · Anonymous · US · Poster

1943 · Anonymous · US · Magazine cover

Donald R. Dohner and J. Gordon Lippincott establish the design company **Dohner & Lippincott** in New York City

1943 · Henry Koerner · AT/US · Poster

1943 · H. Lawrence Hoffman · US · Book cover

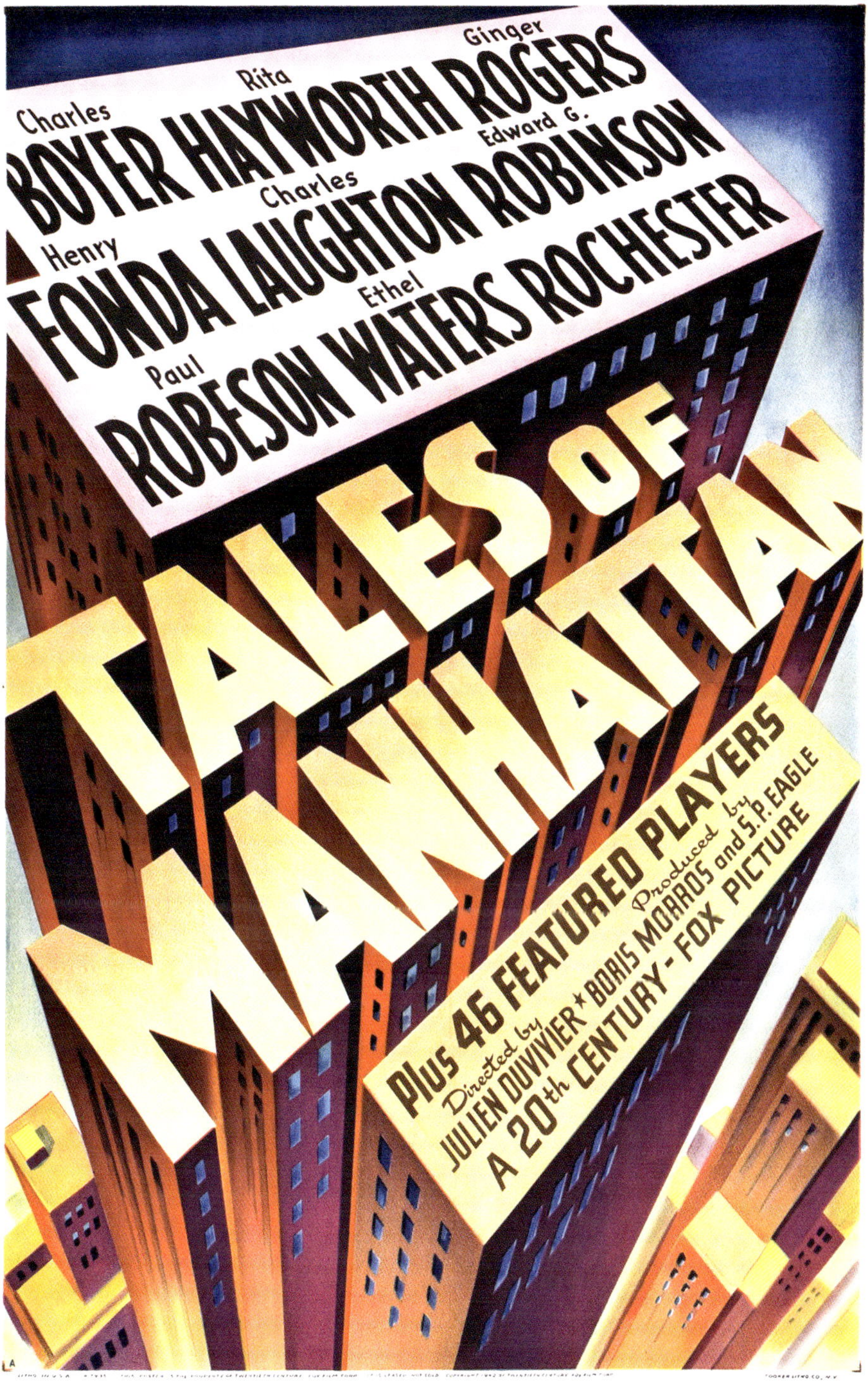

1943 · Anonymous · US · Poster

After the Second World War, innovative posters featuring photorealistic images of objects and products quickly gained in popularity—especially in Switzerland. Graphic designers such as Donald Brun and Fritz Bühler led a movement which had begun in the 1930s in a quest to develop a neutral, down-to-earth, almost photographic style of illustration, although it was only with the advances in printing technology of the 1960s that it became possible to reproduce real color photographs in poster formats. The designs from the late 1940s display a kind of hyperrealism, a forerunner to the perfectly staged advertising photographs of later years.

Nach dem Zweiten Weltkrieg wurden vor allem in der Schweiz neuartige Plakate populär, die Objekte und Produkte in fotorealistischer Form inszenierten. Grafikdesigner wie Donald Brun oder Fritz Bühler führten eine bereits in den 1930er-Jahren eingeleitete Entwicklung fort, die einen der Fotografie nahekommenden sachlich-neutralen Illustrationsstil verfolgte. Erst in den 1960er-Jahren sollte es mit fortschreitender Reproduktionstechnik möglich sein, echte Farbfotografien im Plakatformat wiederzugeben. Die Arbeiten aus den späten 1940er-Jahren nahmen eine Art Hyperrealismus vorweg, die Perfektion der inszenierten Werbefotografie späterer Jahre.

Après la Seconde Guerre mondiale, principalement en Suisse, des affiches d'un nouveau genre deviennent populaires et mettent en scène des objets et des produits sous une forme photoréaliste. Des graphistes comme Donald Brun ou Fritz Bühler poursuivent ainsi une évolution amorcée dès les années 1930 et qui visait à un style d'illustration objectif, neutre, proche de la photographie. Il faudra en effet attendre les années 1960 pour que l'évolution des techniques d'impression permette d'imprimer de vraies photographies en couleurs au format d'affiche. Les réalisations de la fin des années 1940 préfiguraient une sorte d'hyperréalisme – la perfection des mises en scène de la future photographie publicitaire.

1942 · Peter Birkhäuser · CH · Poster

»The industrial product became, so to speak, a symbolic beacon of hope for change and the future. Even today, 'straight' photography, New Objectivity, and New Vision are strongly associated with modernity.« Gerda Breuer, *The Magic of Things*, 2012

1949 · Anonymous · CH · Poster

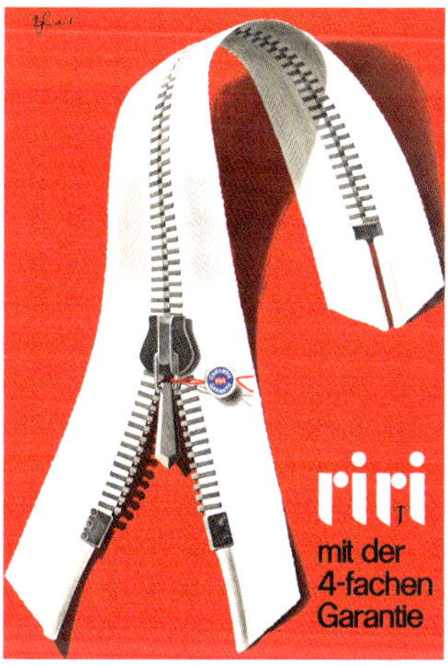

1945 · Pierre Gauchat · CH · Poster

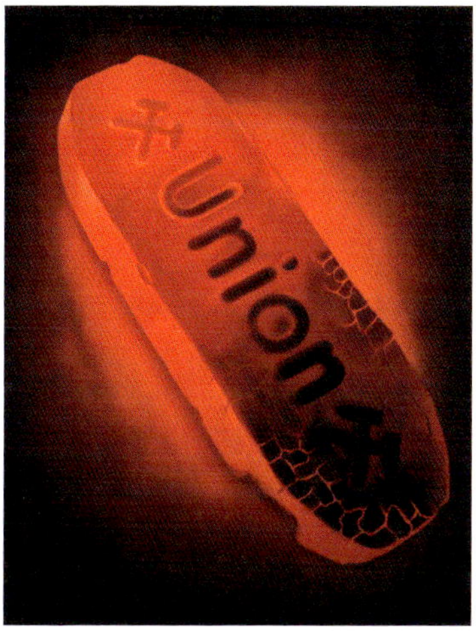

1943 · Fritz Bühler · CH · Poster

1942 · Hans Aeschbach · CH · Poster

1941 · Peter Birkhäuser · CH · Poster

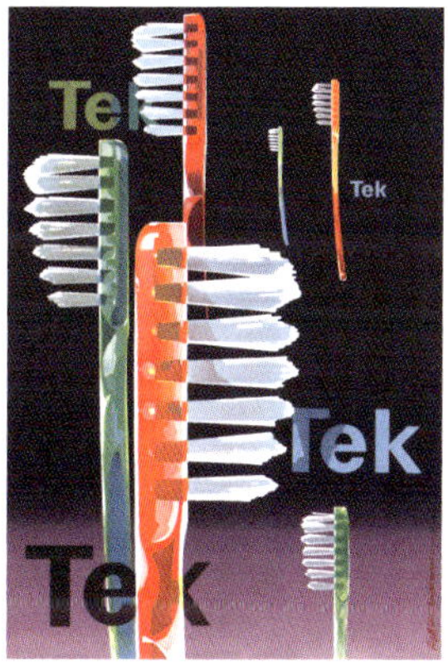

1947 · Fritz Bühler · CH · Poster

1947 · Peter Birkhäuser · CH · Poster

1944

Graphis design magazine is founded in Zurich by Walter Herdeg and Walter Amstutz

The **Design Council** is established in the United Kingdom

1944 · Anonymous · US · Poster

1944 · Anonymous · US · Ad

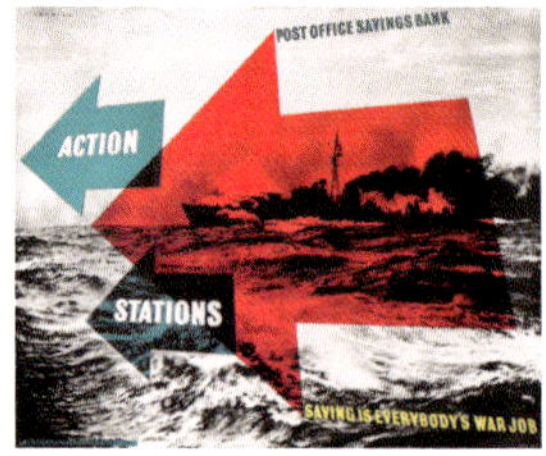

1944 · F. H. K. Henrion · UK · Poster

1944 · Stanley Ekman · US · Poster

1944 · Anonymous · FR · Poster

1944 · Patrick Cokayne Keely · UK · Poster

1945

The **Italian Association of Visual Communication Design** (AIAP) is founded

1945 · "Espert" · MX · Poster

1945 · Alex Steinweiss · US · Magazine cover

1945 · Havas Paris · FR · Poster

1945 · Rolf Rappaz · CH · Poster

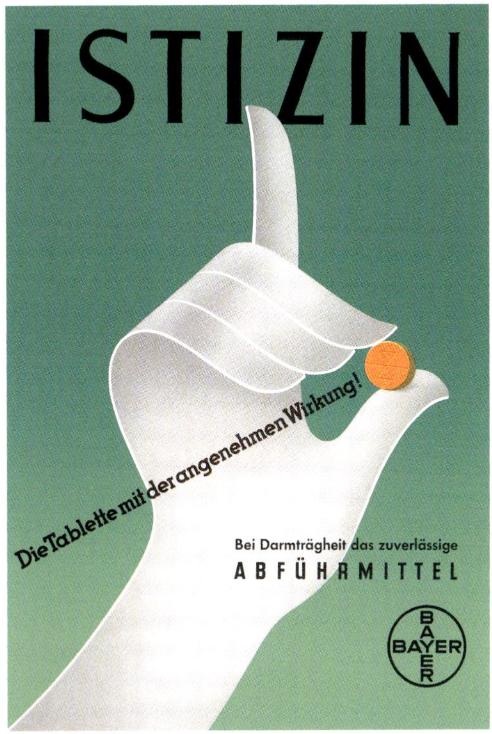

1945 · Anonymous · DE · Brochure cover

1945 · Herbert Matter · CH/US · Magazine cover

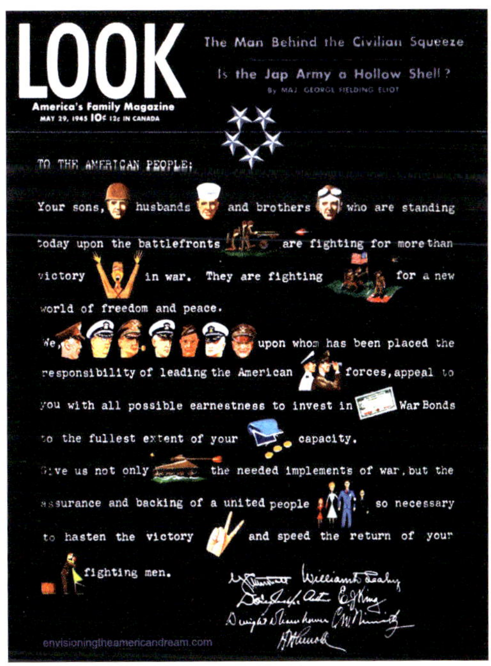

1945 · Fred Chance · US · Magazine cover

1946

Herbert Bayer becomes art director of the CCA (Container Corporation of America)

Saul Bass moves from New York to Los Angeles to open a design studio

1946 · Hans Neuburg · CH · Jean Oertli Werkzeuge

1946 · Lee Elliott · UK · Logo · Imperial Airways

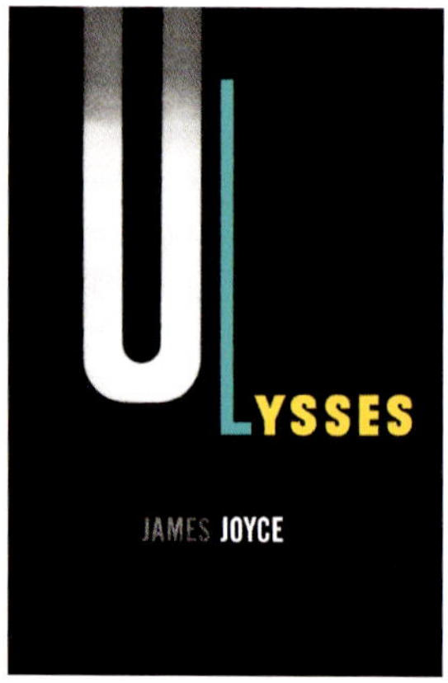

1946 · Edward McKnight Kauffer · US · Book cover

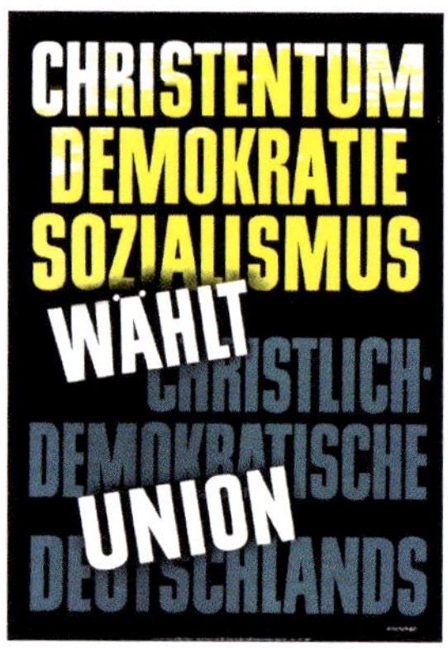

1946 · Heinz Schwabe · DE · Poster

1946 · R. Géroudet · CH · Poster

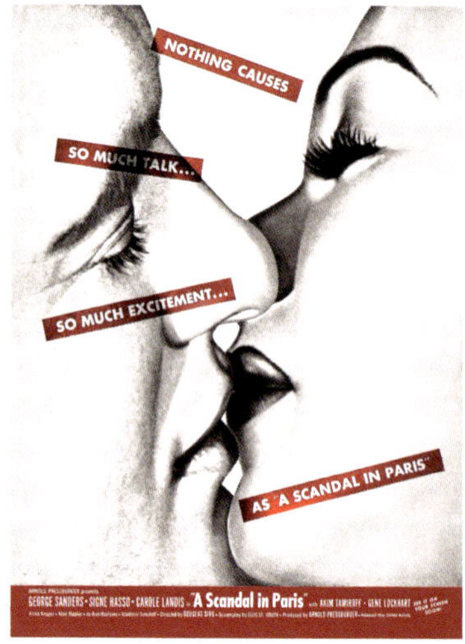

1946 · Anonymous · US · Ad

1946 · Frank Robbins · US · Poster

The New York **Type Directors Club** (TDC) is founded

The Walker Art Center launches its Everyday Art Quarterly, which is renamed in 1954 as **Design Quarterly**

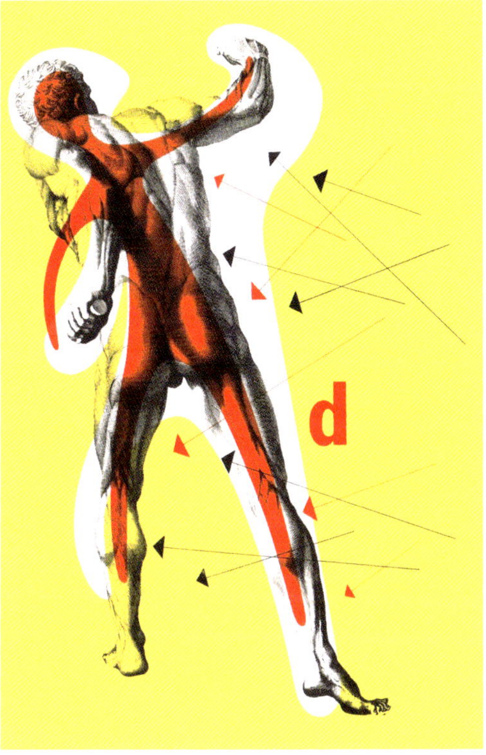

1946 · Matthew Leibowitz · US · Brochure cover

1946 · Victor Rutz · CH · Poster

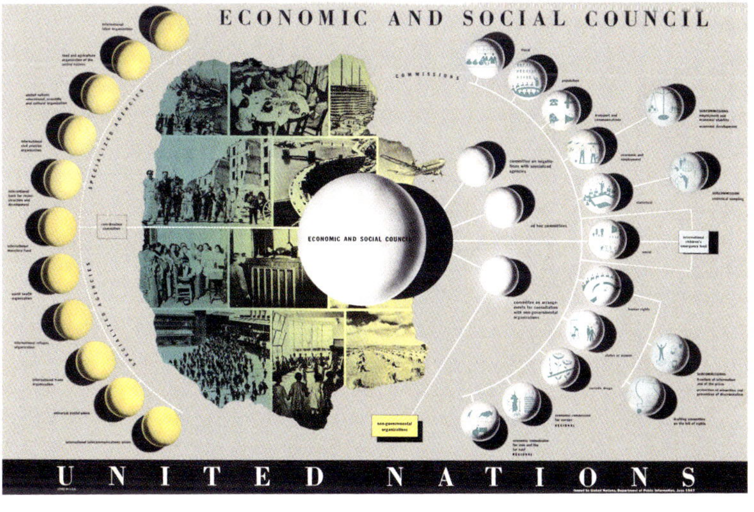

1946 · Ladislav Sutnar · US · Poster/Infographic

1947

Armin Hofmann joins **Emil Ruder** as a teacher at the Basel School of Design

Paul Rand's book **Thoughts on Design** is published

Penguin Books hires Jan Tschichold as a design consultant

1947 · Lou Frimkess · US · Logo · Helipot Corporation

1947 · Gert Sellheim · DE/AU · Logo · Quantas Airlines

1947 · Paul Baudouin · FR · Poster

The **School of Visual Arts** is founded in New York City, originally called the Cartoonists and Illustrators School

1947 · Alvin Lustig · US · Book cover

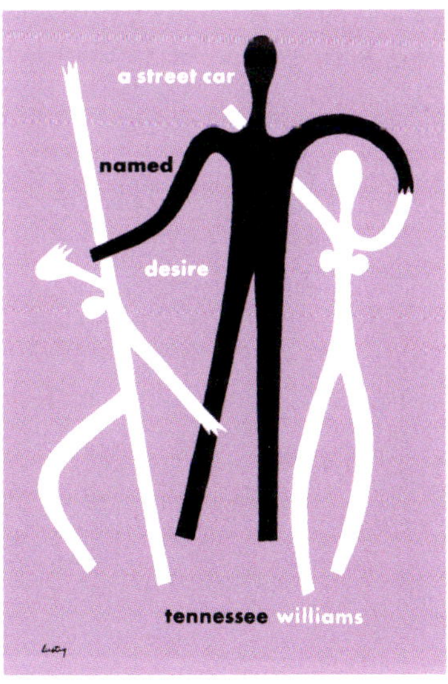

1947 · Alvin Lustig · US · Book cover

1947 · Vedat Tan · TR · Poster

1947 · "Kereszty" · HU · Poster

1947 · Co-op 2 · US · Book cover

1947 · Anonymous · US · Brochure cover

1947 · Reyn Dirksen · NL · Poster

Alexey Vyacheslavovich Brodovitch (1898, Ogolichi, Belarus – 1971, Le Thor, France) was a Russian photographer and designer, known for art directing fashion editorials for *Harper's Bazaar* between 1934 and 1958. Self-taught in the arts, he fought for the Russian army, and later against the Bolsheviks, before fleeing to France. He was exposed to all the art movements of the time in Paris and readily embraced design, winning a poster competition in 1924—with Picasso getting second place. Starting off at magazines, such as producing layouts for *Cahiers d'Art* and *Arts et Métiers Graphiques*, Brodovitch later consolidated his work at *Harper's*.

Alexey Vyacheslavovich Brodovitch (1898, Ogolichi, heute Weißrussland – 1971, Le Thor, Frankreich) war ein russischer Fotograf und Grafikdesigner, der von 1934 bis 1958 insbesondere als Artdirector der Modestrecken in *Harper's Bazaar* bekannt wurde. Er hatte für die russische Armee und später gegen die Bolschewiki gekämpft, ehe er nach Frankreich floh, wo er in Paris mit allen Kunstströmungen der Zeit in Kontakt kam und sich als künstlerischer Autodidakt dem Grafikdesign zuwandte. So gewann er 1924 einen Plakatwettbewerb, aus dem Picasso als Zweiter hervorging. Bei seiner Arbeit für Zeitschriften gestaltete er zunächst Layouts für *Cahiers d'Art* und *Arts et Métiers Graphiques*, eine Tätigkeit, die er später bei *Harper's* noch ausweitete.

Alexey Tcheslavovitch Brodovitch (1898, Ogolichi, Biélorussie – 1971, Le Thor, France) fut un photographe et designer russe connu comme directeur artistique éditorial chez *Harper's Bazaar* entre 1934 et 1958. Artiste autodidacte, il combattit dans les rangs de l'armée russe, et plus tard contre les bolcheviks, avant de se réfugier en France. À Paris, il fut exposé à tous les mouvements artistiques de l'époque et se lança tout naturellement dans le design après avoir remporté un concours d'affiches en 1924 – Picasso avait été deuxième. Travaillant d'abord pour des magazines et metteur en pages pour les *Cahiers d'Art* et *Arts et Métiers Graphiques*, Brodovitch consolida ensuite son travail pour *Harper's*.

1931 · Alexey Brodovitch · US · Magazine cover

1937 · Alexey Brodovitch · US · Poster

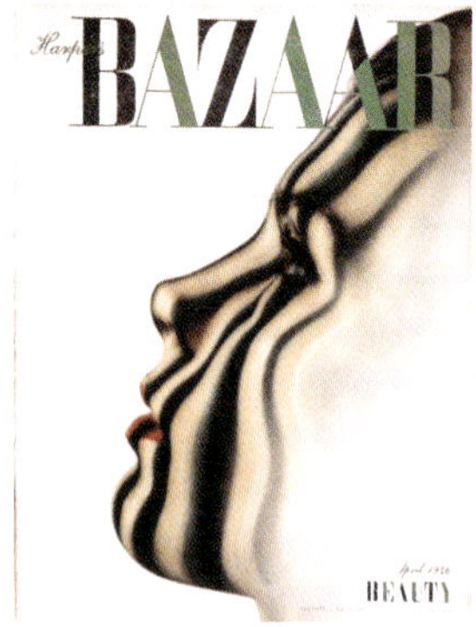

1946 · Alexey Brodovitch (AD) · US · Magazine cover

1947 · Alexey Brodovitch (AD) · US · Magazine cover

1955 · Alexey Brodovitch (AD) · US · Magazine cover

»There isn't a designer or photographer in our time who hasn't felt the influence of Alexey Brodovitch. The waves that went out from *Harper's Bazaar* since his first issue are still rippling.«

Irving Penn, *Alexey Brodovitch and His Influence*, 1972

1950 · Alexey Brodovitch (AD) · US · Magazine spread

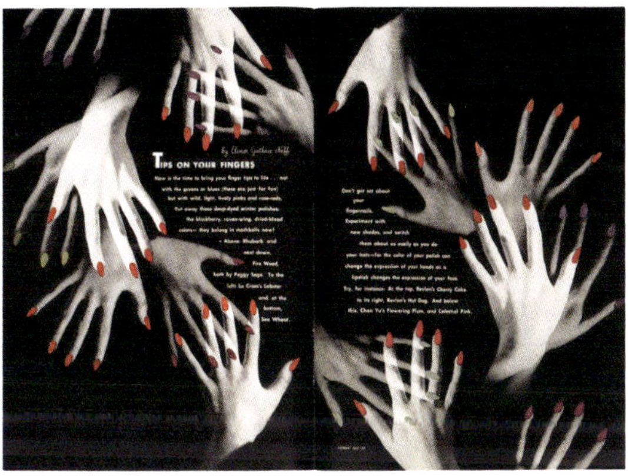

1954 · Alexey Brodovitch (AD) · US · Magazine spread

1954 · Alexey Brodovitch (AD) · US · Magazine spread

1950 · Alexey Brodovitch · US · Magazine cover

1959 · Alexey Brodovitch · US · Book cover

1948

1948 · Bill Ray · US · Warning symbol

The **Trade Gothic** typeface is designed by Jackson Burke

1948 · Max Huber · CH/IT · Poster

1948 · Joseph Binder · AT/CH · Magazine cover

David Ogilvy opens an advertising agency in New York City

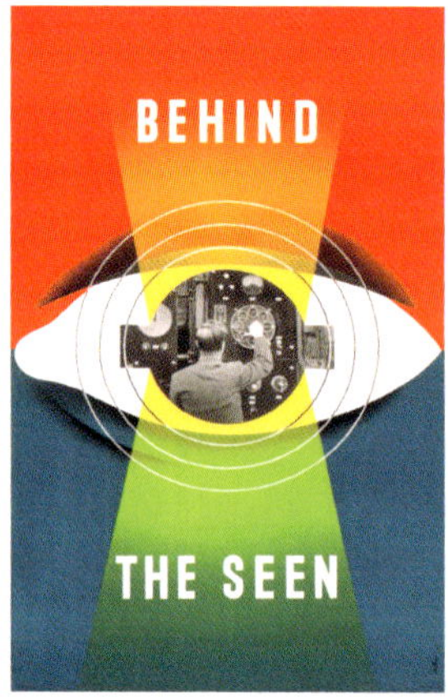

1948 · James Fitton · UK · Poster

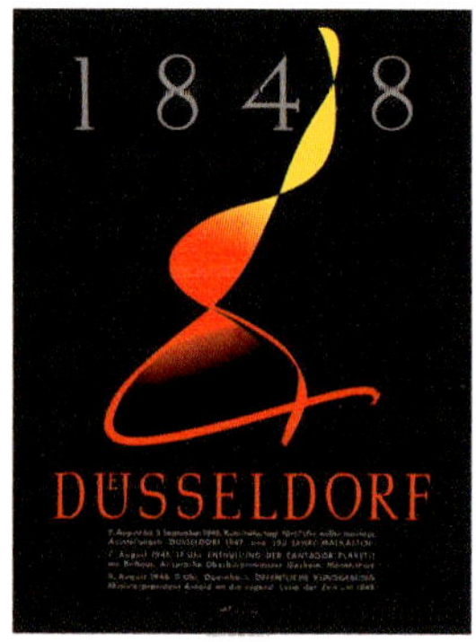

1948 · Wolf D. Zimmermann · DE · Poster

1948 · F. H. K. Henrion · UK · Poster

The **Best Dutch Book Designs** competition is held for the first time

1948 · Karov · US · Book cover

1948 · Guy Demachy · FR · Ad

1948 · Albe Steiner · IT · Magazine cover

1948 · Jan Lewitt, George Him · UK · Poster

1949

Bill Bernbach, Ned Doyle, and Mac Dane start the **Doyle Dane Bernbach** (DDB) advertising agency in New York City

Roger Vershen develops **Highway Gothic**, a standard typeface for use on U.S. traffic signs

1949 · William Belcher · US · Book cover

1949 · Friedrich Binder · DE · Magazine cover

1949 · Anonymous · PT · Poster

1949 · Anonymous · UY · Poster

Herbert Spencer's **Typographica** is first published

The first issue of British magazine **Design** is published

The first **International Design Conference** is held in Aspen, Colorado

The first **phototypesetting** machines are introduced in the United States

1949 · Amand Domènech · ES · Poster

1949 · J. Tonelli · FR · Poster

1949 · Fritz Bühler · CH · Poster

1948 · Cipe Pineles (AD) · US · Magazine cover

1949 · Cipe Pineles (AD) · US · Magazine cover

1954 · Cipe Pineles (AD) · US · Magazine cover

1951 · Cipe Pineles (AD) · US · Magazine cover

Cipe Pineles (1908, Vienna – 1991, New York) was a pioneering Austrian-American editorial designer. Starting her career at Condé Nast, and climbing the ladder of a male-dominated profession during the 1930s and '40s, she became the first woman art director of a mass-market publication at *Glamour*. She also produced groundbreaking work for *Seventeen*, *Charm*, and *Mademoiselle*—notably being the first person to hire fine artists to illustrate popular magazines. Pineles was also the first woman to become a member of the Art Directors Club in New York (1943) and the AGI (1955).

Cipe Pineles (1908, Wien – 1991, New York), geboren in Österreich war eine amerikanische Pionierin im Zeitschriftendesign. Ihre Laufbahn begann bei Condé Nast. In den 1930er- und 1940er-Jahren stieg sie in einer reinen Männerdomäne die Karriereleiter hinauf und wurde bei *Glamour* die erste weibliche Artdirectorin einer Zeitschrift mit großer Auflage. Auch bei *Seventeen*, *Charm* und *Mademoiselle* war ihre Arbeit wegweisend, insbesondere weil sie als Erste bildende Künstler engagierte, um Publikumszeitschriften zu illustrieren. Pineles wurde zudem als erste Frau Mitglied des Art Directors Club in New York (1943) und der AGI (1955).

Cipe Pineles (1908, Vienne – 1991, New York) fut une graphiste éditoriale austro-américaine novatrice. Après un début de carrière chez Condé Nast, pendant les années 1930 et 1940, elle gravit les échelons de la profession dominée par les hommes, jusqu'à devenir la première femme directrice artistique de la publication de masse *Glamour*. Elle produisit aussi un travail pionnier pour *Seventeen*, *Charm* et *Mademoiselle*, et fut notamment la première à engager des artistes pour illustrer des magazines populaires. Pineles fut aussi la première femme à intégrer l'Art Directors Club à New York (en 1943) et l'AGI (en 1955).

»Design is dealing with content. Magazine design should never play second fiddle to advertising. If the editorial content is very interesting and has a reason for being, it attracts advertising. A fashion magazine should report on what the industry has to offer. We are journalists in our special field.«

Cipe Pineles, 1989

1958 · Cipe Pineles (AD) · US · Magazine cover

From 1950 to 1959, Cipe Pineles was the art director at *Charm*, a magazine for independent, working women, and year after year her outstanding editorial design won awards from both the ADC and the AIGA. In 1959, she left to embark on a teaching career, but not before she had completely reshaped the magazine.

Zwischen 1950 und 1959 war Cipe Pineles als Artdirectorin für die Gestaltung von *Charm* verantwortlich, einem Magazin für selbstbewusste berufstätige Frauen. Für das hervorragende Editorial Design gab es fast jedes Jahr Auszeichnungen bei den Awards des ADC und des AIGA. 1959 verabschiedete sich Pineles zugunsten einer langjährigen Karriere als Dozentin aus der Magazinpraxis, realisierte zuvor jedoch noch ein umfassendes Redesign des Hefts.

Entre 1950 et 1959, Cipe Pineles fut directrice artistique de *Charm*, un magazine s'adressant à des femmes conscientes de leur valeur et actives professionnellement. Son design éditorial fut récompensé chaque année par l'ADC et l'AIGA. En 1959, Pineles se retira de cette activité pour se consacrer à une longue carrière d'enseignante – après avoir intégralement redéfini le design éditorial du magazine.

1951 · Cipe Pineles (AD) · US · Magazine spreads

1958 · Ralph E. Eckerstrom · US · Logo · Container Corporation of America

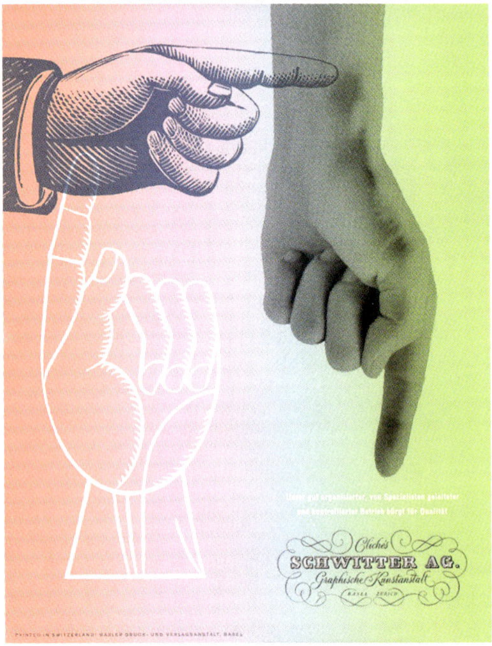

1950 · Anonymous · CH · Ad

1950

1958 · Erberto Carboni · IT · Poster

1952 · Anonymous · CL · Poster

1951 · Peracchi · IT · Book cover

—1959

1958 · Yusaku Kamekura · JP · Logo · Nippon Broadcasting System

In the 1950s many countries were permeated by a tremendous spirit of progress and optimism, even though the Cold War carried the very real threat of a new international conflict. It was, above all, in western societies that television established itself as a mass medium, while more and more people could now afford to buy their own automobile. At the same time, the space race got off to an auspicious start. There was also a feeling of self-confidence in the realm of visual communication, where many new styles emerged: in the United States, the innovative advertising scene which had grown up now developed a new, playful approach to typography, while in Switzerland the knock-on effect of the avant-garde of times past led to layouts which employed minimalist imagery and lettering, signaling the start of the modern era of graphic design. In Poland, a new generation of young designers made its presence felt with a novel kind of quasi-Expressionist posters, and alongside these charismatic and better-known pioneers of international fame, other countries, as yet unobtrusive in the world of graphic design, began to develop their own design culture in step with the modern age.

Die 1950er-Jahre waren in vielen Ländern von ungeheurem Fortschrittsgeist und Optimismus geprägt, auch wenn der Kalte Krieg sich als neuer internationaler Konflikt abzeichnete. Vor allem in westlichen Gesellschaften setzte sich das Fernsehen als Massenmedium durch, immer mehr Menschen konnten sich ein eigenes Auto leisten. Gleichzeitig begann ein vielversprechender Wettlauf ins All. Auch im Bereich der visuellen Kommunikation herrschte Aufbruchsstimmung, zahlreiche neue Tendenzen entstanden. Die innovative US-Werbeszene entwickelte einen neuen spielerischen Umgang mit Typografie. In der Schweiz manifestierten sich, in Fortsetzung der früheren Avantgarde, grafisch wie typografisch reduzierte Arbeiten, diese leiteten nicht weniger als die Moderne im Grafikdesign ein. In Polen trat eine junge Gestaltergeneration mit neuartigen, teils expressionistischen Plakaten erstmals in Erscheinung. Neben diesen Vorreitern mit internationaler Strahlkraft entwickelte sich auch in bislang im Grafiksektor unauffälligen Ländern eine zeitgemäße Designkultur.

Dans bien des pays, les années 1950 sont marquées par un esprit progressiste et un extraordinaire optimisme, même si la guerre froide dessine un nouveau conflit international. Dans les sociétés occidentales surtout, la télévision s'impose en tant que média de masse, et de plus en plus de gens peuvent s'acheter une voiture. En même temps débute une prometteuse concurrence pour la conquête de l'espace. Dans le domaine de la communication visuelle aussi, l'esprit qui prévaut est celui d'un nouveau départ, et d'innombrables nouvelles tendances voient le jour. La scène publicitaire américaine innovante développe un nouveau maniement ludique de la typographie. En Suisse apparaissent des travaux qui présentent un net minimalisme à la fois graphique et typographique dans le sillage de l'ancienne avant-garde, faisant entrer rien moins que la modernité dans le graphisme. Pour la première fois, une jeune génération de designers se manifeste en Pologne avec des affiches nouvelles, en partie expressionnistes. À côté de ces précurseurs au rayonnement international, une culture du design moderne se développe désormais aussi dans des pays restés jusqu'alors discrets dans le domaine du graphisme.

The American graphic designer Saul Bass with a selection of his movie poster designs.

Der amerikanische Grafikdesigner Saul Bass mit einer Auswahl seiner Entwürfe für Filmplakate.

Le graphiste américain Saul Bass devant une sélection de son travail pour des affiches de films.

1950

The first **Kieler Woche** design competition is held in Germany

The German **Gebrauchsgraphik** design magazine is relaunched

1950 · Aerostudio Borghi · IT · Logo · Lavazza

1950 · Edward L. Barnes, Charles Forberg, Ivan Chermayeff · US · Logo · Pan Am

1950 · Hermann Eidenbenz · CH · Logo · Schweizer Filmarchiv

1950 · Arpad Elfer · UK · Poster

1950 · Milner Gray, Design Research Unit · UK · Packaging

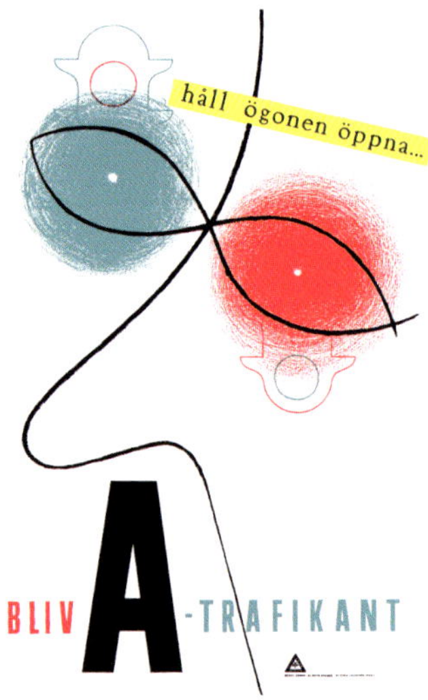

1950 · Arthur L. Bohman · SE · Poster

1950 · "Dohet" · BE · Poster

1950 · Eugen M. Cordier · DE · Poster

1950s · Oskar Spáčil · CZ · Ad

1950 · Paul Rand · US · Poster

1951

The first annual awards for **Best German Books** are held

Henrion Design Associates is founded in London

1951 · Libra Studio · NL · Poster

1951 · Adolf Pražský · CZ · Poster

1951 · Fritjof Pedersen · SE · Poster

1951 · Alexander Wagner · DE · Poster

1951 · Alfredo Alia · IT · Poster

The **Designers Society of Slovenia** is established

The **Japanese Advertising Artists Club** is set up

A prototype model of an **inkjet printer** is presented by the Siemens corporation

1951 · Erik Nitsche · CH/US · Record cover

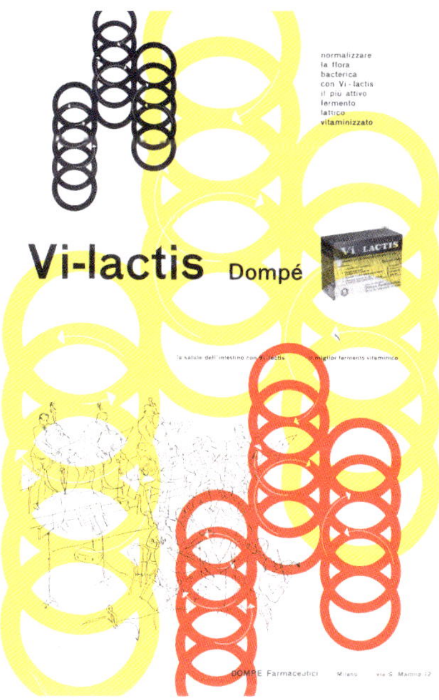

1951 · Anonymous · IT · Ad

1951 · Abram Games · UK · Poster

1951 · William Golden · US · Ads

When Adriano Olivetti took over his father's typewriter factory in the late 1930s he transformed the business, which had been founded in 1908, into a modern concern where design played a central role. Henceforth, the firm's products, retail outlets, manufacturing centers, and, of course, its advertising, came to exemplify a new style of top-quality design. Between 1950 and 1967, Giovanni Pintori, who had worked for Olivetti as a graphic designer since 1936, headed the publicity department. In this capacity he created an instantly recognizable graphic identity for Olivetti with international appeal. His personal design projects were largely based on visual interpretations of the workings of the various products through images which also featured the use of numbers, letters, and words.

Als Adriano Olivetti Ende der 1930er-Jahre die Schreibmaschinenfabrik seines Vaters übernahm, wandelte er das bereits 1908 gegründete Unternehmen in einen modernen Konzern um, bei dem die Gestaltung eine wesentliche Rolle spielte. Produkte, Verkaufsstellen, Produktionsstätten und natürlich die Werbung zeigten fortan ein innovatives und hochwertiges Design. Der bereits seit 1936 für Olivetti tätige Grafikdesigner Giovanni Pintori leitete zwischen 1950 und 1967 die Werbeabteilung. In dieser Position verlieh er dem Unternehmen eine unverkennbare grafische Identität von internationaler Strahlkraft. In seinen persönlich realisierten Arbeiten dominieren visuelle Übersetzungen der Gerätefunktionen mittels grafischer Bilder aus Zahlen, Buchstaben und Sprache.

À la fin des années 1930, quand Adriano Olivetti reprend la fabrique de machines à écrire de son père, il transforme l'entreprise fondée en 1908 en un groupe moderne dans lequel le graphisme va jouer un rôle essentiel. Les produits, points de vente, sites de production, et bien sûr aussi la publicité, présentent désormais un design innovant et de qualité. Le graphiste Giovanni Pintori, qui travaillait pour Olivetti depuis 1936, dirige le département de publicité de 1950 à 1967. C'est à ce poste qu'il confère à l'entreprise une identité visuelle tout à fait unique et au rayonnement international. Dans ses projets personnels domine la traduction visuelle des fonctions des différentes machines en images graphiques constituées de chiffres, de lettres et de mots.

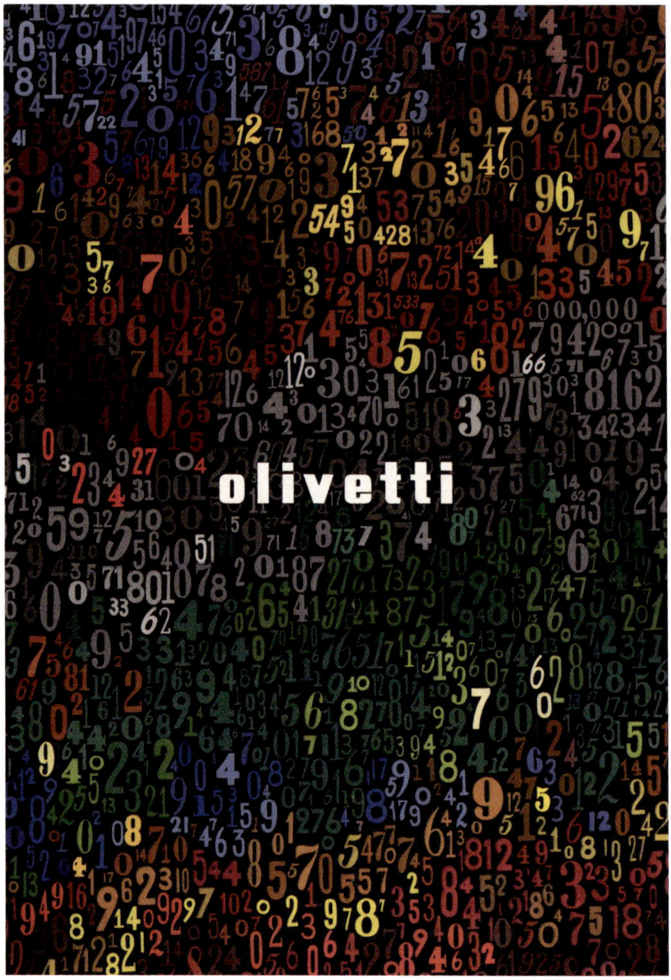

1949 · Giovanni Pintori · IT · Poster

»Olivetti [...] has been responsible for what is perhaps the most complete and successful attempt to date to apply artistic criteria to every visual aspect of a large industrial enterprise.«
Gillo Dorfles, *Graphis* #59, 1955

Giovanni Pintori (1912, Tresnuraghes, Italy – 1999, Milan) was a minimalist Italian graphic designer, mostly recognized for his classic work for Olivetti. With his emblematic use of color and geometrical shapes, Pintori started at the company in 1936 in the advertising department, after graduating from the Higher Institute of Artistic Industries in Monza. Soon after becoming Art Director for Olivetti in 1950, he exhibited at MoMA, in 1952, before leaving the company in 1967. Pintori subsequently opened his own design studio in Milan, working for numerous clients in the surrounding region, before dedicating himself to painting in later life.

Giovanni Pintori (1912, Tresnuraghes, Italien – 1999, Mailand) war ein italienischer Grafikdesigner, der vor allem für seine klassischen Olivetti-Entwürfe im minimalistischen Stil und die emblematische Verwendung von Farbe und geometrischen Formen bekannt ist. Nach dem Abschluss seines Studiums am Istituto Superiore per le Industrie Artistiche in Monza trat Pintori 1936 in die Werbeabteilung der Schreibmaschinenfirma ein. 1952, zwei Jahre nach seiner Ernennung zum Artdirector von Olivetti, fand eine Ausstellung seiner Werke im MoMA statt. 1967 verließ Pintori die Firma und eröffnete sein eigenes Designstudio in Mailand, wo er für zahlreiche Kunden aus der umgebenden Region arbeitete. In seinem späteren Leben widmete sich Pintori ganz der Malerei.

Giovanni Pintori (1912, Tresnuraghes, Italie – 1999, Milan) fut un graphiste italien adepte du minimalisme, connu surtout par son travail pour Olivetti, un classique du graphisme. Après avoir été diplômé de l'Istituto superiore per le Industrie Artistiche de Monza, Pintori entre au département publicitaire d'Olivetti en 1936, où il se fait remarquer par son utilisation emblématique de la couleur et des formes géométriques, avant de devenir directeur artistique en 1950. Il expose au MoMA de New York en 1952 et quitte Olivetti en 1967. Pintori ouvre ensuite son propre studio à Milan et travaille pour de nombreux clients régionaux avant de consacrer la dernière période de sa vie à la peinture.

1957 · Giovanni Pintori · IT · Poster

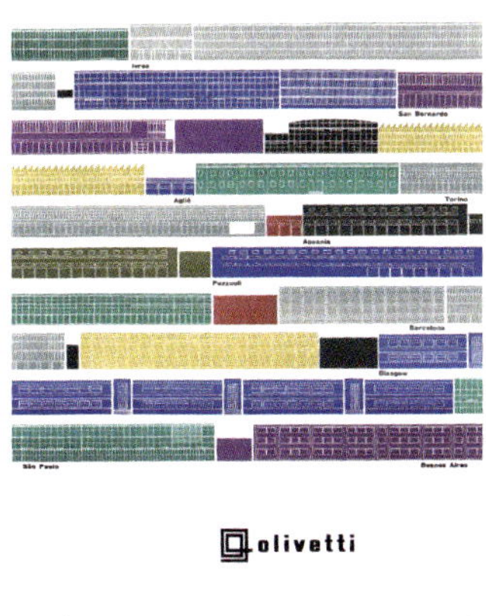

1956 · Giovanni Pintori · IT · Ad

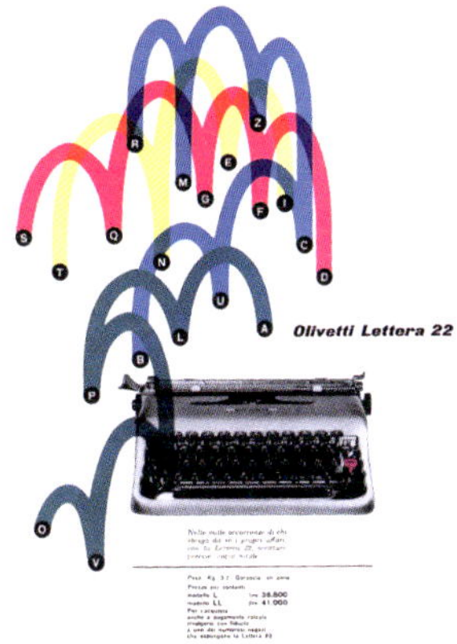

1955 · Giovanni Pintori · IT · Ad

1957 · Giovanni Pintori · IT · Poster

1952

German designer Hermann Zapf creates the **Optima** typeface

Herbert Matter starts teaching at Yale University

1952 · Morton Goldsholl · US · Logo · Motorola

1952 · Robert Bircher · CH · Logo · Swissair

1952 · Heini Fischer · CH · Poster

1952 · Hans & Ruth Albitz · DE · Poster

1952 · Anonymous · US · Opening titles

The Alliance Graphique Internationale (AGI) is incorporated in Paris by Donald Brun, Fritz Bühler, Jean Colin, Jacques Nathan-Garamond, and Jean Picart Le Doux

The first **Graphis Annual** is published

1952 · Lester Beall · US · Poster

1952 · Stan Krol · UK · Poster

1952 · Don Marvine, Robert W. Dunn · US · Poster

1952 · Hans Bolleman · BE · Ad

After 1945, when Poland became a communist-controlled Soviet state, a band of highly talented young designers found that they were able to put their extraordinary talents to practical use. Uninfluenced by the market conditions of capitalist economies, they created, particularly in their poster designs, a new visual language which in many cases was in violent contrast to the friendly, harmonious look of western advertising graphics. Polish graphic design from this period is exemplified by posters for cultural events which hover between functional communication and artistry as an end in itself. The innovative, often dramatic relationship between text and image quickly spread to become the predominant visual style in use behind the Iron Curtain.

Als Polen nach 1945 zu einem kommunistischen Sowjetstaat wurde, bot das System einer Riege hochtalentierter junger Gestalter die Möglichkeit, ihre grafisch außergewöhnlichen Arbeiten in der Praxis anzuwenden. Unbeeinflusst von den Marktbedingungen des Kapitalismus, entwickelte sich vor allem bei der Plakatgestaltung eine neue visuelle Sprache, die in vielen Fällen einen maximalen Gegensatz zur westlichen Werbegrafik und ihrer harmonisch-freundlichen Optik darstellte. Das kulturelle Plakat an der Grenze zwischen kommunikativer Aufgabe und künstlerischem Selbstzweck wurde zum Aushängeschild des polnischen Grafikdesigns. Der neuartige, oft expressive Umgang mit Schrift und Bild fand sich bald auch in anderen Oststaaten und wurde zum vorherrschenden visuellen Stil hinter dem Eisernen Vorhang.

Après 1945, alors que la Pologne est devenue un état soviétique contrôlé par les communistes, un groupe de jeunes graphistes hautement doués découvre qu'il a la possibilité de faire servir son extraordinaire talent. Loin de l'influence des marchés capitalistes, un nouveau langage visuel se développe alors essentiellement dans le domaine de l'affiche et apparaît dans bien des cas comme diamétralement opposé au graphisme publicitaire occidental et à son aspect visuel harmonieux et enjôleur. À la frontière entre mission communicative et propos artistique autonome, l'affiche culturelle devient la marque de fabrique du graphisme polonais. Le maniement inédit et souvent expressif de l'écriture et de l'image est rapidement adopté dans d'autres pays de l'Est jusqu'à devenir le style visuel dominant de l'autre côté du rideau de fer.

1952 · Tadeusz Trepkowski · PL · Poster

1955 · Julian Palka · PL · Poster

»The Polish poster is romantic, that is, romantic in several keys, from the lyrical to the heroic and the pathetic.« Jan Lenica, *Graphis* #88, 1960

1957 · Hanna Huskowska · PL · Poster

1957 · Wojciech Fangor · PL · Poster

1957 · Waldemar Swierzy · PL · Poster

1956 · Eryk Lipiński · PL · Poster

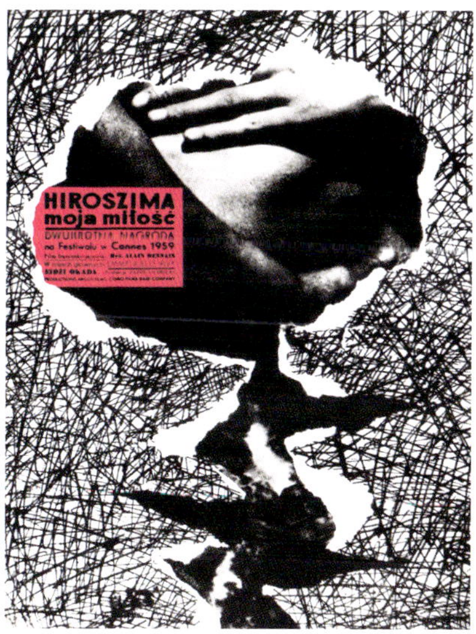

1959 · Stanisław Zagórski · PL · Poster

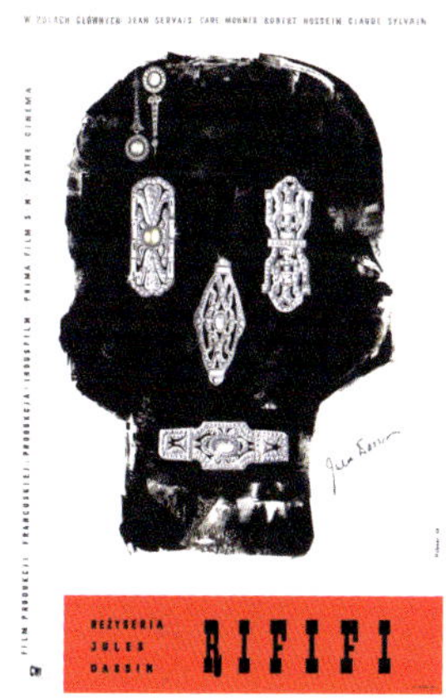

1958 · Maciej Hibner · PL · Poster

1959 · Andrzej Heidrich · PL · Poster

1960 · Wojciech Fangor · PL · Poster

1953

1953 · Arthur Paul · US · Logo · Playboy magazine

The first issue of Japanese design magazine **IDEA** is published

1953 · Wolf D. Zimmermann · DE · Book cover

1953 · Staffan Wirén · SE · Book cover

The **HfG Ulm** design school is founded in Germany by Max Bill, Otl Aicher, and Inge Aicher-Scholl

1953 · José Artigas Ojeda · ES · Packaging

1953 · Erik Bruun · FI · Poster

The **German Design Council** is established

French designer **Roger Excoffon** creates the Mistral typeface

1953 · Leonard Karasakov, Bauman Inc. · US · Ad

1950s · George Tscherny, George Nelson Office · US · Ad

1953 · Takashi Kono · JP · Poster

1953 · Erberto Carboni · IT · Poster

1954

The first issue of **I.D.** design magazine is published in the United States

The first issue of Italian design magazine **Stile Industria** is published

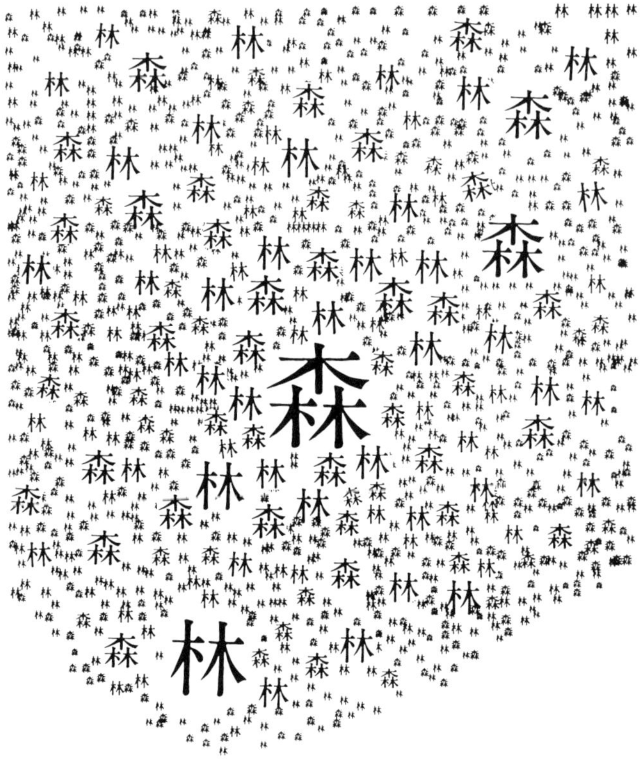

1954 · Ryuichi Yamashiro · JP · Poster

1954 · Anton Stankowski · DE · Logo · Süddeutscher Rundfunk

1954 · Erberto Carboni · IT · Logo · Radio Italiana

1954 · Herbert Matter · CH/US · Logo · New Haven Railroad

More than 100,000 **Linotype machines** are in use worldwide

Push Pin Studios is founded by Seymour Chwast, Milton Glaser, and Edward Sorel in New York City

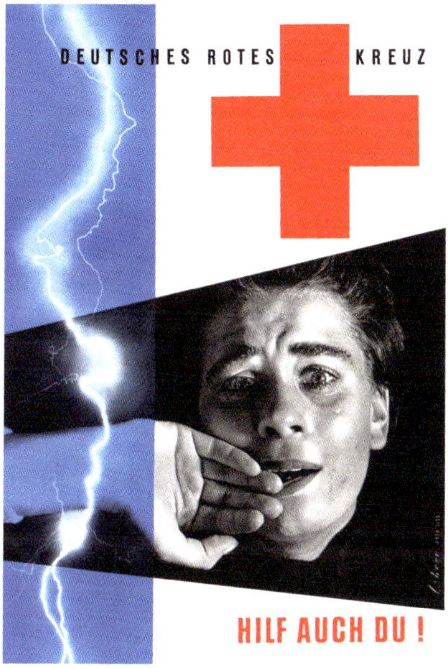

1954 · Hanns Lohrer · DE · Poster

1954 · Jean David · IL · Poster

1954 · Burt Goldblatt · US · Record cover

1954 · "Gersten" · US · Record cover

The worldwide use of humor as a visual device in advertising graphics of the 1950s can be seen as a reaction against the years of fear and deprivation suffered during the war. Whether in Japan, the United States, or Great Britain, for several years a wide range of lovable characters and cartoon-like images played a leading role, especially in product advertising. French graphic designers such as Hervé Morvan and Raymond Savignac were especially skilled at creating the attention-grabbing poster motifs that were just right for advertising drinks, cigarettes, and technical equipment.

Es kann als Reaktion auf die schreckens- und entbehrungsreichen Jahre des Kriegs gedeutet werden, dass in den 1950er-Jahren der Humor als visuelles Mittel der Werbegrafik weltweit auftauchte. Ob in Japan, den USA oder England – speziell in der Produktwerbung dominierten über einige Jahre die freundlichen Charaktere und cartoonesken Visualisierungen. Französische Grafikdesigner wie Hervé Morvan oder Raymond Savignac entwickelten eine besondere Meisterschaft darin, aufmerksamkeitsstarke Plakatmotive zu kreieren, die scheinbar ganz nebenbei für Getränke, Zigaretten oder technische Geräte warben.

L'on peut y voir une réaction aux années d'horreur et de privations de la Seconde Guerre mondiale: dans les années 1950, un peu partout dans le monde, l'humour devient un nouveau vecteur visuel du graphisme publicitaire. Pendant quelques années, que ce soit au Japon, aux États-Unis ou en Angleterre, la publicité de produits notamment est dominée par des personnages sympathiques et des visualisations qui rappellent la bande dessinée. Des graphistes français comme Hervé Morvan ou Raymond Savignac excellent dans ce domaine et créent des affiches dans lesquelles la réclame proprement dite pour des boissons, cigarettes ou appareils est pratiquée de manière presque accessoire.

1946 · John Averill · US · Ad

1950 · Rudi Bass (IL), George Krikorian (AD) · US · Ad

1952 · Kurt Weihs · US · Ad

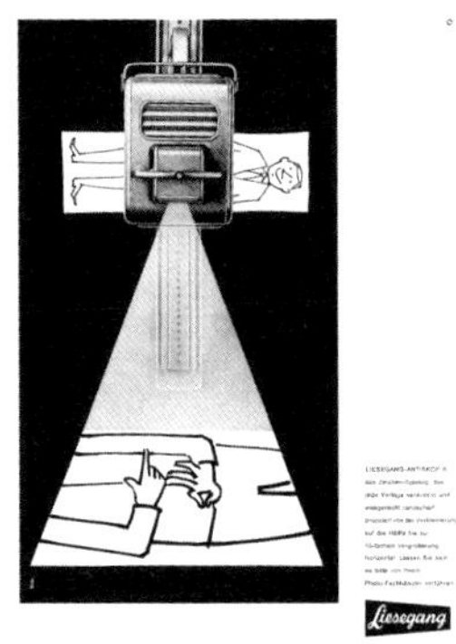

1962 · Gregor Orczykowski · DE · Ad

1953 · Ryu Sakai · JP · Ad

»One of my main concerns is to give the product I am supposed to be advertising a role to play. The product must be more than an unobtrusive object simply added to the presentation. It must become an actor and put on a performance.« Raymond Savignac, *Exempla graphica*, 1968

1950s · Henri Favre · FR · Poster

1950s · Frans Mettes · NL · Poster

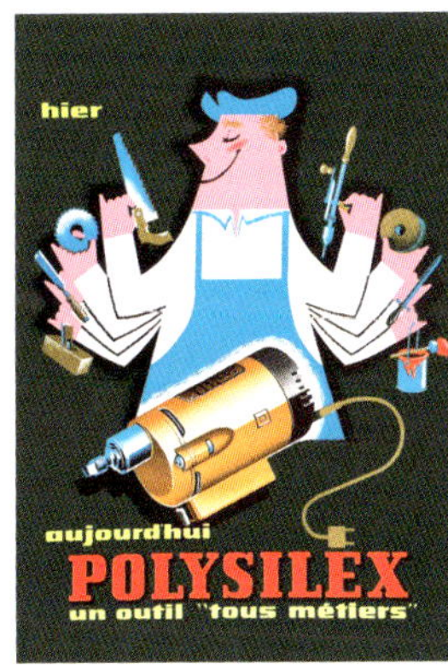

1950s · Michel Robert · FR · Poster

1955 · Erwin Fabian · DE/UK · Poster

Having come through the Great Depression and emerged victorious from the Second World War, the United States entered an era full of optimism. The middle classes in particular benefited from the economic upturn and, predictably, consumer advertising flourished as the industry went in search of novel, eye-catching ways to get the message across. Graphic designers rediscovered photography, and the cleverest of all at using the medium in inventive new ways were the advertising agencies on New York's Madison Avenue. Soon enough, color photography became the mainstay of consumer advertising, bringing to an end a set of artistic principles which had long held sway for illustrated press advertising.

Nach Überwindung der Weltwirtschaftskrise und dem siegreichen Einsatz im Zweiten Weltkrieg begann in den USA eine von Optimismus geprägte Ära. Vor allem die Mittelschicht erlebte einen massiven wirtschaftlichen Aufstieg. Die Konsumwerbung boomte entsprechend und suchte nach neuen Mitteln, um ihre Botschaften sichtbar zu machen. Die Fotografie wurde für die Werbegrafik wiederentdeckt. Besonders die innovativen Werbeagenturen der New Yorker Madison Avenue setzten das Foto in neuer, spielerischer Weise ein. Bald setzte sich die Farbfotografie in der Werbung durch, und damit war eine lange vorherrschende Ästhetik illustrierter Anzeigenwerbung beendet.

Après la crise économique mondiale et l'engagement victorieux dans la Seconde Guerre mondiale, une ère d'optimisme s'ouvre aux États-Unis. La classe moyenne surtout connaît une ascension sociale massive. Parallèlement, une publicité de consommation en plein essor cherche de nouveaux moyens pour visualiser ses messages. La photographie est redécouverte par les graphistes publicitaires. Particulièrement, les agences new-yorkaises innovantes de Madison Avenue exploitent les possibilités de la photographie de manière inédite et ludique. La photographie en couleurs s'impose bientôt dans la publicité, mettant fin aux règles esthétiques de l'illustration publicitaire.

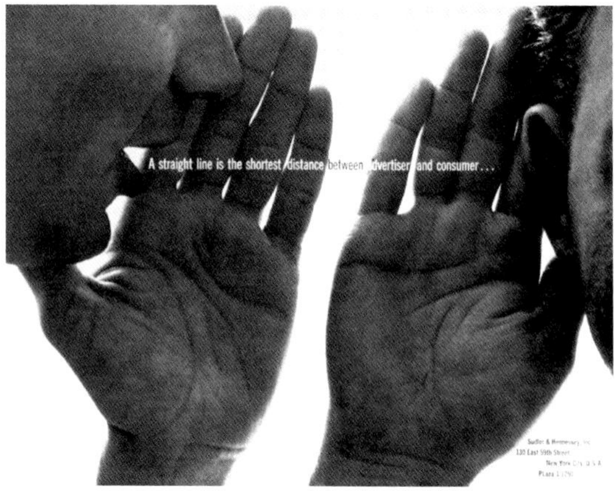

1956 · Herb Lubalin, Carl Fischer (PH) · US · Ad

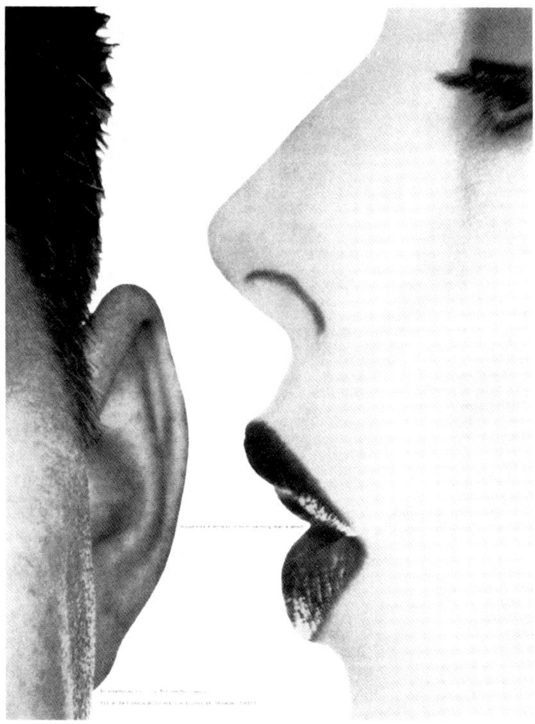

1958 · Norman Gollin, Tommy Mitchell · US · Ad

»Photography dominates the whole field of advertising. By virtue of its presumed objectivity, it is accorded the highest chance of credibility. [...] The photography may also be modified by various technical processes to give the advertisement a poster-like effect.« Kurt Weidemann, *ad 1*, 1966

1953 · Anonymous · US · Ad

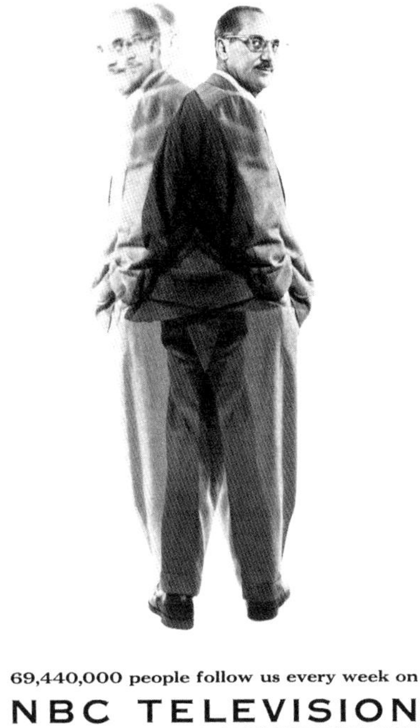

1953 · Robert Dolobowsky (AD), Philippe Halsman (PH) · US · Ad

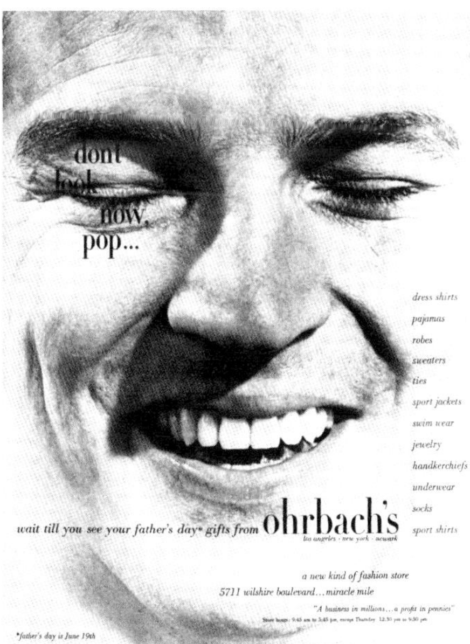

1950 · Joe de Casseres, Robert Gage (AD), DDB · US · Ad

1954 · Robert Gage (AD), DDB · US · Ad

Hiroshi Ohchi (1908–1974, Tokyo) was a Japanese designer and author, whose work ranged from posters, advertising, package and book design, to ikebana (the Japanese art of flower arrangement). After studying at the Tokyo Academy of Fine Arts in 1938, Ohchi worked in advertising before turning to design. Embarking on a freelance career, he traveled and studied widely in Europe and the United States before publishing his third book, *Design Methodology and Tools* (1957). Ohchi also served as the first art director of *IDEA* magazine, the renowned Japanese design publication.

Hiroshi Ohchi (1908–1974, Tokio) war ein japanischer Grafikdesigner und Autor, dessen Werk Plakate, Werbung, Verpackungs- und Buchdesign ebenso umfasste wie Ikebana (die japanische Kunst des Blumenarrangements). Nach dem Studium an der Tokyo Academy of Fine Arts 1938 arbeitete Ohchi zunächst in der Werbung, ehe er sich dem Design zuwandte. Als selbstständiger Grafikdesigner unternahm er ausgedehnte Reisen durch Europa und die Vereinigten Staaten, in deren Verlauf er auch studierte, 1957 dann schrieb sein drittes Buch: *Design Methodology and Tools*. Ohchi war auch der erste Artdirector der renommierten japanischen Designzeitschrift *IDEA*.

Hiroshi Ohchi (1908–1974, Tokyo) fut un designer et auteur japonais dont le champ d'activité s'étendit des affiches et de la publicité au packaging, au design de livres et à l'ikebana (l'art floral japonais). Après des études à l'École des beaux-arts de Tokyo en 1938, Ohchi travailla dans le domaine publicitaire avant de se consacrer au design. Se lançant dans une carrière indépendante, il voyagea et étudia extensivement en Europe et aux États-Unis avant de publier son troisième livre, *Design Methodology and Tools* (1957). Ohchi fut aussi le premier directeur artistique de la revue *IDEA*, la célèbre publication japonaise de design.

1954 · Hiroshi Ohchi · JP · Poster

»It is stunning to see how 'finished,' how definitive and how beyond further development the effect of symmetry is, while asymmetry by its suggested and seemingly 'half finished' solutions, continuously contains new solutions in itself, and Hiroshi Ohchi is the intelligent preserver of its implicit secret.« Anton Sailer, *Gebrauchsgraphik*, 1953

1953 · Hiroshi Ohchi · JP · Logo · Japanese Advertising Artists Club

1954 · Hiroshi Ohchi · JP · Logo · Nichiyu Toy Co.

1957 · Hiroshi Ohchi · JP · Logo · Amateur camera club

1959 · Hiroshi Ohchi · JP · Logo · Namiki Cameras

1954 · Hiroshi Ohchi · JP · Poster

1954 · Hiroshi Ohchi · JP · Poster

1954 · Hiroshi Ohchi · JP · Poster

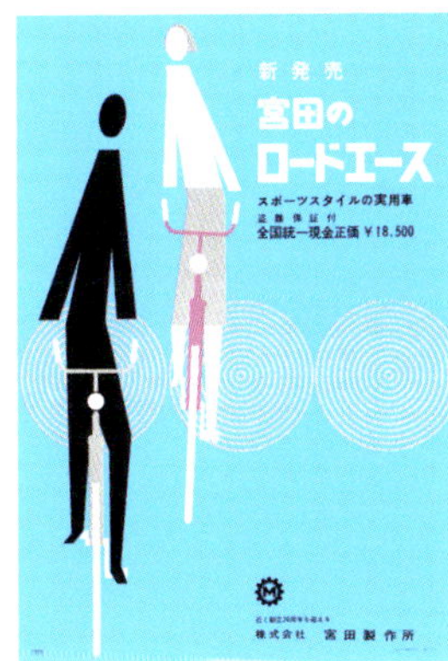

1950s · Hiroshi Ohchi · JP · Poster

1950s · Hiroshi Ohchi · JP · Poster

1955

Dieter Rams starts working for Braun

The **Courier** typeface is created by U.S. designer Howard Kettler

The Swedish design association **Svenska Tecknare** is founded

1955 · Ryszard Sidorowski · PL · Logo · Vita Farmac Pharmaceutical

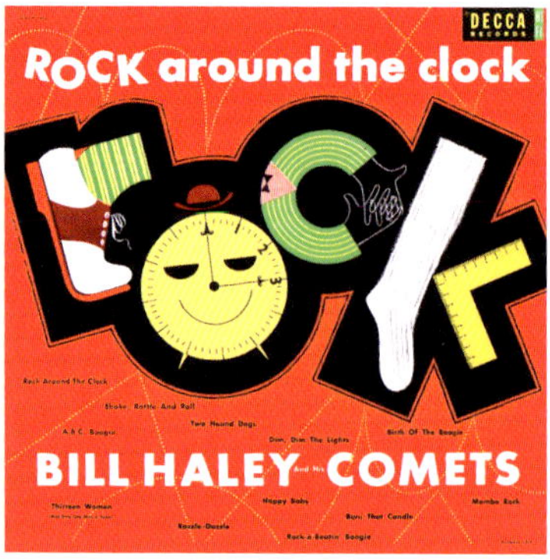

1955 · Anonymous · US · Record cover

1955 · Reginald Mount · UK · Poster

1955 · Ayao Yamana · JP · Ad

1955 · Anonymous · IT · Brochure cover

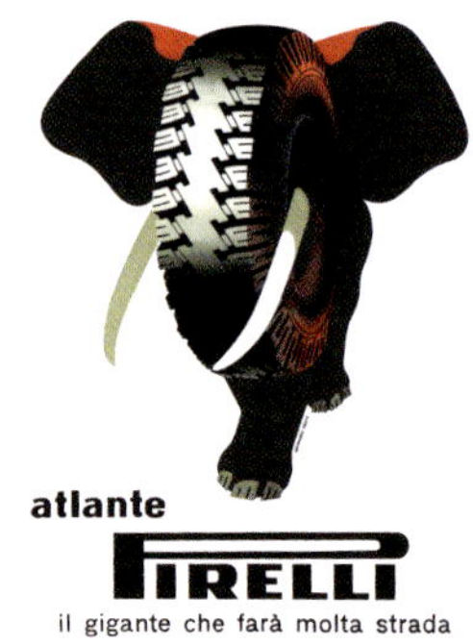

1955 · Armando Testa · IT · Ad

1955 · Jim Flora · US · Record cover

The first exhibition of work by members of the **Alliance Graphique Internationale** (AGI) is held in Paris

The first issue of **Kwadraat-Bladen**, a series of graphic experiments, is published by Pieter Brattinga in the Netherlands

Polish graphic design magazine **Projekt** is launched

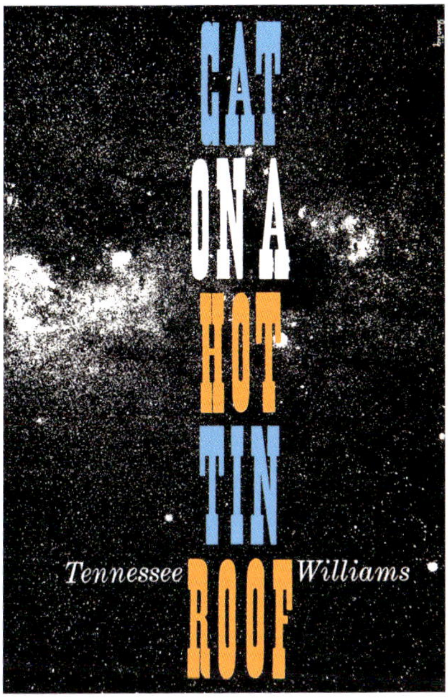

1955 · Alvin Lustig · US · Book cover

1955 · Will Burtin · US · Magazine cover

1955 · Jacques Nathan-Garamond · FR · Poster

1955 · W. S. Crawford Advertising · UK · Ad

1955 · Saul Bass · US · Opening titles

Saul Bass was the designer of both the poster and the opening credits for Otto Preminger's 1955 movie, *The Man with the Golden Arm*. With this work he not only set the case for the value of graphic design to the movie industry, but at the same time he also revolutionized the whole nature of a film's title sequence. Bass's contribution revealed how images and music could, from the very beginning, brilliantly set the mood for the film that followed.

Saul Bass gestaltete sowohl den Printauftritt als auch die Titelsequenz für Otto Premingers Film *Der Mann mit dem goldenen Arm* von 1955. Damit stellte er nicht nur eingehend die hohe Bedeutung einheitlichen grafischen Auftretens im Filmsektor unter Beweis, sondern er revolutionierte gleichzeitig das Medium des Filmvorspanns. Bewegte Grafik und Musik stimmen auf beeindruckende Weise bereits in die Atmosphäre des Films ein.

Saul Bass a réalisé à la fois les affiches et le générique du film d'Otto Preminger *L'Homme au bras d'or* de 1955, démontrant ainsi la valeur du graphisme dans le domaine du cinéma, tout en révolutionnant la nature même du générique. D'emblée, l'impressionnante dynamique des images et de la musique mettent le spectateur dans l'ambiance du film.

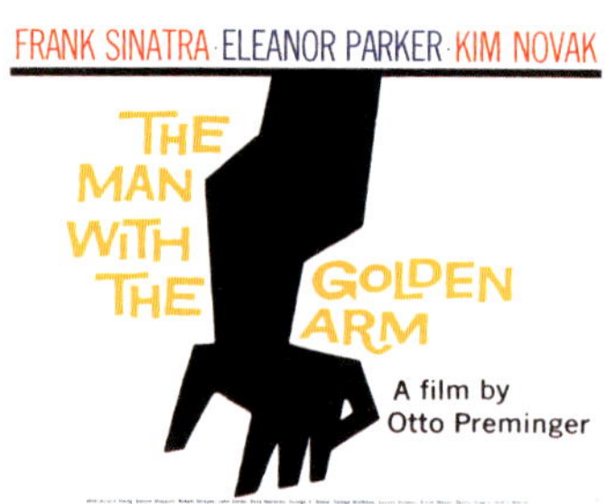

1955 · Saul Bass · US · Poster

1958 · Saul Bass · US · Opening titles

»I have approached the titles with the objective of making them sufficiently provocative and entertaining to induce the theater inhabitants to sit down and watch, because something is really happening on the screen.« Saul Bass, *Graphis* #89, 1960

Saul Bass (1920, New York – 1996, Los Angeles) was a major American graphic designer and filmmaker. He attended the Art Students League in Manhattan before going on to design film advertising in Hollywood in the 1940s. His extensive collaborations with Alfred Hitchcock, Otto Preminger, Stanley Kubrick, and numerous other film directors opened up a new field for graphic designers. His groundbreaking work in the music industry and corporate identity further consolidated his name as one of the new breed of designers in the 20th century. Bass won an Academy Award for Best Documentary for his short film *Why Man Creates* (1968).

Saul Bass (1920, New York – 1996, Los Angeles) war ein bedeutender amerikanischer Grafikdesigner und Filmemacher. Er besuchte die Art Students League in Manhattan und ging in den 1940er-Jahren nach Hollywood, um in der Filmwerbung zu arbeiten. Mit seiner intensiven Zusammenarbeit mit Alfred Hitchcock, Otto Preminger, Stanley Kubrick und zahlreichen anderen Filmregisseuren eröffnete er Grafikdesignern ein neues Tätigkeitsfeld. Seine wegweisenden Leistungen in der Musikindustrie und der Firmenidentität untermauerten seinen Ruf als Vertreter der neuen Designerspezies des 20. Jahrhunderts. Für seinen Kurzfilm *Why Man Creates* (1968) wurde Bass mit einem Oscar für den besten Dokumentarfilm ausgezeichnet.

Saul Bass (1920, New York – 1996, Los Angeles) fut un grand graphiste et réalisateur américain. Après des études à l'Art Students League à Manhattan, il se lança dans le design publicitaire pour le cinéma dans les années 1940. Ses collaborations au long cours avec Alfred Hitchcock, Otto Preminger, Stanley Kubrick et bien d'autres réalisateurs, ont ouvert un nouveau champ d'activité aux graphistes. Son travail révolutionnaire dans l'industrie musicale et l'identité de marque consolida son nom comme un des acteurs clés de la nouvelle génération de graphistes au XXe siècle. En 1969, Bass remporta l'Oscar du meilleur documentaire pour son propre court métrage *Why Man Creates*, réalisé en 1968.

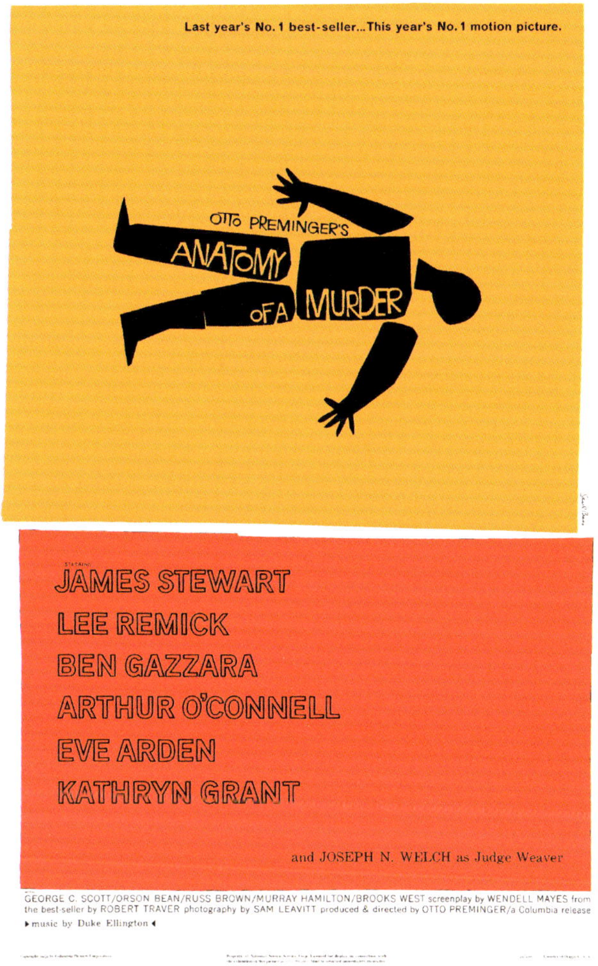

1959 · Saul Bass · US · Poster

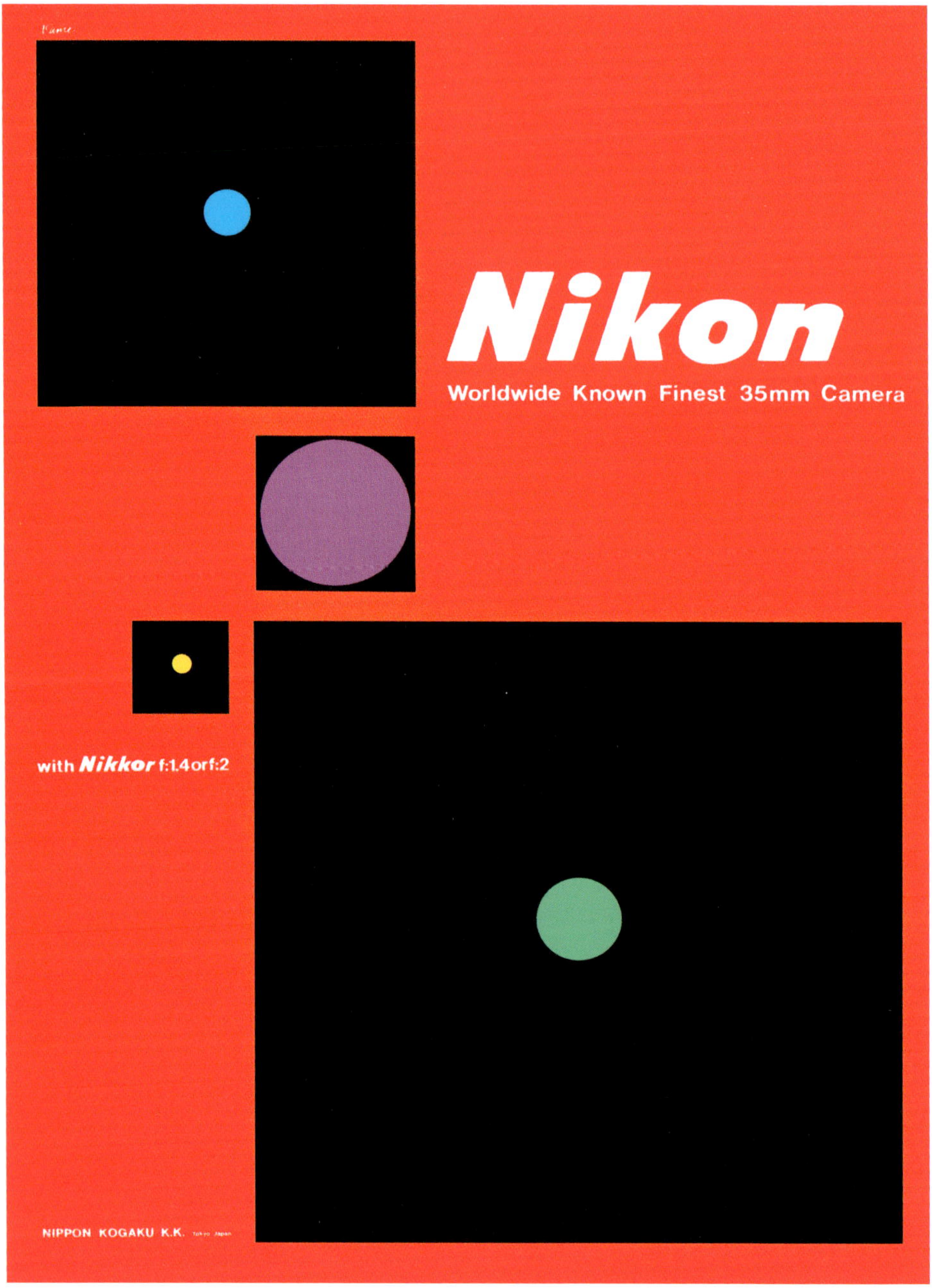

1955 · Yusaku Kamekura · JP · Poster

»Japan's aesthetics and craftsmanship seem to be present in Yusaku Kamekura as in any tradition-bound exponent of those talented people, but he impresses me with his all-out orientation towards today and the future rather than towards the past.« Herbert Bayer, 1971

Yusaku Kamekura was one of the key players in the great modernization movement in Japanese design which began in the mid-20th century. Working for Nikon, the camera manufacturer, he found a client with an open mind that was ready to engage with the avant-garde and to entrust him with the firm's corporate image for many years. The posters and leaflets Kamekura produced show how well the modern style of graphic design developed in Europe harmonizes with traditional Japanese aesthetics.

Yusaku Kamekura gehörte zu den großen Modernisierern des japanischen Designs im 20. Jahrhundert. In dem Kamerahersteller Nikon fand er einen aufgeschlossenen Auftraggeber, der offen für grafische Avantgarde war und ihm über viele Jahre seine visuelle Identität anvertraute. Zumindest auf den ersten Blick hatten Kamekuras Entwürfe wenig mit der traditionellen Bildsprache des Landes zu tun.

Yusaku Kamekura a été un des grands modernisateurs du graphisme japonais, dont les débuts remontent au milieu du XXe siècle. Commanditaire ouvert à l'avant-garde du graphisme, le fabricant d'appareils photo Nikon lui confie son identité visuelle pendant bien des années. Les affiches et brochures produites par Kamekura montrent à quel point le style du graphisme moderne s'harmonise avec l'esthétique japonaise traditionnelle.

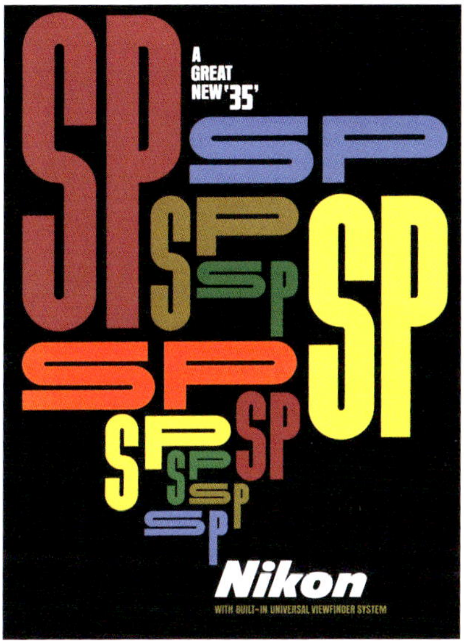

1957 · Yusaku Kamekura · JP · Poster

1960 · Yusaku Kamekura · JP · Poster

Yusaku Kamekura (1915, Niigata – 1997, Tokyo) was a highly acclaimed Japanese graphic artist whose work displayed a distinctive combination of Bauhaus modernity and traditional Japanese forms. Upon graduating from the Institute of New Architecture and Industrial Arts in Tokyo, Kamekura joined the publishers Nippon Kobo, where he looked after *Nippon* magazine and the Thai publication *Kaupapu*. In 1964, he was a pioneer in the use of photography to promote the Olympic Games. Kamekura is often credited with coining the term "corporate identity graphics."

Yusaku Kamekura (1915, Niigata – 1997, Tokio) war ein vielfach anerkannter japanischer Grafikdesigner, dessen Werk sich durch eine unverkennbare Mischung von Bauhaus-Moderne und traditionellen japanischen Formen auszeichnet. Nach dem Studium am Institute of New Architecture and Industrial Arts in Tokio arbeitete er bei dem Verlag Nippon Kobo, wo er für die Zeitschrift *Nippon* sowie die thailändische Publikation *Kaupapu* zuständig war. 1964 lotete er wegweisend die Möglichkeiten aus, die Olympischen Spiele zu Marketingzwecken fotografisch darzustellen. Kamekura wird häufig als Schöpfer des Begriffs „Corporate Identity Graphics" gewürdigt.

Yusaku Kamekura (1915, Niigata – 1997, Tokyo) fut un artiste graphiste japonais hautement acclamé dont le travail présente une combinaison très caractéristique de modernité Bauhaus et de formes japonaises traditionnelles. Diplômé de l'École de design et de nouvelle architecture de Tokyo, Kamekura rejoignit la maison d'édition Nippon Kobo, au sein de laquelle il supervisa l'édition de la revue *Nippon* et la publication thaïlandaise *Kaupapu*. En 1964, il fut pionnier dans l'utilisation de la photographie pour promouvoir les jeux Olympiques. On attribue souvent à Kamekura l'invention du terme «image de marque».

1956

The **Letter Gothic** typeface is designed by Roger Roberson, for use on IBM typewriters

Magnetic ink character recognition is developed by the Stanford Research Institute

1956 · Damian Contreras · ES · Poster

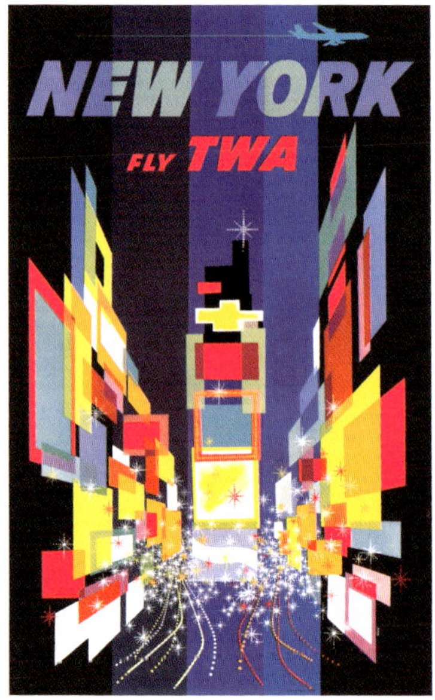

1956 · David Klein · US · Poster

1956 · Anonymous · US · Record cover

Paul Rand's collaboration with **IBM** starts

Swiss graphic designer **Armin Hofmann** starts his visiting lectures at Yale University

The **Society of Graphic Designers of Canada** is founded

1956 · Abram Games · UK · Poster

1956 · Maurice Richards · UK · Magazine cover

1956 · Anonymous · CZ · Poster

1956 · Alex Steinweiss · US · Magazine cover

1956 · Ladislav Sutnar · CZ/US · Brochure cover

1956 · Ernst Fuhrherr · AT · Poster

1956 · Karl Oskar Blase · DE · Poster

1956 · John Alcorn · US · Book cover

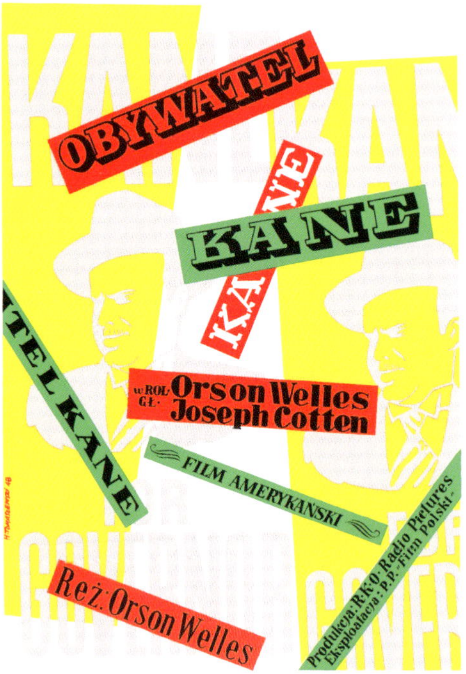

1949 · Henryk Tomaszewski · PL · Poster

1949 · Henryk Tomaszewski · PL · Poster

1953 · Henryk Tomaszewski · PL · Poster

»Poster design primarily releases what there is left of the painter in me, while drawing allows me to mock and laugh, which is essential for my soul.« Henryk Tomaszewski, *Projekt* #163, 1985

Henryk Tomaszewski (1914–2005, Warsaw) was an acclaimed Polish poster artist, satirical cartoonist, and professor. He graduated from the Warsaw Academy of Fine Arts in 1939, becoming its head of poster design from 1952–85. Tomaszewski won multiple awards during his career, including five gold medals at the 1948 International Poster Exhibition in Vienna, alongside subsequent accolades at the International Poster Biennale in Warsaw and the International Poster Triennial in Toyama, Japan. He was made an Honorary Royal Designer for Industry by the Royal Society of Arts in London, and was a member of the AGI.

Henryk Tomaszewski (1914–2005, Warschau) war ein berühmter polnischer Plakatkünstler, Satirecartoonist und Professor. 1939 schloss er sein Studium an der Akademie der Bildenden Künste Warschau ab, von 1952 bis 1985 war er dort Dekan der Abteilung für Plakatkunst. Im Laufe seiner Schaffenszeit wurde Tomaszewski mit zahlreichen Preisen ausgezeichnet, u. a. mit fünf Goldmedaillen bei der Internationalen Plakatausstellung 1948 in Wien. Darauf folgten Auszeichnungen bei der International Poster Biennale in Warschau und der International Poster Triennial in Toyama, Japan. Die Royal Society of Arts in London ernannte ihn zum Honorary Royal Designer for Industry, zudem war er Mitglied der Alliance Graphique Internationale.

Henryk Tomaszewski (1914–2005, Varsovie) fut un affichiste polonais renommé, dessinateur de presse et enseignant. Diplômé de l'Académie des beaux-arts de Varsovie en 1939, il y fut nommé directeur du département de conception d'affiches, poste qu'il occupa de 1952 à 1985. Tomaszewski remporta de nombreux prix tout au long de sa carrière, notamment cinq médailles d'or à l'Exposition internationale de l'affiche (Vienne, 1948), ainsi que des marques de reconnaissance à la Biennale internationale de l'affiche de Varsovie et à la Triennale internationale de l'affiche de Toyama, au Japon. Il fut nommé Royal Designer for Industry honoraire par la Royal Society of Arts de Londres, et fut membre de l'AGI.

1959 · Henryk Tomaszewski · PL · Poster

1963 · Henryk Tomaszewski · PL · Poster

1957

The **Chermayeff & Geismar** design studio is founded in New York by Ivan Chermayeff and Tom Geismar

The **Helvetica** typeface by Max Miedinger and Eduard Hoffmann is released under the name Neue Haas-Grotesk

1957 · Heini Fischer · CH · Poster

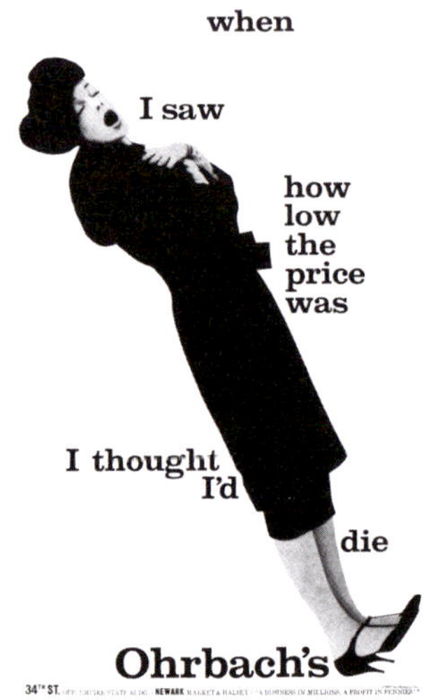

1957 · Robert Gage (AD), Wingate Paine (PH), DDB · US · Ad

1957 · Raymond Loewy · FR · Logo · LU Biscuits

1957 · Weiss-Deswarte · FR · Poster

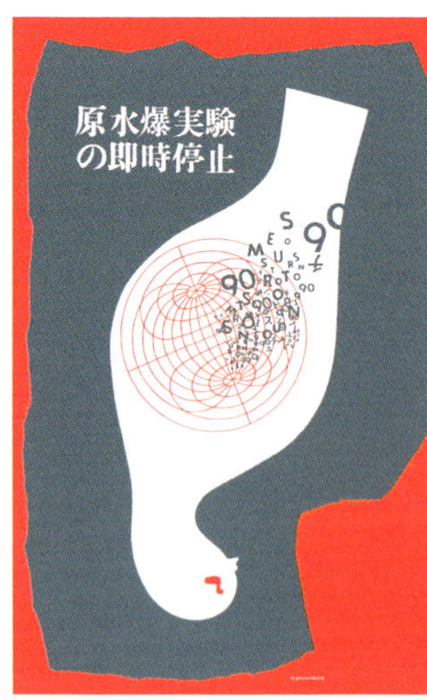

1957 · Yusaku Kamekura · JP · Logo · Good Design

1957 · Ryuichi Yamashiro · JP · Poster

Günther Kieser designs his first concert posters for Lippmann + Rau

McCann-Erickson becomes the first U.S. advertising agency to bill $100 million in TV and radio sales

After six years' work, Swiss designer Adrian Frutiger presents the **Univers** typeface in Paris

The **Good Design Award** is established in Japan

1957 · Hans Hillmann · DE · Poster

1957 · Max Huber · CH/IT · Poster

1957 · Mary Vieira · BR · Poster

1957 · Anonymous · JP · Poster

1958

Neue Grafik (New Graphic) magazine is set up by four Swiss graphic designers to promote modernist ideas

1958 · Hermelindo Fiaminghi · BR · Book cover

1958 · Henrion Design Associates · UK/FR · Logo · Metra International

1958 · Gerald Holtom · UK · Logo · Peace Movement

1958 · Joan Pedragosa · ES · Logo · Fogo Seimex

1958 · Anonymous · RU · Poster

1958 · Kurt Müller · DE-GDR · Book cover

1958 · Anonymous · HU · Poster

1958 · Anonymous · NL · Brochure cover

1958 · George Giusti, Edward Gorey · US · Book cover

1958 · "Beka" · SE · Poster

1958 · "Siné" (Maurice Sinet) · FR · Poster

1958 · Lintas Werbeagentur · CH · Poster

Slowly but surely, during the course of the 1950s a postwar Germany once again became a prosperous nation. Many young designers were now in a position where they could afford their own photographic equipment, while some even had enough money for a darkroom, which enabled them to do their own processing and developing. This gave them the freedom to explore new technical possibilities, such as creating compressed images or silhouettes, and the results led to exciting new poster designs which marked a major step forward in modern graphic work.

Im Laufe der 1950er-Jahre wurde auch im Nachkriegsdeutschland langsam wieder der Wohlstand spürbar. Viele junge Gestalter konnten sich jetzt eine Fotoausrüstung und eine eigene Dunkelkammer leisten. Letztere ermöglichte das Bearbeiten der Fotografie im Entwicklungsprozess selbst. Es entstanden etwa grafisch reduzierte Motive bis hin zu Silhouetten – eine neue technische Möglichkeit, die zu spannenden Plakatlösungen führte und speziell in Deutschland den Schritt hin zum modernen Grafikdesign der Nachkriegsjahre markierte.

Lentement mais sûrement dans les années 1950, le retour de la prospérité commence aussi à se faire sentir dans l'Allemagne d'après-guerre. Beaucoup de jeunes graphistes peuvent désormais se payer un équipement photographique et, pour certains, une chambre noire, afin de faire leurs propres développements. Cette nouvelle possibilité technique a conduit à des solutions passionnantes dans le domaine de l'affiche, comme la création d'images compressées et de silhouettes. Particulièrement en Allemagne, elle marque la transition vers le graphisme moderne d'après-guerre.

1958 · Anonymous · DE · Poster

1962 · Michael Engelmann · DE · Poster

»It is strange: the poster was already reported dead once—somewhat prematurely, it would seem, even though it has indeed lost its former leading role to other advertising media. In spite of this it has lost nothing of its old prestige. Thanks to its vivid colors and its large size the poster is still the most popular and attractive of all pictorial advertising media [...].« Eberhard Hölscher, *Gebrauchsgraphik*, 1960

1960 · Wolfgang Schmidt · DE · Poster

1958 · Werner Weissbrodt · DE · Poster

1958 · Karl Oskar Blase · DE · Poster

1958 · Hans Michel · DE · Poster

1959 · Fischer-Nosbisch · DE · Poster

1961 · Fischer-Nosbisch · DE · Poster

Among the numerous technological innovations introduced by General Dynamics, the American aerospace and defense company, can be counted the first nuclear submarine, the USS *Nautilus*, which was launched in 1954. Pioneering too were the graphics used in their advertising campaigns, designed for many years by the Swiss-born Erik Nitsche.

Zu den vielen Innovationen des amerikanischen Rüstungskonzerns General Dynamics gehörte unter anderem der Bau der USS *Nautilus* – 1954 vom Stapel gelassen, ist sie das erste nukleargetriebene U-Boot. Gleichermaßen progressiv war die Werbegrafik des Unternehmens, die der gebürtige Schweizer Erik Nitsche über viele Jahre prägte.

Parmi les innovations de la société américaine de défense General Dynamics figurait aussi la construction du premier sous-marin à propulsion nucléaire, le USS *Nautilus*, qui fut lancé en 1954. Tout aussi progressiste fut le graphisme publicitaire de l'entreprise, que le Suisse Erik Nitsche a marqué de son empreinte pendant de nombreuses années.

1950s · Erik Nitsche · CH/US · Poster

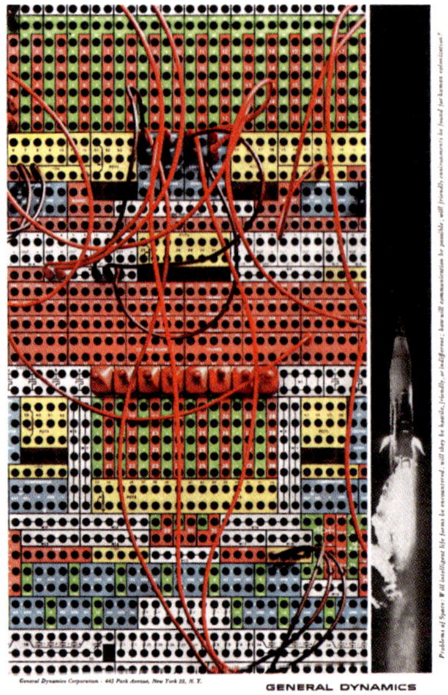

1950s · Erik Nitsche · CH/US · Ad

1950s · Erik Nitsche · CH/US · Ad

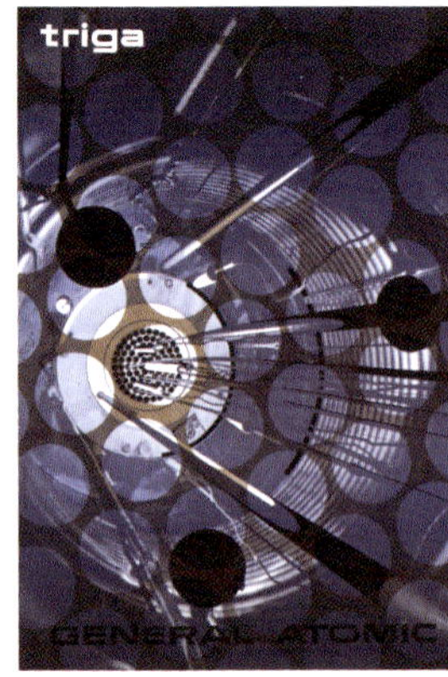

1958 · Erik Nitsche · CH/US · Poster

1958 · Erik Nitsche · CH/US · Poster

1958 · Erik Nitsche · CH/US · Poster

»As a designer, Erik Nitsche has been called a catalyst 'who knows the alphabet of symbols from A to Z.' His effort has always been to identify strongly with the needs of the client, and his affinity for General Dynamics' needs has resulted in a newly romantic and concentrated manner of expression.«
Suzanne Barrey, *Graphis* #79, 1958

Erik Nitsche (1908, Lausanne – 1998, New York) was a Swiss graphic artist whose broad spectrum of work greatly contributed to the development of poster, identity, and editorial design. Coming from an artistic family, Nitsche was influenced by Paul Klee to study art, though chose to study in Munich rather than at the Bauhaus where Klee was a teacher. His characteristic visual language, developed with both modern and classical ideas, is best displayed in his series of works beginning in the 1950s for the engineering company General Dynamics—encompassing corporate identity, posters, and annual reports—which followed his earlier departure for the United States when war broke out. Nitsche also produced children's books throughout his 70-year career.

Erik Nitsche (1908, Lausanne – 1998, New York) war ein Schweizer Grafikdesigner, der mit der großen Bandbreite seines Schaffens die Entwicklung von Plakat-, Identity- und Zeitungsdesign prägte. Er stammte aus einer künstlerisch gesinnten Familie und wurde von Paul Klee ermutigt, Kunst zu studieren, entschied sich allerdings für München und gegen das Bauhaus, wo Klee unterrichtete. Seine unverkennbare visuelle Sprache, für die er moderne ebenso wie klassische Gedanken aufgriff, kommt am besten in den Werken zum Tragen, die er ab den 1950er-Jahren für den Rüstungskonzern General Dynamics gestaltete – Corporate Identity ebenso wie Plakate und Jahresberichte. Nitsche war schon früh, kurz nach Kriegsausbruch, in die USA ausgewandert. Im Lauf seiner 70 Jahre währenden Karriere gestaltete er auch Kinderbücher.

Erik Nitsche (1908, Lausanne – 1998, New York) fut un artiste graphiste dont le vaste éventail de réalisations a fortement contribué au développement de l'affiche, de l'identité de marque et du graphisme éditorial. Issu d'une famille d'artistes, Nitsche subit d'abord l'influence de Paul Klee, qui l'incita à entreprendre des études d'art, mais choisit finalement de faire ses études à Munich plutôt qu'au Bauhaus, où Klee enseignait. Son langage visuel très caractéristique, développé à partir d'idées modernes aussi bien que classiques, ressort le mieux des séries de travaux qu'il commença à réaliser dans les années 1950 pour la société de défense General Dynamics – identité de marque, affiches et rapports annuels – après avoir émigré aux États-Unis au début de la Seconde Guerre mondiale. Tout au long de ses 70 ans de carrière, Nitsche produisit aussi des livres pour enfants.

1950s · Erik Nitsche · CH/US · Poster

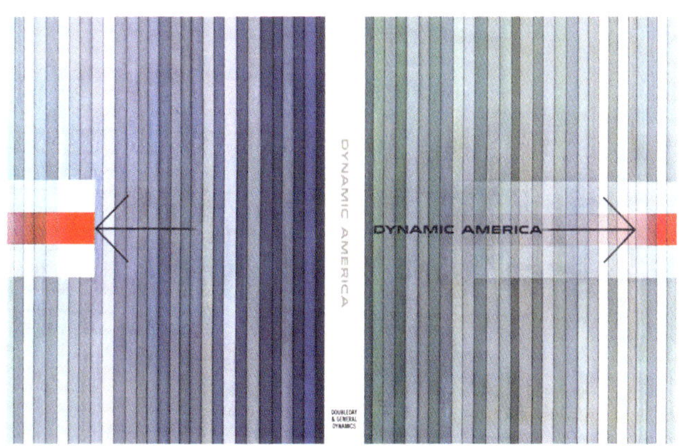

1960 · Erik Nitsche · CH/US · Book cover

1959

Communication Arts magazine is founded by Richard Coyne and Robert Blanchard

Alan Fletcher and **Colin Forbes** start a design studio in London

1959 · Lester Beall · US · Logo · International Paper

1959 · Morton Goldsholl · US · Logo · IMC

1959 · Allan Robb Fleming · CA · Logo · Canadian National Railways

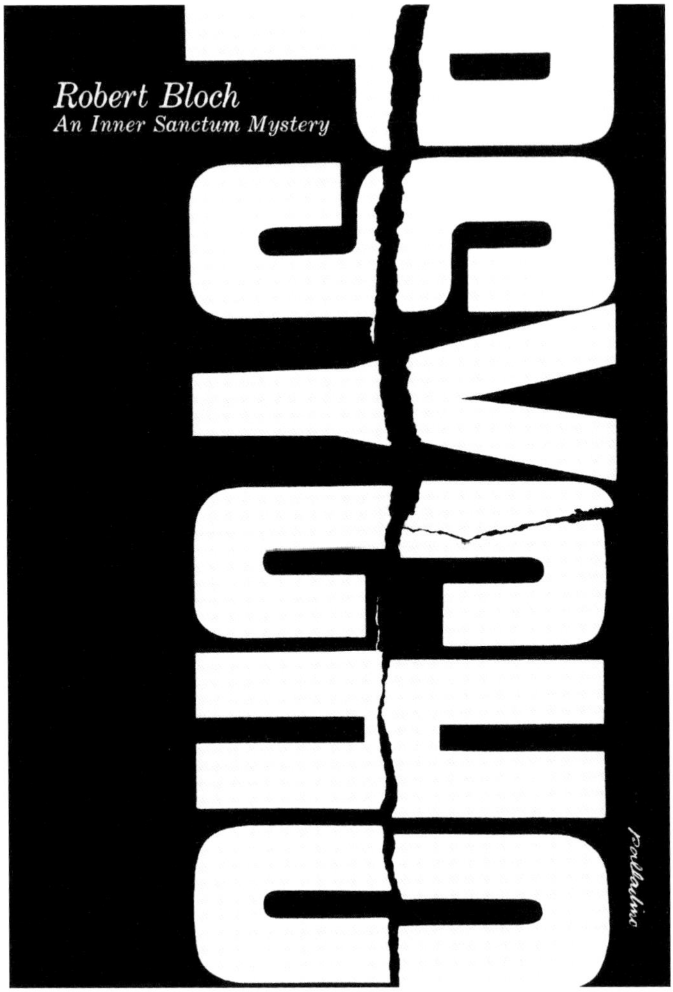

1959 · Tony Palladino · US · Book cover

Swiss design studio and ad agency **Gerstner+Kutter** is founded by Karl Gerstner and Markus Kutter and expands to become GGK with the addition of Paul Gredinger in 1962

The **Letraset** corporation is founded in London

1959 · Wojciech Zamecznik · PL · Poster

1959 · Helmut Krone (AD), DDB · US · Ad

1959 · George Tscherny · US · Ad

1959 · Robert Brownjohn · US · Book cover

When the National Socialist Party seized power in 1933, modernist graphic design was largely suppressed in Germany, where it had previously developed and found its greatest expression. It continued to flourish, however, in neutral Switzerland, and after 1945 Basel and Zurich, with their rival schools, became the capitals of the new modernist movement in graphic design. Posters, books, packaging, and lettering all bore the classic hallmarks of modernism: the use of sanserif fonts, layouts based on coordinated grid systems, and a geometric design vocabulary. Soon this new compositional approach, which became known under the generic heading of "Swiss Style" and featured in several professional publications, proved it was not at all a passing trend but a permanent advance. Its universally applicable visual style continues to this day to inspire graphic designers around the world.

Während die vor allem in Deutschland entwickelte und ausgeprägte Moderne im Grafikdesign mit der Machtübernahme der Nationalsozialisten ab 1933 weitgehend zurückgedrängt wurde, überdauerten diese Ideen besonders in der neutralen Schweiz. Nach 1945 wurden Basel und Zurich mit ihren konkurrierenden Designschulen zu den Metropolen eines neuen grafischen Modernismus. Serifenlose Schriften, im Raster aufeinander abgestimmte Layouts und eine geometrische Formensprache prägten Plakate, Bücher, Verpackungen oder Beschriftungen. Bald unter dem Oberbegriff „Swiss Style" geführt und in zahlreichen Fachpublikationen manifestiert, sollte sich diese neue Gestaltungsweise nicht als kurzlebiger Trend, sondern als nachhaltige Weiterentwicklung erweisen. Diese universell einsetzbare Ästhetik bestimmt bis heute das Aussehen des internationalen Grafikdesigns mit.

Si la modernité, telle qu'elle s'est développée particulièrement en Allemagne dans le domaine du graphisme, est largement réprimée après la prise de pouvoir des nazis en 1933, les idées continuent de se développer en Suisse neutre. Après 1945, Bâle et Zurich et leurs écoles de graphisme concurrentes deviennent les métropoles d'un nouveau modernisme graphique. Des écritures sans serif, des mises en pages harmonisées par des grilles de composition et un langage formel géométrique caractérisent les affiches, livres, emballages et inscriptions. Développée sous l'appellation «style suisse» et appliquée dans de nombreuses publications, cette nouvelle approche du graphisme s'avère bientôt ne pas être qu'une tendance éphémère, mais bien une évolution durable. En tant qu'esthétique universellement applicable, elle détermine aujourd'hui encore en partie l'aspect du graphisme international.

1960 · Robert Bühler · CH · Poster

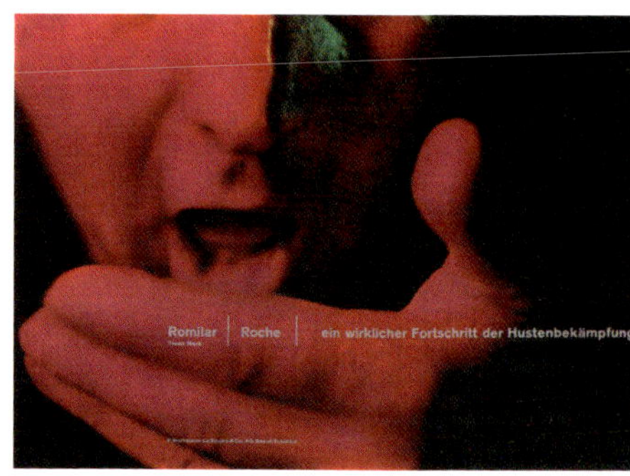

1957 · Carlo L. Vivarelli, René Groebli (PH) · CH · Ad

»What is new in this art is its almost mathematical clarity. Though full of striking details, it relies for effect not upon ornament but on the balance and tension of form and color. The style, which is in a state of continual flux, is the direct product of the theme or the industrial subject.«

Richard P. Lohse, Josef Müller-Brockmann, Hans Neuburg, and Carlo L. Vivarelli, *Neue Grafik* #1, 1958

1950s · Enzo Rösli · CH · Logo · Merck

1957 · Sigi Odermatt · CH · Logo · Grammo Studio

1957 · GGK · CH · Logo · Boîte à Musique

1950s · Marcel Wyss · CH · Logo · Mario Dias Costa

1954 · Emil Ruder · CH · Poster

1957 · Gottlieb Soland · CH · Poster

1956 · Emil Ruder · CH · Brochure cover

1957 · Karl Gerstner · CH · Book cover

1960 · Emil Ruder · CH · Stamp

While a new typography rooted in prewar modernism was being developed in Switzerland, a similar modernization was also taking place in the United States. Here, designers were exploring different ways of handling type which were not so much to do with precision as with a new, creative, and playful approach. Freeing themselves from their basic task of simply providing information, the new generation of young American designers raised typography to the status of a major structural element, in advertising campaigns as well as in product design, such as book jackets. Most of all, it was those practicing their craft in New York's cutting-edge advertising agencies who adopted this completely new approach to typographic design.

Während sich in der Schweiz auf Basis des Vorkriegsmodernismus eine neue Typografie entwickelte, fand eine vergleichbare Modernisierung auch in den USA statt. Hier zeigten sich neue Tendenzen im Umgang mit Schrift, die sich jedoch weniger in Strenge als vielmehr in einem neuartigen spielerisch-kreativen Ansatz niederschlugen. Losgelöst von ihrer fundamentalen Aufgabe, Information zu vermitteln, erhob eine Generation junger amerikanischer Gestalter die Typografie zum tragenden Element, etwa für Anzeigenmotive oder Buchumschläge. Vor allem im Umfeld der innovativen New Yorker Werbeszene erfuhr die typografische Gestaltung einen ganz neuen Ansatz.

Tandis qu'en Suisse, une nouvelle typographie se développe sur la base du modernisme d'avant-guerre, une modernisation similaire se produit aussi aux États-Unis. De nouvelles tendances apparaissent dans le traitement de l'écriture; elles se distinguent moins par la rigueur que par une approche ludique et créative inédite. Dissociée de son propos premier – communiquer de l'information –, la typographie se voit alors élevée au rang d'élément structurel par une nouvelle génération de jeunes graphistes américains, notamment dans des campagnes d'affichage ou des couvertures de livres. C'est surtout dans l'entourage de la scène new-yorkaise innovante que la conception typographique connaît une nouvelle approche.

1959 · Herb Lubalin · US · Ad

1958 · Gene Federico · US · Ad

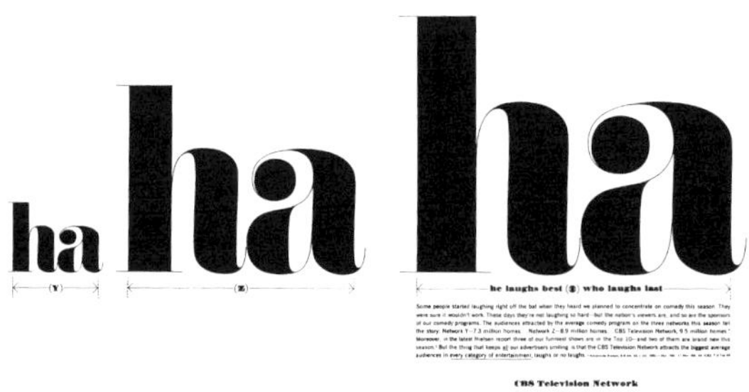

1961 · Louis Dorfsman, Al Amato · US · Ad

»Television has had its effect on the reading habits of the American people. We are becoming more and more accustomed to looking at pictures and less and less interested in lengthy copy. The resulting trend is that our advertising has been towards large pictorial elements and short sparkling headline copy.« `Herb Lubalin,` *`Graphis`* `#82, 1959`

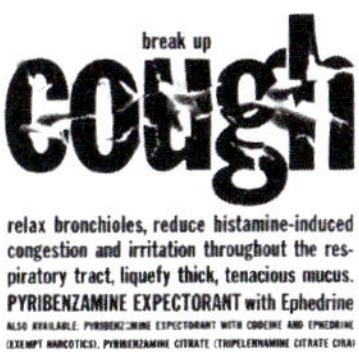

1958 · Herb Lubalin · US · Ad

1960 · Donald Egensteiner, Larry Ottino, Young & Rubicam · US · Ad

1960 · Robert Brownjohn · US · Book cover

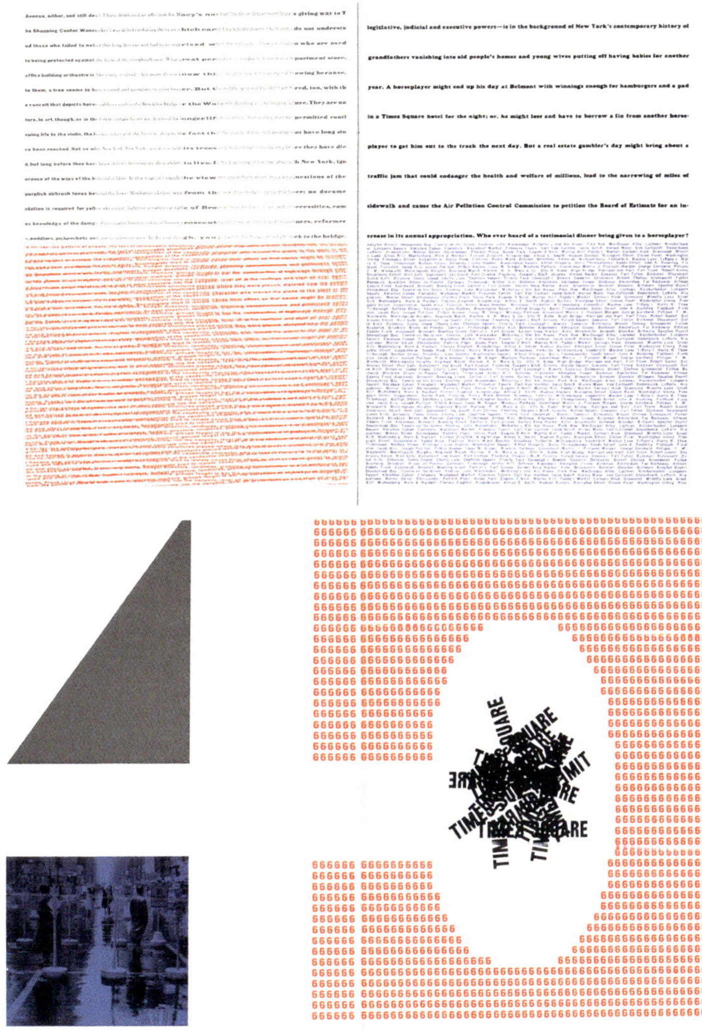

1960 · Brownjohn, Chermayeff & Geismar · US · Brochure spreads

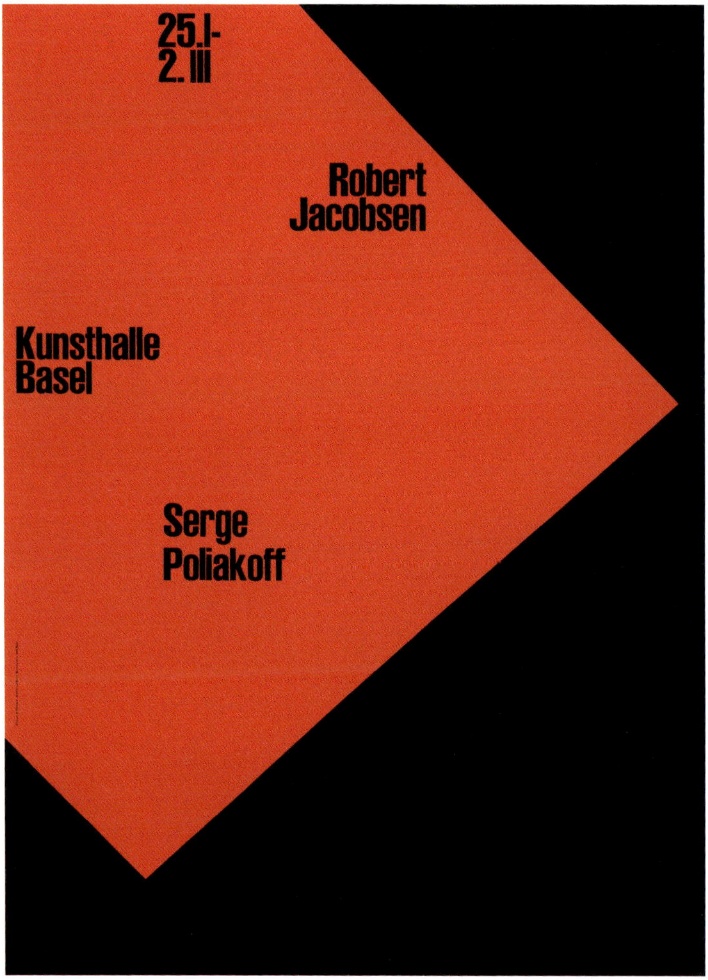

1959 · Armin Hofmann · CH · Poster

1958 · Armin Hofmann · CH · Poster

1960 · Armin Hofmann · CH · Poster

1960 · Armin Hofmann · CH · Poster

»Hofmann's posters collectively epitomize mid-century modernism not because ornament is rejected and mechanical methods are used in place of hand-drawn decoration or illustration, but because they touch the soul of their times.« `Steven Heller, *Poster Collection* #07, 2003`

Armin Hofmann's posters for the Kunsthalle in Basel were among the high points of Swiss graphic design. Using only minimal means, he nevertheless developed innovative ways of creating tension through the interplay of typefaces and space. The illustrations of Hofmann's works here do not include any of those that were included in art exhibitions in which his works were shown; rather, they have been chosen purely as examples of how he injected modern art into graphic design.

Armin Hofmanns Plakate für die Kunsthalle Basel gehörten zu den Höhepunkten der Schweizer Grafik. Auf unvergleichliche Weise entwickelte er spannungsreiche Konstruktionen aus Typografie und Flächen unter Verwendung äußerst reduzierter grafischer Mittel. Die in den Ausstellungen gezeigten Arbeiten werden nicht abgebildet, vielmehr übertragen Hofmanns Arbeiten die Ästhetik moderner Kunst ins Grafikdesign.

Les affiches d'Armin Hofmann pour la Kunsthalle Basel comptent parmi les sommets du graphisme suisse. D'une manière tout à fait incomparable, Hofmann développa des constructions associant typographie et surfaces géométriques avec des moyens graphiques réduits à l'extrême. Les affiches ne montraient pas les œuvres présentées dans les expositions: le travail d'Hofmann traduisait l'esthétique de l'art moderne dans le langage du design graphique.

1961 · Armin Hofmann · CH · Poster

1963 · Armin Hofmann · CH · Poster

1966 · Armin Hofmann · CH · Poster

Armin Hofmann (1920, Winterthur – 2020, Lucerne, Switzerland) was a Swiss designer and educator, instrumental in the development of what is today known as the Swiss Style. Relying on the fundamental elements of point, line, and shape, he articulated a unique visual language to express simplicity as well as complexity and abstraction, and his work ranges from logotypes and sign systems to books, exhibitions, and posters. In 1965 Hofmann published the reference book *Graphic Design Manual*, having taught in Basel from the age of 26 and becoming one of the most respected academics in design. He also brought the Swiss design style to the United States, in the course of a visiting professorship at Yale University.

Armin Hofmann (1920, Winterthur – 2020, Luzern, Schweiz) war ein Schweizer Grafikdesigner und Dozent, der maßgeblich an der Entwicklung des „Swiss Style", wie er heute genannt wird, beteiligt war. Ausgehend von den Grundelementen Punkt, Strich und Form, gestaltete er eine einzigartige visuelle Sprache, die Schlichtheit ebenso wie Komplexität und Abstraktion zu vermitteln vermochte. Die Bandbreite seines Werks umfasst Firmensignets, Zeichensysteme und Bücher, aber auch Ausstellungen und Plakate. Bereits mit 26 Jahren lehrte er in Basel, wurde zu einem der angesehensten Theoretiker im Bereich Grafikdesign und schrieb 1965 das Handbuch *Methodik der Form- und Bildgestaltung*. Im Rahmen einer Gastprofessur an der Yale University machte er den Schweizer Designstil auch in den Vereinigten Staaten bekannt.

Armin Hofmann (1920, Winterthur – 2020, Lucerne, Suisse) fut un designer et enseignant suisse qui a joué un rôle clé dans le développement du «style suisse». Partant des éléments fondamentaux du point, de la ligne et de la forme, il a articulé un langage visuel exprimant à la fois la simplicité, la complexité et l'abstraction, et son travail s'étend du logotype et des systèmes signalétiques à des livres, des expositions et des affiches. En 1965, Hofmann publie son ouvrage de référence *Manuel de création graphique* après avoir enseigné à Bâle depuis l'âge de 26 ans et être devenu un des enseignants les plus respectés dans le monde du design. Il a aussi introduit le style suisse aux États-Unis en qualité de professeur invité à l'université Yale.

1960s · Anonymous · DE · Poster

1960

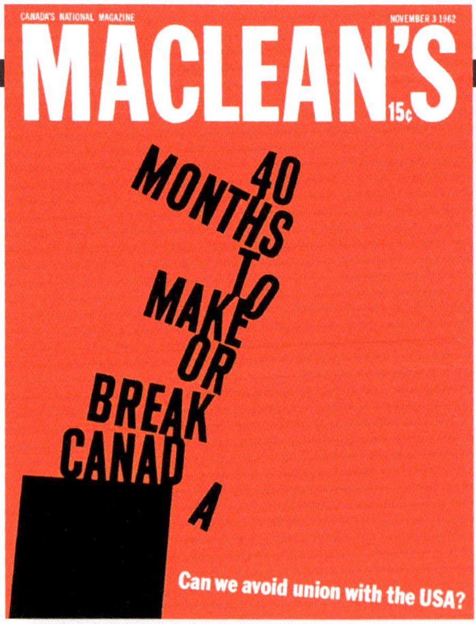

1962 · Allan Robb Fleming · CA · Magazine cover

1962 · Paul Rand · US · Logo · ABC Television

1965 · Wiktor Górka · PL · Poster

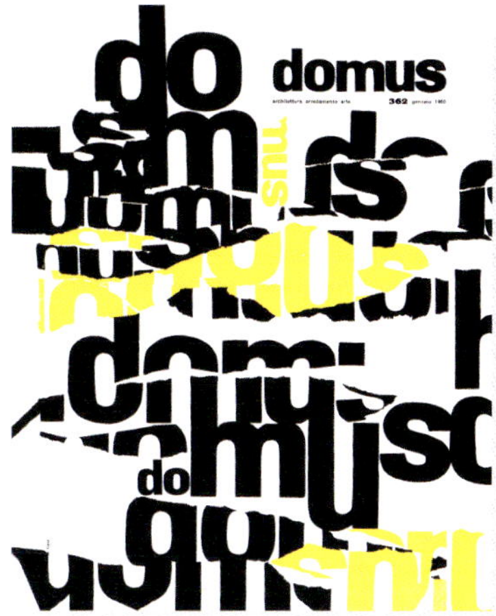

1960 · William Klein · IT · Magazine cover

1969

1963 · Benno Wissing · NL · Poster

The signposting system at Amsterdam's Schiphol Airport, designed in 1967 by Benno Wissing of the agency Total Design.

Das Wegeleitsystem des Amsterdamer Flughafens Schiphol, 1967 von Benno Wissing im Designbüro Total Design entwickelt.

La signalétique de l'aéroport d'Amsterdam-Schiphol développée en 1967 par Benno Wissing au sein de l'agence de graphisme Total Design.

The 1960s saw the heyday of modernist-minimalist graphic design, and at first, Switzerland was in the vanguard. The wide-ranging new style was used in a whole series of different ways—from food packaging and magazine design to signage systems for airports—and was soon picked up right across the world, earning itself the name of International Style. At about the same time the merits of powerful imagery were at last becoming widely accepted, leading to a new standard in brand communication. An international group of designers, including Paul Rand, Otl Aicher, F.H.K. Henrion, and Yusaku Kamekura, made a defining impression on all aspects of graphics, and alongside the austerity of the International Style, the second half of the decade also produced an innovative, emotionally charged visual vocabulary that defied all previous convention. Set against a musical backdrop of jazz, pop, and rock, a new kind of imagery was created which began in western subculture but quickly found its way into the mainstream.

Die 1960er-Jahre waren die Blütezeit der modernistisch-reduzierten Grafik. Tonangebend war hier zunächst vor allem die Schweiz. Der neue Stil fand sich in einem breiten Spektrum unterschiedlichster Anwendungsformen – von Lebensmittelverpackungen und Magazinen bis zu Leitsystemen auf Flughäfen – verbreitete sich aber auch in rasanter Geschwindigkeit überall in der Welt, was ihm den Namen „International Style“ einbrachte. Gleichzeitig setzten sich die Vorzüge eines konsequenten Erscheinungsbildes endgültig durch und führten zu einer neuen Qualität in der Markenkommunikation. Eine Riege internationaler Gestalter wie Paul Rand, Otl Aicher, F.H.K. Henrion oder Yusaku Kamekura prägten dieses neue Arbeitsfeld nachhaltig. Neben aller Strenge stand besonders die zweite Hälfte des Jahrzehnts gleichermaßen auch für ein neuartiges konventionsfreies und emotionsgeladenes Design. Besonders im Umfeld von Jazz-, Pop- und Rockmusik entwickelten sich neue Bildsprachen, die, ausgehend von der westlichen Subkultur, schnell ihren Weg in den Mainstream fanden.

Les années 1960 marquent l'apogée d'un graphisme à la fois minimaliste et moderniste, et le ton est d'abord donné par la Suisse. Le nouveau style trouve alors son application dans les domaines les plus divers, des emballages alimentaires et du graphisme éditorial à la signalétique dans les aéroports, et il se répand à une vitesse effrénée dans le monde entier, ce qui lui vaut le nom de «style international». En même temps, les avantages d'une image plus cohérente s'imposent enfin et conduisent à une nouvelle norme dans la communication de marque. Une série de créateurs internationaux comme Paul Rand, Otl Aicher, F.H.K. Henrion ou Yusaku Kamekura marquent durablement de leur empreinte ce nouveau champ d'activité.
À côté de toute cette rigueur, la seconde moitié de la décennie voit aussi émerger un graphisme inédit, libéré des conventions et véhiculé par un vocabulaire visuel plein d'émotions. Dans le contexte du jazz, de la pop et du rock se développe une nouvelle imagerie qui, partant de la sous-culture, entre rapidement dans le *mainstream*.

1960

A **World Design Conference** (Sekai Dezain Kaigi) is held in Tokyo, featuring speakers from all over the world

1960 · Kazumasa Nagai · JP · Logo · Nippon Design Center

1960 · Anton Stankowski · DE · Logo · Viessmann

1960 · Yusaku Kamekura · JP · Logo · Japan Architects Association

1960 · Roger-Virgil Geiser · CH · Poster

1960 · Franz Fässler · CH · Poster

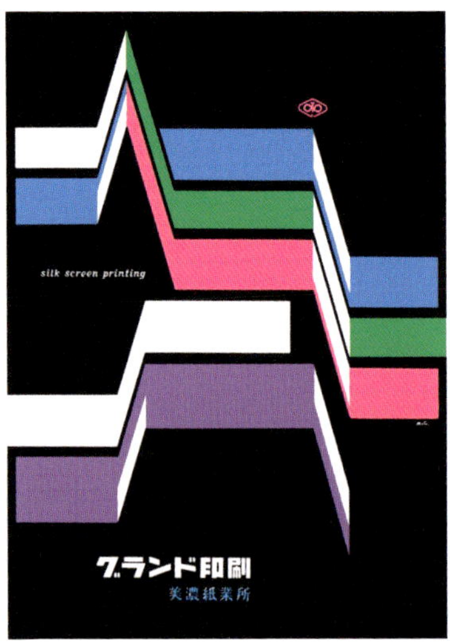

1960 · Mitsutomo Ishikawa · JP · Poster

1960 · Pieter Brattinga · NL · Poster

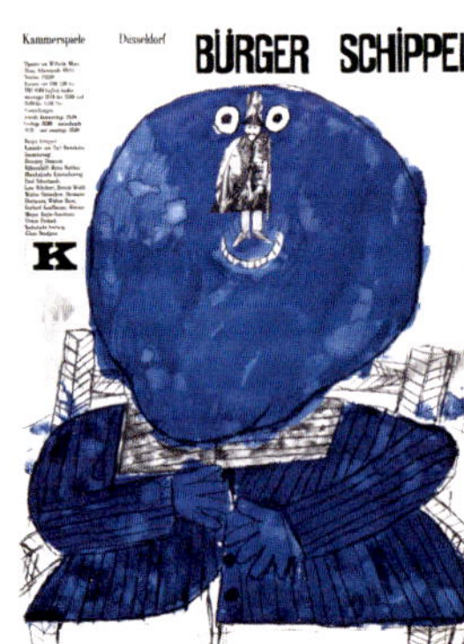

1960 · Heinz Edelmann · DE · Poster

1960 · Emil Ruder · CH · Poster

1960 · Franco Grignani · IT · Ad

1960 · Sebastião Rodrigues · PT · Magazine cover

1960 · Wojciech Zamecznik · PL · Poster

1960 · Wojciech Zamecznik · PL · Poster

Swiss graphic design is a particularly telling example of how, in the age of analog technology, developments in visual imagery could catch on internationally and rapidly spread from one country to another. Only a few years after it was first conceived in its native Switzerland in the mid-1950s, similar, or in some cases identical forms of visual expression emerged worldwide. In the course of the 1960s, in Poland, as in Greece, Argentina, or Japan, the functional style first coined in Basel and Zurich became globally accepted as one that could be applied without restriction in any number of contexts. Consequently, the name "Swiss Style" was quickly replaced by the term "International Style."

Wie schnell und über nationale Grenzen hinweg sich bereits im analogen Zeitalter visuelle Entwicklungen verbreiteten, zeigt die Internationalisierung der Schweizer Grafik besonders eindrucksvoll. Nur wenige Jahre nach ihrer nationalen Etablierung Mitte der 1950er-Jahre tauchten weltweit vergleichbare Arbeiten auf, die ähnliche oder sogar identische Gestaltungsmaximen zeigten. Ob in Polen, Griechenland, Argentinien oder Japan: Die in Basel und Zürich geprägte funktionale Stilistik fand im Laufe der 1960er-Jahre globale und vor allem thematisch uneingeschränkte Anwendung. Der Name „Swiss Style" wurde folgerichtig bald durch den Begriff „International Style" vielfach abgelöst.

La vitesse à laquelle les évolutions visuelles ont pu se diffuser au-delà des frontières nationales dès l'ère analogique est illustrée de manière saisissante par le cas du graphisme suisse. Quelques années après l'avènement du style suisse dans son pays d'origine au milieu des années 1950, des travaux similaires, voire identiques, apparaissent déjà un peu partout dans le monde. Que ce soit en Pologne, en Grèce, en Argentine ou au Japon, le style fonctionnel d'empreinte bâloise ou zurichoise connaît dans les années 1960 une application globale et surtout thématiquement illimitée. Très logiquement, l'appellation «style suisse» devient alors «style international».

1962 · Juan Carlos Distéfano · AR · Ad

1966 · Burton Kramer · CA · Packaging

»To be a Modernist is to rely not on the solutions and stylistic quirkiness of the past, but to become part of creating an idiom of today and tomorrow. It is to be convinced that there is a way to improve what exists, and to be part of an ongoing process that does not, without understanding, revere or accept what has gone before.« Burton Kramer, *Burton Kramer Identities*, 2008

1960s · Waldemar Świerzy · PL · Poster

1963 · Iannis Svoronos · GR · Poster

1964 · Leif Frimann Anisdahl · NO · Book cover

1962 · Larry Carter · UK · Book cover

1968 · Jiří Hilmar · CZ · Poster

1965 · Paul Ibou · BE · Brochure cover

In 1959, Adolf Theobald and Stephan Wolf came up with the idea of a new magazine designed for young adults. Without the backing of a publisher, the two of them put together a batch of advertising orders and printed and distributed issue one of *twen* without knowing whether a second would be forthcoming. In the years that followed, the magazine became the mouthpiece for an entire generation, dealing with a range of social and cultural issues. Willy Fleckhaus's design played a major role in this success story. From the very first issue, the young art director defined the look of the magazine with its striking black covers and pioneering layouts. *twen*'s uncompromising creativity gave it international resonance and made it a trailblazer for modern magazine design.

Adolf Theobald und Stephan Wolf hatten 1959 die Idee zu einem neuartigen Magazin für junge Erwachsene. Ohne den Rückhalt eines Verlages sammelten die beiden Anzeigenaufträge und realisierten in Eigenregie den Druck einer Nullnummer. In den folgenden Jahren wurde *twen* zum Sprachrohr einer ganzen Generation, behandelt wurden gesellschaftliche wie kulturelle Themen. Eine wesentliche Rolle in dieser Erfolgsgeschichte spielte die Gestaltung von Willy Fleckhaus. Von der ersten Ausgabe an definierte der junge Artdirector das Aussehen des Hefts mit seinen markanten schwarzen Covern und radikal modernen Layouts. Die kompromisslose Gestaltung machte *twen* zum Vorreiter moderner Magazingestaltung und erfuhr internationale Resonanz.

En 1959, Adolf Theobald et Stephan Wolf eurent l'idée de créer un magazine d'un genre inédit destiné à de jeunes adultes. Sans le soutien d'aucun éditeur, il recueillirent des commandes publicitaires et réalisèrent l'impression d'un numéro un sans savoir si un deuxième suivrait. Au cours des années suivantes, *twen* devint le porte-parole de toute une génération grâce à ses sujets de société et culturels. Le graphisme de Willy Fleckhaus a joué un rôle essentiel dans cette éclatante réussite: dès le premier numéro, le jeune directeur artistique définit l'aspect visuel de la revue, avec ses couvertures noires marquantes et ses mises en pages inédites. Son graphisme sans concession fit de *twen* un précurseur du design éditorial de magazines et connut un impact international.

1963 · Willy Fleckhaus · DE · Magazine cover

»A magazine is something three-dimensional, it is not just a matter of the height and width of the page, but is much more than that: it is an adventure.«
Willy Fleckhaus, Typography Symposium Stuttgart, 1980

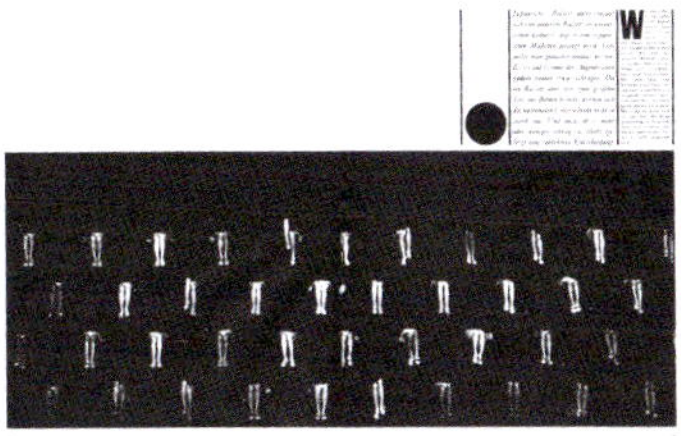

1963 · Willy Fleckhaus · DE · Magazine spreads

Willy Fleckhaus (1925, Velbert, Germany – 1983, Castelfranco di Sopra, Italy) was one of the most influential German designers from the 1950s to the 1980s. Also a journalist, Fleckhaus was a prominent book and newspaper designer, and professor of visual communications in the universities of Essen and Wuppertal. After serving in the military in WWII, he worked in various editorial positions before taking over the design direction for *Aufwärts* magazine in 1953. Fleckhaus worked closely with the Photokina photography fair for over two decades, co-founded *twen* magazine, and served as president of the German Art Directors Club from 1972–73.

Willy Fleckhaus (1925, Velbert, Deutschland – 1983, Castelfranco di Sopra, Italien) war ab den 1950er-Jahren bis zu seinem Tod einer der einflussreichsten deutschen Grafikdesigner. Zudem war er Journalist, Buch- und Zeitungsgestalter und Professor für Kommunikationsdesign an den Universitäten Essen und Wuppertal. Nach dem Militärdienst im Zweiten Weltkrieg arbeitete Fleckhaus in mehreren Redaktionen in unterschiedlichen Positionen, bis er 1953 die gestalterische Leitung der Zeitschrift *Aufwärts* übernahm. Über zwanzig Jahre lang arbeitete er zudem eng mit der Fotografiemesse Photokina zusammen, war ein Mitbegründer der Zeitschrift *twen* und diente 1972/73 als Präsident des deutschen Art Directors Club.

Willy Fleckhaus (1925, Velbert, Allemagne – 1983, Castelfranco di Sopra, Italie) fut un des graphistes allemands les plus influents des années 1950 aux années 1980, mais aussi journaliste et professeur de communication visuelle aux universités d'Essen et de Wuppertal. Après avoir servi dans l'armée pendant la Seconde Guerre mondiale, il occupa différents postes éditoriaux avant d'assurer la direction conceptuelle de la revue *Aufwärts* en 1953. Fleckhaus a collaboré étroitement avec la Photokina pendant plus de deux décennies, fut cofondateur du magazine *twen* et président de l'Art Directors Club allemand en 1972–73.

1959 · Willy Fleckhaus · DE · Magazine cover

1962 · Willy Fleckhaus · DE · Magazine cover

1963 · Willy Fleckhaus · DE · Magazine cover

Paul Rand (1914, New York – 1996, Norwalk, Connecticut) was an American designer who embraced the guidelines of modernism, and became renowned for his many corporate identities, including IBM, UPS, Westinghouse, and ABC. Educated at the Pratt Institute, and later a teacher at Yale University, Rand was initially influenced by the European graphic design pioneers of the 1920s and '30s. By his early 20s, Rand was already at the forefront of the graphic design field, and was art-directing several publications. In 1947, he published *Thoughts on Design*, a fundamental reference in visual communication.

Paul Rand (1914, New York – 1996, Norwalk, Connecticut) war ein amerikanischer Grafikdesigner, der sich die Leitlinien der Moderne zur Aufgabe machte und durch seine zahlreichen Logos für Unternehmen wie IBM, UPS, Westinghouse und ABC bekannt wurde. Rand, der seine Ausbildung am Pratt Institute erhielt und später an der Yale University unterrichtete, war ursprünglich von den Vorreitern des europäischen Grafikdesigns der 1920er- und 1930er-Jahre beeinflusst. Bereits als Anfang 20-Jähriger spielte er im Bereich des Grafikdesigns eine führende Rolle und fungierte bei mehreren Publikationen als Artdirector. 1947 veröffentlichte er sein Standardwerk zur visuellen Kommunikation *Thoughts on Design*.

Paul Rand (1914, New York – 1996, Norwalk, Connecticut) fut un graphiste américain qui reprit à son compte les lignes directrices du modernisme et se rendit célèbre par ses nombreuses images de marque, parmi lesquelles IBM, UPS, Westinghouse et ABC. Après une formation à l'Institut Pratt, et devenu professeur à l'université Yale, Rand fut d'abord influencé par les pionniers européens du graphisme des années 1920 et 1930. Dès le début de sa vingtaine, Rand était déjà chef de file dans le domaine et le directeur artistique de plusieurs publications. En 1947, il publia *Thoughts on Design*, référence fondamentale en matière de communication visuelle.

1960 · Paul Rand · US · Identity · Westinghouse

»Simple ideas, as well as simple designs are, ironically, the products of circuitous mental purposes. Simplicity is difficult to achieve, yet worth the effort.«

Paul Rand, *AIGA Journal of Graphic Design*, 1991

In the 1960s, Rand developed the corporate identities of both Westinghouse and IBM. With these two pioneering projects, he set the international standard of design in this newly burgeoning sector. A key part of Rand's approach was to seize upon the practice Peter Behrens had first employed in 1908, namely creating for a company its own individual corporate typeface.

In den 1960er-Jahren entwickelte Paul Rand die Firmenidentitäten für Westinghouse und IBM. Damit legte er zwei international wegweisende Projekte dieses gerade aufblühenden Sektors vor. Rand griff dabei die um 1908 von Peter Behrens erstmals praktizierte Vorgehensweise wieder auf, für ein Unternehmen eine eigene individuelle Hausschrift zu entwickeln.

Dans les années 1960, Paul Rand développa les images de marque de Westinghouse et d'IBM. Il réalisa ainsi deux projets internationaux révolutionnaires dans un secteur économique en plein boom. Pour ce faire, il reprit la démarche que Peter Behrens avait adoptée pour la première fois en 1908 lorsqu'il fut chargé de développer la signature visuelle spécifique d'une entreprise.

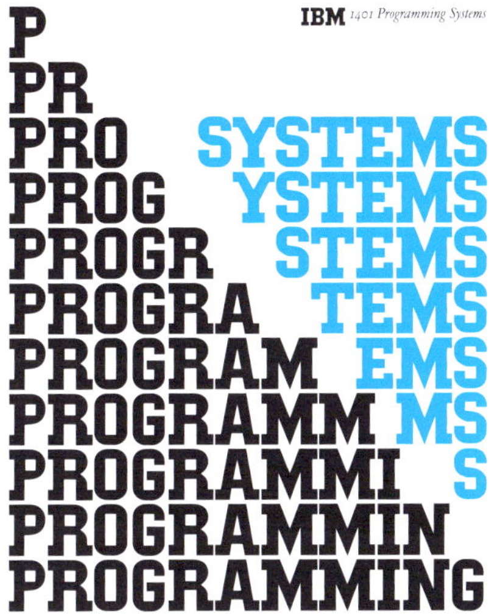

1959 · Paul Rand · US · Brochure cover

1962 · Paul Rand · US · Identity · IBM

1974 · Paul Rand · US · Packaging

1964 · Paul Rand · US · Brochure cover

1956 · Paul Rand · US · Logo · IBM

1967 · Paul Rand · US · Logo · IBM

1967 · Paul Rand · US · Logo · IBM

1961

Former Bauhaus teacher Johannes Itten creates the **Farbkreis** (color wheel)

Hans Hillmann is appointed to a professorship at the Werkkunstschule Kassel and lays the foundations for the Kassel School of Posters

1961 · A.M. Cassandre · FR · Logo · Yves Saint Laurent

1961 · Yasuo Kuroki · JP · Logo · Sony

1961 · Paul Rand · US · Logo · United Parcel Service

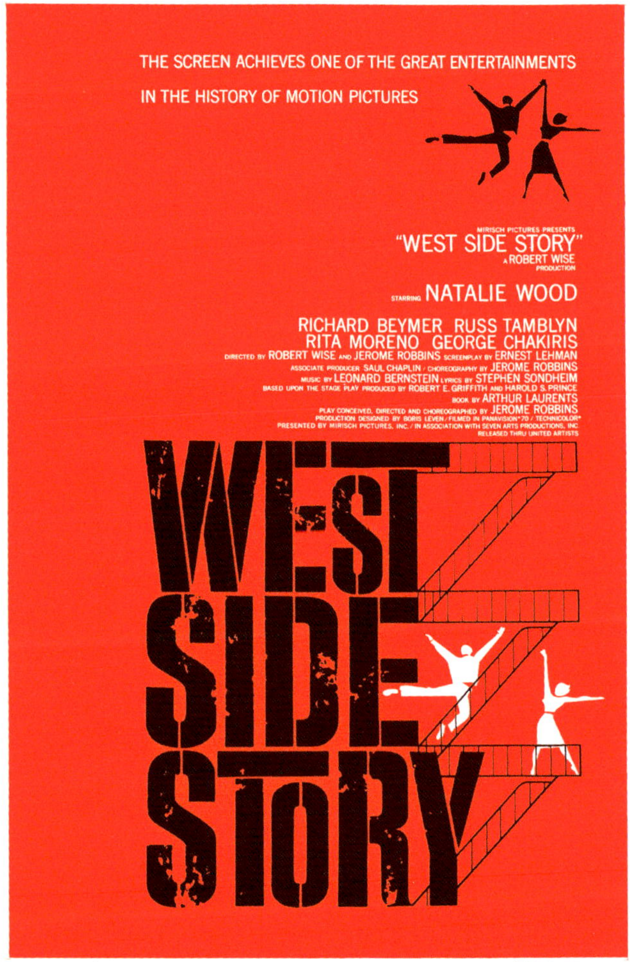

1961 · Joseph Caroff · US · Poster

Josef Müller-Brockmann's book **The Graphic Artist and His Design Problems** is published

Pierre Mendell and Klaus Oberer set up their design studio **Mendell & Oberer** in Munich

The **California Institute of the Arts** is established

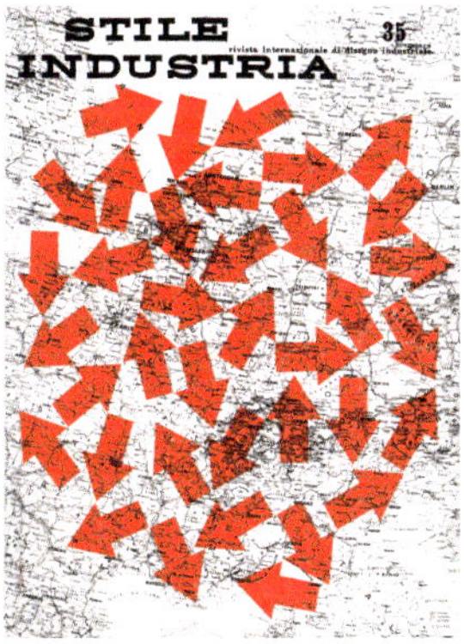

1961 · Enzo Mari · IT · Magazine cover

1961 · Józef Mroszczak · PL · Poster

1961 · Ruedi Külling · CH · Poster

1961 · Henry Wolf · AT/US · Magazine cover

1961 · Erich Strenger · DE · Poster

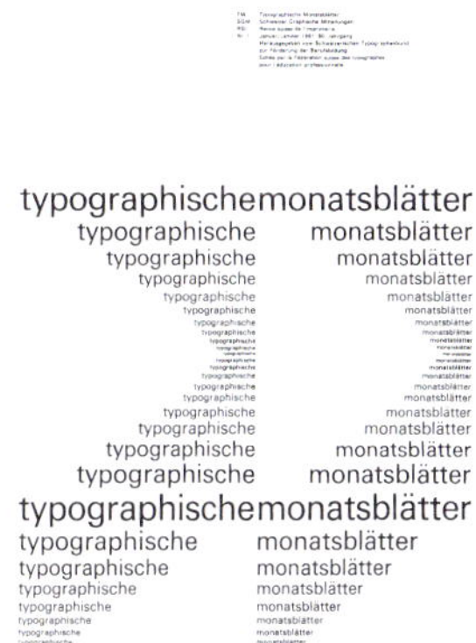

1961 · Emil Ruder · CH · Magazine covers

1961 · Hans Hillmann · DE · Poster

1961 · Kazumasa Nagai · JP · Poster

1962

The **Eurostile** typeface is created by Italian designer Aldo Novarese

The **Fletcher Forbes Gill** design studio is set up in London

George Lois designs his first cover for **Esquire** magazine

1962 · Herb Lubalin · US · Logo · Sudler, Hennessey & Lubalin Advertising

1962 · Marcel Wyss · CH · Logo · Electrolux

1962 · Lippincott & Margulies · US · Logo · Chrysler

1962 · Anonymous · US · Poster

The Italian graphic design magazine **Pagina** is founded

Polish designer **Jan Lenica** creates the animated short film *Labyrinth*, which is shown around the world

Otl Aicher and his students create a new identity for **Lufthansa** airlines

The **D&AD** organization is founded in London

1962 · Reid Miles, Francis Wolff (PH) · US · Record cover

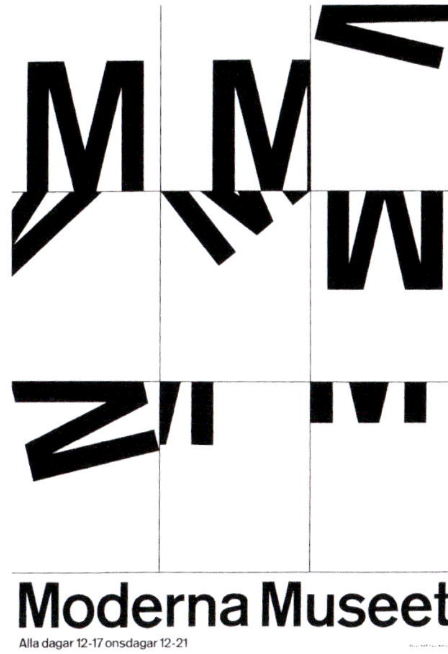

1962 · John Melin, Anders Österlin · SE · Poster

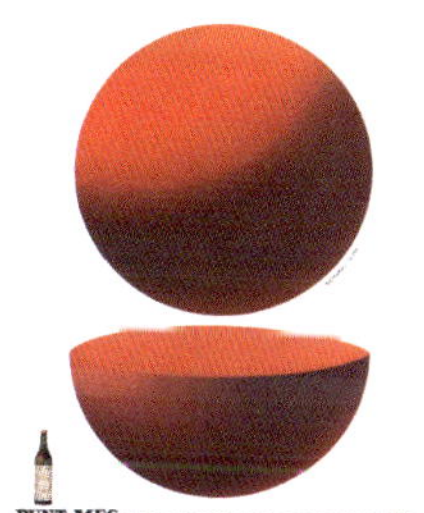

1962 · Armando Testa · IT · Ad

1962 · Eryk Lipiński · PL · Poster

1962 · Novum · DE · New year's card

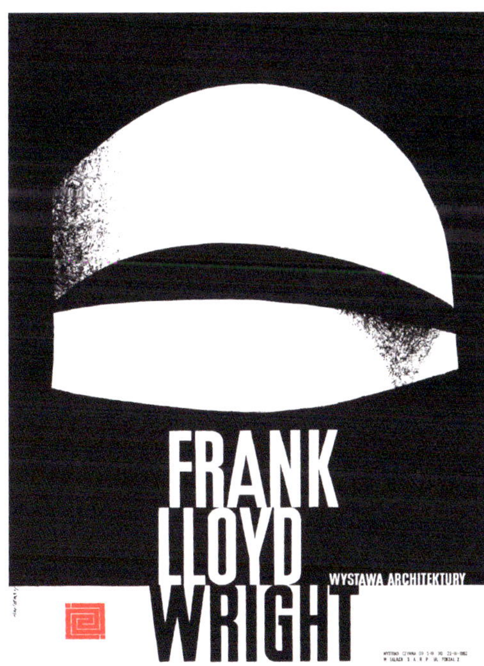

1962 · Waldemar Świerzy · PL · Poster

1963

The design studio **Total Design** is founded by Wim Crouwel, Benno Wissing, and Friso Kramer in Amsterdam

The **Icograda** (International Council of Graphic Design Associations) is founded in London

1963 · Bob Noorda · NL/IT · Logo · Metropolitana Milanese

1963 · Otto Treumann · NL/IL · Logo · El Al Airlines

1963 · Fletcher Forbes Gill · UK · Logo · D&AD

1963 · Wojciech Zamecznik · PL · Poster

1963 · Michael Engelmann · DE · Poster

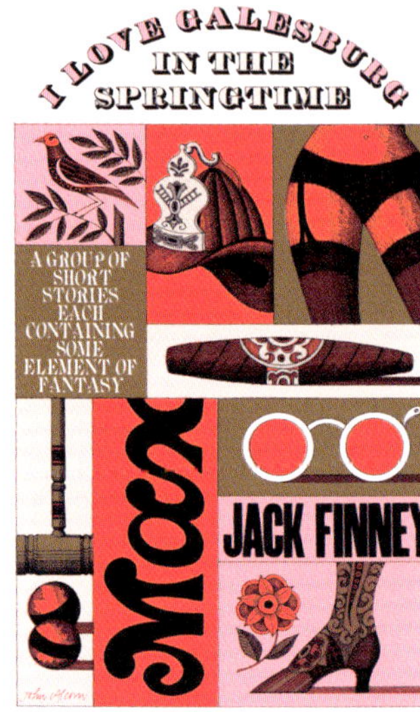

1963 · John Alcorn · US · Book cover

1963 · Wolfgang Schmidt · DE · Poster

Josef Albers's color theory **Interaction of Color** is published

Karl Gerstner publishes his book **Programme entwerfen** (Designing Programs)

The book **Graphic Design: Visual Comparisons** by Alan Fletcher, Colin Forbes, and Bob Gill is published

The **Pantone** color matching system is introduced

1963 · Armin Hofmann · CH · Poster

1963 · Roger Mayer · CH · Packaging

1963 · Otl Aicher, E5 · DE · Design manual

When taking a retrospective look at many design trends, it is often impossible to determine with any certainty who came up with the idea in the first place. This is the situation with skewed typefaces, which function with the help of photographic means, and are a design feature first seen in the early 1960s including on the cover of the Italian magazine *domus* and in the opening credits of the second James Bond movie, *From Russia with Love*. Over the following decade, designers from all over the world used different techniques to produce this kind of arresting effect, and even today the same ideas are still being applied in a whole variety of ways.

Bei vielen gestalterischen Trends lässt sich rückblickend nicht mehr mit Sicherheit ermitteln, wer eine Idee tatsächlich zum allerersten Mal aufbrachte. So auch im Fall der mithilfe fotografischer Mittel verzerrten Typografie. Erstmalig lässt sich dieses Gestaltungsmittel Anfang der 1960er-Jahre ausmachen, unter anderem auf dem Cover der italienischen Zeitschrift *domus* oder im Vorspann des zweiten James-Bond-Films *Liebesgrüße aus Moskau*. In den folgenden zehn Jahren generierten Gestalter auf der ganzen Welt auf diese Weise Texte zu plakativen Bildmotiven, und bis heute taucht die Idee immer wieder in den unterschiedlichsten Anwendungsformen auf.

Bien des tendances du graphisme ne permettent pas de déterminer à coup sûr qui fut la première personne à en avoir l'idée. Tel est le cas pour les distorsions typographiques réalisées à l'aide de moyens photographiques. Elles apparaissent pour la première fois au début des années 1960, notamment en couverture de la revue italienne *domus*, ou encore dans le générique du deuxième James Bond *Bons Baisers de Russie*. Au cours des dix années suivantes, des graphistes du monde entier ont employé des techniques pour obtenir des motifs visuels accrocheurs, et encore aujourd'hui, cette idée réapparaît régulièrement sous diverses formes.

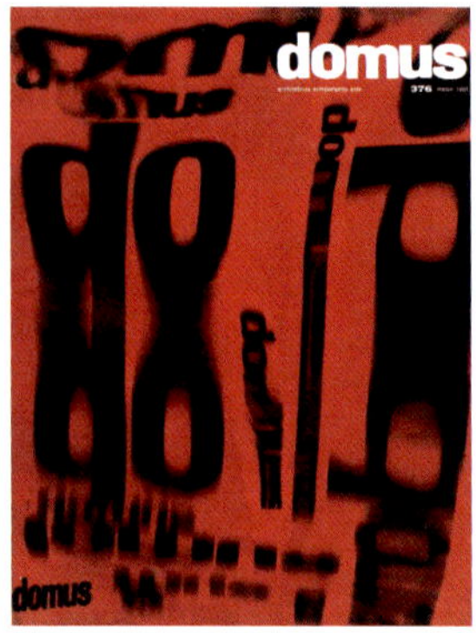

1961 · William Klein · US/IT · Magazine cover

1963 · Gérard Miedinger · CH · Poster

1963 · Heinz Edelmann · DE · Poster

1967 · Gilbert Lesser · US · Magazine cover

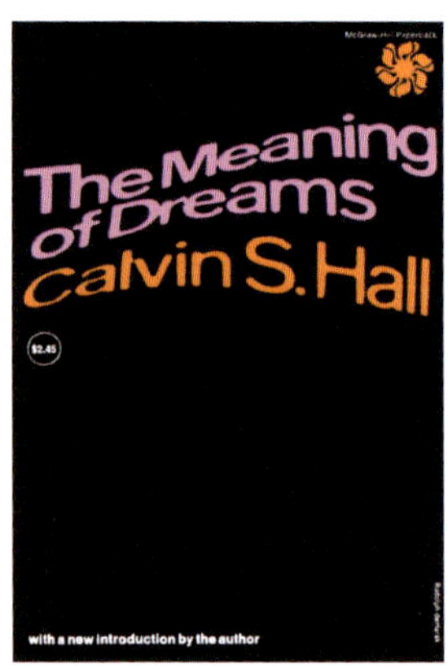

1966 · Rudolph de Harak · US · Book cover

1963 · Franco Grignani · IT · Book cover

»With photographs, nowadays we can express everything better and so much more quickly than is possible with words or in writing. Consequently, the photo block has joined the letters and various lines in the printer's case cabinet as a modern but highly distinct element of typographical composition.«
Tobias M. Barthel, *Photo Graphik*, 1965

1967 · Mendell & Oberer · DE · Poster

1969 · Brian Stones · UK · Ad

1965 · Robert Massin · FR · Book spread

1965 · Zdeněk Ziegler · CZ · Poster

1968 · Anonymous · ES · Poster

1968 · Michael Tucker · UK · Logo · Achille Serre

1968 · Don Bender · US · Book cover

1965 · Daniel Gil · ES · Book cover

1963 · John Murello · US · Record cover

1961 · Ernst Roch · CA · Brochure cover

1964 · Toshihiro Katayama · JP · Brochure cover

1960 · Otaka Takeshi · JP · Packaging

The use of geometric forms in graphic design that began with the Swiss Style became one of the most commonly encountered basic approaches in the design work of the 1960s. Overlapping multicolored circles, triangles, and other shapes were to be seen as often on the labels of discs released by Brazilian record producers as on Japanese packaging design.

Ausgehend vom „Swiss Style" wurde die Arbeit mit geometrischen Formen zu einem der populärsten Gestaltungsansätze der 1960er-Jahre. Sich überlagernde mehrfarbige Kreise, Dreiecke und dergleichen fanden sich auf Schallplatten brasilianischer Musikhersteller ebenso wie im japanischen Verpackungsdesign.

Partant du style suisse, le travail avec des formes géométriques devint une des approches graphiques les plus populaires des années 1960. Superpositions de cercles, triangles et autres formes multicolores du même ordre se retrouvaient alors aussi bien sur les pochettes de disques de labels musicaux brésiliens que dans du packaging japonais.

1963 · Hans Michel · DE · Poster

1965 · Carlos Prósperi · BR · Record cover

1964 · Karl Gerstner · CH · Ad

1962 · Harry Boller · CH · Ad

1971 · Giancarlo Iliprandi · IT · Poster

1964 · Karl Gerstner · CH · Ad

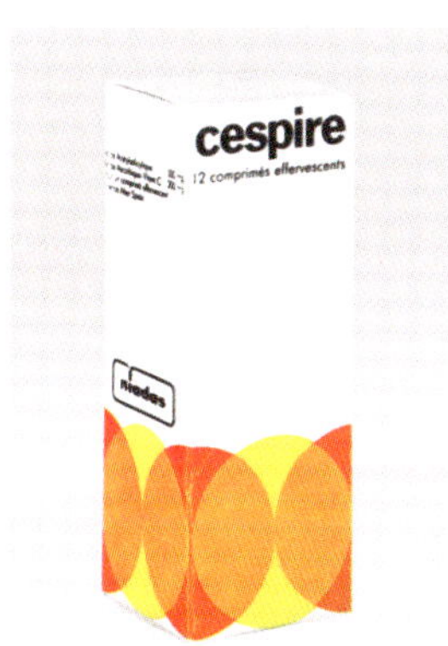

1970 · J. Angelopoulos, Frederick V. Carabott (AD) · GR · Packaging

1956 · Bob Noorda · NL/IT · Poster

1964

Herb Lubalin sets up his own studio in New York City

The first Czechoslovak Exhibition of Poster and Promotional Graphics is held, which later evolves to become the **Brno International Biennial of Graphic Design**

1964 · Franco Grignani · IT · Logo · Woolmark International

1965 · Anonymous · US · Record cover

1964 · Kurt Wirth · CH · Logo · Buri

1964 · Massimo Vignelli · IT · Poster

1964 · James Rosenzweig · US · Book cover

1964 · Jean-Marie Chourgnoz, Henry Chaney, Erich Brenzinger · FR · Logo · Elf Aquitaine

Ken Garland publishes the **First Things First** manifesto on the values of graphic design, which is backed by over 400 artists and graphic designers

Lou Dorfsman becomes director of design at CBS

Pablo Ferro Films is founded and produces the opening titles of the Kubrick film *Dr. Strangelove*

1964 · Rolf Harder · DE/CA · Brochure cover

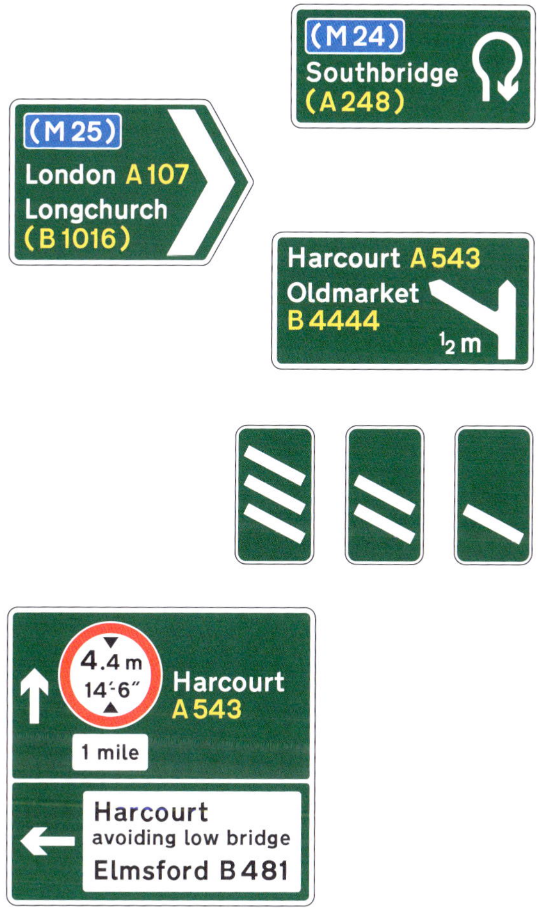

1964 · Jock Kinneir, Margaret Calvert · UK · Identity, Signage

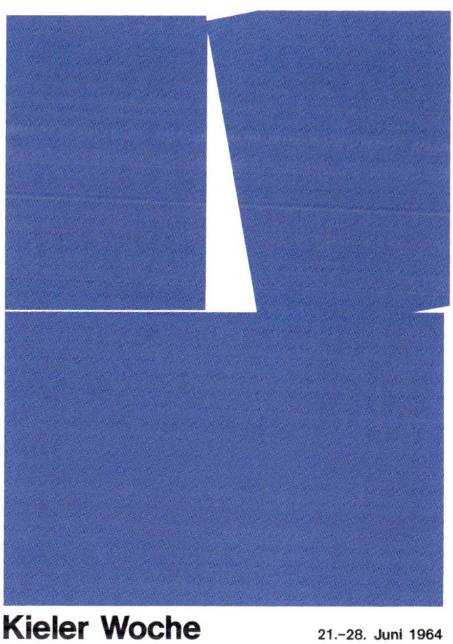

1964 · Hans Hillmann · DE · Poster

1964 · Roger Excoffon · FR · Poster

1965

Armin Hofmann's **Graphic Design Manual** is published

International brand consultancy **Wolff Olins** is founded in London by Michael Wolff and Wally Olins

1965 · Raymond Loewy, CEI · FR/UK · Logo · British Petroleum

1965 · James Pilditch, John Harris, Allied International Designers · UK · Logo · Albert Heijn

1965 · Kinneir, Calvert & Associates · UK · Logo · Glasgow Airport

1965 · Peter von Arx · CH · Poster

1965 · Anonymous · CZ · Poster

1965 · Anonymous · HU · Poster

1965 · Bronislaw Zelek · PL · Poster

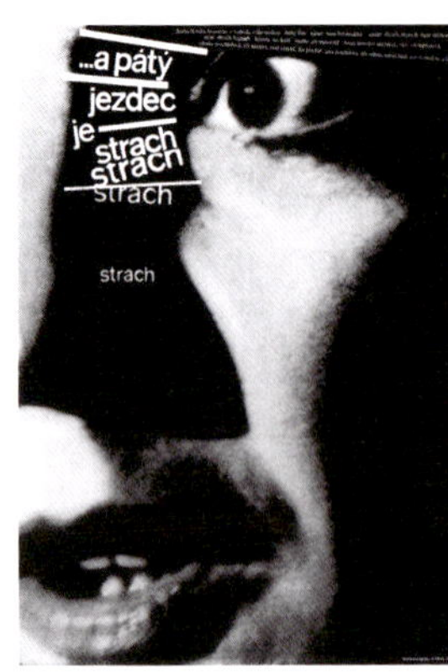

1965 · Zdeněk Ziegler · CZ · Poster

The **Unimark International** branding corporation is founded by Massimo Vignelli, Bob Noorda, and four other partners with offices in Chicago, Milan, and New York

1965 · Hiroshi Tanaka · JP · Poster

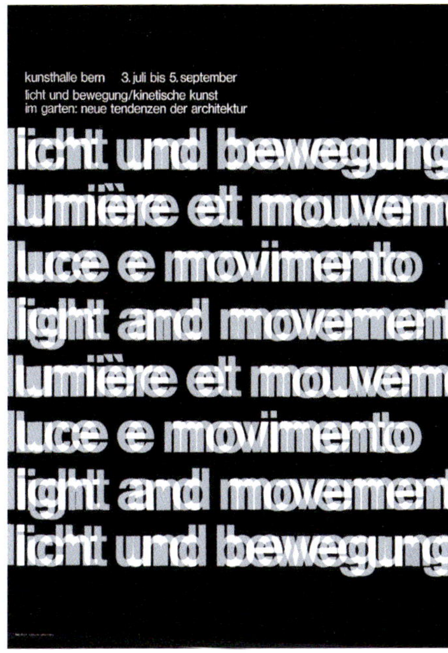

1965 · Peter Megert · CH · Poster

1965 · Bruno Munari · IT · Poster

1965 · Chermayeff & Geismar · US · Magazine cover

1966

1966 · Bob Noorda · NL/IT · Logo · Venice Biennial

1966 · Yvon Laroche · CA · Logo · Cinema

1966 · Anonymous · SE · Logo · Ikea

The first **International Poster Biennale** is held in Warsaw

1966 · Dave Chaston · UK · Magazine cover

1966 · Art Paul (AD), Larry Gordon (PH) · US · Magazine cover

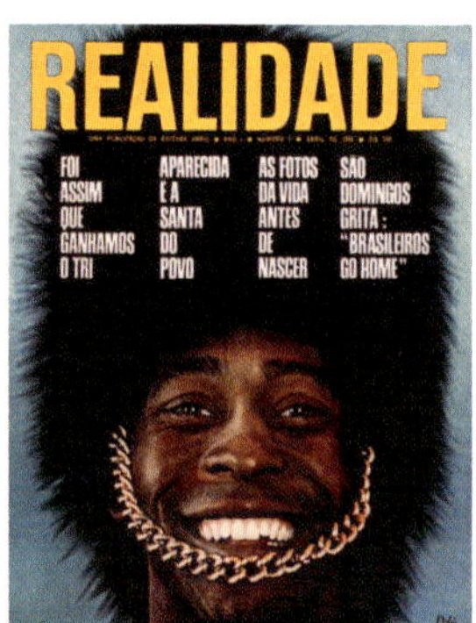

1966 · Eduardo Barreto Filho · BR · Magazine cover

Bruno Munari's book **Design as Art** is published

1966 · Vignelli Associates · US · Identity · American Airlines

1966 · Wolfgang Schmidt · DE · Poster

The design studio **Gottschalk+Ash** is founded in Montreal by Stuart Ash and Fritz Gottschalk

Günter Gerhard Lange begins his work on an update of the **Akzidenz Grotesk** typeface

1966 · Reid Miles, Francis Wolff (PH) · US · Record cover

1966 · Hans Hillmann · DE · Poster

1966 · Wes Wilson · US · Poster

1966 · Klaus Voormann · DE/UK · Record cover

1967

Armin Hofmann becomes head of the design department at the Allgemeine Gewerbeschule Basel

Emil Ruder's influential book **Typographie** is first published

1967 · Till Neuburg · CH/IT · Logo · Bit magazine

1967 · Herb Lubalin · US · Logo · Mother & Child

1967 · Bob Gill · UK · Logo · AGM

1967 · Edgardo Giménez · AR · Poster

German illustrator **Heinz Edelmann** moves to London to work on the animated Beatles movie *Yellow Submarine*

Marshall McLuhan's book **The Medium Is the Massage** is published

The **Graphic Artists Guild** is founded in New York City

1967 · Wim Crouwel · NL · Brochure cover

1967 · John Van Hamersveld · US · Poster

1967 · Seymour Chwast · US · Poster

1967 · Vignelli Associates · US · Poster

1967 · Andy Warhol · US · Record cover

Milton Glaser · United States

With his poster which accompanied Bob Dylan's 1967 *Greatest Hits* album, Milton Glaser created not only a classic of graphic design, but at the same time took a big step forward in consolidating the connection between music and graphics. Glaser created several concert posters for other big names in American music, such as Stevie Wonder and Simon & Garfunkel.

Mit einem beigelegten Poster im *Greatest-Hits*-Album von 1967 von Bob Dylan schuf Milton Glaser nicht nur eine Ikone des Grafikdesigns, sondern bereitete gleichzeitig den Weg für die damals noch nicht selbstverständliche Verbindung von Musik und Grafik. Glaser gestaltete zahlreiche Konzertplakate für andere Größen der US-Musik wie Stevie Wonder oder Simon & Garfunkel.

Avec le poster joint à l'album de Bob Dylan *Greatest Hits* en 1967, Milton Glaser créa non seulement une icône du graphisme, mais contribua aussi à affirmer la relation entre musique et illustration. Glaser créa de nombreuses affiches de concert pour d'autres grands noms de la musique américaine comme Stevie Wonder et Simon & Garfunkel.

1967 · Milton Glaser · US · Poster

»When does 'high art' meet 'low art'? Is everything above this demarcation 'art' and everything below 'non-art'? Shall we call the material below the line craft, applied art, commercial art, decoration? Who invented this question? Who is served by the distinction? Does it matter?«

Milton Glaser, *Commercial Art*, 1989

1969 · Milton Glaser · US · Poster

Milton Glaser (1929–2020, New York) was one of the most important American designers of the modern age. A graduate of Cooper Union, Glaser studied at the Academy of Fine Arts in Bologna before returning to New York to co-found in 1954 the groundbreaking Push Pin Studios. In 1977 he designed the "I Love New York" logo, which has become one of the most recognizable marks in history and also earns the state $30 million each year. Glaser has taught and exhibited widely, and during his career has designed in excess of 300 posters; he was also awarded the National Medal of Arts by Barack Obama in 2009.

Milton Glaser (1929–2020, New York) war einer der bedeutendsten amerikanischen Grafikdesigner der jüngeren Geschichte. Als Absolvent der Cooper Union School of Art studierte er anschließend an der Accademia di Belle Arti in Bologna, ehe er nach New York zurückkehrte und 1954 die wegweisenden Push Pin Studios mitbegründete. 1977 entwarf er das Logo „I Love New York", das zu einem der markantesten Logos in der Geschichte wurde und dem Staat jährlich 30 Millionen US-Dollar einbringt. Glaser hat vielfach unterrichtet und ausgestellt und im Laufe seiner Karriere mehr als 300 Plakate entworfen; 2009 wurde er von Barack Obama mit der National Medal of Arts ausgezeichnet.

Milton Glaser (1929–2020, New York) fut un des grands designers américains de l'époque moderne. Diplômé de la Cooper Union, Glaser étudie ensuite à l'Académie des beaux-arts de Bologne avant de rentrer à New York, où il cofonde le révolutionnaire Push Pin Studios en 1954. En 1977, il dessine le logo «I Love New York», qui est devenu une des marques les plus reconnaissables de l'histoire, et qui rapporte chaque année 30 millions de dollars à l'État. Glaser a enseigné et exposé dans de multiples lieux et il a conçu plus de 300 affiches au fil de sa carrière. En 2009, il a reçu la National Medal of Arts des mains de Barack Obama.

1967 · Milton Glaser · US · Poster

1967 · Milton Glaser · US · Poster

1968 · Milton Glaser · US · Poster

1967 · Milton Glaser · US · Poster

1968

The first issue of **Avant Garde** magazine is published under the art direction of Herb Lubalin

Adrian Frutiger designs **OCR-B**, a font computers could recognize and which was accepted as a worldwide standard in 1973

1968 · Stewart K. Widdess · US · Logo · Target

1968 · George Lois, Carl Fischer (PH) · US · Magazine cover

1968 · Robert Noyce, Gordon Moore · US · Logo · Intel

1968 · Heinz Schwabe · DE · Logo · Eurocheque

1968 · Raymond Loewy, CEI · FR · Logo · New Man

Siegfried Odermatt and Rosmarie Tissi set up their studio **Odermatt+Tissi** in Zurich

The exhibition **50 Jahre Bauhaus** (50 Years of Bauhaus) is held in Stuttgart

The **Ulm School of Design** is shut down because of financial problems

The international poster exhibition **Word and Image** is held at MoMa, New York

1968 · Wim Crouwel · NL · Poster

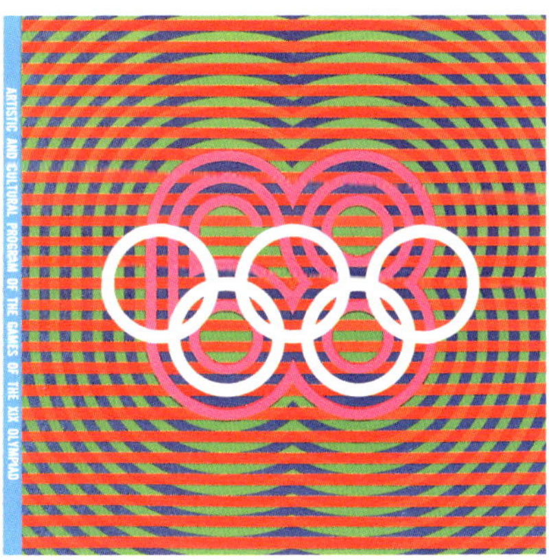

1968 · Lance Wyman · US/MX · Brochure cover

1968 · Kazumasa Nagai · JP · Poster

1968 · Steve Frankfurt · US · Poster

1968 · Gunter Rambow · DE · Poster

1968 · Anonymous · US · Magazine cover

1968 · Antonio Reboiro · CU · Poster

1968 · Heinz Edelmann · DE · Poster

Released in 1968, the Beatles' animated movie *Yellow Submarine* became an instant classic, perfectly capturing how it felt to be alive at that particular moment in history. The film was produced under art director Heinz Edelmann, and its Pop Art fairy tale was one of many international projects to present the zeitgeist of the late 1960s, achieved amongst other things by deploying almost identical types of graphics to those that appeared in happening contexts in the wider world at the time.

Der 1968 veröffentlichte Beatles-Zeichentrickfilm *Yellow Submarine* wurde sofort nach seinem Erscheinen zu einem Klassiker, der punktgenau das Lebensgefühl einer bestimmten Zeit konservierte. Das unter Artdirector Heinz Edelmann entstandene Pop-Art-Märchen war eine von vielen internationalen Arbeiten, die den Zeitgeist mit nahezu identischen grafischen Mitteln visualisierten.

Le film d'animation *Yellow Submarine* sorti en 1968 autour des Beatles devint immédiatement un classique du genre qui capturait au détail près l'air du temps. Ce conte pop art créé sous la direction artistique de Heinz Edelmann a toutefois été une des nombreuses réalisations internationales qui ont illustré l'esprit de l'époque avec des moyens graphiques plus ou moins identiques à ceux qui émergeaient dans le reste du monde.

1968 · John Alcorn · US · Book cover

1968 · Tadanori Yokoo · JP · Poster

1968 · Crosby Fletcher Forbes · UK · Logo · Yes

With the seismic sociopolitical shifts that took place across the world in 1968, many designers and artists saw the opportunity to use their skills to amplify the messages of discontent amid rising oppression. In France, a group of artists from the distinguished École des Beaux-Arts became part of this movement when on May 16 they took over the school and formed the Atelier Populaire (Popular Workshop). Making use of very simple iconography, they responded to the strikes of May 1968, producing over 200 different posters, printed up in quantities from hundreds to thousands using a one-color silkscreen process. With their messages of resistance, anti-colonialism, pro-immigration, and workers' rights, Atelier Populaire became part of the collective visual consciousness of the wider student movement. Noted for its historical importance, the group's work has subsequently been exhibited in several countries.

Aufgrund der seismischen soziopolitischen Veränderungen, die sich 1968 in aller Welt ereigneten, brachten sich auch viele Designer und Maler ein, um inmitten zunehmender Repressionen die Botschaft der Unzufriedenen zu verbreiten. In Frankreich schloss sich eine Gruppe Künstler von der angesehenen École des Beaux-Arts der Bewegung an, übernahm die Schule am 16. Mai und gründete das Atelier Populaire (Volkswerkstatt). Ihre Reaktion auf die Streiks vom Mai 1968 kam in einer sehr schlichten Ikonografie zum Ausdruck, die Künstler gestalteten über 200 Plakate, von denen in einfarbiger Siebdrucktechnik Hunderte, bisweilen auch Tausende gedruckt wurden. Mit seiner Botschaft von Widerstand, Antikolonialismus, Immigrationsfreundlichkeit und Arbeiterrechten ging das Atelier Populaire in das kollektive visuelle Bewusstsein der allgemeinen Studentenbewegung ein. Aufgrund der historischen Bedeutung wurden die Arbeiten der Gruppe in der Folge in mehreren Ländern ausgestellt.

Dans le cadre des bouleversements socio-politiques qui se produisent un peu partout dans le monde en 1968, nombre de graphistes et d'artistes saisissent l'occasion pour mettre leur talent au service des messages d'exaspération liés à une répression croissante. En France, un groupe d'artistes de la vénérable École nationale supérieure des beaux-arts de Paris participe au mouvement en occupant l'école le 16 mai et en proclamant l'Atelier populaire des Beaux-Arts. Avec une iconographie des plus simples, ils font écho aux grèves de mai 1968 en produisant plus de 200 affiches distinctes tirées à des centaines et parfois des milliers d'exemplaires à l'aide d'un procédé sérigraphique monochrome. Par ses appels à la résistance anticolonialiste, pro-immigration et sa défense des droits des travailleurs, l'Atelier populaire devient un acteur important de la conscience visuelle collective du mouvement étudiant. Reconnu pour son importance historique, le travail du groupe sera exposé plus tard dans plusieurs pays.

1968 · Atelier Populaire · FR · Poster

1968 · Atelier Populaire · FR · Poster

»There was no formal organization behind this uprising. It was everyday people who had been pushed too far, showing a solidarity that jumped the shackles of class, age, and education. The kind of revolution of everyday life leading to a societal dialogue where people truly functioned as a collective brain, pulse, and heart.« Johan Kugelberg, *Creative Review*, 2008

1968 · Atelier Populaire · FR · Poster

1968 · Atelier Populaire · FR · Poster

1968 · Atelier Populaire · FR · Poster

1968 · Atelier Populaire · FR · Poster

1968 · Atelier Populaire · FR · Poster

1969

Saul Bass receives an Academy Award for his short film **Why Man Creates**

The **KECD** (Korean Ensemble of Contemporary Design) design association is founded in South Korea

1969 · Alan Siegel, Siegel+Gale · US · Logo · NBA

1969 · Anonymous · US · Logo · DHL

1969 · Lippincott · UK/IT · Logo · Barilla

1969 · Fred Troller · US · Poster

1969 · Dan Reisinger · IL · Poster

1969 · "SPN" · IT · Packaging

1969 · Ivan Picelj · HR · Poster

The **Japan Institute of Design Promotion** is founded

1969 · Waldemar Świerzy · PL · Poster

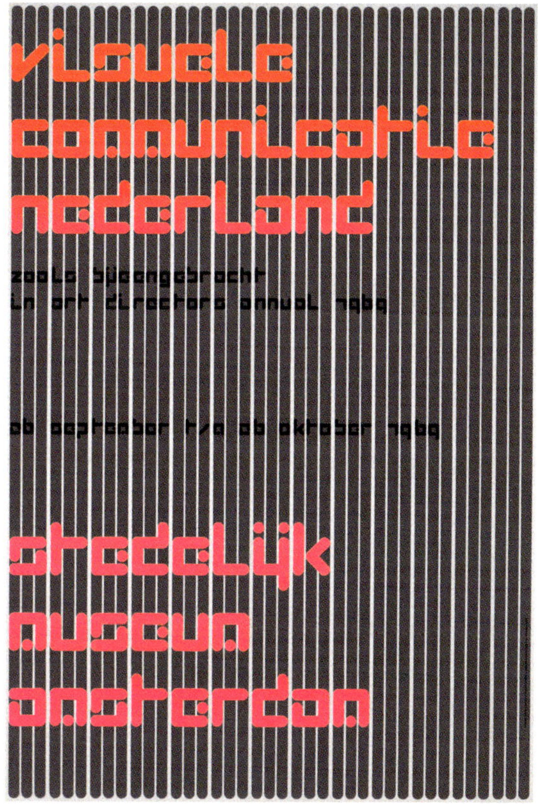

1969 · Wim Crouwel · NL · Poster

1969 · Hubert Hilscher · PL · Poster

1969 · Mihajlo Arsovski · HR · Poster

1970 · Hans Förtsch, Sigrid von Baumgarten · DE · Poster

1970—

1972 · Walter Bernard (AD), Milton Glaser (AD), Henry Wolf (PH) · US · Magazine cover

1977 · Mitsuo Katsui · JP · Logo · National Museum of Ethnology

1979 · Ernst Roch · CA · Brochure cover

1973 · Christoph Ehbets · GDR · Record cover

1979

1978 · Gustavo Pedroza, Estudio MMB · AR · Design manual

1971 · Hamid Samandarian · IR · Poster

The continuation and consolidation of the paths laid down in the previous decade, when modernism and the International Style finally broke through into the mainstream, was the template for the 1970s, as this became the age of strong corporate identities and a time when experimental design thrived throughout the cultural sector. To some degree, this new set of priorities forced commercial and cultural design to strike out in different directions. As a result of the professionalization of the visual arts by large corporations, outstanding pieces of work by individual designers became increasingly rare, especially in consumer advertising. Now, new imagery and the continuing revolution in the visual arts mostly appeared in the context of theater, music, and film, and it was in these environments that commissioning clients could often try out experimental photomontages or eye-catching illustrations with few, if any, restrictions. So it was with punk, a spur-of-the-moment, unpredictable, and bloody-minded form of visual communication, and a totally distinctive stylistic trope that creatives regularly refer back to even today.

View of an exhibition staged by Pentagram at the London Design Centre in 1973. On show was the new monitor-based messaging system designed for the Reuters news agency.

Blick in eine 1973 von Pentagram gestaltete Ausstellung im London Design Centre. Präsentiert wurde ein neues monitorbasiertes Nachrichtensystem der Presseagentur Reuters.

Vue d'une exposition conçue en 1973 par Pentagram au Design Centre de Londres. L'exposition présentait un nouveau système de messagerie conçu pour l'agence de presse Reuters à partir de moniteurs.

Die 1970er-Jahre setzen die im Jahrzehnt zuvor eingeschlagenen Pfade fort – die Moderne und der „International Style" etablieren sich im Mainstream. Es ist die Zeit der konsequenten Erscheinungsbilder ebenso wie der erblühenden experimentellen Kulturgrafik. In gewisser Weise forcierte diese Schwerpunktsetzung, dass kommerzielle und kulturelle Grafik unterschiedliche Richtungen einschlugen. Die visuelle Professionalisierung großer Unternehmen führte dazu, dass vor allem im Bereich der Konsumwerbung herausragende grafische Einzelarbeiten seltener entstehen konnten. Neue Bildsprachen und visuelle Fortentwicklungen zeigten sich nun vor allem im Kontext von Theater, Musik oder Film. Experimentelle Fotomontagen oder expressive Illustration konnten hier oftmals ohne nennenswerte Einschränkungen durch die Auftraggeber ausprobiert werden. So entstand etwa mit dem Punk eine improvisiert, imperfekt und rotzig wirkende visuelle Ausdrucksform, auf die seither als Stilmittel immer wieder einmal zurückgegriffen wird.

Les années 1970 développent les acquis de la décennie précédente, quand se sont imposés le modernisme et le style international, et leur donnent largement droit de cité. C'est l'époque des images de marque fortes, aussi bien que d'un graphisme expérimental florissant dans la sphère culturelle. D'une certaine manière, ce nouvel accent fait prendre au graphisme commercial et culturel des directions différentes. Avec la professionnalisation des grandes entreprises en matière d'arts visuels, les excellentes créations de designers individuels se font rares, surtout dans le domaine de la publicité de consommation. Dès lors, les progrès en termes d'images et de languages visuels s'apprécient principalement dans les domaines du théâtre, de la musique ou du cinéma, où les commanditaires se permettent des photomontages expérimentaux et des illustrations expressives souvent sans grandes restrictions. Ainsi, le mouvement punk donne naissance à une forme d'expression visuelle d'apparence improvisée, imprévisible et hargneuse, créant une figure stylistique caractéristique que les créateurs actuels emploient encore.

1970

Adrian Frutiger creates a standard typeface for the signage for Paris airport, later expanded to become the **Frutiger** typeface, released in 1975

The French design collective **Grapus** is established

1970 · Minale, Tattersfield, Provinciali · UK · Logo · Baric Computing Services

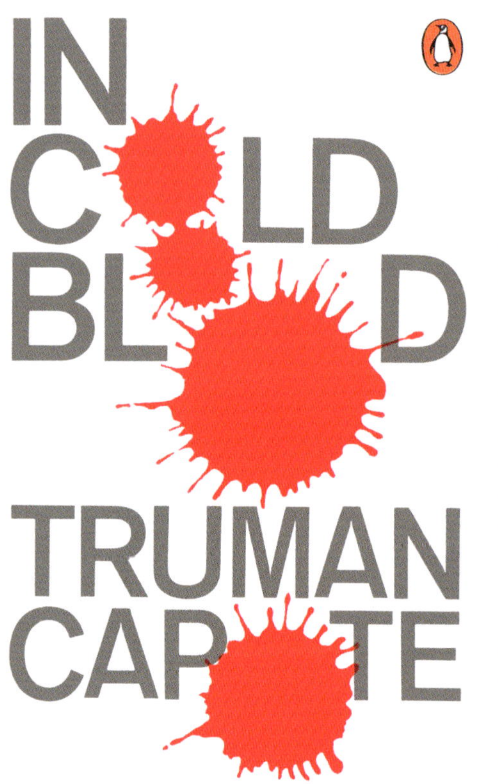

1970 · David Pelham · UK · Book cover

1970 · Bass & Associates · US · Logo · Avery

1970 · Gary Anderson · US · Logo · Recycling Symbol

1970 · René Azcuy · CU · Poster

1970 · Rafał Jasionowicz · PL · Poster

The type foundry **ITC** (International Typeface Corporation) is formed by Herb Lubalin and Aaron Burns

1970 · Stellan Kristenson · SE · Book cover

1970 · Jaroslav Fišer · CZ · Poster

1970 · Keisuke Nagatomo · JP · Poster

1970 · Hubert Hilscher · PL · Poster

1970 · Anonymous · JP · Poster

Since Harry Beck and Bob Noorda developed their respective maps of the London Underground and the Milan Metro, many public transportation systems have adopted their schematic visual approach. In 1970, Unimark International was commissioned by the Metropolitan Transportation Authority (MTA) to improve the map of the New York City Subway, which had been in operation since 1904. Under the direction of Massimo Vignelli and Bob Noorda, the project was approved by the MTA that same year, although Vignelli then left Unimark in 1971 to start his own practice. The new signage system was launched on August 4, 1972, and is considered one of Vignelli's masterpieces; the project is still revered today as an artistic work, and one of the best examples of extensive use of the Helvetica typeface. The design has subsequently gone through a series of modifications.

Seit Harry Beck und Bob Noorda ihre Pläne der U-Bahn in London bzw. Mailand entwarfen, haben zahlreiche Verkehrsbetriebe deren schematische Darstellungsweise übernommen. 1970 erhielt Unimark International von der Metropolitan Transportation Authority (MTA) den Auftrag, den Plan der 1904 in Betrieb genommenen New Yorker U-Bahn zu verbessern. Unter der Leitung von Massimo Vignelli und Bob Noorda wurde das Projekt im selben Jahr von der MTA gebilligt, obwohl Vignelli 1971 Unimark verließ, um sein eigenes Büro zu gründen. Das neue System der Ausschilderung wurde am 4. August 1972 eingeführt und gilt als eines der Meisterwerke Vignellis. Das Projekt wird heute noch als Kunstwerk betrachtet und ist eines der besten Beispiele für den durchgängigen Gebrauch der Schrifttype Helvetica. Der Entwurf wurde seitdem mehrmals angepasst.

Depuis que Harry Beck et Bob Noorda ont développé leurs plans respectifs des métros de Londres et de Milan, nombre de systèmes de transports ont adopté leur approche visuelle schématique. En 1970, Unimark International fut chargée par la Metropolitan Transportation Authority (MTA) d'améliorer le plan de métro de la ville de New York en usage depuis 1904. Le projet dirigé par Massimo Vignelli et Bob Noorda reçut l'approbation de la MTA la même année, bien que Vignelli eut quitté Unimark en 1971 pour ouvrir son propre studio. La nouvelle signalétique lancée le 4 août 1972 est considérée comme un des chefs-d'œuvres de Vignelli. Le projet est encore acclamé aujourd'hui comme une véritable création artistique et un des meilleurs exemples d'utilisation intensive de la police de caractères Helvetica. Plus tard, le graphisme a subi toute une série de modifications.

1970 · Massimo Vignelli, Bob Noorda, Unimark International · US · Identity

1970 · Massimo Vignelli, Bob Noorda, Unimark International · US · Signage

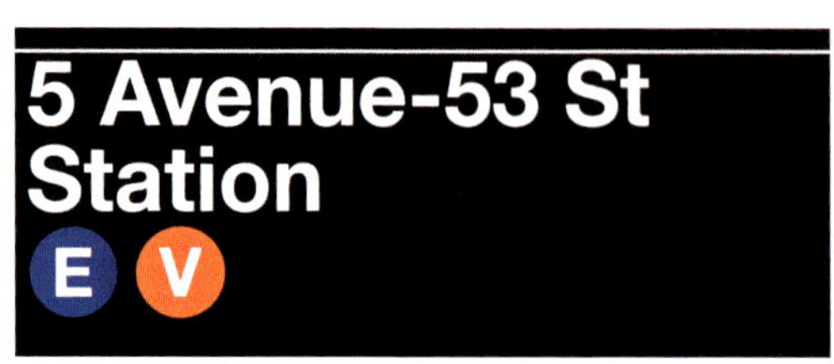

1970 · Massimo Vignelli, Bob Noorda, Unimark International · US · Signage

»Syntactic consistency is of paramount importance in graphic design as it is in all human endeavors. Grids are one of the several tools helping designers to achieve syntactical consistency in graphic design.«
Massimo Vignelli, *The Vignelli Canon*, 2010

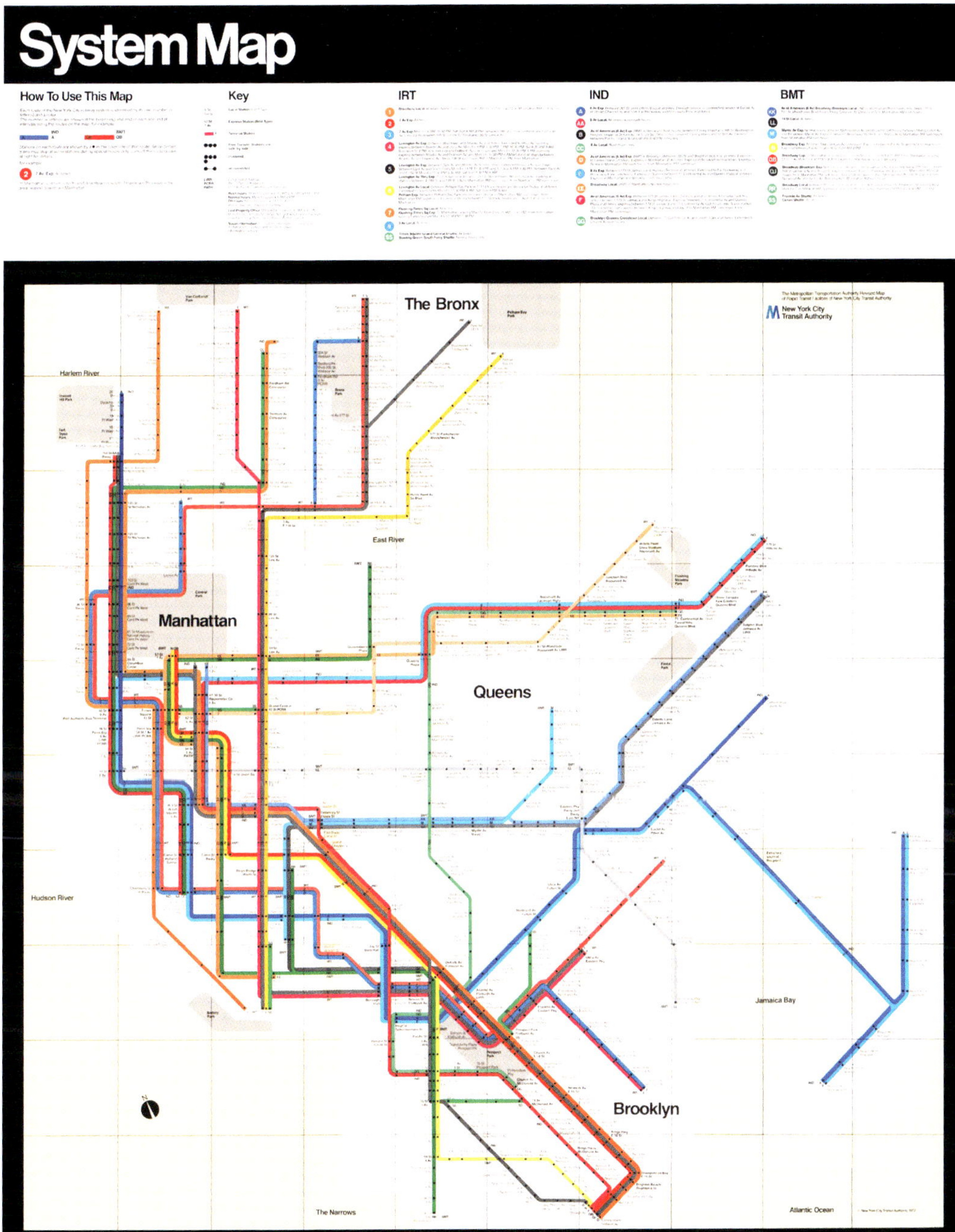

1970–72 · Massimo Vignelli, Joan Charysyn, Unimark International · US · Information graphic

1984 · Félix Beltrán · CU/MX · Logo · Nuñez Architecture

1964 · Félix Beltrán · CU · Logo · Cruz Roja Internacional

1971 · Félix Beltrán · CU · Logo · Instituto Cubano del Libro

1969 · Félix Beltrán · CU/JP · Logo · Asociación para la Solidaridad con Cuba

1967 · Félix Beltrán · CU · Logo · New Year 1968

1972 · Félix Beltrán · CU · Logo · Hormicuba

1965 · Félix Beltrán · CU · Logo · Nacional Importadora

1985 · Félix Beltrán · CU/MX · Logo · Apple México

1973 · Félix Beltrán · CU · Logo · Mincex Havanna

»Félix Beltrán knows that simplicity is the first prerequisite of universally comprehensible and effective communication.«
Hans Kuh, *Gebrauchsgraphik*, 1971

Félix Beltrán (1938, Havana – 2022, Mexico City) was a Cuban visual artist who studied in New York, Paris, and Madrid, before becoming one of the most important poster artists in Latin America. Starting off in advertising at McCann Erickson in the years 1953–56, Beltrán later produced numerous posters for cultural events in Cuba, where he also taught at the Instituto Superior de Arte from 1976–82. In the mid-1980s he moved to Mexico City and became curator of the Archivo Gráfico Internacional at the Universidad Autónoma Metropolitana, a historical visual archive.

Félix Beltrán (1938, Havanna – 2022, Mexico City) war ein kubanischer Künstler, der in New York, Paris und Madrid studierte und zu einem der bedeutendsten Plakatkünstler Lateinamerikas werden sollte. Seine Berufslaufbahn begann Beltrán in den Jahren 1953–1956 als Werbegrafiker bei McCann Erickson und entwarf später zahlreiche Plakate für Kulturveranstaltungen in Kuba, wo er von 1976 bis 1982 auch am Instituto Superior de Arte unterrichtete. Mitte der 1980er-Jahre zog er nach Mexico City und wurde Kurator des Archivo Gráfico Internacional an der Universidad Autónoma Metropolitana.

Félix Beltrán (1938, La Havane – 2022, Mexico) était un artiste visuel cubain qui a étudié à New York, Paris et Madrid avant de devenir un des plus importants affichistes d'Amérique latine. Après des débuts dans la publicité chez McCann Erickson dans les années 1953–56, Beltrán a ensuite produit de nombreuses affiches pour des événements culturels organisés à Cuba, où il a aussi enseigné à l'Instituto Superior de Arte de 1976 à 1982. Au milieu des années 1980, il s'installe à Mexico et devient conservateur de l'Archivo Gráfico Internacional, une archive visuelle historique de la Universidad Autónoma Metropolitana.

1971 · Félix Beltrán · CU · Poster

1971

Design student Carolyn Davidson creates the **Nike** swoosh for $35 USD

Victor Papanek's book **Design for the real world** is published

1971 · Ricardo Blanco · AR · Logo · Equipamento de Hoy

1971 · Salvatore Gregorietti, Unimark International · IT · Logo · Agip

1971 · Carolyn Davidson · US · Logo · Nike

1971 · Ben Bos, Total Design · NL · Poster

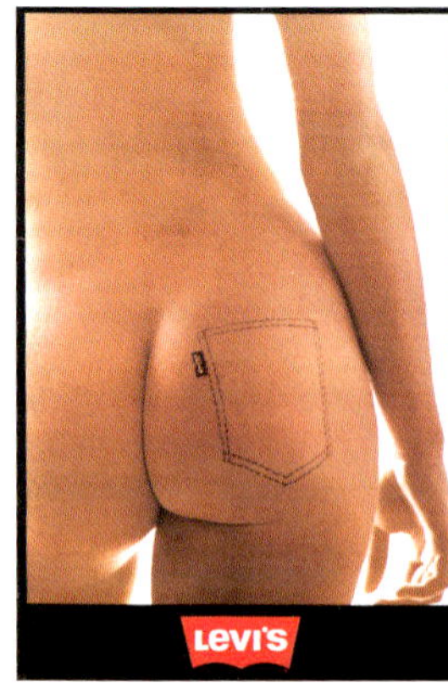

1971 · Ida van Bladel · BE · Poster

1971 · Neukomm+Pinschewer · CH · Poster

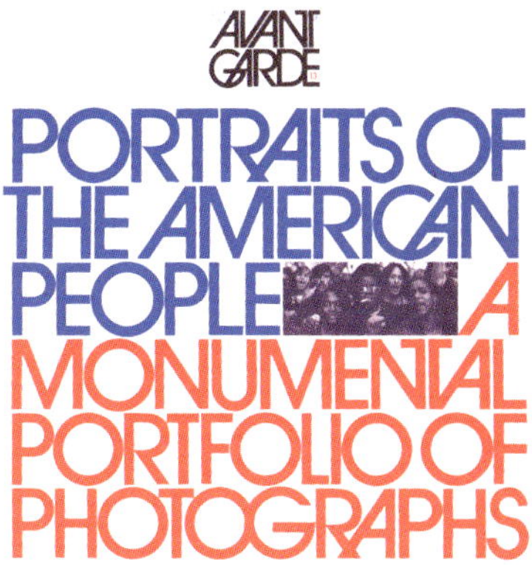

1971 · Herb Lubalin · US · Magazine cover

1971 · Anonymous · GDR · Packaging

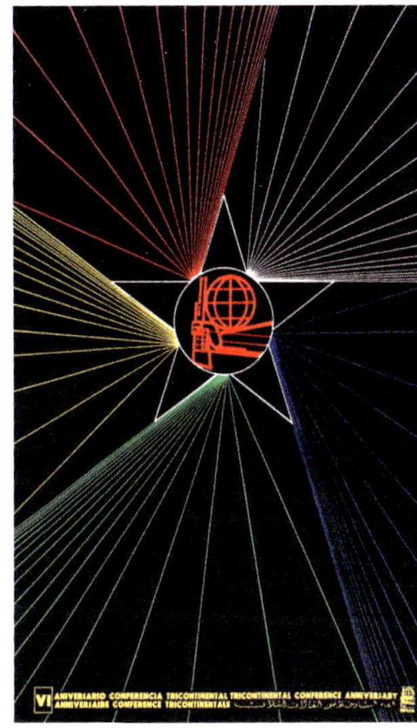

1971 · Lázaro Abreu · CU · Poster

1971 · Walter Breker · DE · Poster

1971 · Jerzy Flisak · PL · Poster

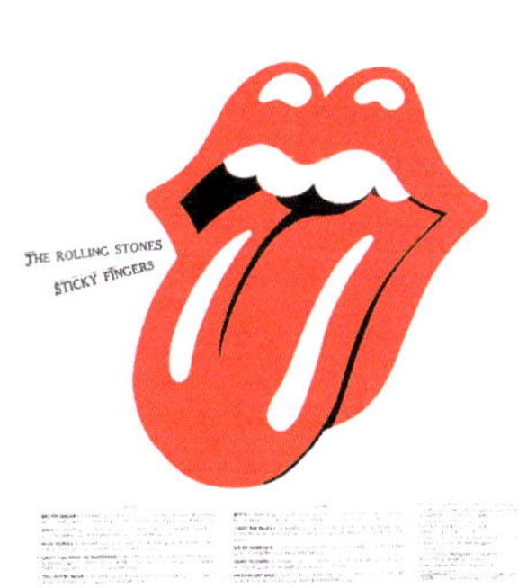

1971 · John Pasche · UK · Record cover

1972

The **Pentagram** design partnership is set up in London

The works of Japanese graphic artist **Tadanori Yokoo** are shown in a solo exhibition at MoMa in New York

1972 · Victor Vasarely · HU/FR · Logo · Renault

1972 · George Opperman, Opperman-Harrington · US · Logo · Atari

1972 · Anonymous · DE · Logo · Adidas

1972 · David Pelham · UK · Book cover

1972 · Isaac Díaz Pardo · ES · Poster

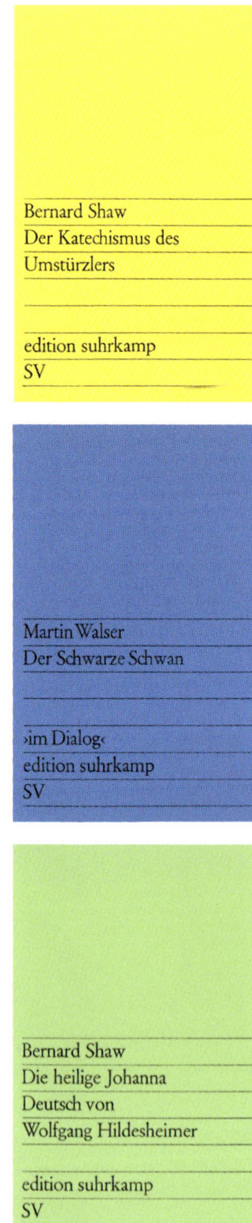

1972 · Willy Fleckhaus · DE · Book covers

Paula Scher is hired as an in-house designer by CBS Records, where she created up to 150 album covers a year

The **Hong Kong Designers Association** (HKDA) is founded

The **Swiss Graphic Designers** (SGD) is founded, also known as the Arbeitsgemeinschaft Schweizer Grafiker (ASG)

1972 · Jerome Gould, James Camperos, Kent Maxson · US · Packaging

1972 · Anonymous · RU · Poster

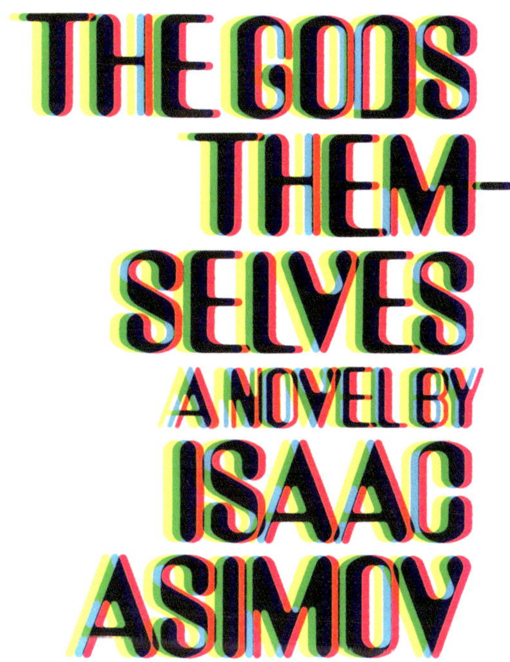

1972 · David November · US · Book cover

1972 · Pierre Mendell, Mendell & Oberer · DE · Book covers

1973 · Alan Fletcher, Pentagram · UK · Poster

?entagram

Colin Forbes will show work and answer questions about the new Pentagram Design Partnership on Wed 15 Nov at 7.30pm at Byggecentrum, Gyldenløvesgade 19. Entrance fee Kr 10.00, SIF members free Arrangement SIF Selskabet for Industriel Formgiving, Nikolaj Plads 9, 1067 København K, 01-152285

1972 · Colin Forbes, Pentagram · UK · Invitation card

1982 · Alan Fletcher, Pentagram · UK · Poster

1981 · John McConnell, Pentagram · UK · Logo · Faber & Faber

1985 · Peter Harrison, Kaspar Schmid, Pentagram · UK · Logo · Science Management Corporation

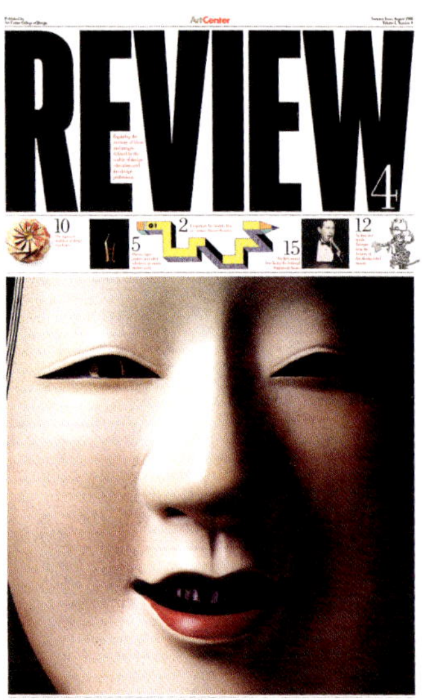

1988 · Kit Hinrichs, Pentagram · US · Magazine cover

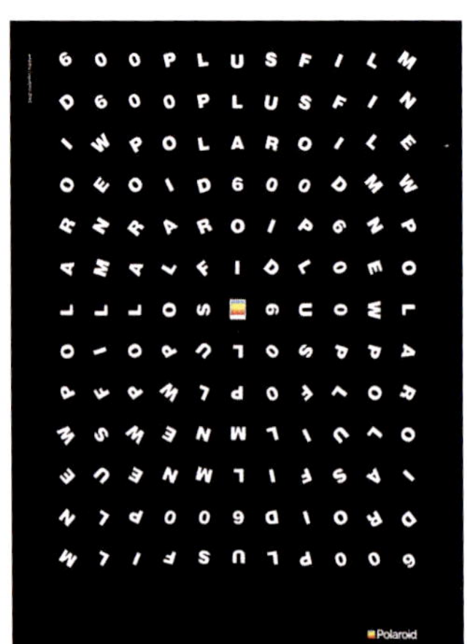

1988 · Mervyn Kurlansky, Patrick O'Sullivan, Pentagram · UK · Poster

ABB

1987 · Alan Fletcher, Pentagram · UK · Logo · Asea Brown Boveri

»Pentagram reflects the contemporary need for co-ordinated design teams able to meet the challenge and opportunities of very large-scale exercises with diverse design abilities and sophistication in the services which they provide.«

Herbert Spencer, *Graphis* #158, 1972

Pentagram (1972, London) is a full-service design firm begun by Alan Fletcher (1931, Nairobi – 2006, London), Theo Crosby (1925, Mafeking, South Africa – 1994, London), Colin Forbes (1928, London), Mervyn Kurlansky (1936, Johannesburg), and Kenneth Grange (1929, London). They established a unique form of partnership and interdisciplinary work and the company has since managed to remain independent with more than 40 partners throughout its history. Pentagram's copious work has produced hundreds of identities for many of the world's most famous brands, campaigns, and exhibitions, as well as countless books, magazines, and packaging designs, as a result of their many long-term client relationships.

Pentagram (1972, London) ist ein Fullservice-Designbüro der Gründer Alan Fletcher (1931, Nairobi – 2006, London), Theo Crosby (1925, Mafeking, Südafrika – 1994, London), Colin Forbes (1928, London), Mervyn Kurlansky (1936, Johannesburg) und Kenneth Grange (1929, London). Sie bildeten eine einzigartige Form der Partnerschaft mit einer interdisziplinären Arbeitsweise. Das Studio ist nach wie vor unabhängig und hatte im Lauf seiner Geschichte bislang über vierzig Partner. Zu den unzähligen Arbeiten des Studios gehören aufgrund der langjährigen Kundenbeziehungen Hunderte Identitäten für viele weltberühmte Marken, Kampagnen und Ausstellungen sowie zahllose Bücher, Zeitschriften und Verpackungsdesigns.

Pentagram (1972, Londres) est un studio de design polyvalent fondé par Alan Fletcher (1931, Nairobi – 2006, Londres), Theo Crosby (1925, Mahikeng, Afrique du Sud – 1994, Londres), Colin Forbes (1928, Londres), Mervyn Kurlansky (1936, Johannesbourg) et Kenneth Grange (1929, Londres). Ensemble, ils élaborèrent un type de partenariat et de travail interdisciplinaire entièrement inédit. Depuis, la firme a su préserver son indépendance avec plus de 40 associés tout au long de son histoire. L'énorme production de Pentagram compte des centaines d'identités, campagnes et expositions pour une foule de marques les plus célèbres au monde, ainsi que d'innombrables livres, magazines et emballages, tous fruits des relations à long terme avec leurs clients.

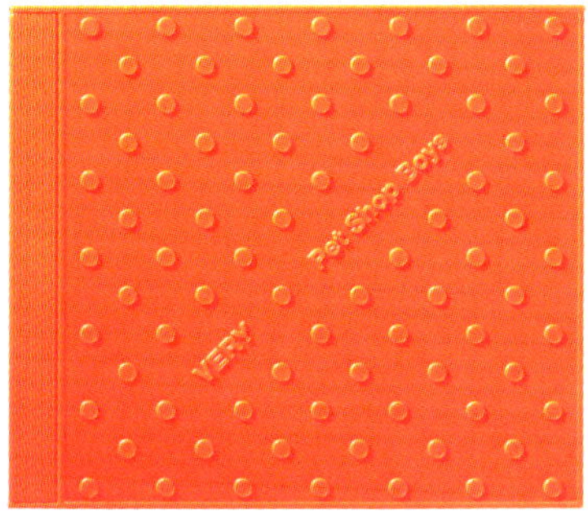

1993 · Daniel Weil, Pentagram · UK · Record cover

2001 · Woody Pirtle, Pentagram · US · Poster

2017 · Natasha Jen, Pentagram · US · Packaging

2018 · Luke Powell, Jody Hudson-Powell, Pentagram · UK · Identity · London Fashion Week

1997 · Justus Oehler, Pentagram · DE/US · Logo · Star Alliance

2004 · John Rushworth, Pentagram · UK · Logo · Mothercare

2016 · Emily Oberman, Pentagram · US · Logo · DC Entertainment

2016 · Michael Bierut, Luke Hayman, Pentagram · US · Logo · Mastercard

When Munich won the bid to host the Summer Olympics of 1972, the organizers were determined to create a program in complete contrast to that of the 1936 Munich games, which were hijacked by the Nazis as a vehicle for their political ends. Otl Aicher, a pacifist and deserter from the Wehrmacht, was chosen in 1967 to design the identity system for this major sporting event. He put together a team with whom he firstly developed a systematic corporate image on which to base all printed matter, merchandise, and uniforms for the games. For all the simplicity of their designs, the overall effect was dynamic as well as easy on the eye, with a visual rigor that set new standards.

Als München den Zuschlag zur Ausrichtung der Olympischen Sommerspiele 1972 erhielt, wollten die Organisatoren ein Gegenprogramm zu den von den Nationalsozialisten missbrauchten Spielen von 1936 präsentieren. Der Pazifist und Kriegsdeserteur Otl Aicher wurde 1967 ausgewählt, um die visuelle Identität des Sportevents zu entwickeln. Er stellte ein Team zusammen, mit dem er zunächst ein systematisches Erscheinungsbild entwickelte und auf dieser Basis sämtliche Drucksachen, Merchandisingartikel und Uniformen der Spiele ausarbeitete. Bei aller gestalterischen Strenge entstand ein höchst lebendiger und freundlicher Gesamtauftritt, dessen visuelle Stringenz neue Standards setzte.

Lorsque Munich fut retenue pour organiser les jeux Olympiques d'été de 1972, les organisateurs voulurent se démarquer totalement du programme des jeux de 1936, qui avaient été politiquement détournés par les nazis. En 1967, le pacifiste et déserteur de la Wehrmacht Otl Aicher fut chargé de concevoir l'identité visuelle de l'événement. Il constitua une équipe et commença par élaborer une image systématique comme base de travail pour tous les imprimés, articles de merchandising et uniformes des jeux. Malgré la simplicité de la conception visuelle, il en résulta globalement une image extrêmement vivante et chaleureuse dont la cohérence établit de nouveaux standards.

1972 · Coordt von Mannstein (symbol), Otl Aicher · DE · Logo

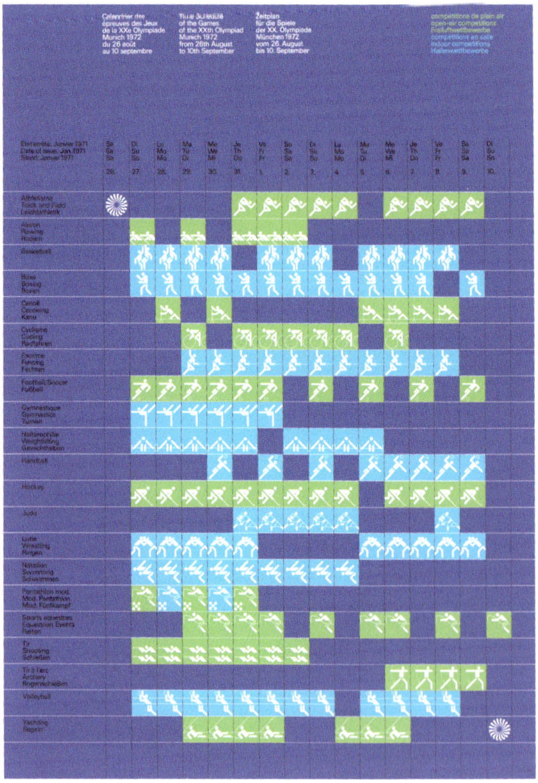

1972 · Otl Aicher · DE · Poster

1972 · Otl Aicher · DE · Identity

1973

Graphis magazine publishes a first feature on computer-generated graphics

1973 · Angelo Sganzerla · IT · Logo · Multhipla

1973 · Peter Seitz · US · Logo · Jefferson Buslines

1973 · Benoy Sarkar · IN · Logo · Indian Airlines

1973 · Les Mason · AU · Magazine cover

1973 · Franco Maria Ricci · IT · Poster

1973 · Antonio Reboiro · CU · Poster

1973 · Anonymous · ES · Poster

1973 · José Santamarina · ES · Poster

1973 · Hipgnosis, George Hardie (ILL) · UK · Record cover

1973 · Morteza Momayez · IR · Poster

1973 · Morteza Momayez · IR · Poster

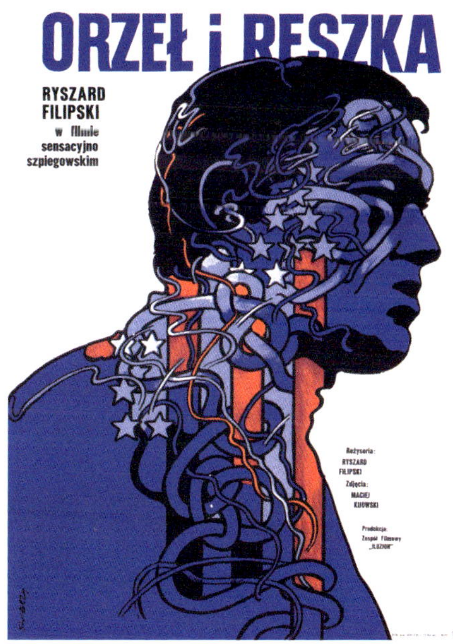

1974 · Waldemar Świerzy · PL · Poster

The first issue of *Ms.* appeared in the summer of 1972, and with the comic-book heroine Wonder Woman gracing the cover it was a clear statement that *Ms.* had nothing in common with traditional women's magazines. This was the first time a publication designed to have popular appeal would focus on feminism and the women's movement, and in support of that aim Bea Feitler developed a uniquely personal style for the magazine's illustrations.

Im Sommer 1972 erschien die Erstausgabe von *Ms.* Das Cover zeigt die Comicheldin Wonder Woman und unterstreicht so, dass das Magazin mit traditionellen Frauenzeitschriften nichts gemein hat. Erstmals beschäftigte sich ein populär aufgemachtes Heft mit Themen der Frauenbewegung und des Feminismus. Bea Feitler entwickelte dafür einen ganz eigenen visuellen Stil.

C'est à l'été 1972 que parut le premier numéro de *Ms.* La couverture montrait l'héroïne de bande dessinée Wonder Woman, soulignant le fait que le magazine n'avait rien à voir avec ceux de la presse féminine traditionnelle. Pour la première fois, une revue à vocation populaire abordait des thèmes du mouvement féministe. Bea Feitler développa pour ces illustrations un style visuel tout à fait personnel qui servait la cause.

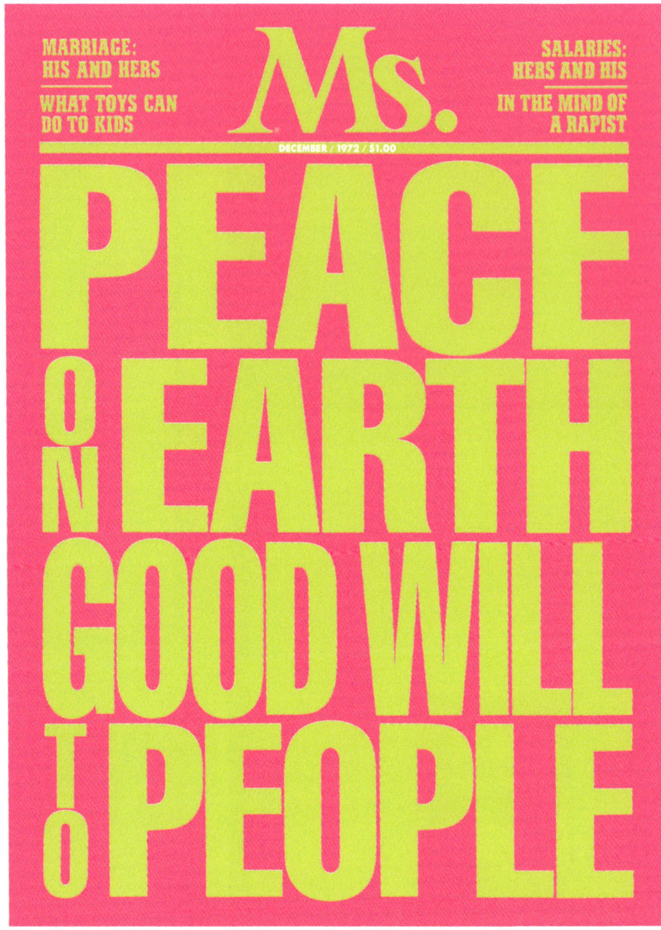

1972 · Bea Feitler · BR/US · Magazine cover

1972 · Bea Feitler · BR/US · Magazine cover

1972 · Bea Feitler · BR/US · Magazine cover

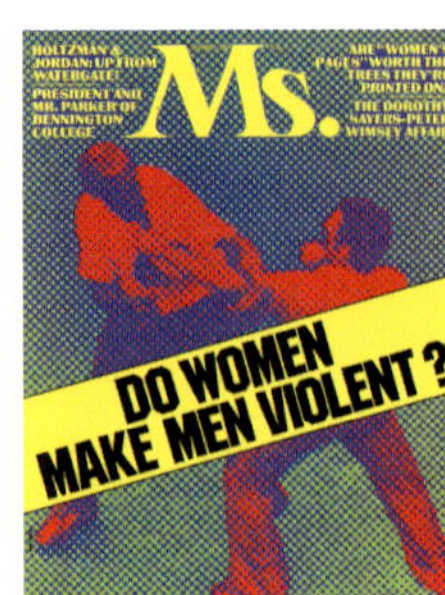

1974 · Bea Feitler · BR/US · Magazine cover

»There's so much visual material in today's world that people can't judge what's good and what's bad. It's up to the graphic designers to set standards.« Bea Feitler, *Idea* #151, 1978

Bea Feitler (1938–1982, Rio de Janeiro) was a visionary Brazilian art director who greatly pushed the boundaries of editorial design. Feitler studied at Parsons School of Design, where her use of photography and her experimental approach soon made her name on the New York design scene, securing commissions for books, record sleeves, and fashion brands. Her extensive work on magazines, notably for *Harper's Bazaar* and *Rolling Stone*, sealed her reputation. In 1982, Feitler redesigned the new *Vanity Fair*, though died of cancer before it was published at the age of only 44.

Bea Feitler (1938–1982, Rio de Janeiro) war eine visionäre brasilianische Artdirectorin, die die Grenzen des Zeitschriftendesigns radikal erweiterte. Feitler studierte an der Parsons School of Design in New York, wo sie sich mit ihrer Verwendung von Fotografie und ihrem experimentellen Ansatz schon bald einen Namen in der dortigen Designszene machte, was ihr Aufträge für Bücher, Plattencover und Modemarken einbrachte. Ihr umfangreiches Schaffen im Zeitschriftensektor, namentlich für *Harper's Bazaar* und *Rolling Stone*, trug zur Festigung ihres Rufs bei. 1982 gestaltete Feitler das neue Erscheinungsbild von *Vanity Fair*, starb aber schon vor der Veröffentlichung mit nur 44 Jahren an Krebs.

Bea Feitler (1938–1982, Rio de Janeiro) fut une directrice artistique brésilienne visionnaire qui repoussa fortement les limites du graphisme éditorial. Feitler suivit des études à la Parsons School of Design, où son utilisation de la photographie et son approche expérimentale lui permirent de se faire un nom sur la scène du design new-yorkais. S'ensuivirent des commandes pour des livres, des pochettes d'albums et des marques de mode. Son travail de grande envergure pour des magazines, particulièrement pour *Harper's Bazaar* et *Rolling Stone*, assurèrent sa réputation. En 1982, Feitler redessina le nouveau *Vanity Fair*, mais succomba à un cancer avant sa publication, à l'âge de seulement 44 ans.

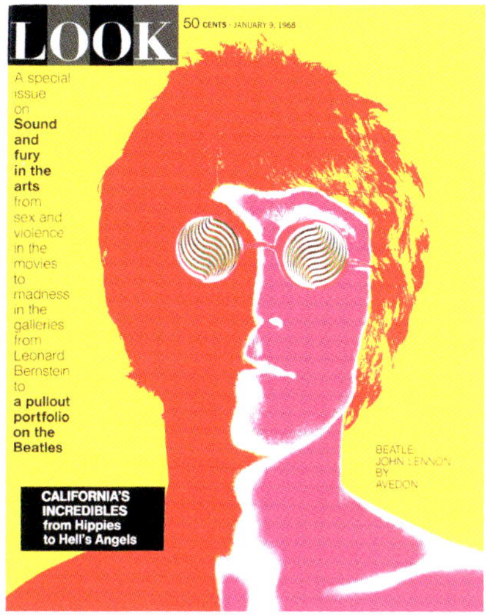

1968 · Bea Feitler, Richard Avedon (PH) · BR/US · Magazine cover

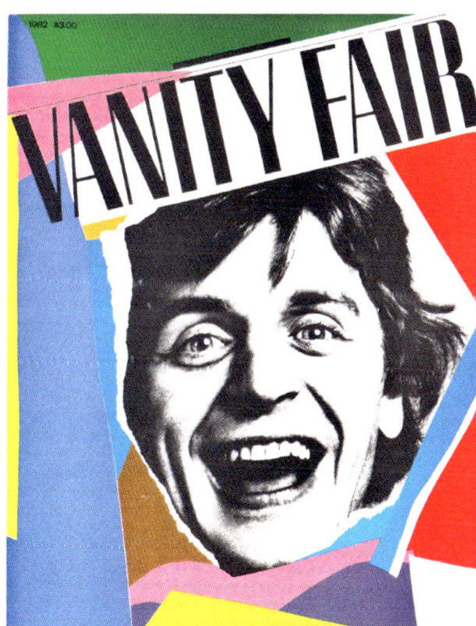

1982 · Bea Feitler · BR/US · Magazine cover

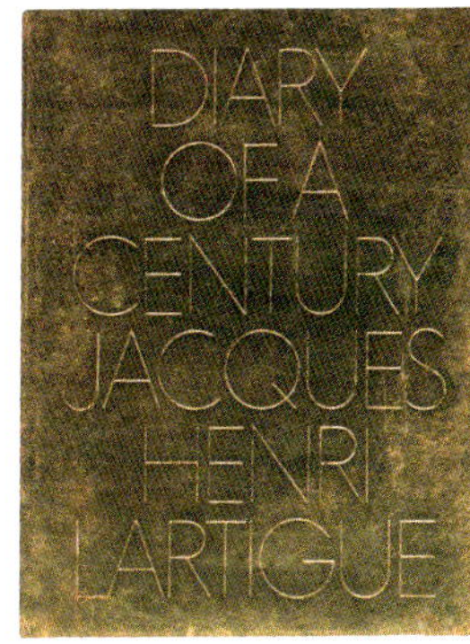

1970 · Bea Feitler · BR/US · Book cover

1976 · Bea Feitler, Helmut Newton (PH) · BR/US · Book cover

1980 · Bea Feitler · BR/US · Book cover

1974

John Murphy and his wife open the branding consultancy Novamark, which evolves to become **Interbrand** in 1979

The first issue of the typography magazine **Upper and Lower Case** is published

1974 · Danne & Blackburn · US · Logo · NASA

1974 · Otl Aicher · DE · Logo · Erco

1974 · Anton Stankowski · DE · Logo · Deutsche Bank

1974 · Italo Lupi, Liliana Collavo · IT · Magazine cover

1974 · Helmut Schmidt-Rhen · DE · Poster

1974 · Peter Geitner · DE · Record cover

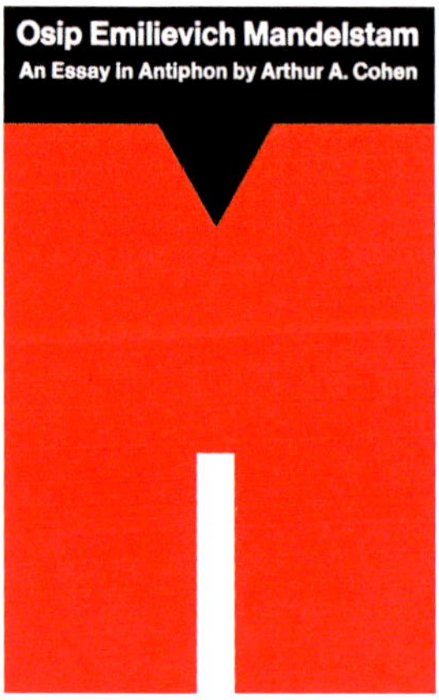

1974 · Elaine Lustig · US · Book cover

1974 · Mihajlo Arsovski · HR · Poster

1974 · David Hillman, Harri Peccinotti (PH) · UK · Magazine cover

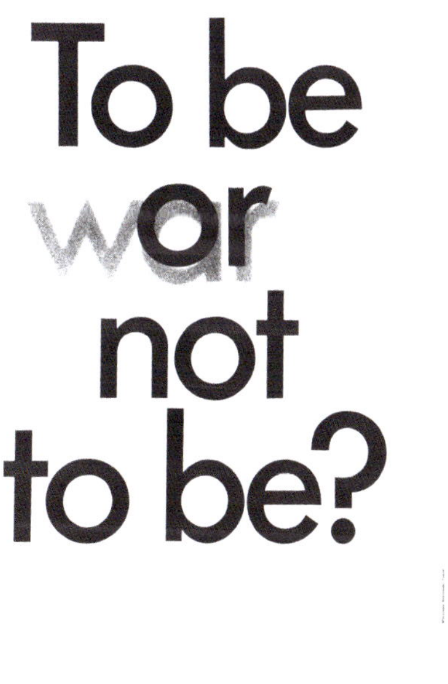

1974 · Mieczysław Wasilewski · PL · Poster

1974 · Burton Kramer · CA · Identity · Canadian Broadcasting Corporation

1975

1975 · Bruno K. Wiese · DE · Logo · German Aerospace Center

1975 · Anne Lund · DK · Logo · The Smiling Sun

1975 · Hans Donner · DE/BR · Logo · Rede Globo

Austrian designer Othmar Motter creates **Motter Tektura**, a typeface later used in the identities of Apple and Reebok

1975 · Mario Lovergine · IT · Poster

1975 · Marcelino Vespeira · PT · Poster

1975 · George Tscherny · US · Poster

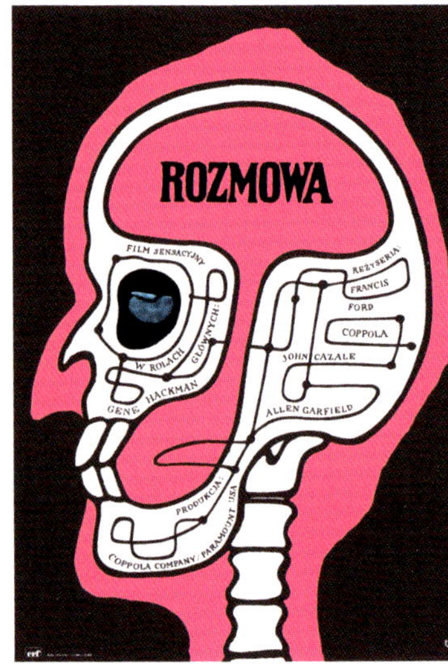

1975 · Jerzy Flisak · PL · Poster

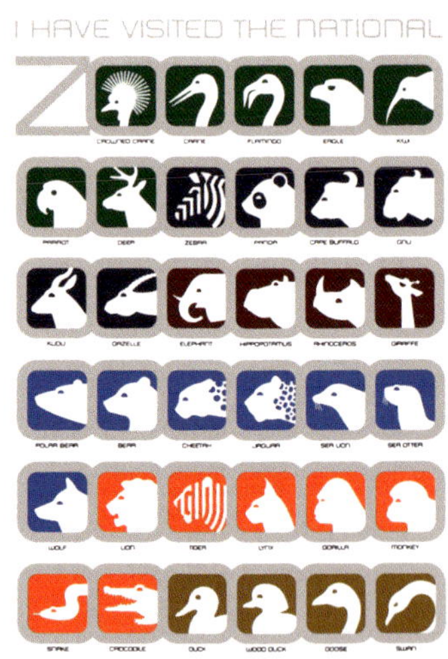

1975 · Lance Wyman · US · Identity · Washington Zoo

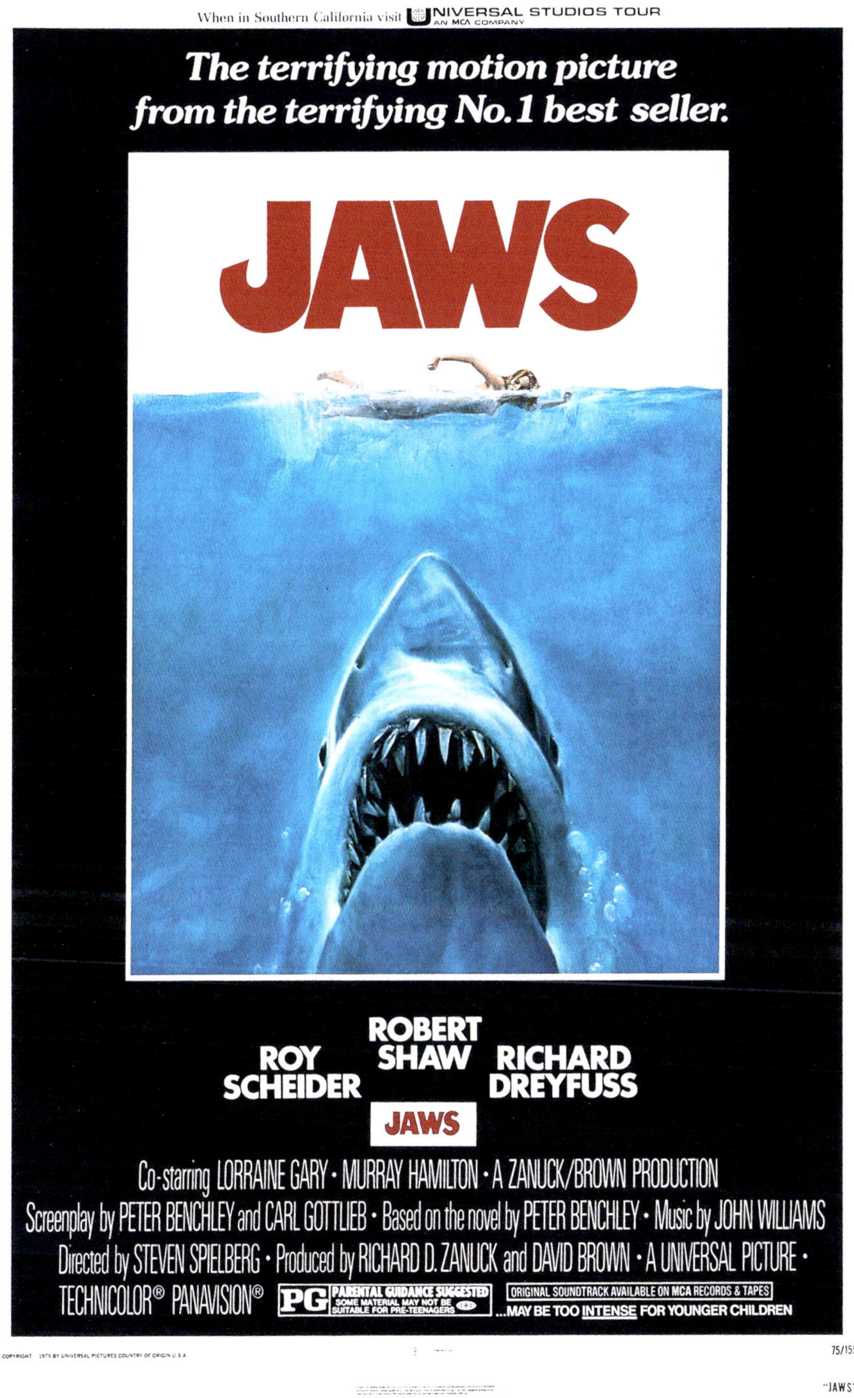

1975 · Roger Kastel · US · Poster

Whilst its main areas of research lie in the humanities, technology, and engineering, MIT had already set up a graphic design program as early as the 1950s. One offshoot of the new degree course in this subject was the establishment of the institute's own design department, which was responsible for university publications and campus announcements. In the 1970s, Jacqueline Casey, Ralph Coburn, and Dietmar Winkler were the team who created MIT's graphic identity, with their fascinating, modernist designs taking inspiration from the Swiss Style. Originally only intended for display around the Boston campus of MIT, the posters and brochures soon found international recognition from experts in the field, who were full of enthusiasm for the graphics produced at the university, which showed a dazzling modernity that is still impressive today.

Bereits in den 1950er-Jahren etablierte das eigentlich auf Geisteswissenschaften, Technik und Maschinenbau spezialisierte MIT ein Grafikdesignprogramm. Ein Ableger des neuen Studiengangs war eine eigene Designabteilung, die für Hochschulpublikationen und Campusankündigungen zuständig war. In den 1970er-Jahren prägten Jacqueline Casey, Ralph Coburn und Dietmar Winkler den grafischen Auftritt des MIT. Inspiriert vom „Swiss Style", realisierten sie faszinierende modernistische Arbeiten. Ursprünglich nur für den Aushang am Bostoner Campus gedacht, fanden die Plakate und Broschüren schnell auch internationale Beachtung in der Fachwelt, die von der bis heute bestechenden Modernität der universitären Grafik begeistert war.

Dès les années 1950, le MIT, spécialisé dans les sciences humaines, la technologie et l'ingénierie, développa un programme de graphisme. Un des aspects de ce nouveau cursus était la création du département de graphisme de l'établissement, chargé des publications de l'école et des annonces du campus. Dans les années 1970, Jacqueline Casey, Ralph Coburn et Dietmar Winkler définirent l'identité visuelle du MIT. Inspirés par le style suisse, ils réalisèrent des travaux modernistes passionnants. Conçues à l'origine pour le seul campus de Boston, leurs affiches et brochures attirèrent rapidement l'attention des experts en la matière, enthousiasmés par la modernité du graphisme des universitaires, qui a conservé tout son attrait jusqu'à aujourd'hui.

1975 · Jacqueline S. Casey · US · Poster

1973 · Jacqueline S. Casey · US · Poster

»My job is to stop anyone I can with an arresting or puzzling image, and entice the viewer to read the message in small type and above all to attend the exhibition.«

Jacqueline S. Casey, *Women in Design*, 1988

1969 · Dietmar R. Winkler · US · Poster

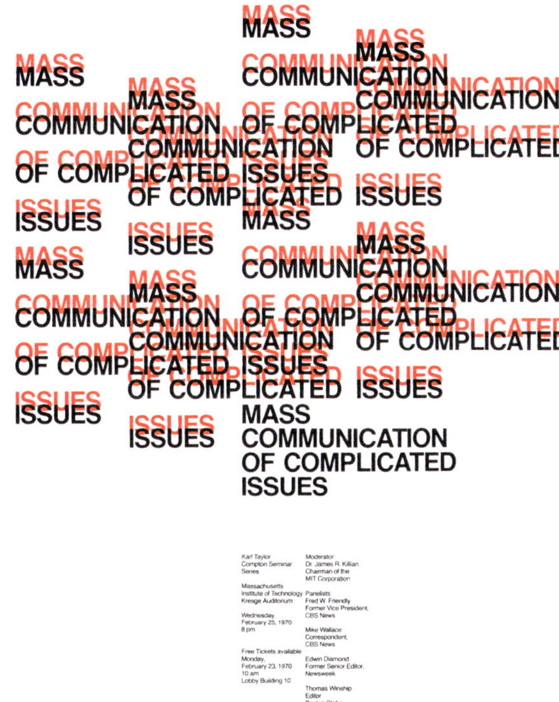

1970 · Dietmar R. Winkler · US · Poster

1973 · Jacqueline S. Casey · US · Poster

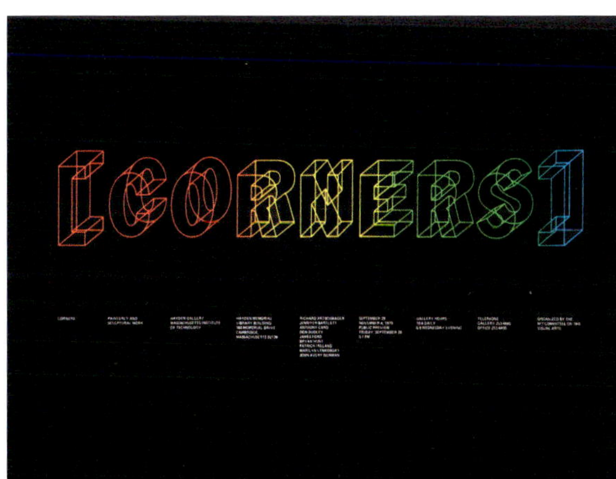

1979 · Jacqueline S. Casey · US · Poster

When similar design solutions appear at the same time it's often hard to say whether this is down to the zeitgeist, or to simple chance, or to the influence of comparable (or contrasting) imagery. One particularly interesting example of this situation is the rainbow symbol, which was used for the first time by Polaroid in the early 1970s, then in the Apple logo created in 1976, and in the LGBT (lesbian, gay, bisexual, and transgender) community's rainbow flag, introduced in 1978.

Es ist schwer zu sagen, ob zur gleichen Zeit entstandene ähnliche Gestaltungslösungen dem Zeitgeist, dem Zufall, gleichen oder gegenseitigen Einflüssen geschuldet sind. Ein besonders interessantes Beispiel sind das Anfang der 1970er-Jahre erstmals verwendete Regenbogenmotiv von Polaroid, das 1976 eingeführte Design von Apple und die 1978 etablierte Regenbogenflagge der LGBT-Community.

Il est difficile de déterminer si la similarité de certaines solutions graphiques apparues à une même époque se doit à l'esprit du temps, au hasard, ou encore à des influences comparables ou opposées. Un exemple particulièrement intéressant en est le motif arc-en-ciel utilisé pour la première fois au début des années 1970 par Polaroid, puis pour le logo d'Apple créé en 1976 et pour le drapeau de la communauté LGBT (lesbiennes, gays, bisexuels et transgenres) établi en 1978.

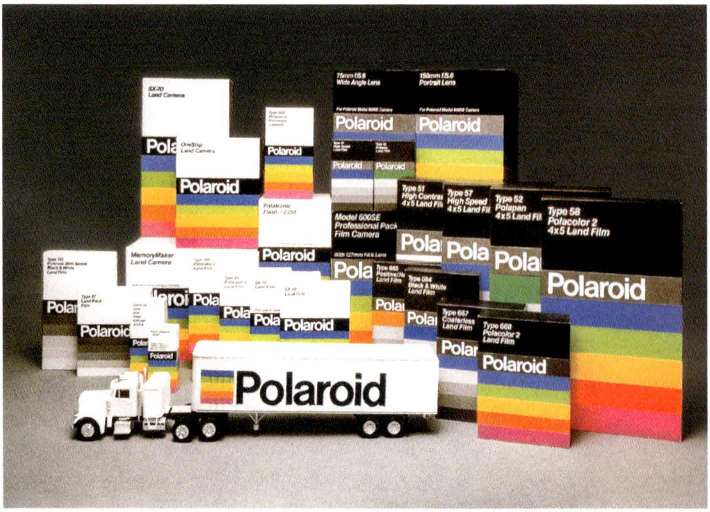

1980 · Roy Alan Hughes (AD) · US · Packaging

apple computer

1976 · Rob Janoff · US · Logo

1977 · Anonymous · US · Ad

1976 · Anonymous · US · Packaging

1978 · Anonymous · US · Flag

1975 · Tapani Aartomaa · FI · Poster

1976

1976 · Milton Glaser · US · Logo · New York City

1976 · Chermayeff & Geismar · US · Identity ·American Revolution Bicentennial

1976 · Piero Gratton · IT · Logo · Rai 2 Television

The **Alliance of German Designers** (AGD) is founded as an association for freelance professionals

1976 · Félix Beltrán · CU · Poster

1976 · Georges Huel, Yvon Laroche, Pierre-Yves Pelletier · CA · Poster

1976 · Anton Zelger · AT · Poster

The **Lebanese Graphic Design Syndicate** (LGDS) is founded

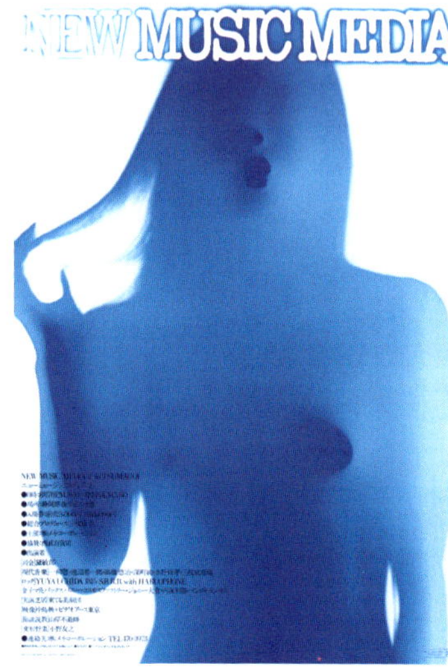

1976 · Shin Matsunaga · JP · Poster

1976 · Milton Glaser · US · Poster

The first commercial **laser printer** is introduced by IBM

1976 · Wim Crouwel · NL · Stamps

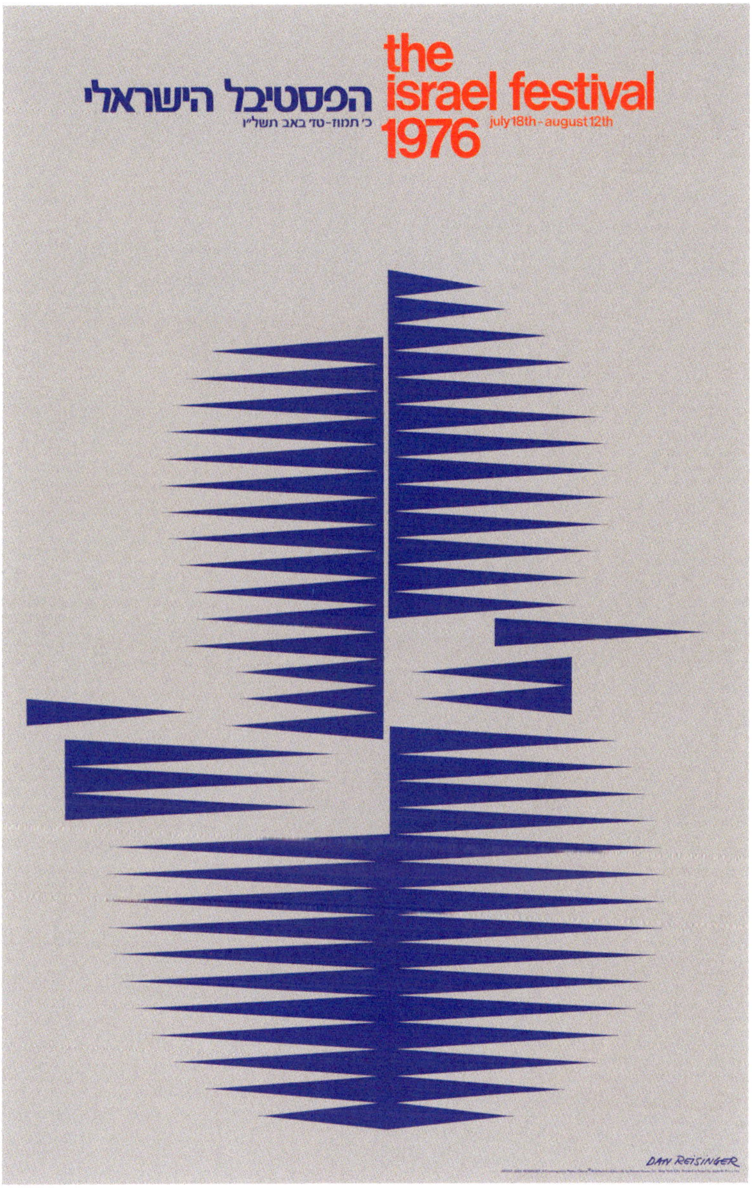

1976 · Dan Reisinger · IL · Poster

Shigeo Fukuda · Japan

Shigeo Fukuda (1932–2009, Tokyo) was a significant Japanese designer and visual artist, known for his use of optical illusions. Employing extreme simplicity in his posters, Fukuda captivated his audience's attention with powerful messages conveyed with graphic wit. He was born into a family of toymakers, and studied fine arts in Tokyo until graduating in 1956; in 1987 he became the first Japanese designer to be inducted into the New York Art Directors Club Hall of Fame. With limited commercial work, Fukuda excelled in designing for social and cultural institutions, including Amnesty International, and also illustrated a column for *Asahi Shimbun* newspaper entitled "Ryu Mita Ka?" (Have You Seen the Dragon?).

Shigeo Fukuda (1932–2009, Tokio) war ein bedeutender japanischer Grafikdesigner und Künstler, der durch die Verwendung optischer Täuschungen bekannt wurde. Dank der äußersten Schlichtheit seiner Plakate, erregte Fukuda die Aufmerksamkeit der Betrachter mit prägnanten, durch grafischen Witz vermittelten Botschaften. Der Sohn einer Familie von Spielzeugherstellern absolvierte ein Kunststudium in Tokio, das er 1956 abschloss; 1987 wurde er als erster japanischer Grafikdesigner in die New Yorker Art Directors Club Hall of Fame aufgenommen. Fukuda, dessen kommerzielle Arbeit eher beschränkt war, brillierte mit Entwürfen für soziale und kulturelle Institutionen – unter anderem für Amnesty International – und illustrierte auch eine Kolumne für die Tageszeitung *Asahi Shimbun* mit dem Titel „Ryu Mita Ka?" (Hast du den Drachen gesehen?).

Shigeo Fukuda (1932–2009, Tokyo) fut un important designer et artiste visuel japonais qui se distingua par son utilisation des illusions d'optique. Appliquant la plus grande simplicité dans ses affiches, Fukuda attirait l'attention du public par des messages puissants doublés d'une grande intelligence graphique. Issu d'une famille de fabricants de jouets, il étudia les beaux-arts à Tokyo et obtint son diplôme en 1956. En 1987, il fut le premier designer japonais accueilli au sein du New York Art Directors Club Hall of Fame. Avec un travail commercial limité, Fukuda excella dans le design pour des institutions sociales et culturelles, notamment pour Amnesty International. Il illustra aussi une colonne du journal *Asahi Shimbun* intitulée «Ryu Mita Ka?» (Avez-vous vu le dragon?).

1976 · Shigeo Fukuda · JP · Poster

1993 · Shigeo Fukuda · JP · Poster

1971 · Shigeo Fukuda · JP · Poster

1981 · Shigeo Fukuda · JP · Poster

1985 · Shigeo Fukuda · JP · Poster

»The poster is intended to be completely clear, to be understood by as many members of the public as possible. Yet it results from its creator's strictly subjective intellectual attitude, it is a visual record of an artist's experience, his knowledge of the world and the rules governing the workings of the human mind.« Shigeo Fukuda, *Projekt* #160, 1985

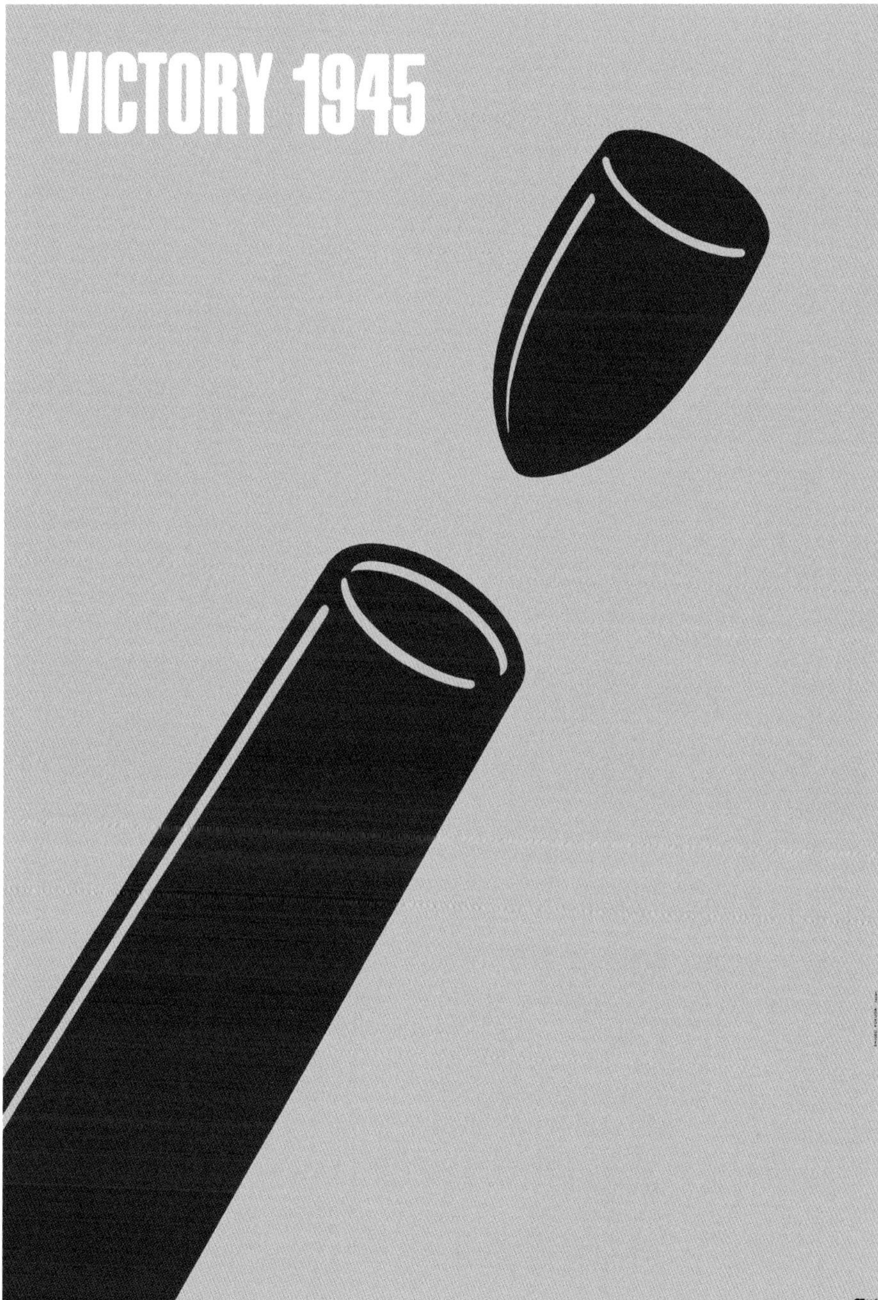

1976 · Shigeo Fukuda · JP · Poster

1977

asics

1977 · Herb Lubalin, PAOS · US/JP · Logo · Asics

Silit

1977 · Anton Stankowski · DE · Logo · Silit

datalink

1977 · Siegfried Odermatt, Odermatt+Tissi · CH · Logo · Datalink

The **R/GA** design studio is established in New York City by brothers Richard and Robert Greenberg

1977 · Vicente Rojo · MX · Magazine cover

1977 · Richard Bird · UK · Poster

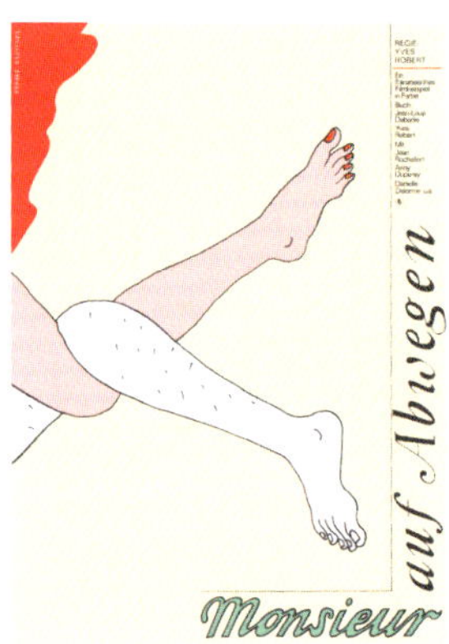

1977 · Erhard Grüttner · GDR · Poster

Studio Dumbar is founded in The Hague by Gert Dumbar

10th maccabiah

1977 · Dan Reisinger · IL · Poster

1977 · Rostislav Vaněk · CZ · Poster

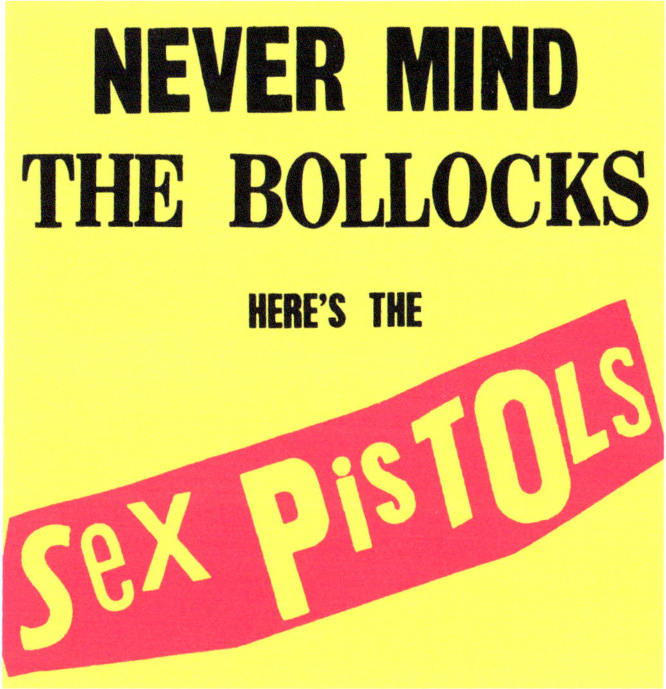

1977 · Jamie Reid · UK · Record cover

1977 · Jamie Reid · UK · Record cover

1977 · R. Tuten, W. Bostedt · US · Poster

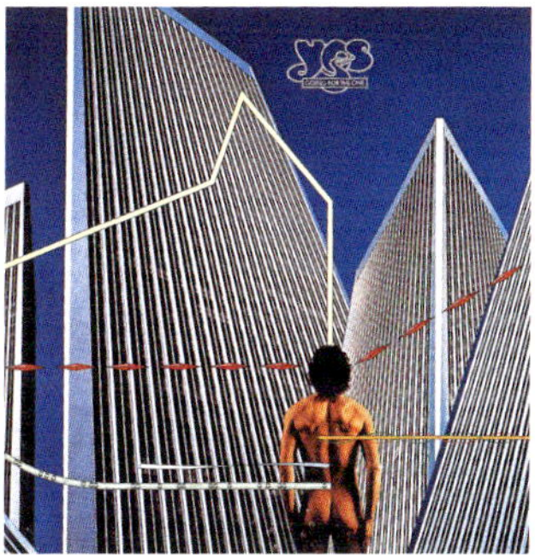

1977 · Hipgnosis · UK · Record cover

1977 · Stan Martin, Tom Nikosey · US · Record cover

In the 1970s there was a short-lived trend for adapting the attention-grabbing effects of neon signs to create similarly eye-catching graphic design. At the time, the music world's emerging craze for disco provided the perfect opportunity for trying out these glitzy, sometimes over-the-top forms of visual imagery.

In den 1970er-Jahren machte sich ein kurzzeitiger Trend breit, bei dem man die plakative Wirkung von Neonschriftzügen für das Printdesign adaptierte. Die gerade bahnbrechende Discowelle in der Popmusik jener Zeit war ein ideales Anwendungsfeld für die schwungvollen und oft übertrieben ausgestalteten Wortbilder.

Au début des années 1970 s'est répandue une tendance éphémère qui adaptait l'effet tape-à-l'œil des enseignes au néon au domaine du design graphique. La vague disco qui déferlait alors dans la sphère musicale de l'époque fut un champ d'application idéal pour ces créations visuelles clinquantes et parfois excessives.

1977 · Diener Hauser Bates Advertising · US · Poster

1972 · John Casado · US · Logo · Joyce Jacobsen

1974 · Michael McMahon · US · Logo · Mike McMahon

1978 · Jean Larcher · FR · Logo · Karen Cheryl

1970s · Rod Dyer · US · Logo · Smokey

1970s · Rod Dyer · US · Logo · Mama Lion

1979 · Anonymous · DE · Record cover

1978 · Jean Larcher · FR · Logo · Contacts

1980 · Jay Vigon · US · Logo · Super Funtastic

1978 · John Georgopoulos · US · Record cover

1978

The **Bell Centennial** typeface by Matthew Carter is released on the occasion of AT&T's 100th anniversary

The **Japan Graphic Designers Association** is established

1978 · Mátyás Gál · HU · Poster

1978 · Anonymous · US · Logo · *Life* magazine

1978 · Henrion & Associates · UK · Logo · Beiersdorf

1978 · Siegel+Gale · US · Logo · 3M

The Turkish design association **Grafik Tasarımcılar Meslek Kuruluşu** is founded

1978 · Burton Kramer · CA · Brochure cover

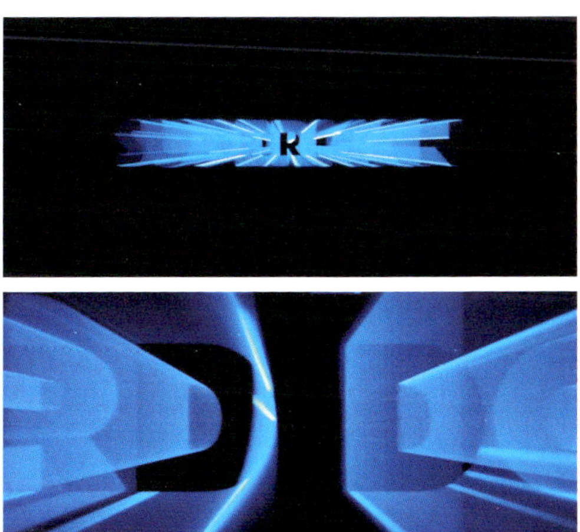

1978 · Richard Greenberg, R/GA · US · Opening titles

1978 · Emil Schult · DE · Record cover

1978 · Hipgnosis · UK · Record cover

1978 · Fred Jordan · BR · Poster

1979

MetaDesign is founded in West Berlin by Gerhard Doerrié, Florian Fischer, Dieter Heil, and Erik Spiekermann

The first issue of the typography magazine **Baseline** is published as a corporate publication of Letraset

1979 · George Tscherny · US · Logo · Fidelity Group of Funds

1979 · Jill Mumford · UK · Record cover

1979 · Tomás Vellvé · ES · Logo · Instituto Nacional de Industria Barcelona

1979 · Rolf Müller · DE · Logo · IHK (Industrie- und Handelskammer)

1979 · Mirko Ilić · BA · Record cover

Tibor Kalman, Carol Bokuniewicz, and Liz Trovato start the design firm **M & Co.** in New York City

Steven Heller's first book on graphic design is published, **Artists' Christmas Cards**

1979 · April Greiman, Jayme Odgers · US · Magazine cover

1979 · Frank Devino · US · Magazine cover

1979 · Mike Wade · UK · Record cover

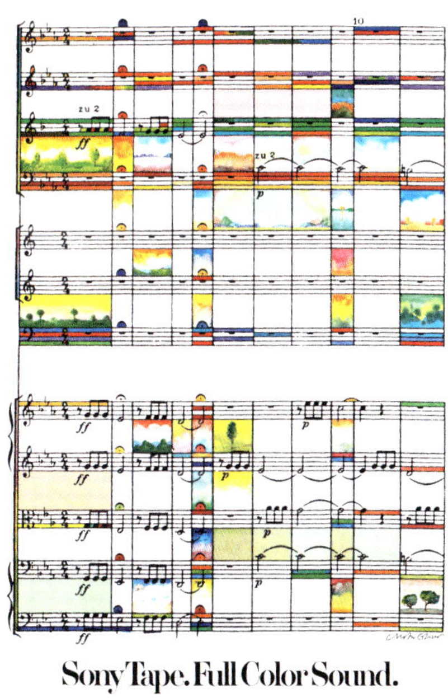

1979 · Milton Glaser · US · Poster

1989 · Anton Furst · UK/US · Poster

1985 · Rolf Müller · DE · Magazine cover

1980

1987 · Anonymous · UK · Magazine cover

1986 · Shigeo Fukuda · JP · Poster

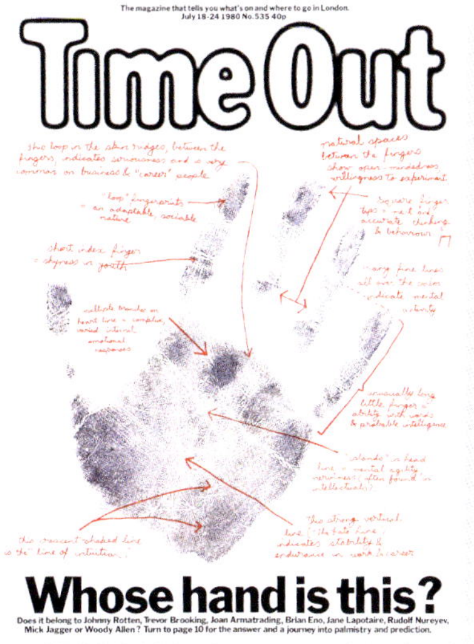

1980 · Pearce Marchbank · UK · Magazine cover

1989

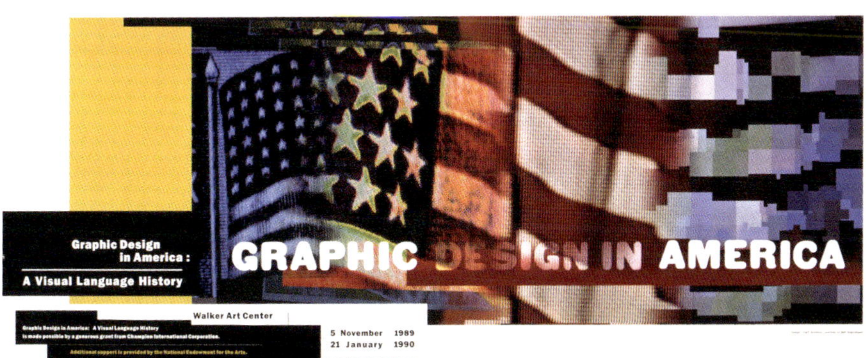

1989 · April Greiman · US · Poster

The new generation of young designers who appeared in the 1980s found that the modernist developments of the post-war decades now seemed largely antiquated. In their search for fresh approaches to design, they rebelled in a variety of ways against the basic notion that graphics must be spare and sober. Technological innovation, including the rapid rise of desktop publishing, came at just the right moment, and in 1984 Apple Macintosh brought out the first graphics-oriented computer. PageMaker, which appeared a year later, was the first software to enable people to design and set up whole magazines and books in digital form. Programs for processing graphics and photos followed and immediately changed the entire face of the creative industry. Although it initially seemed that only the tools of the trade had disappeared, this first digital revolution found expression in an array of new works, many of them characterized by the sheer joy of trying out fresh possibilities.

In den 1980er-Jahren trat eine junge Generation von Gestalterinnen und Gestaltern in Erscheinung, denen die modernistische Entwicklung der Nachkriegsjahrzehnte als veraltet erschien. Auf der Suche nach neuen Ansätzen im Grafikdesign rebellierten sie auf unterschiedliche Art und Weise gegen die Maxime der aufgeräumten und sachlichen Grafik. Die technischen Innovationen, die das aufkommende Desktop-Publishing mit sich brachte, kamen da gerade zur rechten Zeit. 1984 wurde der Apple Macintosh als erster grafikorientierter Computer auf den Markt gebracht. Ein Jahr später erschien mit PageMaker eine Softwarelösung, die es erstmals ermöglichte, komplette Magazine und Bücher in digitaler Form zu realisieren. Programme zur Grafik- und Fotobearbeitung folgten und veränderten innerhalb kürzester Zeit die gesamte Kreativbranche. Auch wenn scheinbar nur das Handwerkszeug verändert wurde, schlug sich diese erste digitale Revolution auch in den realisierten Arbeiten nieder, die in vielen Fällen von der Experimentierfreude mit den neuen Möglichkeiten geprägt waren.

La nouvelle génération de jeunes graphistes qui émerge dans les années 1980 juge désuète l'évolution moderniste des décennies d'après-guerre. À la recherche de nouvelles approches, ils se rebellent de différentes manières contre la maxime d'un graphisme sobre et épuré. Dans ce contexte, des innovations technologiques comme le développement de la PAO arrivent à point nommé. Avec son Macintosh, Apple met sur le marché en 1984 le premier ordinateur à interface graphique. Un an plus tard, PageMaker devient le premier logiciel permettant de composer des magazines ou des livres complets sous forme numérique. Des programmes de traitement graphique et de retouche photo suivent et transforment l'ensemble du secteur créatif en un temps record. Même si seuls les outils de travail semblent avoir changé, cette révolution numérique se traduit aussi dans les réalisations, qui dénotent souvent le plaisir de l'expérimentation offert par les nouvelles technologies.

M & Co., founded by Tibor Kalman and based in New York, was regarded as one of the most innovative design studios of its time.

Blick in das New Yorker Designbüro M & Co. von Tibor Kalman, das als eines der innovativsten Büros seiner Zeit gilt.

Vue de l'agence de graphisme new-yorkaise M & Co. fondée par Tibor Kalman et considérée comme une des plus innovantes de son époque.

1980

The first issue of the British graphic design magazine **Creative Review** is published

The **Union des Designers en Belgique** (UDB) is founded, for graphic designers based in Belgium

1980 · Karl Gerstner · CH · Logo · Ringier

1980 · Stefan Kanchev · BG · Logo · Technica Books

1980 · Shawn Stüssy · US · Logo · Stüssy

1980 · Walter Bernard (AD), Brad Holland (ILL) · US · Magazine cover

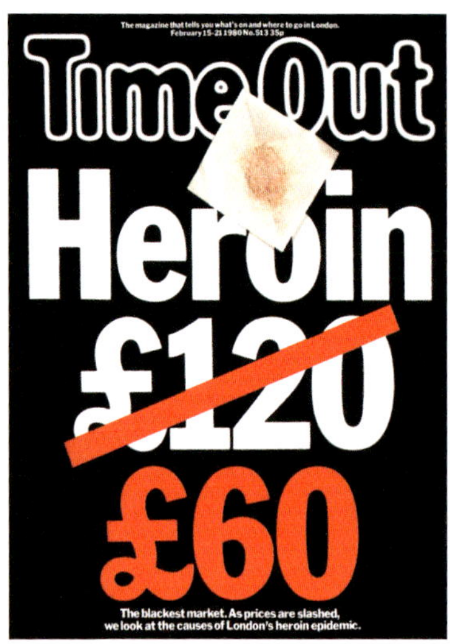

1980 · Pearce Marchbank · UK · Magazine cover

1980 · Anonymous · YU · Magazine cover

1980 · Christine Jones, Edward Bell · UK · Magazine cover

1980 · Fuki Ito · JP · Poster

1980 · Takenobu Igarashi · JP · Poster

1980 · Helmut Schmid · DE/JP · Packaging

1980 · Jan Solpera · CZ · Poster

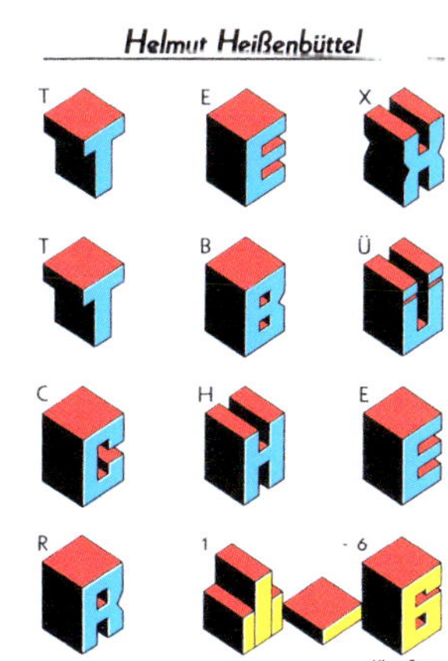

1980 · Heinz Edelmann · DE · Book cover

1980 · Anonymous · RU · Poster

1981 · Wolfgang Weingart · CH · Poster

1981 · Wolfgang Weingart · CH · Poster

1981 · Wolfgang Weingart · CH · Poster

1984 · Wolfgang Weingart · CH · Poster

Wolfgang Weingart (1941–2021, Constance, Germany) was a designer and typographer whose expressive work evolved out of the earlier Swiss Style. Following studies at the Merz Academy in Stuttgart, he trained as a typographer, then studied at the Basel School of Design under Emil Ruder and Armin Hofmann. With an insatiable appetite for experimentation, Weingart instigated a wholesale renewal of typography through his posters and radical cover designs for the *Typographische Monatsblätter* magazine, while teaching at the Basel School of Design. His courses at Yale and lectures around the world have earned him an international reputation. In 2014, the Museum of Design in Zurich presented a retrospective of Weingart's work.

Wolfgang Weingart (1941–2021, Konstanz) war ein Grafikdesigner und Typograf, dessen ausdrucksstarkes Werk aus dem früheren „Swiss Style" hervorgeht. Auf sein Studium an der Merz-Akademie in Stuttgart folgte zunächst eine Lehre als Schriftsetzer, dann studierte er in Basel an der Schule für Gestaltung bei Emil Ruder und Armin Hofmann. Mit leidenschaftlicher Experimentierfreudigkeit führte Weingart eine Rundumerneuerung der Typografie herbei, wie seine Plakate und die radikalen Entwürfe für die Titelseite der Zeitschrift *Typographische Monatsblätter* verdeutlichen. Gleichzeitig unterrichtete er an der Schule für Gestaltung in Basel. Durch seine Seminare in Yale und seine Vorträge in aller Welt ist er international anerkannt. 2014 richtete das Museum für Gestaltung Zürich eine Retrospektive seines Schaffens aus.

Wolfgang Weingart (1941–2021, Constance, Allemagne) était un designer et typographe dont le style expressif s'est développé à partir du style suisse. Après des études à la Merz Akademie à Stuttgart, il suit une formation de typographe, puis étudie à l'école de design de Bâle auprès d'Emil Ruder et d'Armin Hofmann. Habité par un appétit insatiable pour l'expérimentation, Weingart a motivé un renouveau global de la typographie avec ses affiches et ses couvertures radicales pour la revue *Typographische Monatsblätter*, tout en enseignant à l'école de design de Bâle. Ses cours à l'université Yale et les conférences qu'il a données dans le monde entier lui ont valu une notoriété internationale. En 2014, le musée du design de Zurich a présenté une rétrospective du travail de Weingart.

»From 1968 my work became the opposite of 'Swiss Typography'; I was the rebel of the Basel School. In the mid-1970s, many designers copied the Basel approach to create the so-called 'New Wave.' But I never wanted to create a fixed style, so I radically changed the way I worked from that point on.«

Wolfgang Weingart, *AIGA*, 2005

1978 · Wolfgang Weingart · CH · Poster

As a founding member and art director of the legendary independent British label Factory Records, Peter Saville accessed a mass audience through pop music, best exemplified in the series of record sleeves he created for Joy Division and New Order between 1979 and 1993. His radical designs seemed to break all the rules, omitting information about artists or titles and fundamentally questioning modes of consumption and communication.

Als Gründungsmitglied und Artdirector des legendären britischen Independent-Labels Factory Records erreichte Peter Saville durch die Popmusik ein Millionenpublikum. Anschaulichstes Beispiel dafür sind die Plattencover, die er zwischen 1979 und 1993 für Joy Division und New Order gestaltete. Bei seinen radikalen Entwürfen brach er mit sämtlichen Regeln, verzichtete auf Informationen zu Musikern oder Titeln und stellte die Konsum- und Kommunikationskultur grundsätzlich infrage.

En tant que membre fondateur et directeur artistique du légendaire label de musique indépendant britannique Factory Records, Peter Saville a pu toucher un public de masse à travers la musique pop, comme l'illustrent le mieux les pochettes d'albums qu'il a créées entre 1979 et 1993 pour Joy Division et New Order. Ses graphismes absolus semblaient rompre avec toutes les règles établies, omettant une partie de l'information sur les artistes ou les titres, et questionnant fondamentalement les modes de consommation et de communication.

1983 · Peter Saville · UK · Record cover (front)

1983 · Peter Saville · UK · Record cover (back)

»Saville's greatest strength, by his own admission, has always been his sensitivity to cultural currents, and his perspective on visual culture is deeply respected.« Adam Wray, *ssense.com*, 2018

Peter Saville (1955, Manchester) is a British artist and designer whose contribution to culture has been unique. After graduating from Manchester Polytechnic in 1978 he founded his own studio in London. Saville is recognized for creating pioneering work in the fields of music, fashion, sports, and politics, and his achievements were celebrated in *The Peter Saville Show* at the Design Museum in London in 2003. His first major show in a contemporary art museum was at the Migros Museum in Zurich in 2005 and he continues to exhibit internationally. Saville is a Royal Designer for Industry and won the London Design Medal in 2013.

Peter Saville (1955, Manchester) ist ein britischer Künstler und Grafikdesigner, der einen einzigartigen Beitrag zur Kultur geleistet hat. Nach abgeschlossenem Studium an der Manchester Polytechnic im Jahr 1978 gründete er in London sein eigenes Grafikbüro. Saville gilt als Schöpfer bahnbrechender Arbeiten in den Bereichen Musik, Mode, Sport und Politik, seine Leistungen wurden 2003 mit der *Peter Saville Show* im Design Museum in London gewürdigt. Seine erste große Ausstellung in einem Museum für zeitgenössische Kunst folgte 2005 im Migros Museum in Zürich, seitdem ist er immer wieder weltweit durch Ausstellungen vertreten. Saville ist ein Royal Designer for Industry und wurde 2013 mit der London Design Medal ausgezeichnet.

Peter Saville (1955, Manchester) est un artiste et graphiste britannique qui a apporté à la culture une contribution unique en son genre. Après avoir obtenu son diplôme de la Manchester Polytechnic en 1978, il ouvre son propre studio à Londres. Saville est connu pour son travail pionnier dans les domaines de la musique, de la mode, du sport et de la politique, et ses réalisations ont été célébrées en 2003 dans l'exposition «The Peter Saville Show» présentée au Design Museum de Londres. Sa première grande exposition dans un musée d'art contemporain s'est tenue au Musée Migros à Zurich en 2005, et il continue d'exposer au niveau international. Saville a reçu la distinction de Royal Designer for Industry et a remporté la London Design Medal en 2013.

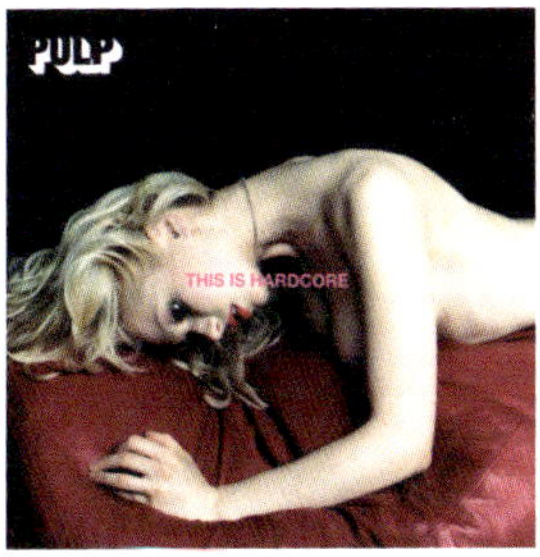

1998 · Peter Saville, John Currin, Horst Diekgerdes (PH) · UK · Record cover

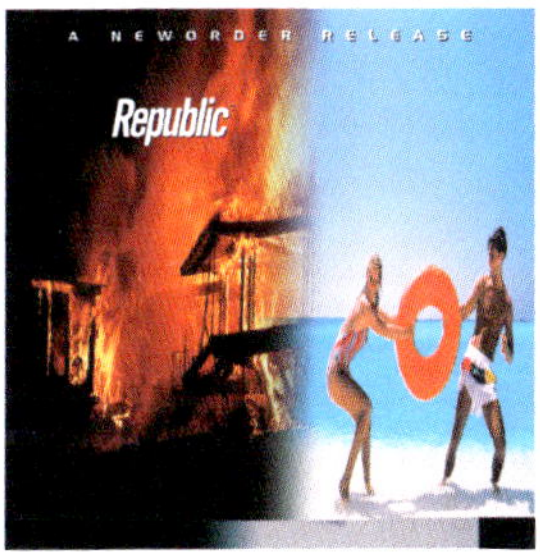

1993 · Peter Saville, Brett Wickens · UK · Record cover

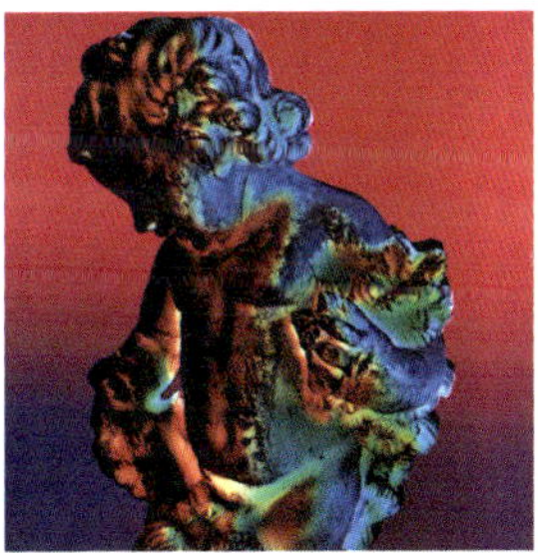

1989 · Peter Saville, Trevor Key · UK · Record cover

2006 · Peter Saville · UK · Sneaker

1979 · Peter Saville · UK · Promotional sticker

1991 · Peter Saville · UK · Ad

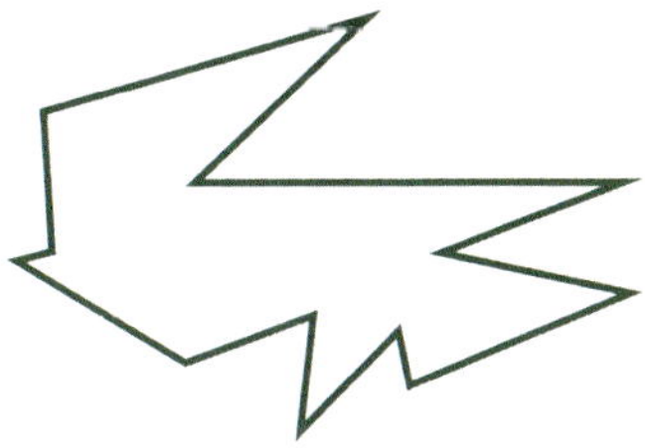

2013 · Peter Saville · UK/FR · Experimental logo · Lacoste

1981

Josef Müller-Brockmann's theoretical work **Rastersysteme für die visuelle Gestaltung** (Grid Systems in Graphic Design) is published

Neville Brody becomes art director of **The Face** magazine

1981 · Fernando Medina · ES · Logo · Ertoil

1981 · Asher Kalderon · IL · Logo · Jewish Youth Games

1981 · Thales Pereira · BR · Logo · BRB Engineering

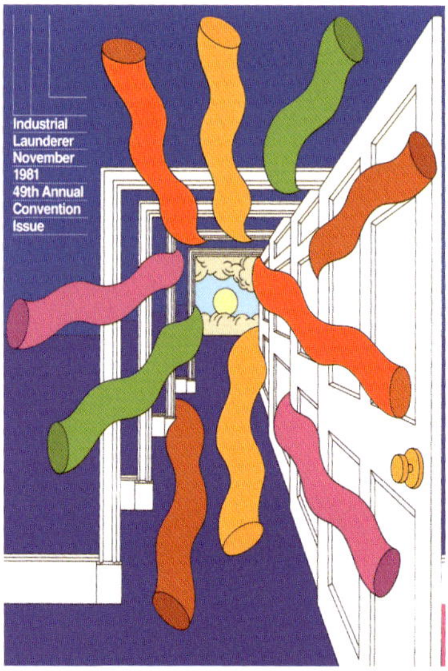

1981 · Jack Lefkowitz · US · Magazine cover

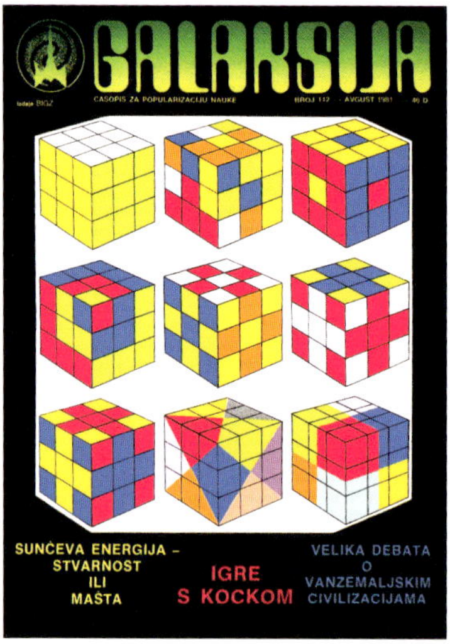

1981 · Anonymous · YU · Magazine cover

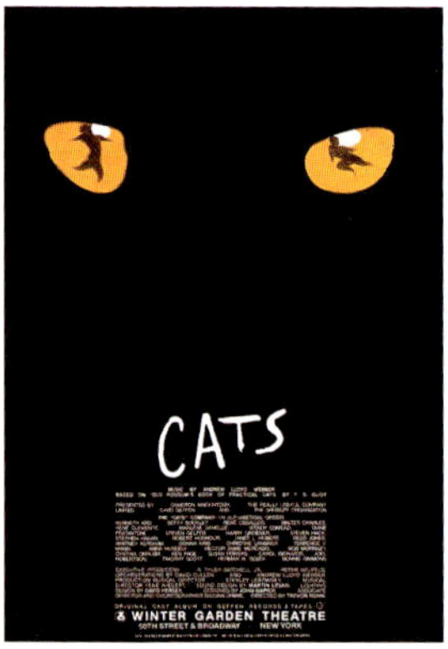

1981 · Anonymous · US · Poster

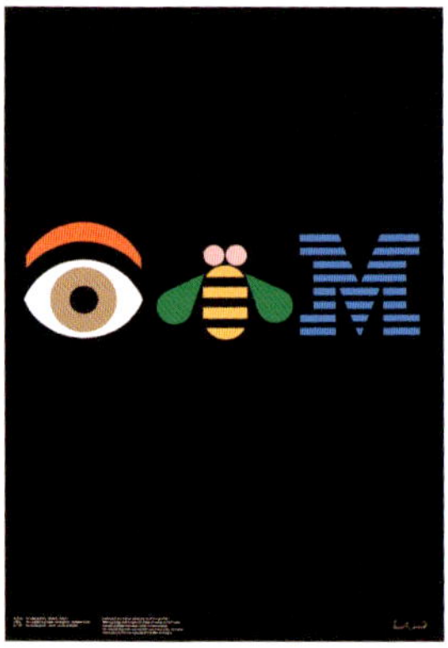

1981 · Paul Rand · US · Poster

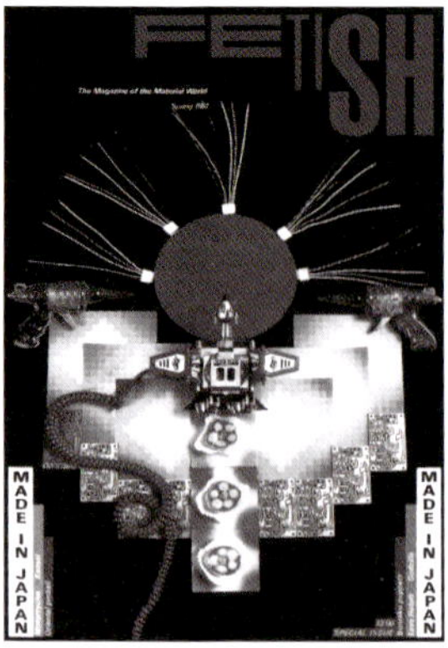

1981 · Jane Kosstrin, David Sterling · US · Magazine cover

1981 · Paula Scher · US · Poster

1981 · Miguel Calatayud · ES · Poster

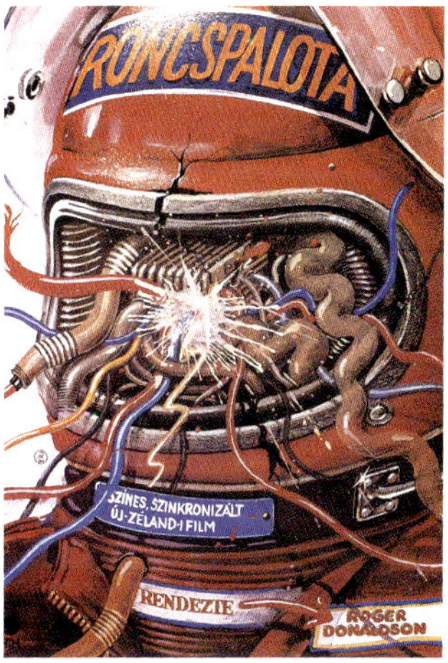

1981 · Eri J. Tamás · HU · Poster

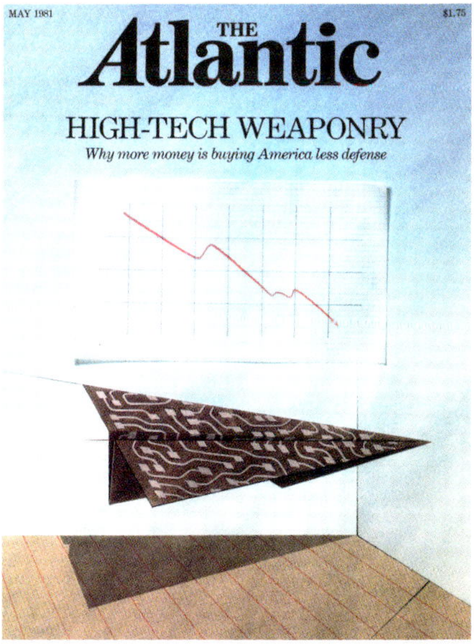

1981 · Walter Bernard (AD), André Thijssen (ILL) · US · Magazine cover

1981 · Lorraine Ferguson · US · Poster

1981 · GGK München · DE · Poster

Although the music channel MTV has lost some of the pulling power it could boast during its heyday in the 1980s, its logo has become a pop-cultural icon. Much of this is down to the introduction, a few years after broadcasting began, of animated versions of the logo, which were aired between music videos. These sequences, often lasting only seconds, turned the 1960s rule of "Don't play with the logo" completely on its head. Many artists, filmmakers, and graphic designers have done the craziest and most bizarre things with the MTV logo, thereby creating a vibrant brand identity which is made even more memorable because it breaks all the rules.

Obwohl der Musiksender MTV nicht mehr die Strahlkraft seiner Hochzeit in den 1980er-Jahren besitzt, ist sein Logo eine Ikone der Popkultur geworden. Maßgeblichen Anteil daran hatte das wenige Jahre nach dem Sendestart entwickelte Konzept animierter Logos, die zwischen jedem Musikvideo gezeigt wurden. In oft nur wenige Sekunden dauernden Sequenzen wurde die in den 1960er-Jahren formulierte Regel „Don't play with the logo" ins Gegenteil verkehrt. Zahlreiche Künstler, Filmemacher und Grafikdesigner stellten die verrücktesten und absurdesten Dinge mit dem MTV-Markenzeichen an und schufen dabei eine höchst lebendige Identität, die gerade durch ihre Nonkonformität einprägsam wurde.

Même si la chaîne musicale MTV a perdu de l'aura qui était la sienne à son apogée dans les années 1980, son logo est resté une icône de la culture populaire. L'introduction quelques années après les débuts de la chaîne de logos animés apparaissant entre chaque vidéoclip y a largement contribué. Ces séquences souvent limitées à quelques secondes déjouaient la règle «On ne joue pas avec le logo» formulée dans les années 1960. De nombreux artistes, réalisateurs et graphistes créèrent alors les choses les plus folles et absurdes à partir du logo MTV, donnant ainsi lieu à une identité des plus dynamiques qui frappa les esprits précisément par son anticonformisme.

MTV MUSIC TELEVISION®

1981 · Pat Gorman, Frank Olinsky, Patti Rogoff, Manhattan Design · US · Logo

»Probably the most revolutionary part of the story came when they were asked to come up with the 'corporate colors' for the logo. The decision was made that there weren't any, and that the logo should always change.« Frank Olinsky, 2008

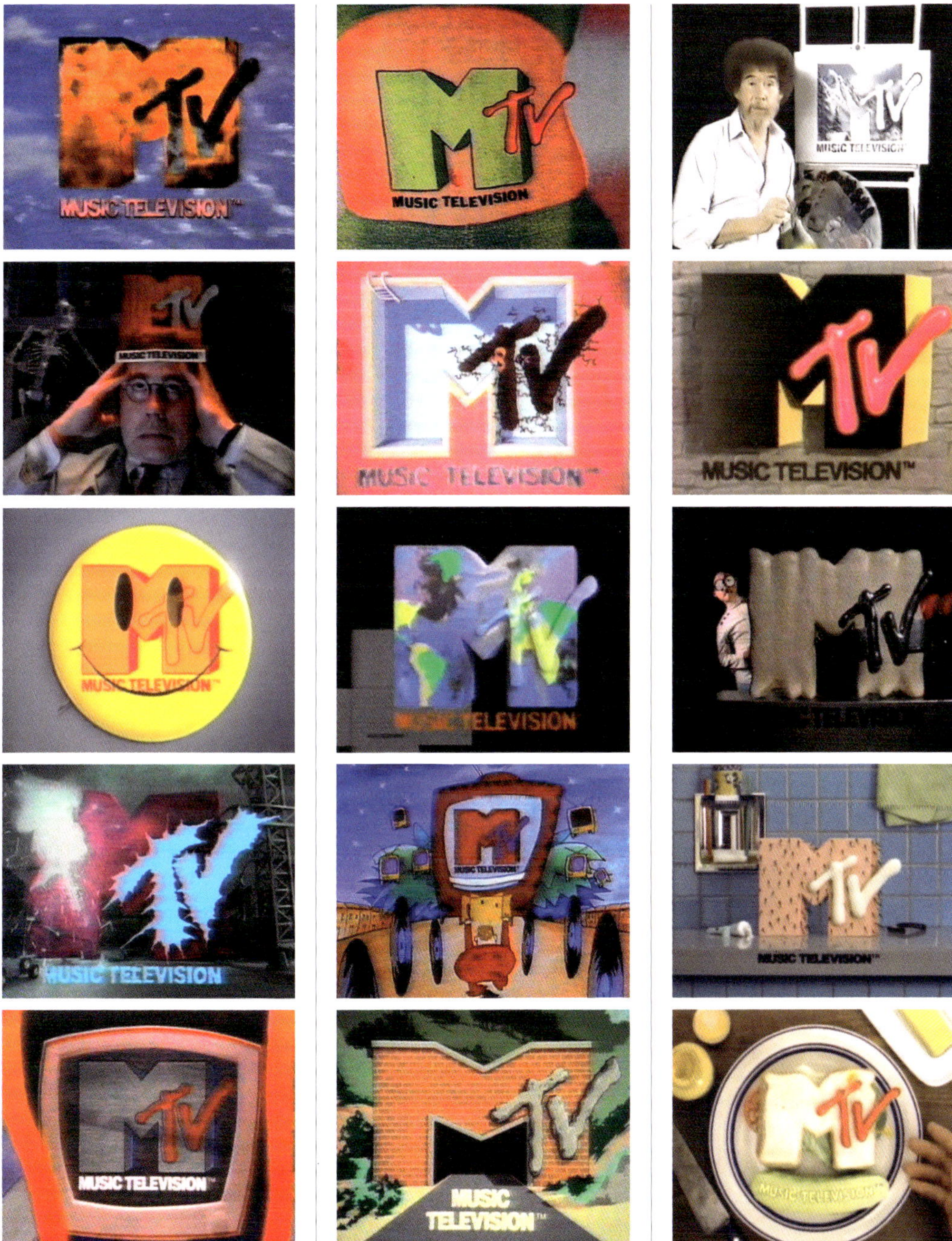

1980s · Various · US · Television graphics

1982

The **Adobe Corporation** is founded by John Warnock and Charles Geschke

The **Arial** typeface is designed by Robin Nicholas and Patricia Saunders for Monotype, for use on low-definition computer displays

1982 · Terry Moore · UK · Logo · Ericsson

1982 · Félix Beltrán, Teresa Echartea · CU/MX · Tequila Mexicano

1982 · Paul Rand · US · Logo · AIGA

1982 · Anonymous · DE · Record cover

1982 · Oliviero Toscani · IT · Ad

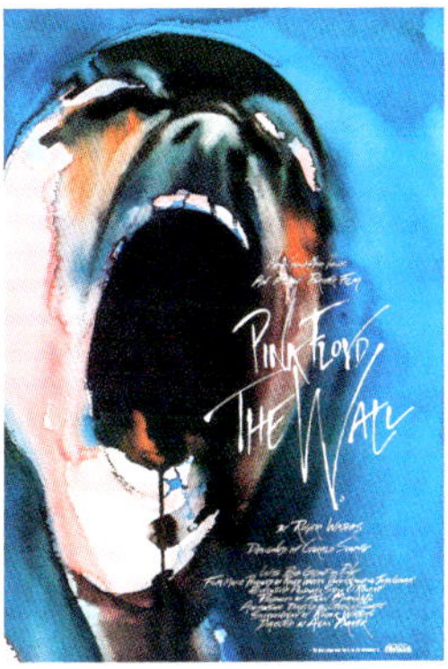

1982 · Gerald Scarfe · UK · Poster

1982 · Nancy Donald, Robert Peak · US · Record cover

1982 · Volker Pfüller · GDR · Poster

1982 · Yarom Vardimon · IL · Poster

1982 · Louise Fili · US · Book cover

1982 · Hugh Ricks · US · Poster

1982 · Anonymous · JP · Ad

1982 · Barney Bubbles · UK · Record cover

1983

Designer **Lars Müller** founds a publishing company in Zurich for books on design, art, and architecture

Philip B. Meggs's book **A History of Graphic Design** is published

1983 · Ernst Roch · CA · Logo · Canadian Pacific

SECURITY

1983 · Peter Adam · CA · Logo · Security Trust

OEA

1983 · Félix Beltrán · CU · Logo · Oea Campaign

1983 · Henry Steiner · HK · Identity · HSBC

Lisa, the first personal computer with a Graphical User Interface (GUI), is introduced by Apple

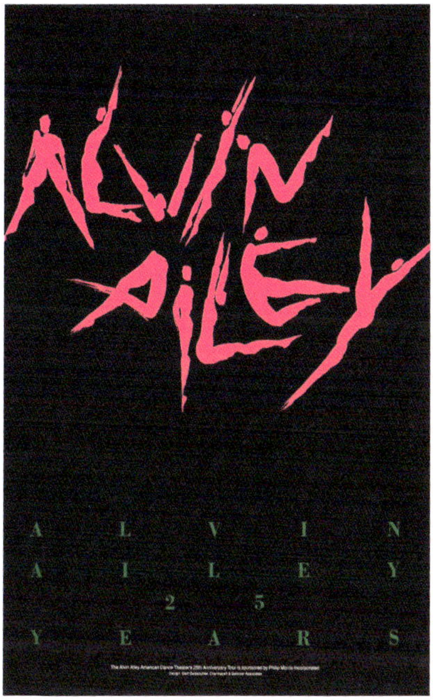

1983 · Steff Geissbuhler, Chermayeff & Geismar · US · Poster

1983 · Martti Mykkänen · FI · Poster

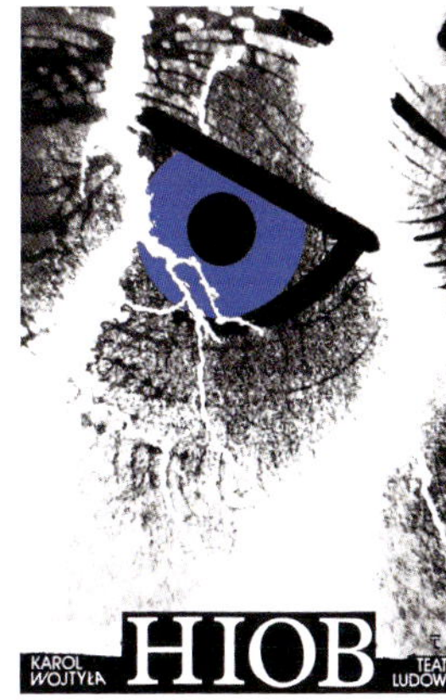

1983 · Władysław Puta · PL · Poster

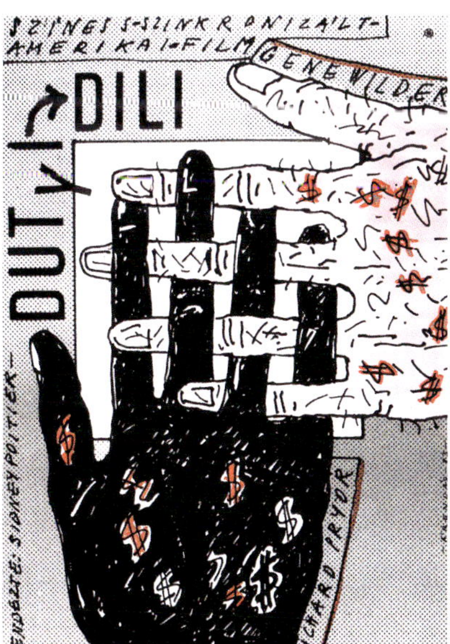

1983 · József Árendás · HU · Poster

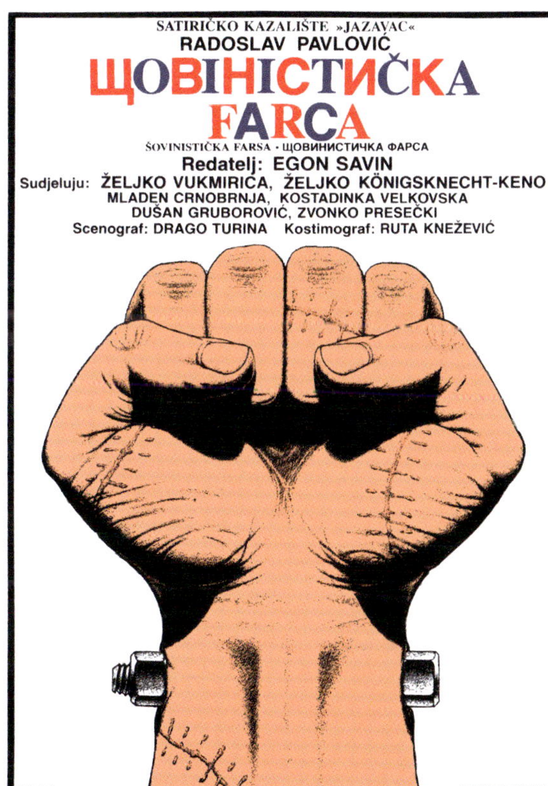

1983 · Mirko Ilić · BA · Poster

1984

Emigre is set up as a type foundry and a magazine by Rudy VanderLans and Zuzana Licko

A **Graphic Design Archive** is established at Rochester Institute of Technology

1984 · Paul Ibou · BE · Logo · Pittors video services

1984 · Mervyn Kurlansky · UK · Logo · Museum of Modern Art, Oxford

1984 · Tony Lunn · AU · Logo · Qantas Airways

1984 · Uwe Loesch · DE · Poster

1984 · Ott+Stein · DE · Poster

1984 · Susan Kare · US · Icons

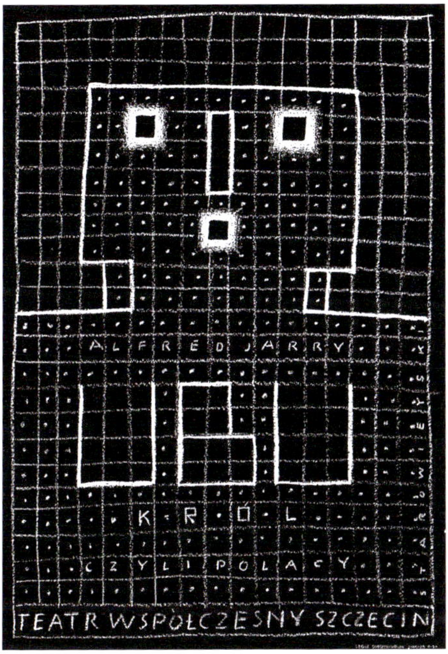

1984 · Franciszek Starowieyski · PL · Poster

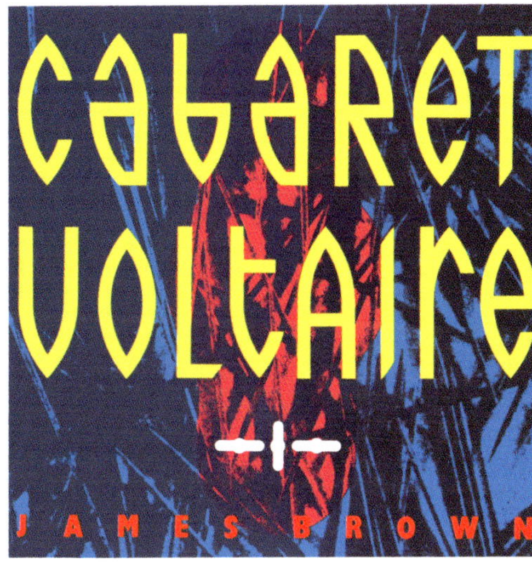

1984 · Neville Brody · UK · Record cover

1984 · Marisa Rizzato · IT · Poster

1984 · Louise Fili · US · Book cover

The Face, founded in London by Nick Logan in 1980, focused on current developments in music, fashion, and similar cultural areas. A year after it was launched, the designer Neville Brody joined the team at the monthly magazine, and it was his innovative layouts that challenged readers and raised the written content to an entirely different level. An unmistakable design vocabulary, coupled with specially designed typefaces, became *The Face*'s unique selling point, while Brody became one of the first magazine designers to venture way beyond the usual range of design elements, creating in the process a periodical with what he referred to as "a core design DNA."

The Face, 1980 von Nick Logan in London gegründet, beschäftigte sich mit aktuellen Entwicklungen in Musik, Mode und Kultur. Ein Jahr nach der Gründung stieß Neville Brody als Gestalter zum Team des monatlich erscheinenden Magazins. Seine neuartigen Layouts stellten die Leser vor Herausforderungen und verlichen den Inhalten eine zusätzliche Ebene. Eine unverkennbare Formensprache in Verbindung mit seiner speziell entwickelten Typografie für die Headlines wurde zum Alleinstellungsmerkmal von *The Face*. Neville Brody war damit einer der ersten Magazingestalter, der, weit über wiederkehrende Gestaltungselemente hinausgehend, einem Heft eine integrale visuelle DNA verlieh.

The Face, fondé à Londres en 1980 par Nick Logan, traitait des nouveautés des mondes de la musique, de la mode et de la culture. Un an après le lancement du mensuel, le graphiste Neville Brody en rejoignait l'équipe. Ses mises en page inédites allaient régulièrement défier les habitudes du lecteur et ajouter un niveau supplémentaire aux contenus. Un langage conceptuel incomparable associé à une typographie spécialement conçue pour les gros titres devinrent l'argument de vente de *The Face*. Neville Brody fut ainsi un des premiers graphistes éditoriaux à conférer à un magazine un ADN visuel qui allait bien au-delà des aspects graphiques habituels.

1985 · Neville Brody, Jamie Morgan (PH) · UK · Magazine cover

»Magazines are 3D items in space and time—there's a connection between page 5 and page 56 and 57, a continuum.« `Neville Brody, 1988`

1984 · Neville Brody · UK · Magazine cover

1983 · Neville Brody · UK · Magazine cover

1984 · Neville Brody · UK · Magazine cover

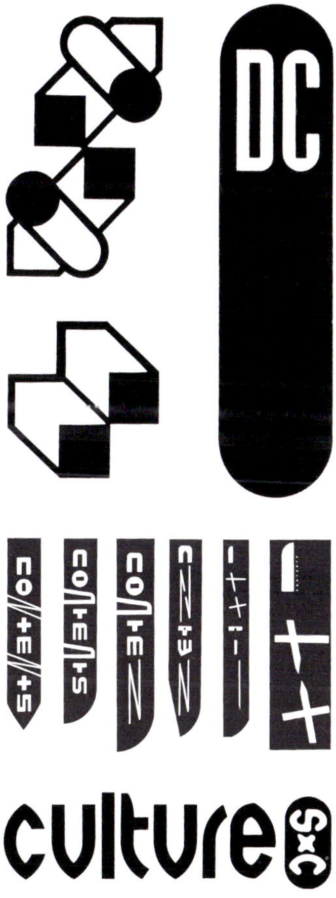

1985 · Neville Brody · UK · Magazine graphics

Neville Brody (1957, London) is a leading British designer and dean of the School of Communication at the Royal College of Art in London. After attending the London College of Printing, Brody gained recognition in the early 1980s art-directing *The Face* magazine and designing record covers for acts such as Depeche Mode. He founded Research Studios in 1994 (rebranded as Brody Associates in 2014), producing groundbreaking work in the areas of editorial, identity, and typography; the *FUSE* project he established with Jon Wozencroft in 1991 became an exploratory ground for new typography. Brody's list of clients has included HSBC, Samsung, and *The Times*.

Neville Brody (1957, London) ist ein führender britischer Grafikdesigner und Dekan der School of Communication am Royal College of Art in London. Nach dem Besuch des London College of Printing wurde er Anfang der 1980er-Jahre als Artdirector der Zeitschrift *The Face* bekannt, aber auch durch seine Plattencover für Bands wie Depeche Mode. 1994 gründete er die Research Studios (2014 zu Brody Associates umfirmiert) und legte bahnbrechende Arbeiten vor, ob im Bereich Editorial Design, CI oder Typografie: Das *FUSE*-Projekt, das er 1991 mit Jon Wozencroft ins Leben rief, wurde zur Versuchsanordnung für neue Typografie. Zu Brodys Auftraggebern zählen unter anderem HSBC, Samsung und *The Times*.

Neville Brody (1957, Londres) est un graphiste britannique chef de file et doyen de l'école de communication du Royal College of Art à Londres. Après des études au London College of Printing, Brody s'est fait connaître au début des années 1980 avec la direction artistique du magazine *The Face* et par les pochettes d'albums qu'il a conçues notamment pour Depeche Mode. En 1994, il fonde Research Studios (rebaptisé Brody Associates en 2014) et produit des travaux révolutionnaires dans les domaines de l'édition, de l'identité et de la typographie. Le projet *FUSE* qu'il a lancé en 1991 avec Jon Wozencroft est devenu une base exploratoire pour une nouvelle typographie. Les clients de Brody incluent notamment HSBC, Samsung et *The Times*.

1985

The **8vo** design studio is set up in London by Simon Johnston, Mark Holt, and Hamish Muir

The **Herb Lubalin Study Center of Design and Typography** is established at Cooper Union school in New York City

1985 · Stipe Brčić, CIO Design · YU · Logo · SRCE

1985 · Tim Girvin · US · Logo · Heat Wave

1985 · Phil Gips, Frankfurt Gips Balkind · US · Logo · ESPN Television

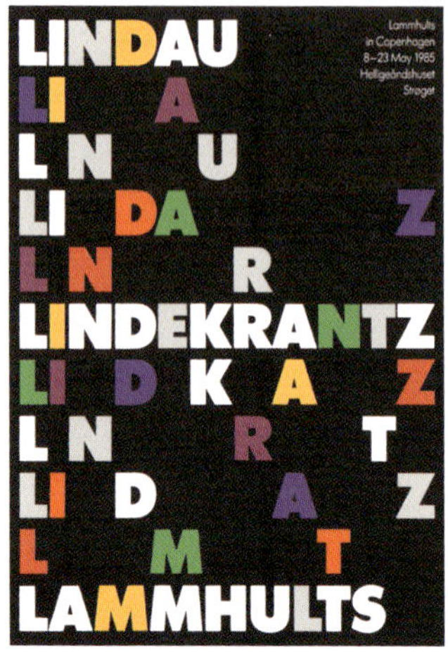

1985 · Hans-Christer Ericson · SE · Poster

1985 · Pierre Mendell · DE · Identity · Videon

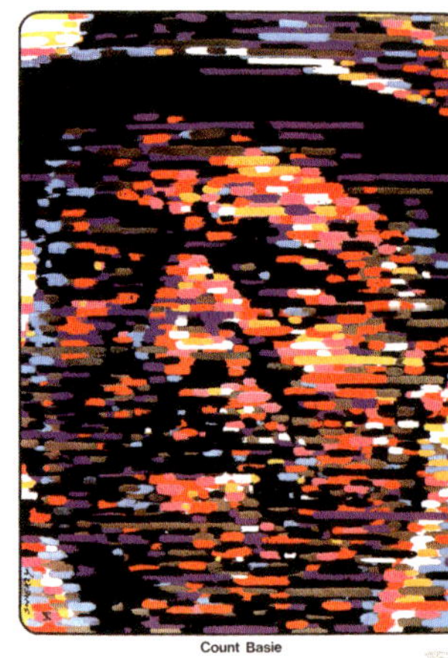

1985 · Waldemar Świerzy · PL · Poster

1985 · Pierre Neumann · CH · Poster

The first desktop layout software **PageMaker** is released by Aldus

The first **Toyama Poster Triennial** is held in Japan

The first issue of **HQ** design magazine is published, designed, and edited by Rolf Müller

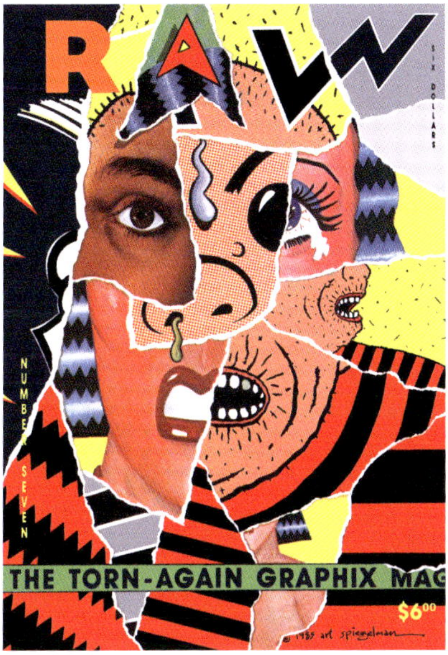

1985 · Art Spiegelman · US · Magazine cover

1985 · Carol Thompson, Eamonn McCabe, Terry Jones · UK · Magazine cover

1985 · Shigeo Fukuda · JP · Poster

1985 · Drew Struzan (ILL) · US · Poster

1985 · Erhard Grüttner · GDR · Poster

1985 · Leif Frimann Anisdahl · NO · Identity · Posten Norge

1986

1986 · Richard Rockwood, Autograph Design Partnership · UK · Logo · Jones

1986 · Lance Anderson · US · Logo · THX

1986 · Paul Rand · US · Logo · Next

April Greiman designs an issue of the magazine **Design Quarterly** using only a computer

1986 · Anonymous · US · Record cover

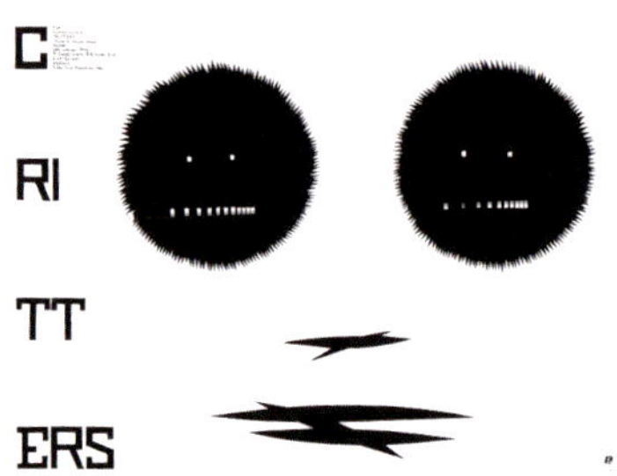

1986 · Mieczysław Wasilewski · PL · Poster

1986 · Thales Pereira · BR · Invitation card

The first issue of typography magazine **Octavo** is published in the United Kingdom

1986 · Shin Matsunaga · JP · Poster

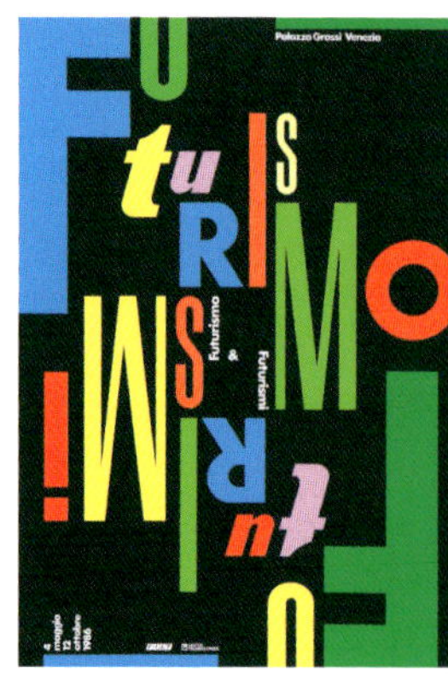

1986 · Pierluigi Cerri · IT · Poster

1986 · Peter Saville Associates · UK · Record cover

Omnicom Group, a global marketing and corporate communications holding controlling BBDO, TBWA, and other global advertising agencies, is established in New York City

The **Ginza Graphic Gallery** for graphic design opens in Tokyo

1986 · Act Up · US · Poster

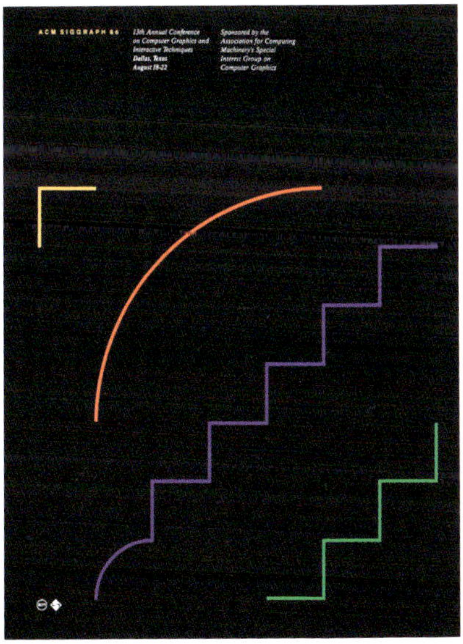

1986 · Woody Pirtle, Pirtle Design · US · Brochure cover

1986 · Yusaku Kamekura · JP · Poster

1986 · Makoto Saito · JP · Poster

As soon as it became possible to work out her design ideas on an Apple Mac, the Californian designer April Greiman turned to this new technology with drive and enthusiasm. In a 1986 edition of *Design Quarterly* she presented one of the first digitally produced layouts, while other new possibilities, such as the use of video stills, led to the creation of a comprehensive and completely independent visual language.

Sobald es möglich war, Gestaltungsideen auf einem Macintosh umzusetzen, wendete sich die kalifornische Grafikdesignerin April Greiman dieser neuen Technik zu. Mit einer Ausgabe von *Design Quarterly* legte sie 1986 eines der ersten vollständig digital erzeugten Layouts vor. Neue Möglichkeiten wie die Verwendung von Videostills führten zu einer ganz eigenständigen Bildsprache.

Dès qu'il fut possible d'élaborer des idées graphiques sur un Macintosh, la graphiste californienne April Greiman adopta avec enthousiasme cette nouvelle technologie. En 1986, elle présenta dans un numéro de *Design Quarterly* une des premières mises en page entièrement réalisées sur ordinateur. Des possibilités inédites comme l'utilisation d'images vidéo ouvrirent la voie à un langage visuel entièrement indépendant.

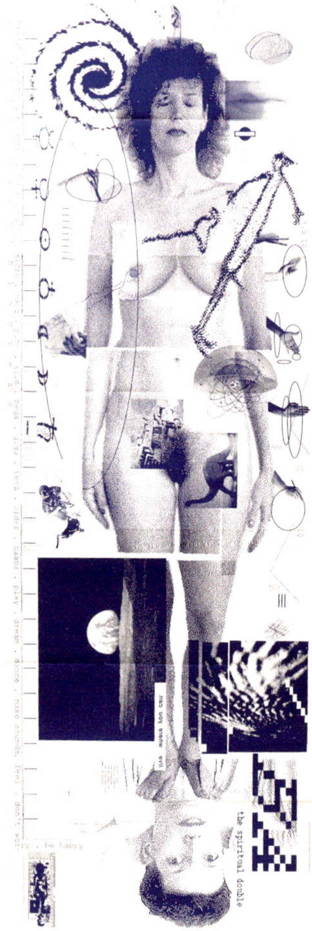

1986 · April Greiman · US · Magazine (outside)

1986 · April Greiman · US · Magazine (inside)

»I'm sort of tagged 'New Wave/Postmodern' and I think that the vast majority of work that came after is probably the most important work, with a bigger scope. Definitely the work we've been doing in the last five years is much more complex. I've sort of coined the phrase 'trans-media' for that. I really think that's what our strength is and what I've been interested in.« April Greiman, *idsgn*, 2009

April Greiman (1948, New York) is an American designer based in Los Angeles, where she heads the design consultancy Made in Space. A pioneering advocate for the use of computer technology as a design tool, Greiman played a major role in developing New Wave design in the United States. After attending Kansas City Art Institute in Missouri, she studied at the Basel School of Design under Armin Hofmann and Wolfgang Weingart. Notable amongst her works are posters for CalArts (1977, with Jayme Odgers) and the 1984 Los Angeles Olympics. In 1982 Greiman became head of the design department at CalArts, two years later changing its name to Visual Communications and thus broadening its influence.

April Greiman (1948, New York) ist eine amerikanische Grafikdesignerin, die in Los Angeles die Design Consulting Agentur Made in Space leitet. Als Vorreiterin beim Einsatz von Computertechnik in der Gestaltung spielte sie in den Vereinigten Staaten eine maßgebliche Rolle bei der Entwicklung von New-Wave-Design. Nach dem Besuch des Kansas City Art Institute in Missouri studierte sie an der Schule für Gestaltung in Basel bei Armin Hofmann und Wolfgang Weingart. Am bekanntesten sind ihre Plakate für CalArts (1977, mit Jayme Odgers) und für die Olympischen Spiele 1984 in Los Angeles. 1982 übernahm Greiman die Leitung der Designabteilung an der CalArts, die sie zwei Jahre später in „Visuelle Kommunikation" umbenannte und damit deren Einflusssphäre vergrößerte.

April Greiman (1948, New York) est une graphiste américaine résidant à Los Angeles, où elle supervise le cabinet de conseil en design Made in Space. Pionnière et ardente promotrice des technologies numériques dans le domaine du design, Greiman a joué un rôle majeur dans le développement du design New Wave aux États-Unis. Après des études au Kansas City Art Institute (Missouri), elle étudie à l'école de design de Bâle auprès d'Armin Hofmann et de Wolfgang Weingart. Parmi ses travaux les plus remarqués figurent ses affiches pour le CalArts (1977, avec Jayme Odgers) et pour les jeux Olympiques de Los Angeles en 1984. En 1982, Greiman est devenue directrice du département de design du CalArts. Deux ans plus tard, elle l'a rebaptisé de communication visuelle, étendant ainsi son influence.

1983 · April Greiman · US · Poster

1981 · April Greiman · US · Poster

1981 · April Greiman · US · Magazine cover

1986 · April Greiman · US · Poster

1985 · April Greiman · US · Poster

While graphic design of the 1960s and '70s often sought to turn away from the homespun styles of earlier times, 1980s designers made a conscious choice to revive them. Many works from the period confirmed the preference for using a minimal design vocabulary to create maximum emotional impact. Endless variations on what once seemed a contradictory connection have continued to be applied ever since.

Während die Grafik der 1960er- und 1970er-Jahre oftmals eine Abkehr von der handgemachten Stilistik früherer Epochen verfolgte, wurde genau diese in den 1980er-Jahren wieder ganz bewusst als Stilmittel eingesetzt. Viele der Arbeiten dieser Zeit verbanden dabei die kommunikativen Vorzüge reduzierter Formensprache mit der emotionalen Anmutung des Gezeichneten. Seither wird diese zunächst widersprüchlich erscheinende Verbindung immer wieder in den unterschiedlichsten Variationen im Grafikdesign verwendet.

Alors que le graphisme des années 1960 et 1970 visait souvent à se démarquer de toute stylistique artisanale d'époques antérieures, c'est précisément cette esthétique que les designers des années 1980 réintroduisirent délibérément. Nombre des réalisations optaient pour un langage réduit en vue d'avoir un impact émotionnel. Depuis, cette combinaison à première vue contradictoire n'a cessé d'être appliquée.

1981 · Tony Lane · US · Record cover

1987 · Richard Greenberg · US · Logo · Dirty Dancing

1984 · Jay Vigon, Ed Thrasher (AD) · US · Logo · Purple Rain

1983 · Joan Miró · ES · Logo · España

1989 · John Hornall, Jack Anderson · US · Logo · Corbis

»The 'avant-garde' spirit of the 1980s is out for individuality, imagination, emotion, shock effect—all the things that the systems and rationale of the previous decades couldn't offer.«
Liz McQuiston and Barry Kitts, *Graphic Design Source Book*, 1987

1984 · Michael Manwaring · US · Poster

1992 · Craig Frazier, Grant Peterson, Frazier Design · US · Logo · Lucas Arts

1980s · Derick Hudspith, John Sorrell, Newell & Sorrell · UK · Logo · Lumino

1990 · George Tscherny · US · Poster

1994 · Javier Romero Design Group · US · Poster

1987 · Lloyd Northover · UK · Packaging

1986 · Duffy Design · US · Packaging

1994 · Béatrice Mariotti · FR · Packaging

1987

The first version of the layout software **QuarkXPress** is released

The **Tokyo Type Directors Club** is established

GALERIES Lafayette

1987 · Bruno Suter · CH/FR · Logo · Galeries Lafayette

CHOCOLATE & CO

1987 · Pat Hansen · US · Logo · Chocolate & Co.

BROOKLYN BREWERY

1987 · Milton Glaser · US · Identity/Packaging · Brooklyn Brewery

The **Random House-Knopf** publishing company establishes an in-house design group, including Barbara deWilde, Carol Devine Carson, Archie Ferguson, and Chip Kidd

1987 · Michael Bierut · US · Poster

1987 · Rostislav Vaněk · CZ · Poster

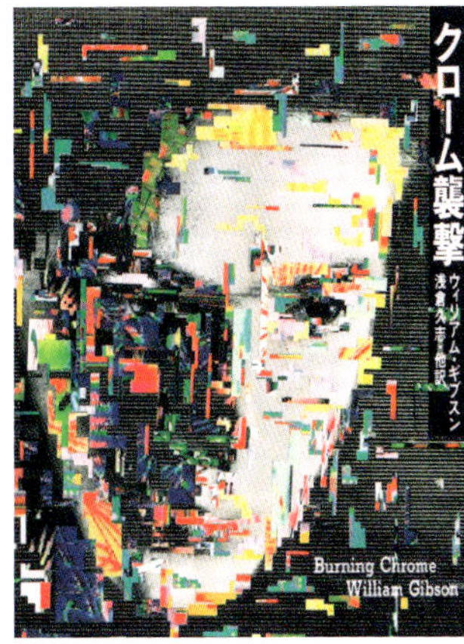

1987 · Yukimasa Okumura · JP · Book cover

1987 · Anonymous · US · Record cover

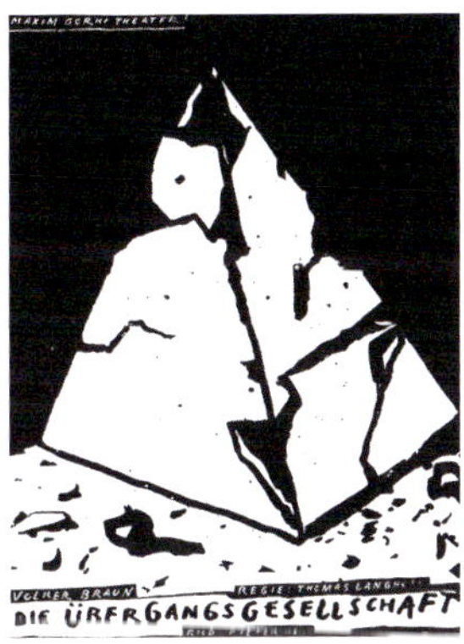

1987 · Erhard Grüttner · GDR · Poster

1987 · Andrzej Pągowski · PL · Poster

1987 · Robert Valentine · US · Poster

1987 · Takenobu Igarashi · JP · Magazine cover

1987 · Henry Marquez, Gary Panter, Nels Israelson (PH) · US · Record cover

1988

The Graphic Language of Neville Brody is published, and with the combined sales of the follow-up volume in 1994 it becomes one of the most successful titles on graphic design

Adrian Frutiger's typeface **Avenir** is released

1988 · David Hillman, Pentagram · UK · Logo · The Guardian

1988 · Scott Idleman · US · Logo · New Music

1988 · Evelyn Grumach · BR · Logo · AT2

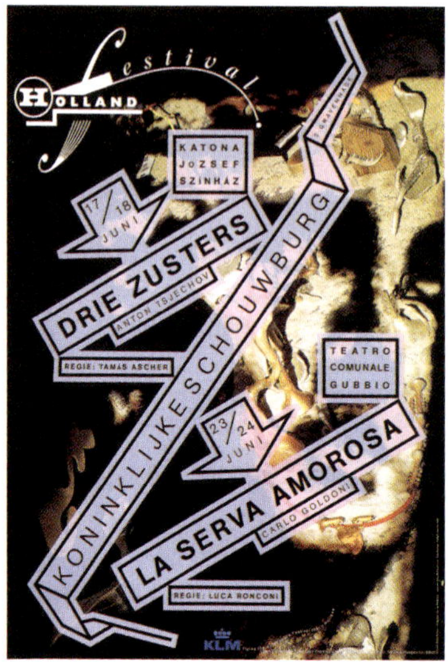

1988 · Studio Dumbar · NL · Poster

1988 · Guto Lacaz, Carlos Baptistella · BR · Magazine cover

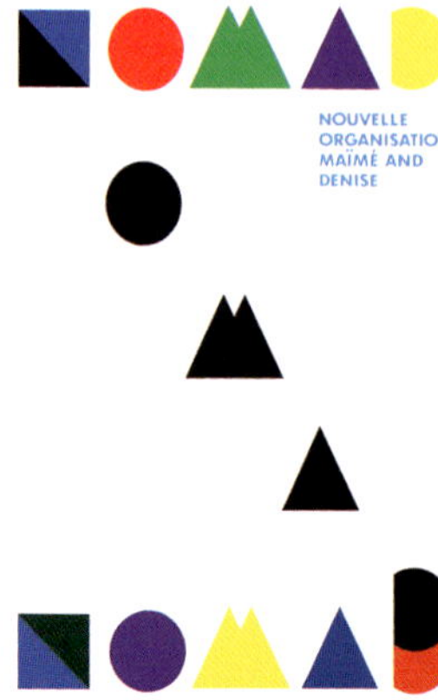

1988 · Ikko Tanaka · JP · Poster

1988 · Emery Vincent Associates · AU · Poster

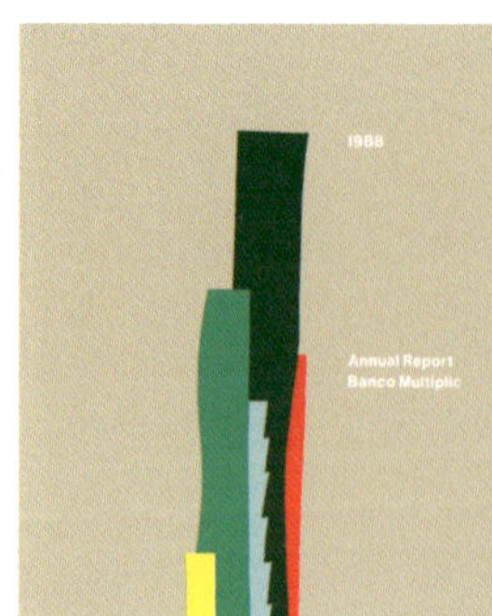

1988 · Kiko Farkas · BR · Brochure cover

The **Rotis** typeface is created by Otl Aicher, becoming one of the most widely used fonts of its time

The **Australian Graphic Design Association** (AGDA) is founded

The first **Tehran International Poster Biennial** is held in Iran

The first version of the vector-based graphic software **FreeHand** is released

1988 · Dusan Junek · SK · Poster

1988 · Studio Dumbar · NL · Design manual

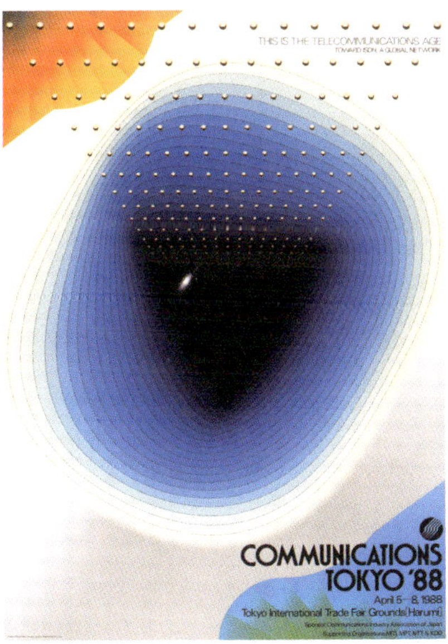

1988 · Mitsuo Katsui · JP · Poster

1988 · Helio Rosas · BR · Ad

1989

The digital type foundy **FontShop** is set up by Joan and Erik Spiekermann in Berlin

The first issue of Japanese design magazine **Creation** is published, edited by Yusaku Kamekura

1989 · Ron Dumas (AD), Gary Nolton (PH), Nike Inc. · US · Poster

1989 · Mengü Ertel · TR · Logo · TRT Television

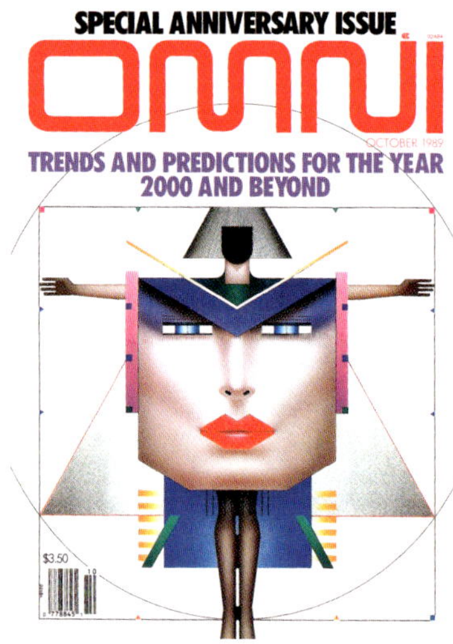

1989 · Anonymous · US · Magazine cover

1989 · Rico Lins · BR · Poster

1989 · Alan Fletcher, Pentagram · UK · Logo ·Victoria & Albert Museum

1989 · The Pushpin Group · US · Logo · Solo Editions

1989 · Neville Brody · UK · Ad

The anti-consumerist **Adbusters Media** is set up in Vancouver

The **Brazilian Graphic Designers Association** (ADG Brasil) is founded

Kurt Weidemann's Corporate **ASE** typeface is released, originally designed for Mercedes-Benz

A **Design Museum** opens in a former banana warehouse in London

1989 · Ott+Stein · DE · Poster

1989 · Georgii N. Kamenskikh · RU · Poster

1989 · Edite Gornova · LV · Poster

1989 · Henry Steiner · HK · Brochure cover

1992 · José Carlos Lollo, Marcello Serpa · BR · Poster

1992 · Javier Mariscal · ES · Poster

1990

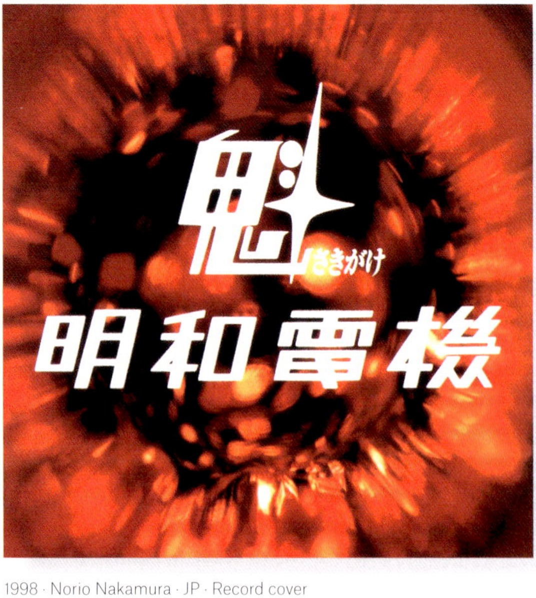

1998 · Norio Nakamura · JP · Record cover

1992 · Nesnadny & Schwartz · US · Brochure cover

1999 · Alejandro Ros · AR · Magazine cover

1999

1993 · Angela Skouras · US · Book cover

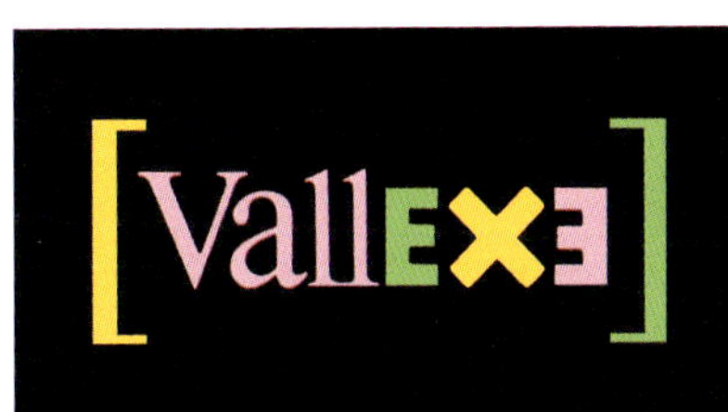

1994 · Roberto Turégano · ES · Logo · Vallexe Jazz Festival

In the early 1990s, the Americans April Greiman and David Carson and Britain's Neville Brody became the design world's new heroes. Their computer-generated works delivered a wealth of uniquely stimulating ideas and new ways of seeing, while in the wider sphere the possibilities offered by computer-based design found favor not only with the new avant-garde but also quickly became part of general contemporary stylistics. The all-encompassing success of the internet, which became apparent as the decade wore on, and the mass-market breakthrough of home PCs, led to even greater progress. Digital media design was a completely new field of application for graphic design, and thanks to simple software applications computer users now had the wherewithal to create their own designs entirely from scratch. The result of this is that, even today, professionals continue to feel the challenge brought about by the knowledge that home users and part-timers may be equally competent and capable designers.

April Greiman und David Carson aus den USA sowie der Brite Neville Brody wurden Anfang der 1990er-Jahre die neuen Helden der Designszene. Ihre digital realisierten Arbeiten lieferten eine Reihe originärer Impulse und brachen mit Sehgewohnheiten des analogen Zeitalters. Die Möglichkeiten der computerbasierten Gestaltung hielten jedoch auch abseits dieser neuen Avantgarde schnell Einzug in die allgemeine Stilistik der Gegenwart. Mit der flächendeckenden Durchsetzung des Internets und dem Durchbruch von Home-PCs am Massenmarkt zur Mitte der Dekade wurde diese Entwicklung noch einmal befeuert. Die Gestaltung digitaler Medien war ein völlig neues Anwendungsfeld von Grafikdesign. Gleichzeitig hatte jeder Computeranwender dank einfach anzuwendender Software die Möglichkeit an der Hand, eigene Entwürfe umzusetzen. Bis heute bleibt diese Egalisierung für Gestalter immer wieder eine Herausforderung.

Uniform of the Dutch police, part of the new visual identity designed by Studio Dumbar in 1993.

Uniform der niederländischen Polizei, die Teil der 1993 neu eingeführten visuellen Identität von Studio Dumbar war.

L'uniforme de la police néerlandaise, qui fait partie de la nouvelle identité visuelle conçue en 1993 par Studio Dumbar.

Au début des années 1990, les Américains April Greiman et David Carson ainsi que le Britannique Neville Brody deviennent les nouveaux héros de la scène du design. Leurs travaux réalisés sur ordinateur livrent une profusion d'idées stimulantes et d'approches inédites. Parallèlement à cette nouvelle avant-garde, les possibilités créatives offertes par le numérique entrent rapidement dans la stylistique générale de l'époque. Vers la fin de la décennie, l'indéniable succès global d'Internet et la percée massive de l'ordinateur personnel sur le marché accélèrent encore davantage cette évolution. La conception via des médias numériques devient un tout nouveau champ d'application du graphisme, et grâce à des solutions logicielles simples, les ordinateurs permettent désormais aux utilisateurs de réaliser de zéro leurs propres projets. C'est pourquoi aujourd'hui encore, les professionnels du graphisme sont conscients que le savoir-faire des amateurs et personnes s'y dédiant à temps partiel peut parfaitement le faire de l'ombre.

1990

1990 · Tel Design · NL · Logo · Gasunie

1990 · Karol Śliwka · PL · Logo · Alfa Chemicals

1990 · Jean Widmer, Bruno Monguzzi · FR · Logo · Musée d'Orsay

The first version of **Adobe Photoshop** is released

1990 · Brunazzi & Associati · IT · Identity · Italia 90

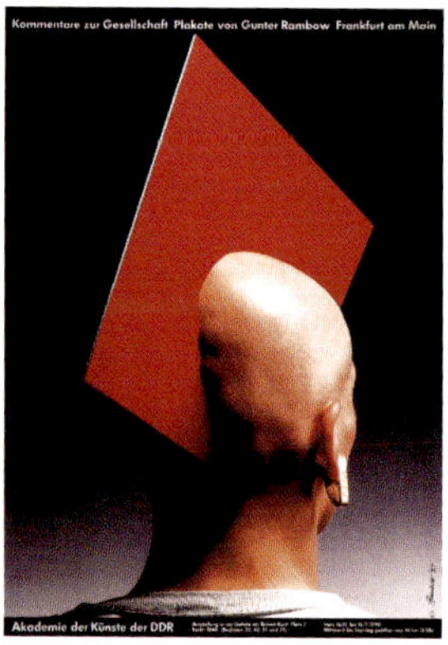

1990 · Gunter Rambow · DE · Poster

1990 · João Machado · PT · Poster

The **Caecilia** typeface is created by Dutch designer Peter Matthias Noordzij

Robert Slimbach's **Minion** typeface is released

1990 · Anonymous · RU · Poster

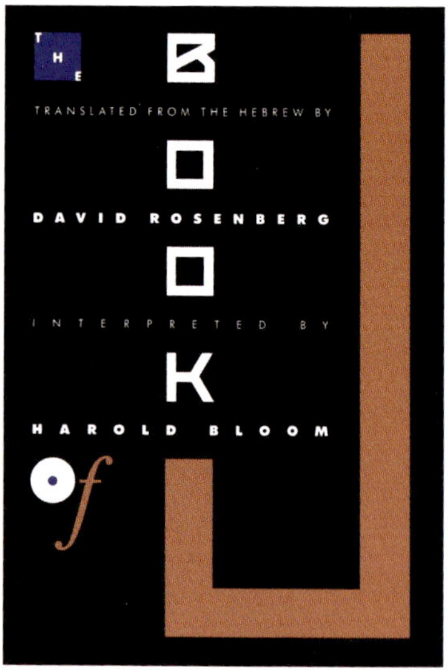

1990 · Carin Goldberg · US · Book cover

The first **International Poster Biennial** in Mexico is held

Michael Bierut becomes a partner at the New York office of **Pentagram**, followed by Paula Scher in 1991

The first **Chaumont Poster Festival** takes place in France

Eye design magazine is launched in London by Rick Poynor

1990 · Chip Kidd · US · Book cover

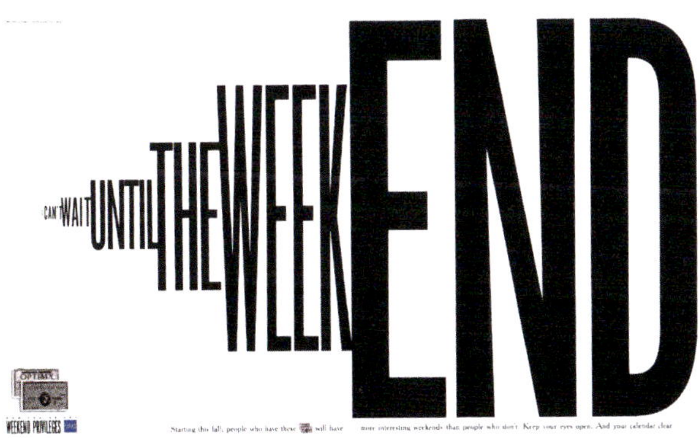

1990 · Ogilvy & Mather · US · Ad

1990 · Burns, Connacher & Waldron Design · US · Poster

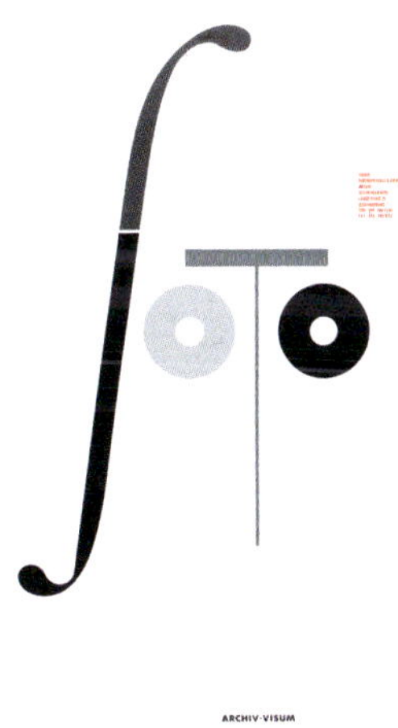

1990 · Ott+Stein · DE · Poster

In 1984, designers Rudy VanderLans and Zuzana Licko launched *Emigre* magazine, a quarterly publication devoted to different aspects of visual communication. Coinciding with the arrival of the Apple Mac, *Emigre* was an early adopter of the new technology and created some of the first digital layouts and typeface designs, for which the duo received both worldwide acclaim and much criticism. The exposure of these typefaces in the magazine eventually led to the creation of Emigre Fonts, one of the first independent type foundries utilizing personal computer technology for design and distribution. Licko and VanderLans thus created the model for the hundreds of small foundries that followed in their footsteps.

Die Grafikdesigner Rudy VanderLans und Zuzana Licko gaben 1984 erstmals das mittlerweile berüchtigte Magazin *Emigre* heraus, eine vierteljährlich erscheinende Publikation zum Thema visuelle Kommunikation. Zur gleichen Zeit kam der Macintosh-Computer auf den Markt, und so gehörte *Emigre* zu den Ersten, die sich die neue Technik aneigneten und einige der allerersten digitalen Layouts und Schriften entwarfen. Dadurch fanden VanderLans und Licko weltweit Anerkennung, stießen aber auch auf nicht minder heftige Kritik. Der Gebrauch ihrer Schriften im Magazin *Emigre* führte schließlich zur Gründung von Emigre Fonts, einem der frühesten unabhängigen Schriftenhersteller, der die Technik des Personal Computer für die Gestaltung und Verbreitung von Schriften nutzte. Das Unternehmen bereitete den Boden für Hunderte kleiner Schriftenhersteller, die seinem Beispiel folgten.

En 1984, les graphistes Rudy VanderLans et Zuzana Licko fondaient le trimestriel *Emigre* consacré à divers aspects de la communication visuelle. Son lancement coïncida avec la naissance des ordinateurs Macintosh et il fut parmi les premiers à adopter la nouvelle technologie pour réaliser des mises en page entièrement numériques et créer des polices de caractères qui ont valu au duo à la fois un accueil enthousiaste dans le monde et un déluge de critiques. L'emploi de ces polices dans la revue *Emigre* conduisit finalement à la création d'Emigre Fonts, une des premières fonderies indépendantes à exploiter la technologie des PC pour concevoir et distribuer des polices de caractères, devenant ainsi un modèle pour les centaines de petites fonderies qui lui ont emboîté le pas.

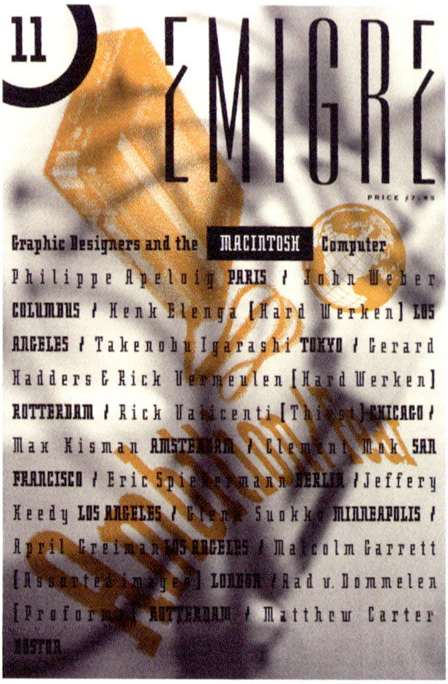

1989 · Rudy VanderLans, Zuzana Licko · US · Magazine cover

1992 · Rudy VanderLans, Zuzana Licko · US · Magazine cover

»I hope that with the story of *Emigre* we can inspire young designers to be critical thinkers, that design is not just about making cool-looking work for cool clients, but that design also offers tremendous potential: that it is a tool for reinvention, for questioning, for independence, for social good, and that you don't always need a client to make work that matters.« Rudy VanderLans, *Page*, 2010

1991 · Rudy VanderLans, Zuzana Licko · US · Magazine cover

1990 · Rudy VanderLans, Zuzana Licko · US · Poster

1995 · Rudy VanderLans, Zuzana Licko · US · Magazine cover

1996 · Rudy VanderLans, Zuzana Licko · US · Magazine cover

1997 · Rudy VanderLans, Zuzana Licko · US · Magazine cover

1998 · Rudy VanderLans, Zuzana Licko · US · Magazine cover

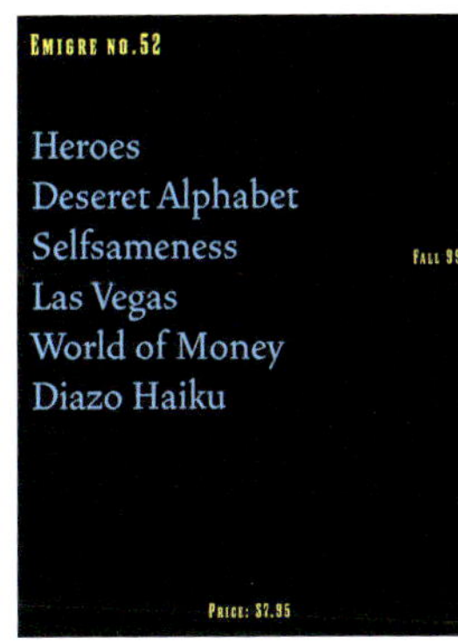

1999 · Rudy VanderLans, Zuzana Licko · US · Magazine cover

2000 · Rudy VanderLans, Zuzana Licko · US · Magazine cover

1991

Erik Spiekermann's **Meta** typeface is released

The **Association of Designers of Russia** (ADR) is founded

1991 · Lo Breier, Neville Brody, Johannes Erler, Büro X · DE · Logo · UFA

1991 · Ken Cato · AU · Logo · SBS Television

1991 · Mike Dempsey, CDT Design · UK · Logo · English National Opera

1991 · Lambie-Nairn · UK · Identity · BBC Two

1991 · Margo Chase · US · Packaging

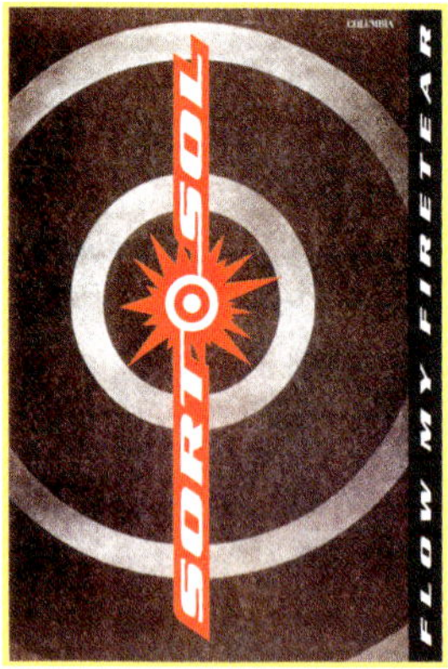

1991 · Michael Jensen · DK · Poster

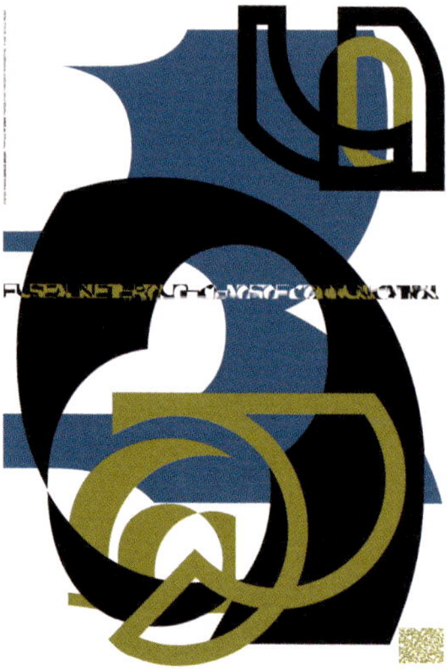

1991 · Neville Brody · UK · Magazine/Poster

1991 · Robert Fisher, Kirk Weddle (PH) · US · Record cover

The experimental typography magazine **FUSE** is launched in London

Erik van Blokland's typeface **Trixie** is released

The **Designers Institute of New Zealand** (DINZ) is established

1991 · Uwe Loesch · DE · Poster

1991 · Ralph Schraivogel · CH · Poster

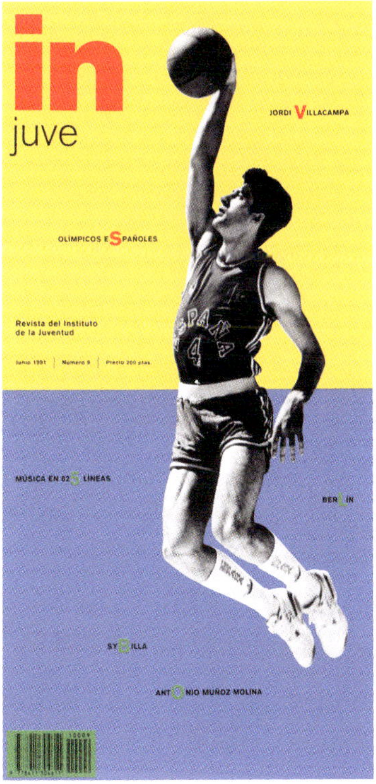

1991 · Summa · ES · Magazine cover

1991 · Tsuguya Inoue, Humichika Kato, Seiai Hirota · JP · Ad

1991 · Tibor Kalman (AD), Oliviero Toscani (PH), Emily Oberman · US/IT · Magazine cover

1991 · Tibor Kalman (AD), Oliviero Toscani (PH), Emily Oberman · US/IT · Magazine spread

Oliviero Toscani, photographer and art director for the Italian fashion label Benetton, looked for a partner in New York to set up an innovative magazine that would be devoted to social issues. In the progressive designer Tibor Kalman he found the ideal person to collaborate with on the project, which appeared just one year later, in 1991, under the title of *Colors*. Funded by Benetton, a company which had become known in the 1980s for its controversial advertising campaigns, the magazine was free to publish issues concentrating entirely on subjects such as AIDS, racism, or religion, and in ways that bypassed the conventions of traditional print media. Challenging articles, flamboyant photography, and, not least, exceptional design made *Colors* a highly respected media phenomenon of the 1990s as the magazine's distribution reached more than 100 countries.

Oliviero Toscani, Fotograf und Artdirector des italienischen Modelabels Benetton, suchte in New York City einen Partner für ein neuartiges Gesellschaftsmagazin. In dem progressiven Designer Tibor Kalman fand er die perfekte Persönlichkeit für dieses Vorhaben, das bereits ein Jahr später, 1991, unter dem Namen *Colors* erschien. Finanziert durch Benetton, ein Unternehmen, das in den 1980er-Jahren mit einer kontroversen Werbekampagne bekannt geworden war, konnte das Magazin in monothematischen Ausgaben Themen wie „Aids", „Rassismus" oder „Religion" ohne die Konventionen traditioneller Printmedien behandeln. Ausgefallene Artikel, extravagante Fotografien und nicht zuletzt die ungewöhnliche Gestaltung machten die in mehr als 100 Ländern vertriebenen Hefte zum viel beachteten Medienphänomen der 1990er-Jahre.

Oliviero Toscani, photographe et directeur artistique de la marque de mode italienne Benetton, cherchait à New York un partenaire pour lancer un magazine d'un genre nouveau traitant de questions sociales. C'est avec le graphiste progressiste Tibor Kalman qu'il devait trouver la personne idéale pour réaliser ce projet apparu en 1991 sous le nom *Colors*. Financé par Benetton, qui s'était fait connaître dans les années 1980 par une campagne publicitaire controversée, le magazine put traiter dans ses numéros monothématiques des sujets de société comme le sida, le racisme ou la religion, sans devoir se plier aux conventions de la presse traditionnelle. Des articles ambitieux, des photographies extravagantes et en bonne partie aussi, un graphisme original, feront de cette revue distribuée dans plus de 100 pays un phénomène médiatique retentissant des années 1990.

»People never talk about things unless you shock them a bit. That's at least the way my relationships have gone on a personal level. Unless my wife shocks me I won't talk to her about anything real, and I think that's what we need as people.« Tibor Kalman, NBC *Today Show*, 1993

1993 · Tibor Kalman (AD) · US/IT · Magazine cover

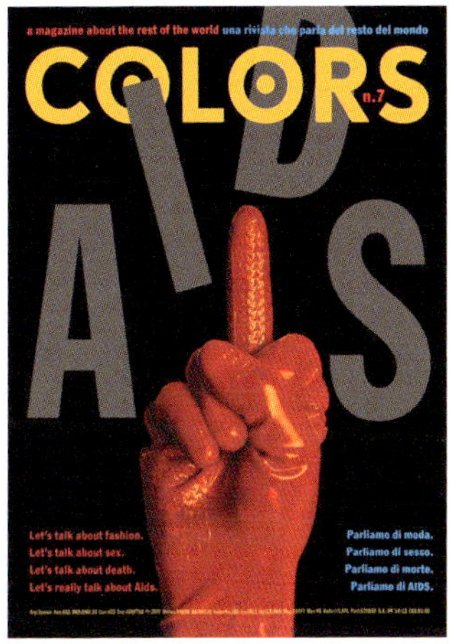

1994 · Tibor Kalman (AD) · US/IT · Magazine cover

Tibor Kalman (1949, Budapest – 1999, Puerto Rico) was a Hungarian-born American art director, who moved to the United States in 1956. After dropping out from studying journalism, Kalman worked for Barnes & Noble (then a single bookstore in New York City), eventually becoming head of its in-house design team. In 1979 he co-founded the design studio M&Co., which became highly influential for its grounding in social activism. This paved the way for his most productive period in the early 1990s, when he moved to Italy to become editor-in-chief for the Benetton-sponsored magazine *Colors*, based at Fabrica, its creative lab in Treviso.

Tibor Kalman (1949, Budapest – 1999, Puerto Rico) war ein in Ungarn geborener amerikanischer Artdirector, der 1956 in die USA auswanderte. Nach einem abgebrochenen Journalismusstudium arbeitete er bei Barnes & Noble (damals ein einzelnes Buchgeschäft in New York), wo er schließlich zum Leiter der hausinternen Designabteilung aufstieg. 1979 gründete er mit anderen das Designbüro M&Co., das sich dem sozialen Engagement verpflichtete und dadurch großen Einfluss ausübte. Das führte zu Kalmans produktivster Phase Anfang der 90er-Jahre, als er nach Italien ging und Herausgeber des von Benetton gesponsorten Magazins *Colors* wurde, das in Fabrica angesiedelt ist, dem Kreativlabor der Firma in Treviso.

Tibor Kalman (1949, Budapest – 1999, Porto Rico) fut un directeur artistique américain d'origine hongroise qui s'installa aux États-Unis en 1956. Après avoir abandonné des études de journalisme, Kalman travailla pour Barnes & Noble (qui n'était alors qu'une simple librairie à New York), avant d'y être engagé comme directeur de l'équipe interne de design. En 1979, il cofonda le studio de design M&Co., qui devint hautement influent du fait de son enracinement dans l'activisme social. Kalman connu alors sa période la plus productive au début des années 1990, quand il s'installa en Italie pour devenir rédacteur en chef du magazine *Colors*, sponsorisé par Benetton et installé au centre de recherche Fabrica, à Trévise.

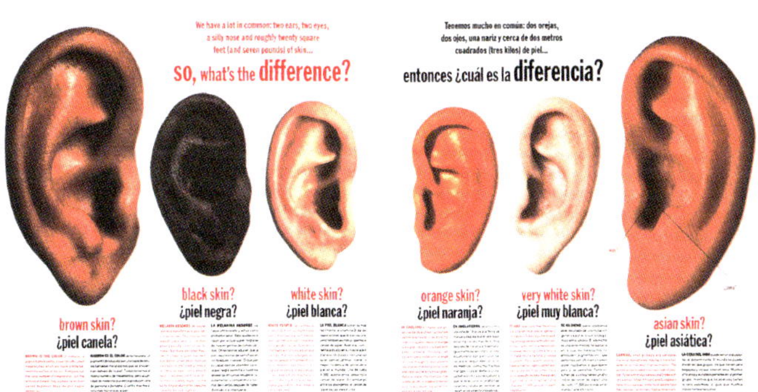

1990s · Tibor Kalman (AD) · US/IT · Magazine spreads

1992

The **JPEG** format for digital image compression is introduced

David Carson becomes art director of **Ray Gun** magazine

The international design magazine **IdN** is launched

1992 · Holly Chasin · US · Logo · E Television

1992 · Mario Gemin · AR · Logo · Kinney Clothing

1992 · Josep M. Trias · ES · Logo · Barcelona 92

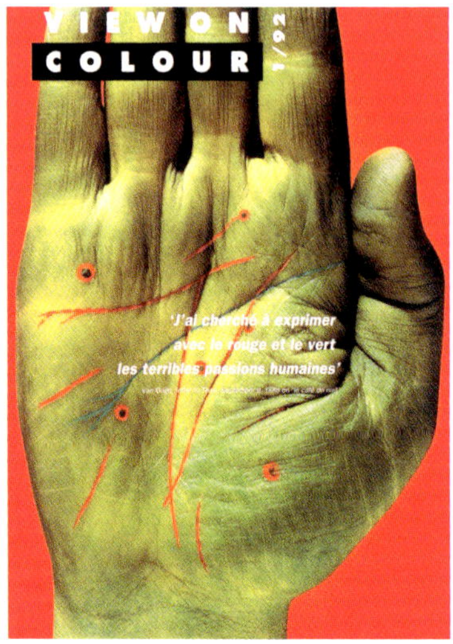

1992 · Anthon Beeke · NL · Magazine cover

1992 · Mevis & Van Deursen · NL · Poster

1992 · Joe Duffy · US · Packaging

1992 · Why Not Associates · UK · Brochure cover

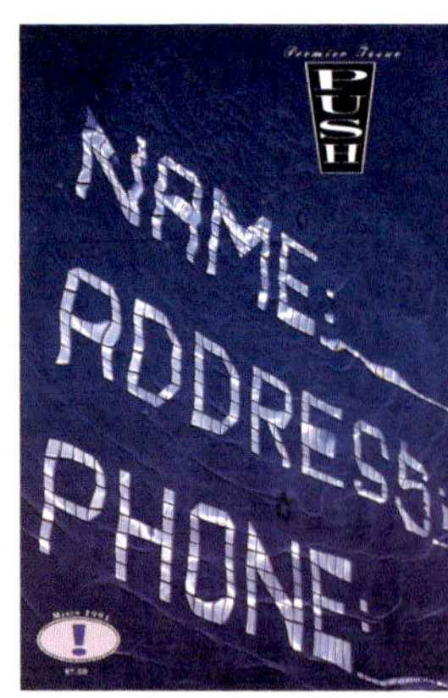

1992 · Lloyd Ziff · US · Magazine cover

The first **Moscow Global Biennale of Graphic Design** (Golden Bee) is held

The **Blur** typeface by Neville Brody is released

Robert Slimbach and Carol Twombly release the **Myriad** typeface

The **Stichting Nederlands Archief Grafisch Ontwerpers** (NAGO) is established

1992 · Peter Bysted · DK · Brochure cover

1992 · Martine Waltzer · FR · Poster

1992 · Mostafa Assadollahi · IR · Poster

1992 · Pierre Mendell · DE · Poster

Margo Chase (1958–2017, Los Angeles) was an American designer, noted for her work in the film and music industries. Originally trained as a biologist, Chase switched to visual communication after taking a course at California Polytechnic State University, later founding the Chase Design Group in 1986. From designing for such entertainment names as Madonna, Cher, *Buffy the Vampire Slayer*, and others, she also expanded into branding, working for Target, Disney, and Nestlé. Departing from a commonly advocated minimalism, Chase's distinctive illustrative style won her multiple awards. She was also a lecturer at CalArts, and Long Beach State University.

Margo Chase (1958–2017, Los Angeles) war eine amerikanische Designerin, die insbesondere durch ihre Arbeiten für die Film- und Musikindustrie bekannt wurde. Als studierte Biologin sattelte sie auf visuelle Kommunikation um, nachdem sie an der California Polytechnic State University einen Kurs besucht hatte. 1986 gründete sie die Chase Design Group. Zunächst gehörten Größen des Entertainments wie Madonna, Cher, *Buffy the Vampire Slayer* und andere zu ihren Auftraggebern, dann dehnte sie ihre Arbeit auch auf Branding aus, u. a. für Target, Disney und Nestlé. Für ihren unverkennbaren illustrativen Stil, der vom vielfach propagierten Minimalismus abweicht, erhielt sie zahlreiche Auszeichnungen. Close unterrichtete an der CalArts und an der Long Beach State University.

Margo Chase (1958–2017, Los Angeles) fut une graphiste américaine remarquée pour son travail dans l'industrie cinématographique et musicale. Après des études initiales de biologie, Chase passa à la communication visuelle suite à un cours à l'université d'État polytechnique de Californie, avant de fonder le Chase Design Group en 1986. Outre son travail pour des noms du spectacle comme Madonna, Cher, *Buffy contre les vampires* et d'autres, Chase étendit son activité au branding, notamment pour Target, Disney et Nestlé. S'écartant du minimalisme habituellement privilégié, son style illustratif distinctif lui valut de multiples récompenses. Chase enseigna au CalArts et à l'université d'État de Californie à Long Beach.

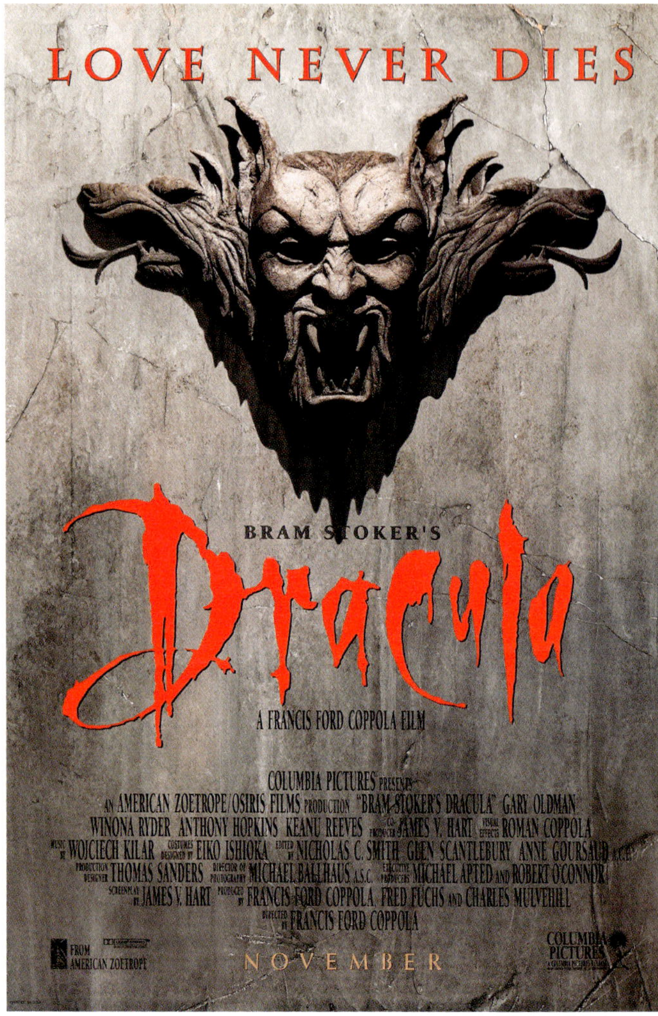

1992 · Margo Chase · US · Poster

»If the designer doesn't feel it, the design won't communicate it.«
Margo Chase, *Idea* #245, 1994

1990 · Margo Chase · US · Logo · Prince – New Power Generation

1994 · Margo Chase · US · Logo · Four Weddings and a Funeral

1997 · Margo Chase · US · Logo · Buffy the Vampire Slayer

1998 · Margo Chase · US · Logo · Charmed

1987 · Margo Chase · US · Record cover

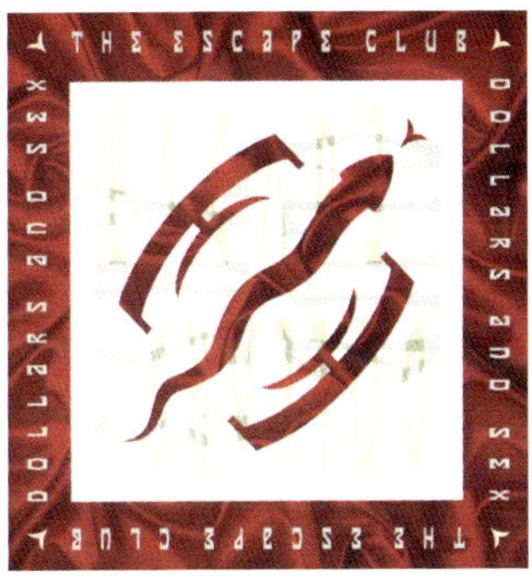

1991 · Margo Chase · US · Record cover

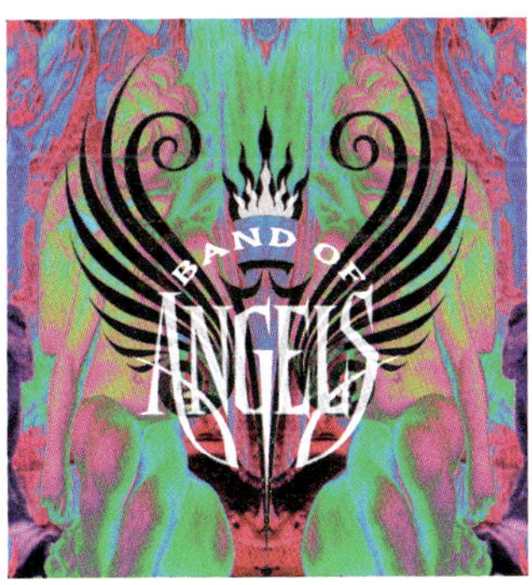

1992 · Margo Chase · US · Record cover

1990 · Margo Chase, Sidney Cooper (PH) · US · Record cover

1991 · Margo Chase, Michele Clement (PH) · US · Record cover

1993 · Margo Chase, Merlyn Rosenberg (PH) · US · Record cover

1993

Adobe introduces the **Portable Document Format** (PDF)

Stefan Sagmeister moves to New York City and opens **Sagmeister Inc.**

1993 · Anonymous · KR · Logo · Samsung

1993 · Chermayeff & Geismar · US · Logo · Casa

1993 · Bart Crosby · US · Logo · Digital Composition

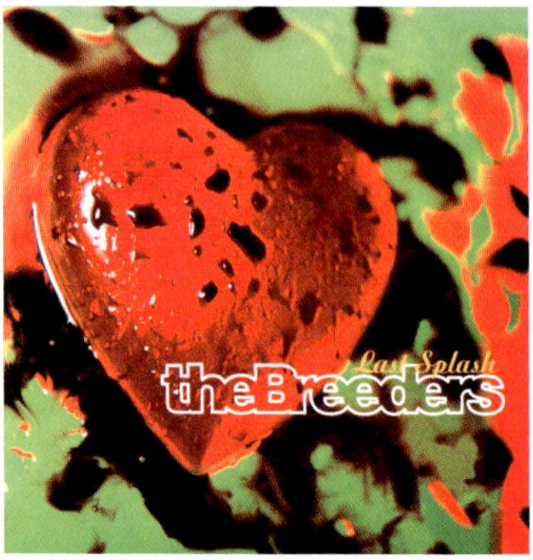

1993 · Vaughan Oliver (AD), Jason Love (PH) · UK · Record cover

1993 · André Baldinger · FR · Poster

The Clinton Mystery

The A.D.L. Under Fire

Its Shift to the Right Has Led to Scandal

It's a Big Lie, Hailed by Anti-Semites

Clinton Voter Stays Glad!

What is wrong with this Presidency?

But what's this about race politics?

The Clinton Challenge

A Fig Leaf on Serbian Genocide

The U.N. looks weak and the West powerless

Progress In Ismailiya

Jefferson Is America — And America Is Jefferson

Racism, our corrosive issue, is evident in what we read and did.

The Administration lacks sex heroes but backbone.

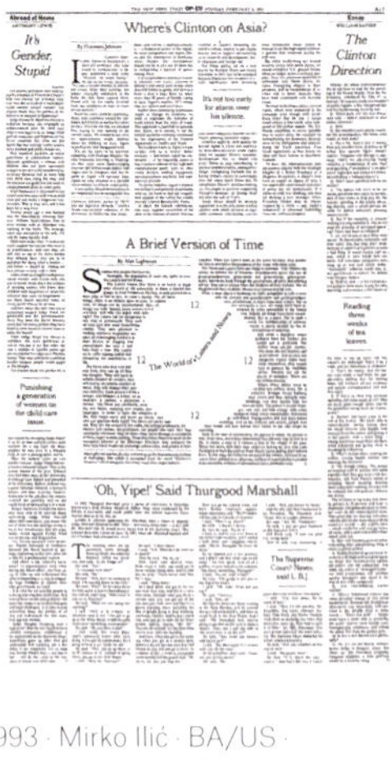
It's Gender, Stupid

Where's Clinton on Asia?

It's not too early for alarm over his silence.

The Clinton Direction

A Brief Version of Time

Punishing a generation of women in the child care issue.

'Oh, Yipe!' Said Thurgood Marshall

The Supreme Court? Never, said L.B.J.

1993 · Mirko Ilić · BA/US · Newspaper spreads

The type foundry **House Industries** is established in the United States

The Swiss type foundry **Lineto** is established

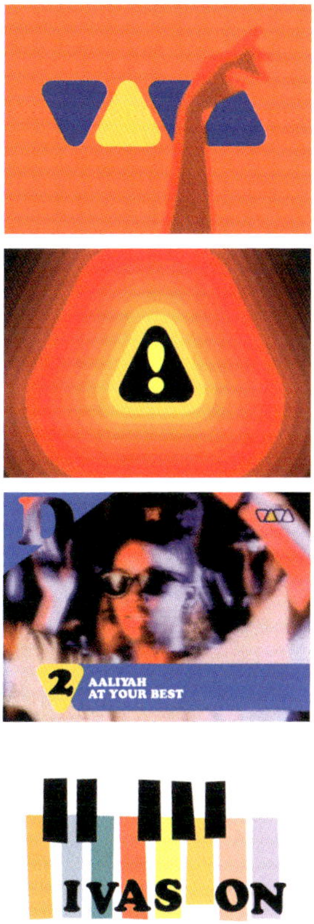

1993–98 · DMC · DE · Motion graphics

1993 · Ott+Stein · DE · Poster

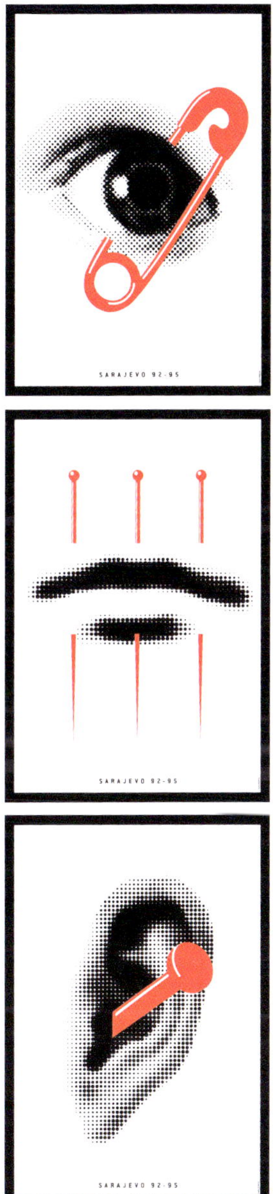

1993 · Sasha Vidakovic · BA · Poster series

1993 · Pierre Mendell, Mendell & Oberer · DE · Identity · Vitra

1993 · Shin Matsunaga · JP · Poster

Ray Gun, the American magazine devoted to the alternative rock scene, first appeared in 1992. With ex-professional surfer and designer David Carson as its art director, the magazine became the prototype for a new kind of nonconformism, while the new digital possibilities that were enabling a breakaway from the hard-and-fast rules of design became *Ray Gun*'s trademark. Carson's decision to set an interview with the musician Bryan Ferry, which he considered to be boring, in illegible Dingbat characters (although the text could be read in a supplement to the magazine), remains the stuff of legend. This sort of boundary-pushing earned the magazine cult status and made Carson one of the most important new voices in contemporary graphic design.

Das US-Magazin *Ray Gun* beschäftigte sich mit der alternativen Rockmusikszene, es erschien erstmals 1992. Unter der Artdirection von Exprofisurfer und Designer David Carson wurde das Magazin zum Prototypen eines neuen Nonkonformismus. Die neuen digitalen Möglichkeiten erlaubten den Bruch feststehender Gestaltungsregeln und wurden zum Charakteristikum von *Ray Gun*. Legendär ist bis heute ein der Redaktion langweilig erscheinendes Interview mit dem Musiker Bryan Ferry, das Carson in der Symbolschrift „Dingbat" umsetzte und damit unlesbar machte (wenngleich es im Anhang des Hefts noch einmal nachzulesen war). Derartige Grenzüberschreitungen verliehen dem Magazin einen Kultstatus und machten Carson zu einer der wichtigsten neuen Stimmen im Grafikdesign seiner Zeit.

Le magazine américain *Ray Gun*, dont le premier numéro parut en 1992, était consacré à la scène rock alternative. Sous la direction artistique de l'ex-surfer professionnel et graphiste David Carson, le magazine devint le prototype d'un nouvel anticonformisme. Les possibilités offertes par le numérique permirent à Carson de rompre avec des règles graphiques strictes et devinrent la marque de fabrique de *Ray Gun*. Jusqu'à ce jour, une interview avec le chanteur Bryan Ferry est restée légendaire: Carson la trouvant inintéressante, il la fit imprimer en dingbats, la rendant ainsi illisible (même si elle était disponible en annexe). Ce genre d'extravagance conféra au magazine un statut culte et fit de Carson une des grandes voix du graphisme de son époque.

1993 · David Carson · US · Magazine cover

1992 · David Carson · US · Magazine cover

1993 · David Carson · US · Magazine cover

»I'm a big believer in the emotion of design, and the message that's sent before somebody begins to read, before they get the rest of the information; what is the emotional response they get to the product, to the story, to the painting—whatever it is.« David Carson, *ted.com*, 2003

1992–94 · David Carson · US · Magazine spreads

David Carson (1954, Corpus Christi, Texas) is a trailblazing American art director, often cited as the godfather of "grunge typography." Carson revolutionized graphic design in the 1990s by defying the boundaries of the grid and challenging modernist logic. A sociology graduate from San Diego State University, he was also a professional surfer, at one point ranking ninth in the world. In 1984 he started working for *Transworld Skateboarding* magazine, but made his professional leap in 1992 when he became the first art director of the alternative music and lifestyle magazine *Ray Gun*.

David Carson (1954, Corpus Christi, Texas) ist ein bahnbrechender amerikanischer Artdirector, der häufig als Pate der „Grunge-Typografie" gilt. In den 1990er-Jahren revolutionierte er das Grafikdesign, indem er sich über die Grenzen des Rasters hinwegsetzte und die Logik der Moderne hinterfragte. Er hatte an der San Diego State University Soziologie studiert, war aber auch ein professioneller Surfer und hatte einmal auf Platz 9 der Weltrangliste gestanden. Ab 1984 arbeitete er für das Magazin *Transworld Skateboarding*, der Durchbruch gelang ihm 1992, als er zum ersten Artdirector der alternativen Musik- und Lifestylezeitschrift *Ray Gun* ernannt wurde.

David Carson (1954, Corpus Christi, Texas) est un directeur artistique américain précurseur, souvent désigné comme le parrain de la «grunge typography». Carson a révolutionné le graphisme dans les années 1990 en transcendant les limites de la grille et en contestant la logique moderniste. Diplômé en sociologie à l'université d'État de San Diego, il a aussi été surfer professionnel, se hissant jusqu'à la neuvième place mondiale. En 1984, il commence à travailler pour le magazine *Transworld Skateboarding*, mais sa carrière fait un bond en 1992 quand il devient le premier directeur artistique du magazine de musique et de société alternatif *Ray Gun*.

1993 · Plunkett+Kuhr · US · Magazine cover

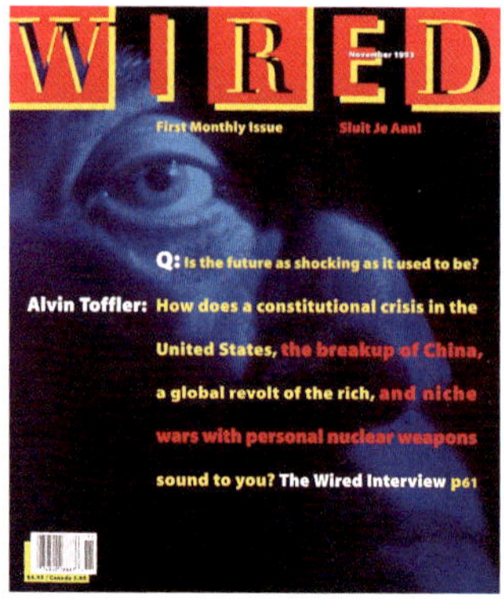

1993 · Plunkett+Kuhr · US · Magazine cover

1993 · Plunkett+Kuhr · US · Magazine cover

1994 · Plunkett+Kuhr · US · Magazine cover

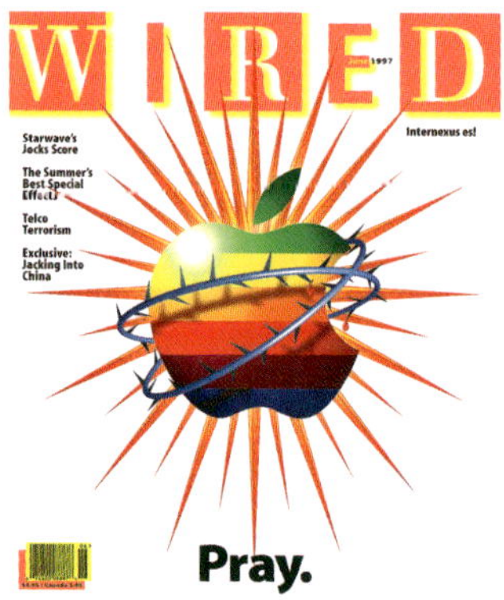

1997 · Plunkett+Kuhr · US · Magazine cover

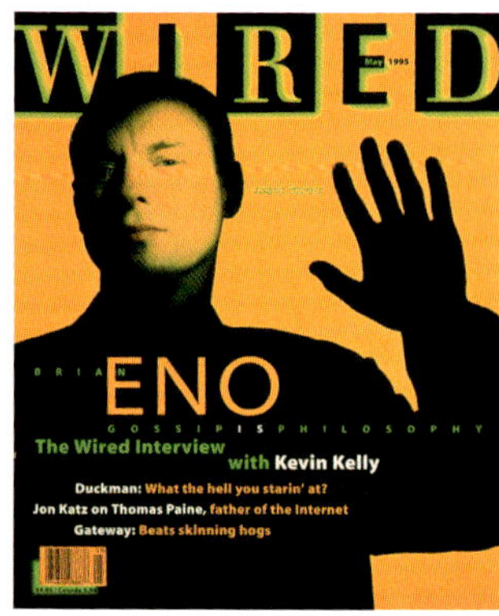

1995 · Plunkett+Kuhr · US · Magazine cover

1990s · Plunkett+Kuhr · US · Magazine spines

»We wanted to avoid the unspoken design taboo: good design = subtle, tasteful, elegant, restrained.«
John Plunkett, *Eye* #28, 1998

In the late 1980s, the American journalist Louis Rossetto became aware of the groundbreaking digital revolution that was then getting under way. In 1991, he and a small team that included the designers John Plunkett and Barbara Kuhr began developing the concept for *Wired*. In terms of both its content and visuals, the magazine, which first appeared in January 1993, documented the early years of PCs, cell phones, and of course the internet more authentically than any other similar publication. Then, in 1994, came the launch of hotwired.com that was originally intended simply as a sideline, but instead became the world's first commercial web magazine.

Der amerikanische Journalist Louis Rossetto wurde Ende der 1980er-Jahre auf die bahnbrechenden digitalen Revolutionen aufmerksam und entwickelte ab 1991 mit einem kleinen Team, darunter die Designer John Plunkett und Barbara Kuhr, das Konzept von *Wired*. Die ab Januar 1993 erschienenen Hefte dokumentierten das gerade anbrechende Zeitalter von PCs, Mobiltelefonen und natürlich des Internets inhaltlich wie visuell so authentisch wie kein anderes Heft. Ganz nebenbei entstand als Ableger der Zeitschrift 1994 unter hotwired.com das weltweit erste kommerzielle Webmagazin.

À la fin des années 1980, le journaliste américain Louis Rossetto comprit qu'une révolution fondamentale était en route avec l'avènement de l'ère numérique. En 1991, il développa en équipe avec les graphistes John Plunkett et Barbara Kuhr le concept de *Wired*. Tant par son contenu que son esthétique, le magazine lancé en janvier 1993 allait documenter les premières années du PC, des téléphones portables et bien sûr d'Internet de manière plus authentique que toute autre publication du même ordre. En 1994 fut lancé hotwired.com, qui ne se voulait à l'origine qu'une activité secondaire, mais qui devint en fait le premier magazine commercial en ligne au monde.

1990s · Plunkett+Kuhr · US · Magazine spreads

Plunkett+Kuhr (1990, Park City, Utah) is a design studio partnership run by Barbara Kuhr (1954, Great Falls, Montana) and John Plunkett (1952, Chicago). Kuhr studied design at Montana State University and was later employed by a number of design studios, including Chermayeff & Geismar. Plunkett studied at Parsons School of Design and CalArts before going on to work for Saul Bass, Louis Danziger, Deborah Sussman, and Colin Forbes. As Plunkett+Kuhr they created designs for the Sundance Film Festival, a number of TED conferences, and for the Carnegie Hall Museum in New York. However, their most influential work has been the designs they developed between 1991 and 1998 for *Wired* magazine, the winner of three National Magazine Awards.

Plunkett+Kuhr (1990, Park City, Utah) ist das gemeinsame Designstudio von Barbara Kuhr (1954, Great Falls, Montana) und John Plunkett (1952, Chicago). Kuhr studierte Design an der Montana State University und war später unter anderem für Chermayeff & Geismar tätig. Plunkett studierte an der Parsons School of Design und an der CalArts. Anschließend arbeitete er für Saul Bass, Louis Danziger, Deborah Sussman und Colin Forbes. Als Plunkett+Kuhr waren sie für das Sundance Filmfestival, die TED-Konferenz und für das Carnegie Hall Museum in New York tätig. Den meisten Einfluss erlebte jedoch ihre Entwicklung des Magazins *Wired* zwischen 1991 und 1998, das mit drei National Magazine Awards prämiert wurde.

Plunkett+Kuhr (1990, Park City, Utah) est un studio de graphisme codirigé par Barbara Kuhr (1954, Great Falls, Montana) et John Plunkett (1952, Chicago). Kuhr a fait des études de graphisme à l'université d'État du Montana avant de travailler dans toute une série d'agences de graphisme parmi lesquelles figure notamment Chermayeff & Geismar. Plunkett a étudié à la Parsons School of Design et au CalArts avant de travailler pour Saul Bass, Louis Danziger, Deborah Sussman et Colin Forbes. Sous le nom Plunkett+Kuhr, les deux associés ont créé pour le festival du film de Sundance, plusieurs conférences TED et le Carnegie Hall Museum à New York. Leur travail le plus influent reste toutefois leurs créations entre 1991 et 1998 pour le magazine *Wired*, lauréat de trois National Magazine Awards.

1994

The **Indonesian Association of Graphic Designers** (ADGI) is founded

The first issue of French design magazine **Étapes** is published

1994 · Lindon Leader, Landor · US · Logo · FedEx

1994 · Pentagram · US · Logo · World Cup '94

1994 · Manabu Sakamoto · JP · Logo · PlayStation

1994 · Janet Levinson, Chris Robinson · US · Record cover

1994 · David High, High Design · US · Poster

1994 · Sergio Liuzzi · BR · Poster

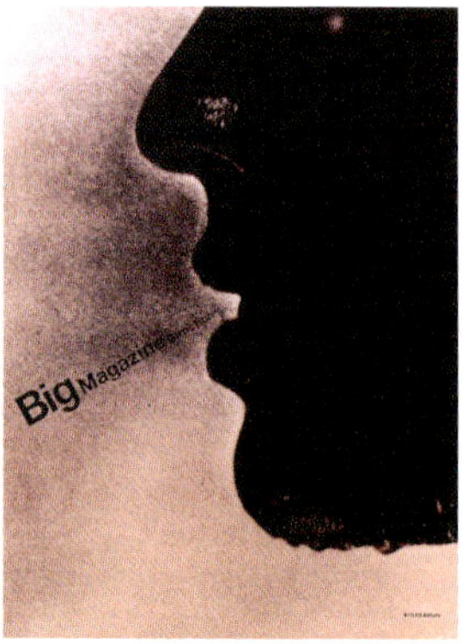

1994 · Vince Frost · UK/CA · Magazine cover

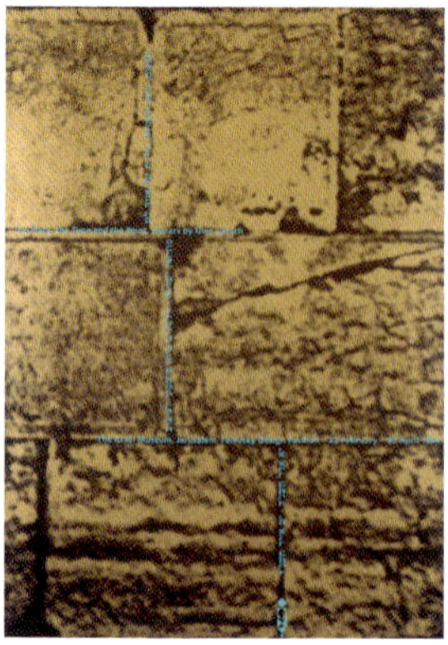

1994 · Uwe Loesch · DE · Poster

The **Comic Sans** typeface by Vincent Connare is released by Microsoft

1994 · David Carson, Davies + Starr (PH) · US · Magazine cover

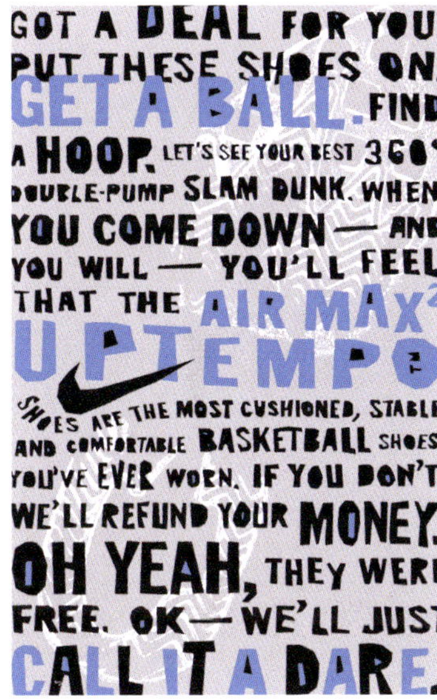

1994 · Dan Richards · US · Poster

1994 · BBH · UK · Ad

1994 · Igor Maistrovsky · RU · Poster

The visual part of the web, including many aspects of the user interface, was initially put together by an army of curious nerds, very often engineers who saw the web as an opportunity to change the way we work, communicate, sell, and interact with one another. The first websites for today's multibillion-dollar corporations such as Amazon and Adobe were built from scratch, one line of code at a time, and carefully designed to process data as quickly as was possible with the dial-up connections that were then all that was available. Templates were unknown, image resolution was low, but companies understood that the web needed designers to improve such things, from the logos of internet-based companies to the layouts of web pages. In an endless history of trial and error, standards in programming, structure, and usability were conceived and reworked in a huge collective effort.

Die visuellen Aspekte des Web, einschließlich vieler Elemente der Bildschirmoberfläche, wurden anfangs von einem Heer schräger Nerds entwickelt, häufig Techniker, die das Web als Möglichkeit begriffen, die Art zu verändern, wie wir arbeiten, kommunizieren, verkaufen und interagieren. Die ersten Websites für die heute Milliarden Dollar schweren Unternehmen wie Amazon und Adobe wurden von Grund auf aufgebaut, eine Codezeile nach der anderen, und umsichtig entworfen, damit Daten so schnell wie möglich über die damals verfügbaren Modemverbindungen per Telefonleitung verarbeitet werden konnten. Templates waren unbekannt, die Bildauflösung war schlecht, aber den Unternehmen war klar, dass das Web Designer brauchte, um diese Aspekte zu verbessern, von den Logos der Internetunternehmen bis zum Layout der Webseiten. In einer endlosen Abfolge von Trial and Error und durch eine gewaltige kollektive Anstrengung wurden die Standards bei der Programmierung, der Struktur und der Bedienungsfreundlichkeit konzipiert und überarbeitet.

La partie visuelle du web, notamment bien des aspects de l'interface utilisateur, fut d'abord compilée par une armée de curieux et de passionnés – souvent des ingénieurs qui considéraient le web comme une opportunité pour changer notre manière de travailler, de communiquer, de vendre et d'interagir. Les premiers sites réalisés pour des entreprises qui pèsent aujourd'hui des milliards de dollars comme Amazon et Adobe furent construits à partir de rien, ligne de code par ligne de code, et soigneusement conçus pour traiter les données le plus rapidement possible à travers les connexions téléphoniques, seules disponibles à l'époque. Les modèles étaient inconnus, la résolution des écrans faible, mais les entreprises avaient conscience que le web devait s'appuyer sur des graphistes pour améliorer des aspects comme les logos des entreprises en ligne ou la composition des pages web. Après maintes tentatives et erreurs, les standards de la programmation, de l'architecture numérique et de l'utilisabilité furent conçus et remaniés grâce à un immense effort collectif.

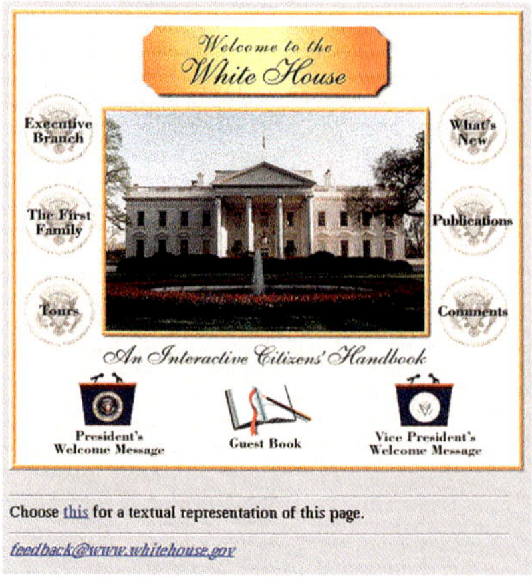

1994 · Anonymous · US · Website

1994 · Plunkett+Kuhr, Max Kisman (ILL) · US · Website

1995 · Anonymous · US · Website

»In the early 1990s, text with blue hyperlinks adorned most websites, as the main focus was sharing information. 1995 saw the start of the dot-com boom with the release of JavaScript, Java, PHP, and MP3. In 1996, websites had more character by using images and animated gifs, and by 1997 Macromedia Flash sites began to transform the web into a vibrant multimedia playground.« Rob Ford, The FWA

1995 · Anonymous · US · Website

1996 · Anonymous · US · Website

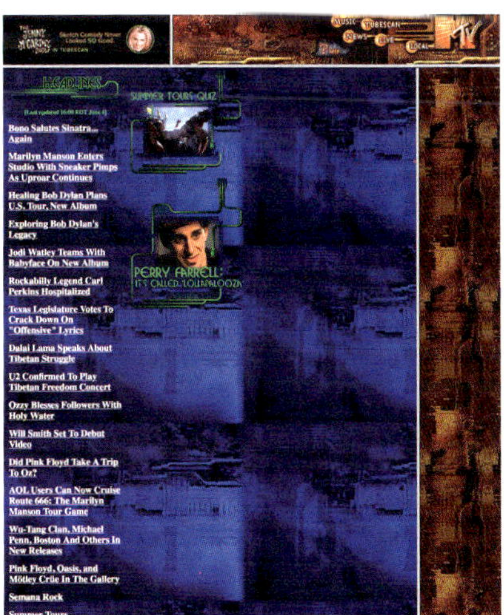

1996 · Anonymous · US · Website

1996 · Anonymous · US · Website

1996 · Anonymous · US · Website

1996 · Anonymous · US · Website

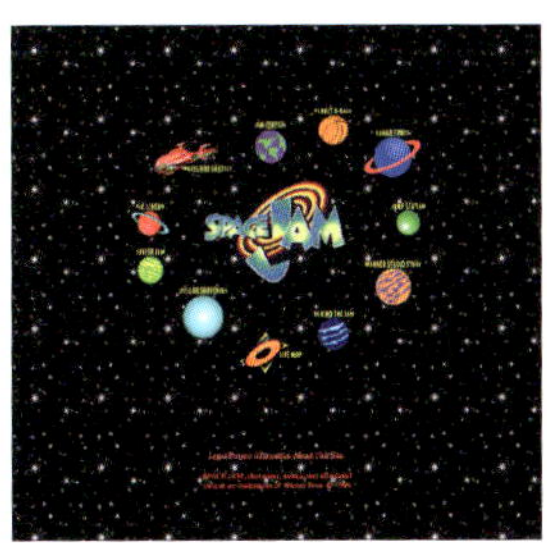

1996 · Anonymous · US · Website

1991 · Anonymous · US · Logo · America Online

1994 · Anonymous · US · Logo · Amazon.com

1996 · Kevin Farnham, Organic · US · Logo · Yahoo!

1996 · Anonymous · US · Logo · Hotbot

Paula Scher (1948, Washington, DC) is one of the most important American graphic designers of modern times. After attending the Tyler School of Art in Pennsylvania, Scher went on to design advertising and record sleeves for CBS and Atlantic, later becoming the first female principal at Pentagram, which she joined in 1991. Her most notable works include identities for Citibank, MoMA, the New York Philharmonic, and the Metropolitan Opera. Scher has taught at the School of Visual Arts, Cooper Union, and Yale University, having widely exhibited both her design and fine art work for over three decades.

Paula Scher (1948, Washington, D.C.) ist im Bereich Grafikdesign eine der bedeutendsten amerikanischen Persönlichkeiten unserer Zeit. Nach dem Besuch der Tyler School of Art in Pennsylvania gestaltete sie Werbung und Plattencover für CBS und Atlantic, 1991 ging sie zu Pentagram und wurde die erste Frau, die diese Designfirma leitete. Zu ihren bemerkenswertesten Arbeiten gehören das CI für die Citibank, das MoMA, das New York Philharmonic und die Metropolitan Opera. Scher unterrichtet an der School of Visual Arts, an der Cooper Union und der Yale University. Seit über dreißig Jahren kommen ihre Arbeiten – sowohl in der Grafik wie in der Malerei – vielfach zur Ausstellung.

Paula Scher (1948, Washington, D.C.) est une des grandes graphistes américaines contemporaines. Après des études à la Tyler School of Art, Pennsylvanie, Scher enchaîne avec la conception publicitaire et des pochettes d'albums pour CBS et Atlantic, devenant plus tard la première femme à intégrer Pentagram, qu'elle rejoint en 1991. Ses travaux les plus remarqués comptent notamment des identités pour Citibank, le MoMA, le New York Philharmonic et le Metropolitan Opera. Scher a enseigné à la School of Visual Arts, à la Cooper Union et à l'université Yale. Elle expose depuis plus de trois décennies ses œuvres de design et d'art.

1994 · Paula Scher, Pentagram · US · Poster

»The Public Theater identity created a complete visual language for an institution beyond just a logo. [...] The main challenge was, and still is, how to make a complex organization understandable to its audience while promoting individual productions.« Paula Scher, *Works*, 2017

1995 · Paula Scher, Pentagram · US · Poster

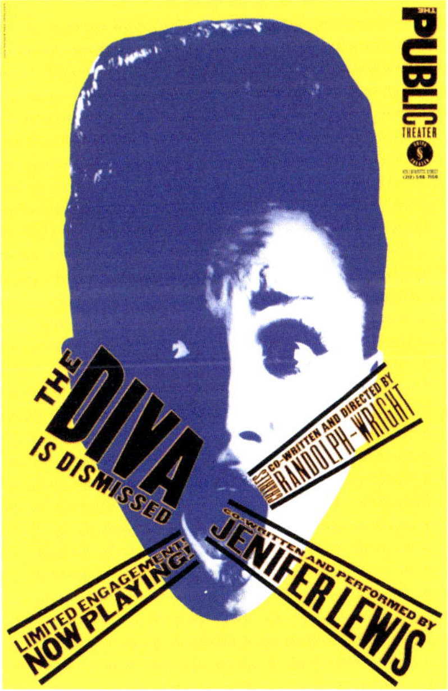

1994 · Paula Scher, Pentagram · US · Poster

In 1994, Scher was awarded the contract to develop a new visual identity for the Public Theater in New York City. With her unconventional visual vocabulary and playful use of typefaces, she managed to introduce an avant-garde aesthetic to a field which all too often tends towards the unadventurous. At the same time, her designs captured the imagination of potential new theater audiences.

Im Jahr 1994 erhielt Paula Scher den Auftrag zur Entwicklung einer neuen visuellen Identität für das Public Theater in New York City. Mit unkonventioneller Bildsprache und spielerisch eingesetzter Typografie gelang es ihr, eine neuartige Ästhetik in diesem ansonsten oft konservativ auftretenden Bereich zu etablieren. Damit ließen sich auch neue Zielgruppen für das Programm begeistern.

En 1994, Paula Scher fut chargée de développer la nouvelle identité visuelle du Public Theater à New York. Son langage visuel anticonformiste et son utilisation ludique de la typographie lui permirent de créer une esthétique d'un nouveau genre dans un secteur qui se donne volontiers une image conservatrice. Cette approche a aussi eu le mérite d'attirer et de passionner de nouvelles cibles pour le programme du théâtre.

1994 · Paula Scher, Pentagram · US · Identity

1990s · Paula Scher, Pentagram · US · Poster

1995 · Paula Scher, Pentagram · US · Poster

1995

Dutch designer Albert-Jan Pool creates a new digital version of the German standard typeface **DIN**, which becomes one of the most influential typefaces of the following years

1995 · Justus Oehler, Pentagram · DE/US · Logo · World Economic Forum

1995 · Neville Brody · UK · Poster

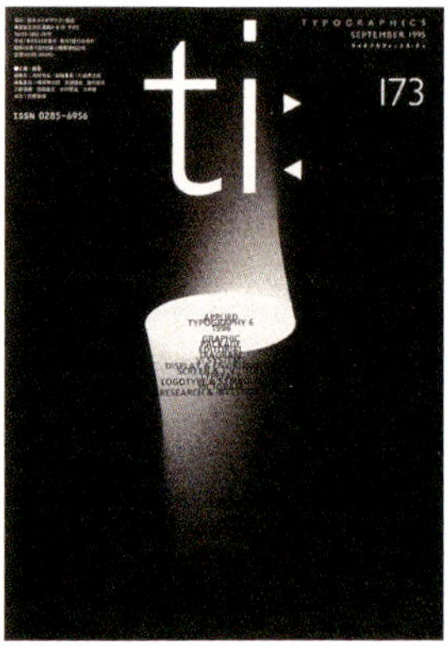

1995 · Yoshimaru Takahashi · JP · Magazine cover

1995 · Vignelli Associates · US/IT · Logo · United Colors of Benetton

1995 · P. Scott Makela, Billy Phelps (PH) · US · Magazine cover

1995 · Michael Bryce · AU · Poster

1995 · Zintzmeyer & Lux · CH/DE · Logo · Deutsche Telekom

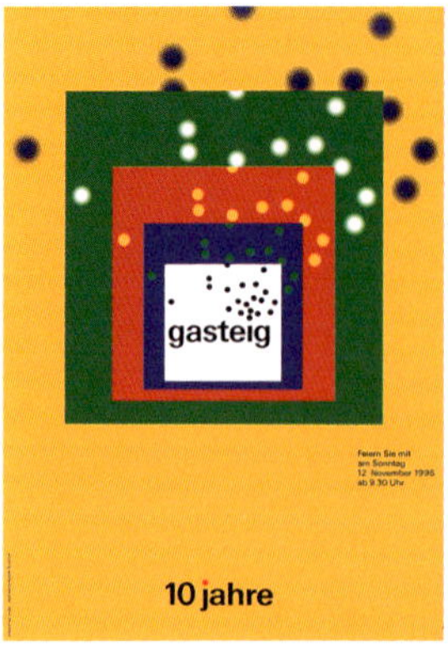

1995 · Rolf Müller · DE · Poster

The FUSE 95 design conference is held, later renamed **TYPO Berlin**

David Carson's book **The End of Print** is published

The **Razorfish** web design company opens for business in New York City

1995 · Erik Spiekermann, MetaDesign · DE · Identity · Audi

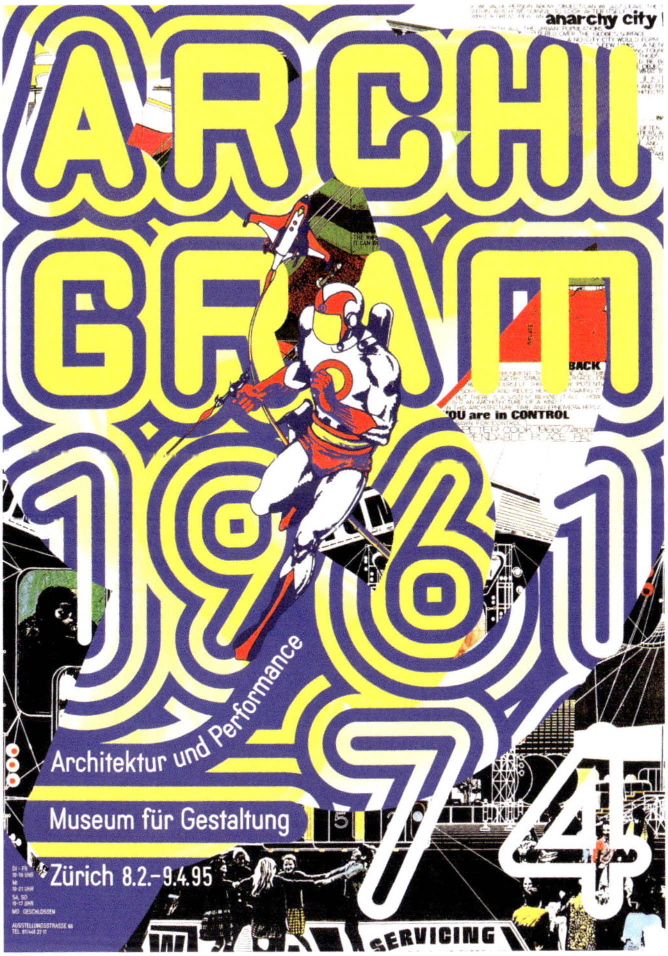

1995 · Ralph Schraivogel · CH · Poster

1995 · Garth Walker · ZA · Magazine covers

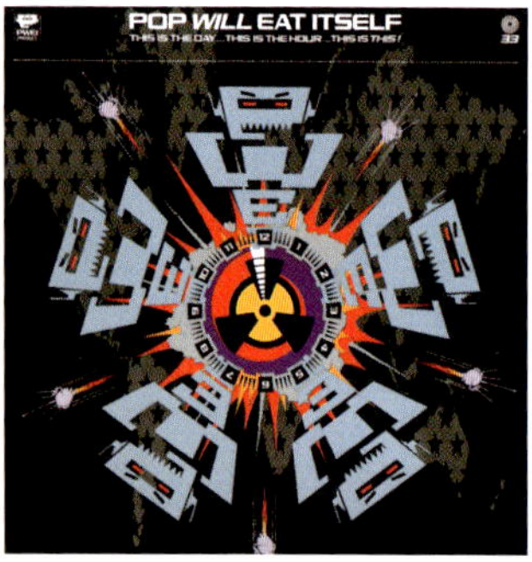

1989 · The Designers Republic™ · UK · Record cover

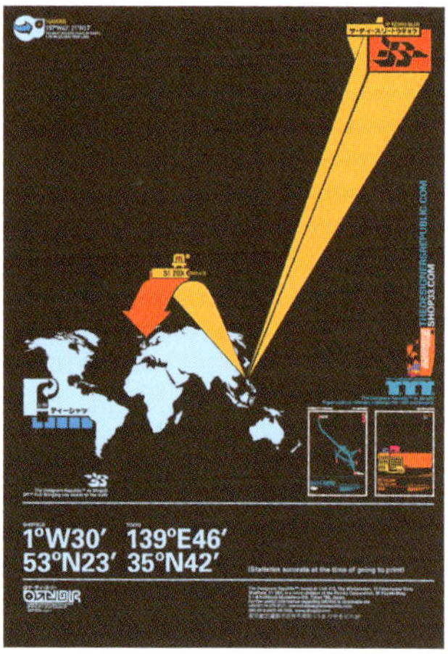

1990s · The Designers Republic™ · UK · Poster

1990s · The Designers Republic™ · UK · Poster

1990s · The Designers Republic™ · UK · Poster

The Designers Republic™ (tDR; 1986, Sheffield, England) was a British multimedia design studio formed by Ian Anderson (1961, London) and Nick Phillips (1962, London). With a subversive take on consumerism and corporate branding, the duo produced groundbreaking work for film festivals, computer games, Sony's AIBO robot pets, and Coca-Cola, while perhaps most notably designing album covers for cult UK electronica label Warp Records. The company closed its doors in 2009, with Anderson relaunching tDR as a slimmed-down enterprise. Their work is in the permanent collections of MoMA and the V&A.

The Designers Republic™ (tDR; 1986, Sheffield, England) war ein britisches Multimediadesignbüro, gegründet von Ian Anderson (1961, London) und Nick Phillips (1962, London). Mit seinem subversiven Blick auf Konsumdenken und Unternehmensbranding schuf das Duo bahnbrechende Arbeiten für Computerspiele, Filmfestivals, Sonys AIBO-Robotertiere und für Coca-Cola; am bekanntesten sind allerdings wohl ihre Albumcover für das britische Electronica-Kultlabel Warp Records. Das Büro wurde 2009 aufgelöst, Anderson eröffnete das Studio im kleineren Format neu. Arbeiten von tDR liegen in der ständigen Sammlung des MoMA und des V&A.

The Designers Republic™ (tDR; 1986, Sheffield, Angleterre) fut un studio de design multimédia britannique formé par Ian Anderson (1961, Londres) et Nick Phillips (1962, Londres). Avec une approche subversive du consumérisme et de l'image de marque, le duo a produit des projets révolutionnaires pour des jeux vidéo, des festivals de cinéma, les chiens robots AIBO de Sony et Coca-Cola. Mais leur travail le plus remarquable reste peut-être les pochettes d'albums pour Warp Records, le très culte label britannique de musique électronique. tDR a fermé ses portes en 2009, Anderson relançant une version réduite de la firme. Leur travail a sa place dans les collections permanentes du MoMA et du V&A.

»The inspiration, motivation, drive, starting point for my work is pop culture: why people do what they do, why they believe what they believe, what enriches their lives, and why and how that can be tapped into—what makes people tick.« Ian Anderson, *Eye* #71, 2009

1995 · The Designers Republic™ · UK · Poster

1989 · The Designers Republic™ · UK · Logo · Warp Records

1990s · The Designers Republic™ · UK · Poster

1994 · The Designers Republic™ · UK · Poster

1992 · The Designers Republic™ · UK · Poster

1996

British designer Matthew Carter creates the **Georgia** and **Verdana** typefaces

Karel Martens publishes his book **Drukwerk**

1996 · April Greiman · US · Logo · Lux Pictures

1996 · Italo Lupi · IT · Logo · Miu Miu

1996 · Koeweiden Postma · NL · Logo · Cineteam

1996 · Mark Blamire, Rob O'Connor, Stylorouge, Lorenzo Agius (PH) · UK · Poster

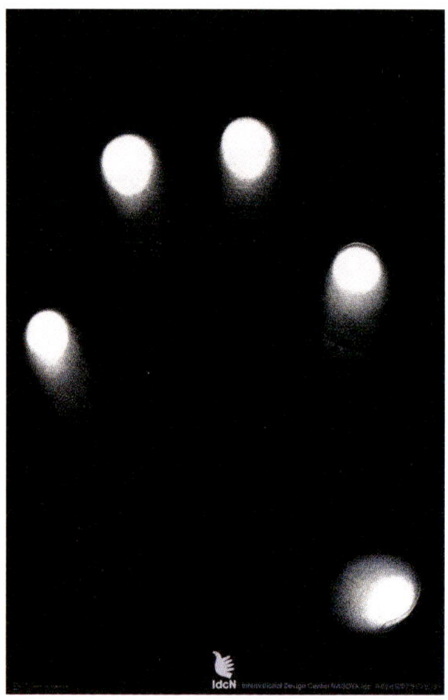

1996 · Koichi Sato · JP · Poster

1996 · Chris Ashworth, Neil Fletcher · UK · Magazine covers

The **Lithuanian Graphic Design Association** (LGDA) is founded

Zuzana Licko creates the **Mrs Eaves** typeface

Imaginary Forces, a motion graphics studio based in Hollywood and New York, is founded by Kyle Cooper, Peter Frankfurt, and Chip Houghton

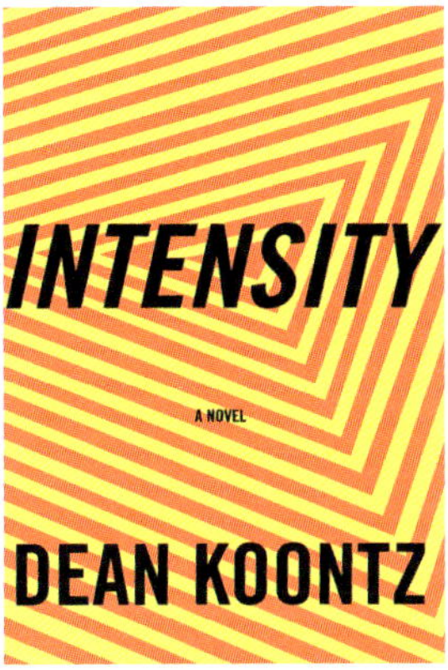

1996 · Chip Kidd · US · Book cover

1996 · Jin Sato · JP · Poster

1996 · Milton Glaser · US · Poster

1996 · Anthony Burrill, KesselsKramer · NL · Ads

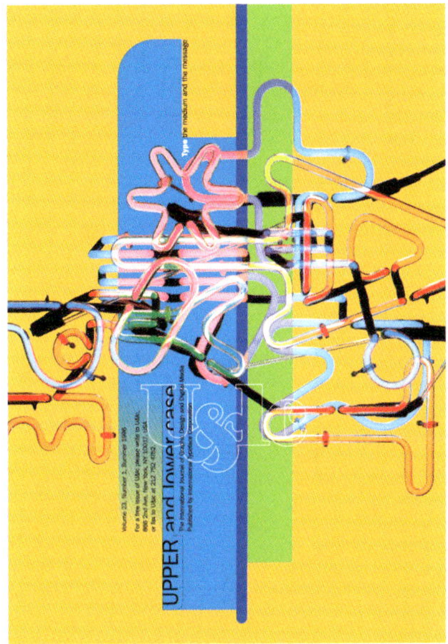

1996 · Why Not Associates · UK · Magazine cover

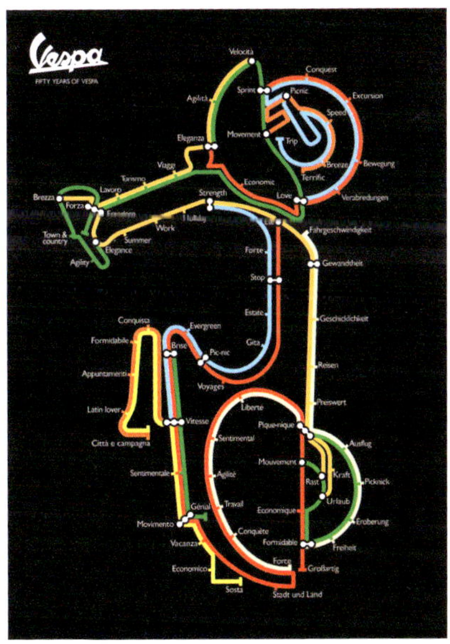

1996 · Italo Lupi · IT · Poster

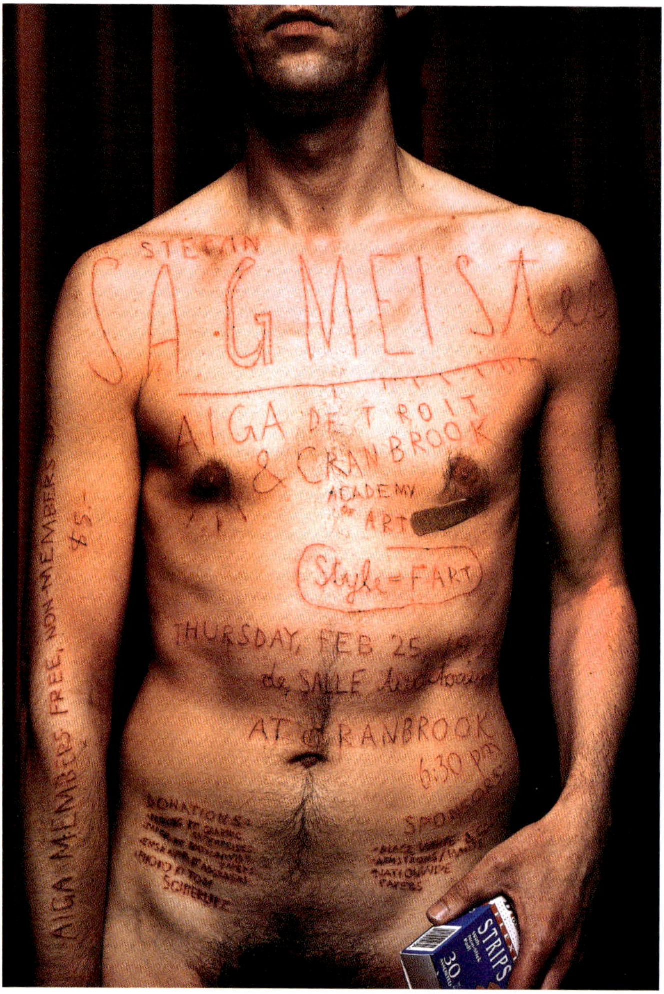

1999 · Stefan Sagmeister · AT/US · Poster

Stefan Sagmeister (1962, Bregenz, Austria) is an Austrian-American designer and typographer based in New York, where he runs Sagmeister & Walsh with Jessica Walsh (1986, New York). Always challenging visual conventions and the reach of a designer's influence, Sagmeister's design work ranges from record covers to software, besides creating new aesthetics and interactions. He has received Grammy Awards for packaging designs for Talking Heads, David Byrne, and Brian Eno. After originally studying in Vienna, and at New York's Pratt Institute, he worked in advertising in Hong Kong and then in New York with Tibor Kalman, before starting Sagmeister Inc. in 1993.

Stefan Sagmeister (1962, Bregenz, Österreich) ist ein österreichisch-amerikanischer Grafikdesigner und Typograf mit Sitz in New York, wo er gemeinsam mit Jessica Walsh (1986, New York) Sagmeister & Walsh leitet. In seiner Arbeit fordert er die visuellen Konventionen und den herkömmlichen Einflussbereich von Design heraus und gestaltet vor diesem Hintergrund Plattencover ebenso wie Software; zudem schafft er eine neue Ästhetik und neue Interaktionen. Für seine Packagingdesigns für Talking Heads, David Byrne und Brian Eno wurde Sagmeister jeweils mit einem Grammy Award ausgezeichnet. Er studierte in Wien und am Pratt Institute in New York, anschließend arbeitete er in Hongkong in der Werbebranche und dann in New York bei Tibor Kalman, ehe er 1993 Sagmeister Inc. gründete.

Stefan Sagmeister (1962, Brégence, Autriche) est un designer et typographe austro-américain basé à New York, où il dirige Sagmeister & Walsh avec Jessica Walsh (1986, New York). Défiant toujours les conventions visuelles et le champ d'influence du designer, le travail de Sagmeister va de pochettes d'albums aux logiciels, sans compter la création de nouvelles esthétiques et interactions. Il a reçu des Grammy Awards récompensant ses designs d'emballages pour Talking Heads, David Byrne et Brian Eno. Après des études à Vienne et l'Institut Pratt de New York, Sagmeister a travaillé dans la publicité à Hong Kong, puis à New York avec Tibor Kalman, avant de lancer Sagmeister Inc. en 1993.

»Beauty is something you have to work at, it doesn't happen automatically. The simpler things are the better, the whole Bauhaus idea involved a lot of jiggery-pokery. If you want to make beautiful things, you must make beauty your ultimate goal.« Stefan Sagmeister, *Novum*, 2016

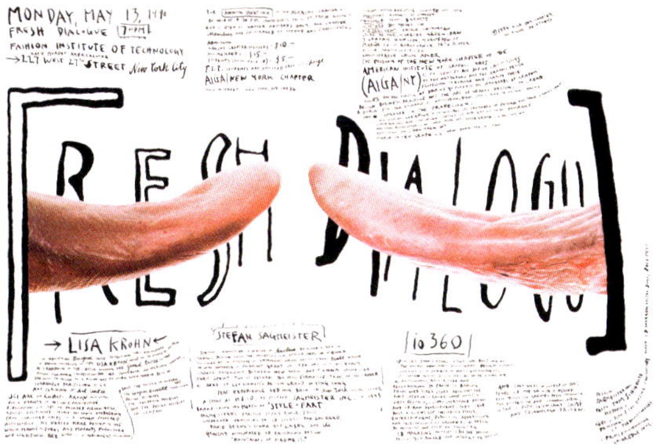

1996 · Stefan Sagmeister · AT/US · Poster

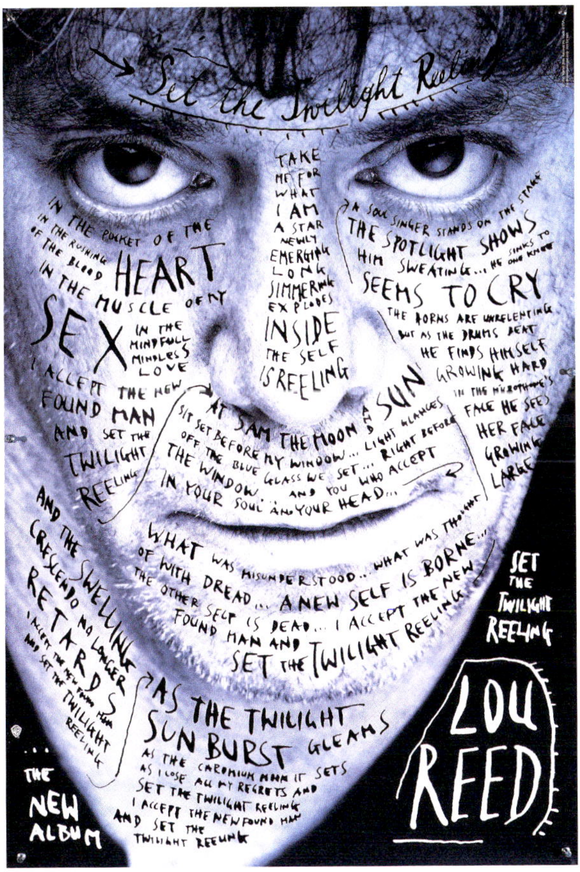

1996 · Stefan Sagmeister · AT/US · Poster

1994 · Stefan Sagmeister · US · Record cover

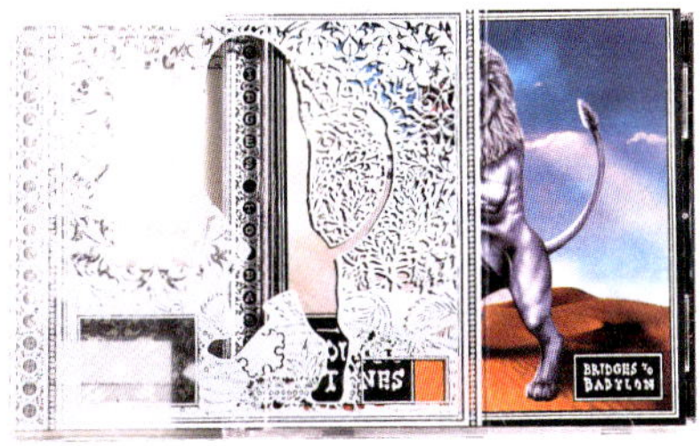

1997 · Stefan Sagmeister · AT/US · Record cover

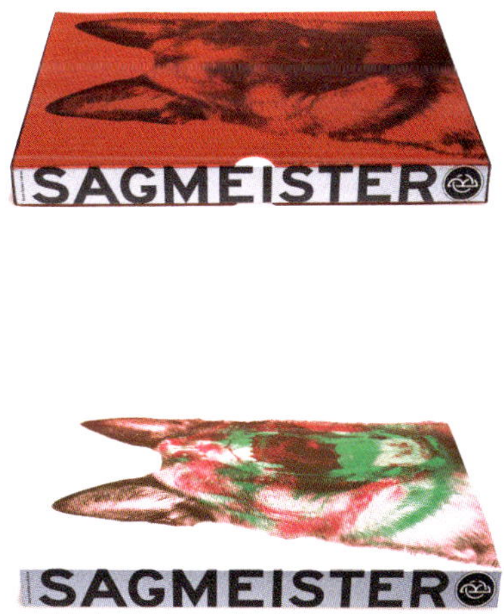

2001 · Stefan Sagmeister · AT/US · Book covers

1997

1997 · Iris Utikal, Michael Gais, Qwer · DE · Logo · Expo 2000 Hannover

1997 · Landor · US · Logo · Fortis

1997 · Enterprise IG · US · Logo · Hilton Hotels

Per Mollerup's book on trademarks is published, **Marks of Excellence**

1997 · TBWA\Chiat\Day · US · Posters

Rene Wanner's **Poster Page** goes online

1992 · David Carson · US/BR · Magazine cover

1997 · Thérèse Troika · FR · Poster

1997 · Vignelli Associates · US · Identity · Guggenheim Museum

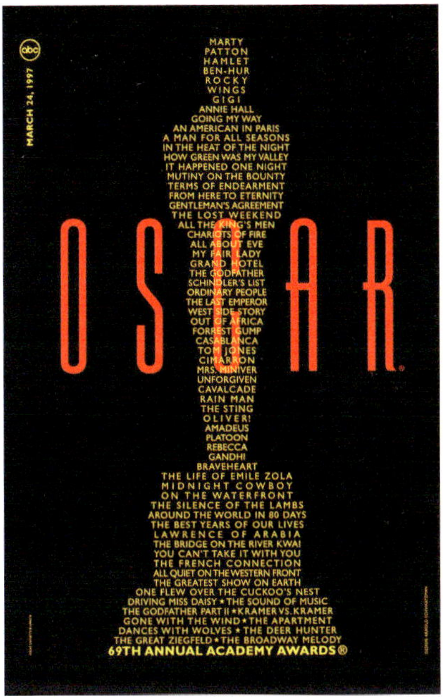

1997 · Arnold Schwartzman · UK/US · Poster

1997 · Stefan Sagmeister · AT/US · Poster

1997 · Felipe Taborda · BR · Poster

1997 · Melchior Imboden · CH · Poster

1998

1998 · Turner Duckworth · US · Logo · SETI Institute

1998 · Stockholm Design Lab · SE · Logo · SAS Scandinavian Airlines

1998 · FutureBrand · AU · Logo · Crown Melbourne

Publication of the reference book **Typography: When Who How** by Friedrich Friedl, Nicolaus Ott, and Bernard Stein

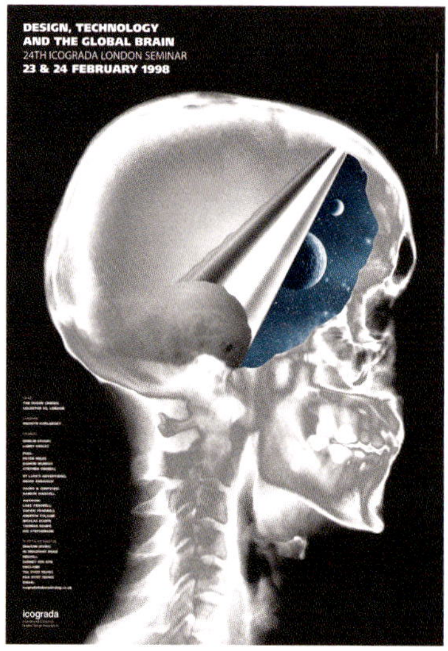

1998 · Mervyn Kurlansky · UK · Poster

1998 · April Greiman · US · Poster

The **Zapfino** typeface by Hermann Zapf is released

1998 · Gunter Rambow, Rambow van de Sand · DE · Poster

1998 · Rosmarie Tissi, Odermatt+Tissi · CH/JP · Poster

1997 · Roman Kalarus · PL · Poster

The international branding corporation **Moving Brands** is founded by graduates of Central Saint Martins College in London

The **Werkplaats Typografie** Master's course in typography is founded in Arnhem, Netherlands, by Wigger Bierma and Karel Martens

1998 · Kit Hinrichs, John Hersey (ILL) · US · Magazine cover

1998 · Jennifer Morla · US · Ad

1998 · Helmut Schmid · DE/KR · Packaging

1998 · Fernando Gutiérrez · ES · Magazine cover

1999

Adbusters magazine updates the **First Things First** manifesto by Ken Garland from 1964, as signed by 33 international graphic designers

The Dutch type foundry **Underware** is established

1999 · Michael Bierut, Pentagram · US · Poster

1999 · Ian Chilvers, Atelier Works · UK · Logo · Integrity

1999 · April Greiman · US · Logo · Roto Architects

1999 · Paula Scher, Pentagram · US · Logo · Citibank

1999 · Patrick Mitchell · US · Magazine cover

Jonathan Hoefler and Tobias Frere-Jones establish the **Hoefler & Frere-Jones** type foundry in New York City

The book **Radical Graphics/Graphic Radicals** presents an overview of recent developments in graphic design

The Malaysian graphic design association **WREGA** is founded

1999 · Concept Arts · US · Poster

1999 · Lawrence Azerrad (AD), Sonya Koskoff (PH) · US · Record cover

1999 · Daniel Kleinman · UK · Opening titles

1999 · Andy Dreyfus, Apple Inc. · US · Packaging

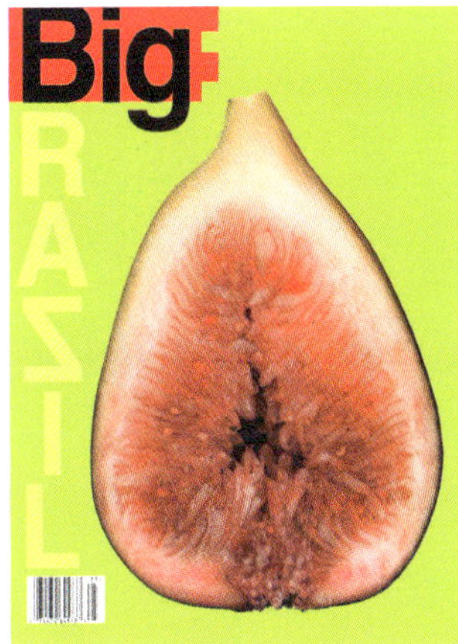

1999 · Rico Linc · BR · Magazine cover

1999 · Oscar Mariné · ES · Poster

2007 · Melchior Imboden · CH · Poster

2000

2008 · "Obey" (Shepard Fairey) · US · Poster

2006 · Karel Martens · NL · Magazine cover

2005 · Jonathan Gray · UK · Book cover

2009

2004 · Ostengruppe · RU · Poster

2004 · Victor Candia · PY · Magazine cover

Whether it could be attributed to the sometimes overwhelming surfeit of computer graphics, or was a reaction to the flood of digitally produced imagery, at the turn of the millennium there was a clear return to austere, minimalist solutions in graphic design. Following the initiative of a few innovative design studios in central Europe, 1960s modernism was rediscovered and reinvented in a new contemporary guise. The heroes of the Swiss Style and Dutch Design were celebrated in major retrospectives and even Helvetica, the typeface long regarded as no more than "reliable," enjoyed a revival, which included a highly respected film documentary made to mark its 50th birthday. Simultaneously, huge progress was made in media design. For example, it was now perfectly simple to animate a design or to make your own short movie. The internet and the increasing use of broadband also speeded up connections with designers working in other parts of the world, making the discovery of new visual trends and technological advances still quicker and easier.

The exterior of the New Jersey Performing Arts Center, created by the American graphic designer Paula Scher and completed in 2001.

Fassade des New Jersey Performing Arts Center, 2001 von der amerikanischen Designerin Paula Scher gestaltet.

Façade du New Jersey Performing Arts Center, conçue en 2001 par la graphiste américaine Paula Scher.

Möglicherweise aus Überdruss an der teils überbordenden Menge an Computergrafik, vielleicht auch als Reaktion auf die Flut an visuellen Eindrücken durch digitale Medien: Etwas hat während der Jahrhundertwende zu einer Rückbesinnung auf strenge und reduzierte Lösungen im Bereich des Grafikdesigns geführt. Ausgehend von einigen innovativen Designbüros in Mitteleuropa, wurde der Modernismus der 1960er-Jahre wiederentdeckt und in einer neuen und zeitgemäßen Form wiederbelebt. Die Helden der Schweizer Grafik oder des niederländischen Designs wurden in großen Retrospektiven gefeiert, und selbst die lange als ausschließlich zweckmäßig angesehene Schrift Helvetica erlebte zu ihrem fünfzigsten Geburtstag ein Revival, inklusive einer viel beachteten Filmdokumentation. Gleichzeitig entwickelten sich die Möglichkeiten digitaler Gestaltung enorm weiter. Es war nun beispielsweise ganz einfach möglich, Entwürfe zu animieren oder eigene kleine Filme zu produzieren. Das Internet und der Ausbau der Breitbandkommunikation förderten zudem die Vernetzung der internationalen Designszene und sorgten für eine beschleunigte Wahrnehmung visueller Trends und neuer Entwicklungen.

Que ce soit en raison d'une saturation face à la masse d'infographies, ou en réaction au flot incessant d'images numériques, le changement de millénaire fut témoin d'un clair retour à des solutions austères et minimalistes en matière de graphisme. Des studios de design innovants d'Europe centrale eurent cette initiative et de là, on redécouvrit le modernisme des années 1960, qui connut un revival sous une forme contemporaine. Les héros du style suisse ou du design néerlandais furent célébrés dans de grandes rétrospectives, et même l'Helvetica, longtemps considérée comme une police de caractères purement utilitaire, fêta sa renaissance, notamment dans un documentaire très remarqué à l'occasion de son cinquantième anniversaire. En parallèle, les possibilités du graphisme numérique se multiplièrent et il était désormais facile d'animer un graphisme ou de produire de petits films. Internet et l'emploi croissant du haut débit favorisèrent en outre la mise en réseau de la scène internationale du design et la découverte de nouvelles tendances visuelles et évolutions technologiques.

2000

The visual culture magazine **Dot Dot Dot** is launched

Graphic designers Jan Wilker of Germany and Hjalti Karlsson of Iceland open the design firm **Karlssonwilker** in New York City

2000 · FHA Image Design · AU · Logo · Sydney Olympic Games

2000 · Paula Scher, Pentagram · US · Logo · Whitney Museum of American Art

2000 · Hiroshige Fukuhara · JP · Logo · Walkman

2000 · Helmut Schmid · DE/JP · Poster

Steven Heller's monograph on Paul Rand is published

2000 · Germán Montalvo Aguilar · MX · Poster

2000 · Yuri Surkov · RU · Poster

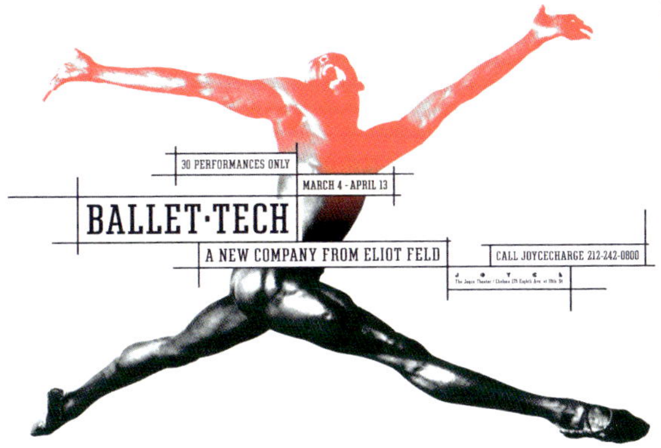

2000 · Paula Scher, Pentagram · US · Poster

2000 · NB Studio · UK · Poster

2000 · Michael Bierut, Pentagram · US · Poster

Michael Bierut (1957, Cleveland, Ohio) is a leading American designer who was vice president of graphic design at Vignelli Associates before becoming a partner at Pentagram in 1990. Bierut has been a prolific educator and senior critic in design at Yale School of Art; the author of a number of books on design, his own works have been acquired by major institutions worldwide. Notable achievements have ranged from the redesign of *The Atlantic* magazine to the signage system for Lower Manhattan, while Bierut has also served as the president of AIGA, and was a founding member of the *Design Observer* blog.

Michael Bierut (1957, Cleveland, Ohio) ist ein führender amerikanischer Grafikdesigner, der als Vizepräsident bei Vignelli Associates tätig war, ehe er 1990 Partner bei Pentagram wurde. Bierut hat vielfach Lehrtätigkeiten ausgeübt und ist Senior Critic in Grafikdesign an der Yale School of Art. Zum Thema Design hat er zudem eine Reihe von Büchern verfasst; seine eigenen Arbeiten wurden von führenden Institutionen in aller Welt erworben. Zu seinen bedeutendsten Projekten gehören das Redesign der Zeitschrift *The Atlantic* ebenso wie das Beschilderungssystem in Lower Manhattan. Zudem ist Bierut Präsident des AIGA und ein Gründungsmitglied des Blogs *Design Observer*.

Michael Bierut (1957, Cleveland, Ohio) est un graphiste américain de premier plan qui a été vice-président du département de graphisme chez Vignelli Associates avant de s'associer à Pentagram en 1990. Bierut a été un enseignant prolifique et intervenant principal en design à la Yale School of Art. Auteur de nombreux livres sur le graphisme, ses propres œuvres ont été acquises par de grandes institutions du monde entier. Ses réalisations les plus remarquées vont de la refonte du magazine *The Atlantic* au système de signalisation dans Lower Manhattan. Bierut a aussi présidé l'AIGA et a été membre fondateur du blog *Design Observer*.

»Fifteen years in and counting, including encounters with a few fonts I may never use again, our posters for Yale Architecture still surprise even me.« Michael Bierut, *How to*, 2015

2007 · Michael Bierut, Pentagram, Marian Bantjes (TY) · US · Poster

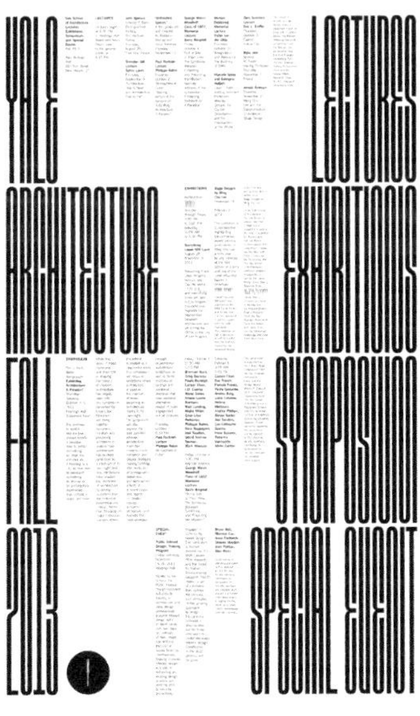

2013 · Michael Bierut, Pentagram · US · Poster

2014 · Michael Bierut, Pentagram · US · Poster

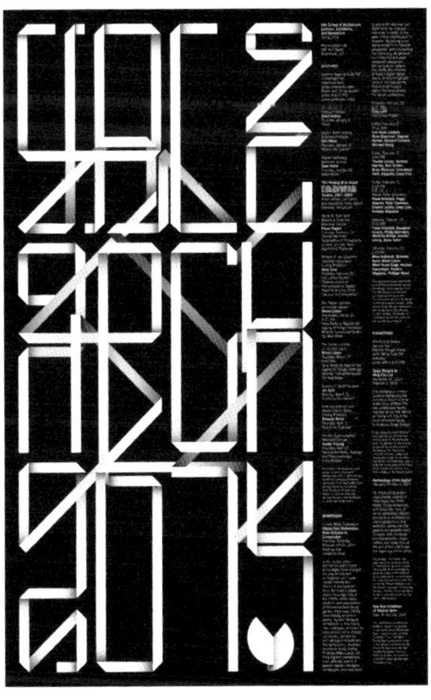

2014 · Michael Bierut, Pentagram · US · Poster

The lecture series at the Yale School of Architecture have been notable for many reasons but their significance for graphic design dates back to 1998, when Michael Bierut started designing the posters. They quickly became collectible items in their own right for the detailed and inventive typographic work involved, and were all produced in black and white until 2015, after which another printed color was introduced for the backgrounds.

Die Vortragsreihen an der Yale School of Architecture sind aus vielen Gründen bemerkenswert, doch ihre Bedeutung für das Grafikdesign geht auf das Jahr 1998 zurück, als Michael Bierut erstmals die Plakate gestaltete. Wegen der detailreichen, fantasievollen Verwendung von Typografie wurden die Poster sehr bald zu Sammlerstücken. Bis Ende 2015 waren sie alle in Schwarz-Weiß gehalten, danach wurde eine weitere Druckfarbe für den Hintergrund eingeführt.

Si les cycles de conférences de la Yale School of Architecture ont été remarquables à bien des titres, leur importance dans le domaine du graphisme remonte à 1998, quand Michael Bierut commença à concevoir les affiches de l'école. Celles-ci devinrent rapidement des pièces de collection à part entière du fait de leur approche typographique détaillée et ingénieuse. Elles ont toutes été produites en noir et blanc jusqu'en 2015, après quoi une couleur fut adoptée pour l'arrière-plan.

2001

The German **100 Best Posters** competition is extended to Austria and Switzerland

Peter Bilak starts the creation of the **Fedra** family of typefaces

2001 · Paula Scher, Pentagram · US · Logo
The High Line, New York

2001 · Lambie-Nairn · UK · Logo · O2

2001 · Eden · NL · Logo · Furore

2001 · Milton Glaser · US · Poster

2001 · Michael Bierut, Pentagram · US · Identity · New York Jets

2001 · Uwe Loesch · DE · Poster

2001 · Andreas Uebele, Büro Uebele · DE · Poster

As early as the 1970s, designers had begun to create the first examples of what became known as "supergraphics," whose typography and abstract graphics appeared on the broad faces of various public buildings. Whether intended simply as a way of catching the consumer's eye with logos that took up much more space, or as a more particular signposting system, by the turn of the 21st century this field of graphic design once again experienced a boom, which in turn generated a variety of outstanding results. The starting point for this special manifestation of the designer's art often alternates between aesthetic considerations and user orientation.

Bereits in den 1970er-Jahren realisierten Gestalterinnen und Gestalter erstmals Arbeiten aus dem Bereich der sogenannten Supergraphics, bei dem öffentliche Gebäude zum Spielfeld von Typografie und abstrakter Grafik werden. Ob einfach nur als Blickfang, als räumliche Erweiterung des Brandings oder als Wegeleitsystem, erlebte dieses Feld in den 2000er-Jahren einen neuen Boom und brachte eine Vielzahl herausragender Lösungen hervor. Die Arbeiten dieser besonderen Ausprägung von Grafikdesign bewegen sich nicht selten zwischen ästhetischen und nutzungsorientierten Ansatzpunkten.

Dès les années 1970, des graphistes réalisaient les premiers travaux relevant de ce qui allait être baptisé «supergraphics», où les façades de bâtiments publics deviennent le terrain de jeu de la typographie et du graphisme abstrait. Simple accroche visuelle à l'aide de logos démesurés ou signalétiques plus ciblées, cette approche graphique connut dans les années 2000 un véritable essor et donna d'excellents résultats. Il n'est pas rare que ce type d'expression évolue aux confins de réflexions esthétiques et d'une volonté d'orientation.

2001 · Paula Scher, Pentagram · US · Environmental graphics

2011 · Andreas Uebele, Carolin Himmel, Büro Uebele · DE · Environmental graphics

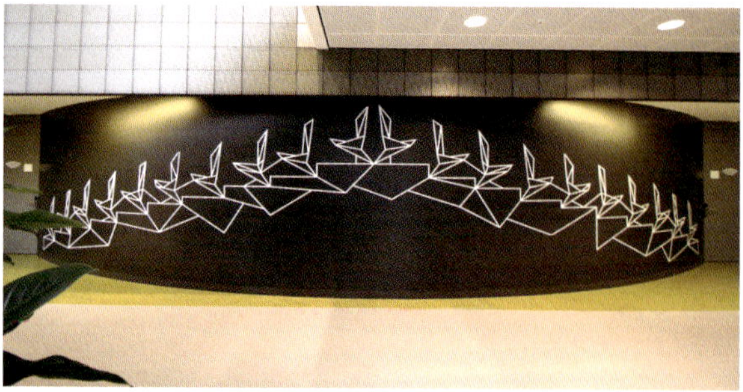

2016 · Lava · NL · Environmental graphics

»Nowadays the term supergraphics is almost completely divorced from its origins in architectural theory; today, it means big graphics in an architectural setting, and is now more commonly referred to as environmental graphics.« Adrian Shaughnessy, *Supergraphics*, 2010

2004 · Andreas Uebele, Gerd Häußler, Büro Uebele · DE · Environmental graphics

2007 · April Greiman · US · Environmental graphics

2000s · Paula Scher, Pentagram · US · Environmental graphics

1995 · April Greiman · US/JP · Environmental graphics

2002

Christian Schwartz's **Neutraface** typeface is released, which became one of the most popular fonts of the 2010s

Lars Müller's book **Helvetica: Homage to a Typeface** is published

2002 · Angus Hyland, Pentagram · UK · Logo · EAT

2002 · Interbrand · UK · Logo · British Library

2002 · Graphic Thought Facility · UK · Logo · Habitat

2002 · Gabor Palotai · SE · Poster/Identity

2002 · Ostengruppe · RU · Poster

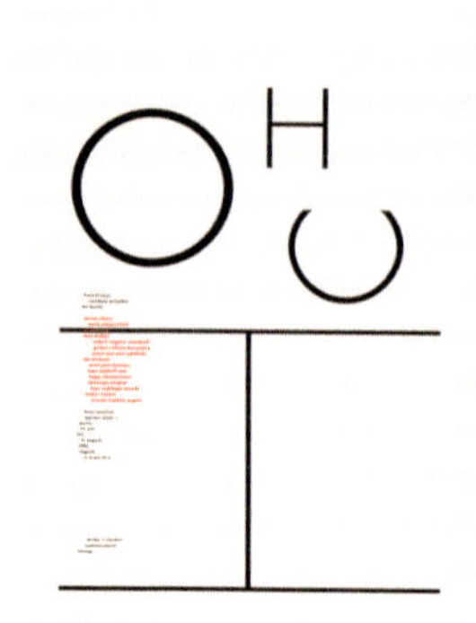

2002 · Ott+Stein · DE · Poster

2002 · Fritz Gottschalk · CH · Poster

2002 · Jonathan Gray · US · Book cover

2002 · Jonathan Barnbrook · UK ·
Record cover

2002 · R2 · PT · Poster

2002 · Antoine+Manuel · FR · Poster

2002 · Marcelo Pallotta · BR · Poster

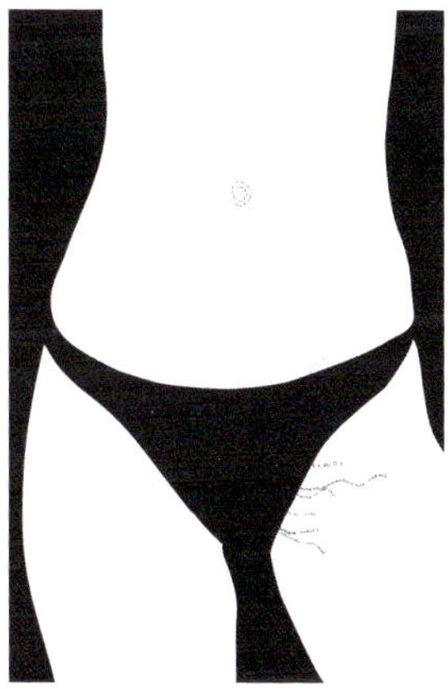

2002 · Fons Hickmann · DE · Poster

2003

The first issue of Iranian design magazine **Neshan** is published

A group of prominent German designers initiate the **11 Designer** campaign in protest against the official FIFA logo for the 2006 Soccer World Cup in Germany

2003 · Anna Berkenbusch · DE · Poster

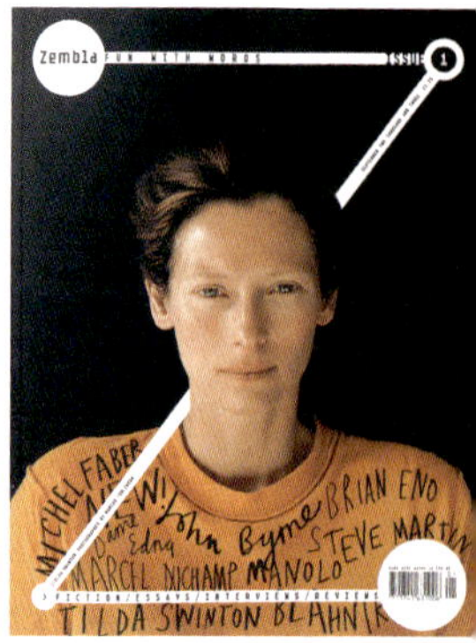

2003 · Frost* Design · AU · Magazine cover

2003 · Skype design team · LU · Logo · Skype

2003 · TBWA · US · Poster

2003 · FutureBrand · US · Logo · UPS

2003 · Goebel Weyne · BR · Poster

2003 · Suburbia · UK · Logo · *Pop* magazine

2003 · Ralph Schraivogel · CH · Poster

The widely acclaimed book **Tell Me Why** is published, on the first 24 months of New York-based graphic design studio Karlssonwilker

2003 · Reza Abedini · IR · Poster

2004

2004 · Chermayeff & Geismar · US · Logo · Opet

2004 · Luke Hayman, Pentagram · US · Logo · New York magazine

2004 · Michael Johnson · UK · Logo · Shelter

Swiss designer Laurenz Brunner creates the **Akkurat** typeface

2004 · James Goggin · UK · Poster

2004 · Kosuke Niwano, Shinmura Design Office · JP · Poster

2004 · Ahn Sang-Soo · KR · Poster

Ellen Lupton's book **Thinking with Type** is published

2004 · Chen Zhengda · CN · Poster

2004 · Jürg Lehni · CH · Magazine cover

The type foundry **Commercial Type** is established by Paul Barnes and Christian Schwartz in New York and London

The first issue of Swiss graphic design magazine **Idpure** is published

004 · Intégral Ruedi Baur · CH/DE · Identity, Signage · Cologne Bonn Airport

004 · Atlas · ES · Brochure spreads

2004 · 2x4 · US · Identity · Brooklyn Museum

2004 · Danny Yount, Prologue Films · US · Opening titles

Throughout the history of design there have always been phases in which attempts were made to break or bend the centuries-old basic rules of typography. Such experiments took place in the 1920s with the New Typography movement and in the 1990s, with the dawn of the computer age. Then, around 2000, the fresh possibilities offered by digital image manipulation, and by the ability to create completely computer-generated images with 3D software, heralded another completely new era in offbeat typographic designs. Alongside obviously computer-generated solutions, many projects deliberately deployed an analog aesthetic, and several designers discovered exciting associations between type and nature. Among these was Stefan Sagmeister, who caused a major stir with the experimental typo-installations in his highly regarded book, *Things I Have Learned in My Life So Far*, published in 2008.

In der Designgeschichte gab es immer wieder einzelne Phasen, in denen das traditionelle und seit Jahrhunderten geprägte Regelwerk der Typografie zu überwinden oder zu erweitern versucht wurde – sei es durch die Bewegung der „Neuen Typografie" in den 1920er-Jahren oder durch die wilden Jahre der frühen Computerzeit in den 1990er-Jahren. Die neuen Möglichkeiten digitaler Bildmanipulation oder gar vollständig digitaler Bilderzeugung mit 3-D-Software läuteten um das Jahr 2000 noch einmal eine ganz neue Phase nonkonformistischer Gestaltung mittels Schriften an. Neben offensichtlich digital erzeugten Lösungen entstanden zahlreiche Arbeiten, die ganz bewusst analoge Ästhetik einsetzten. Viele Gestalter entdeckten die spannungsreiche Verbindung von Schrift und Natur, so auch Stefan Sagmeister, der die Designszene mit seinen experimentellen Typo-Installationen in dem viel beachteten Buch *Things I Have Learned In My Life So Far* von 2008 begeisterte.

L'histoire du graphisme a régulièrement été ponctuée de tentatives pour enfreindre ou contourner un corpus de règles typographiques marqué par une tradition séculaire. Ce fut notamment le cas au début des années 1920 avec le mouvement «La Nouvelle Typographie» et avec la folie des débuts de l'ère informatique dans les années 1990. Vers 2000, les nouvelles possibilités offertes par la manipulation d'images et les images entièrement générées à l'aide de logiciels de 3D ont proclamé une phase inédite de création typographique non conformiste. À côté de solutions entièrement numériques, de nombreux travaux faisaient délibérément appel à une esthétique analogique. Beaucoup de graphistes ont découvert la relation fascinante entre caractères et nature, comme Stefan Sagmeister, qui enthousiasma la scène du graphisme avec les installations typographiques expérimentales de son livre très remarqué *Things I Have Learned In My Life So Far*, paru en 2008.

2006 · Stephen Doyle, Doyle Partners · US · Poster

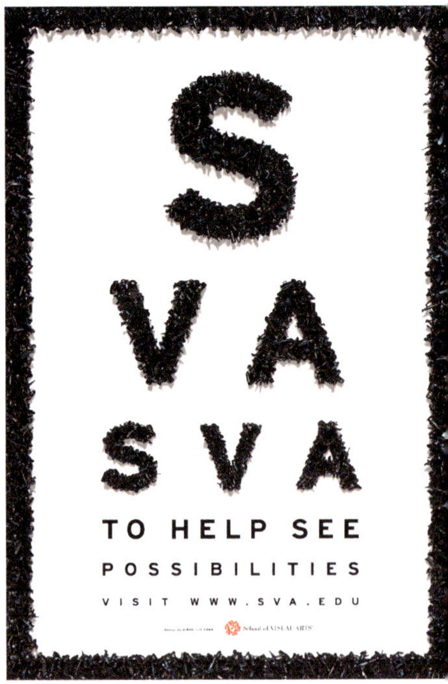

2009 · Mirko Ilić · BA · Poster

»When a sense of adventure, of seeking out unfamiliar territory, is cultivated by the typographer, then what are being promoted are ideals that equate novelty with value. Naturally, and surely to be expected of experimental typography, this is a demanding composite.«

Roger Fawcett-Tang, *New Typographic Design*, 2004

2004 · Stefan Sagmeister · AT/US · Poster

2007 · Grandpeople · NO · Poster

2003 · Oded Ezer, Shaxaf Haber (PH) · IL · Poster

2006 · Stefan Sagmeister · AT/US · Book cover and spread

2005

2005 · Spin · UK · Logo · More4

2005 · Chad Hurley · US · Logo · YouTube

2005 · Joe Kral, Cuban Council, Test Pilot Collective · US · Logo · Facebook

Adrian Shaughnessy's influential book **How to be a Graphic Designer, without Losing Your Soul** is published

2005 · Lava · NL · Poster

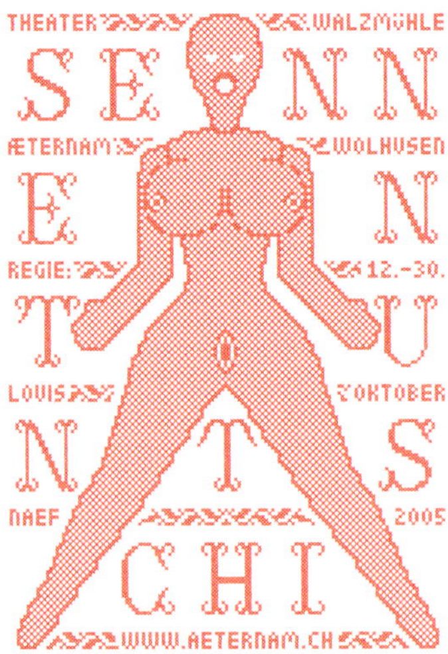

2005 · Erich Brechbühl · CH · Poster

The first issue of **Slanted** design magazine is published

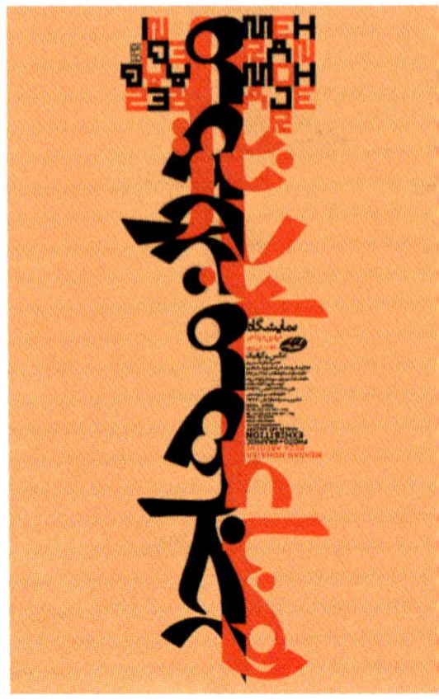

2005 · Reza Abedini · IR · Poster

2005 · Frank Arbelo · CU/BO · Poste

2005 · Sascha Lobe, Ina Bauer · DE
Book series

2006 · Kashiwa Sato · JP · Identity · Uniqlo

2005 · Intégral Ruedi Baur · FR · Identity · La Cinémathèque Française

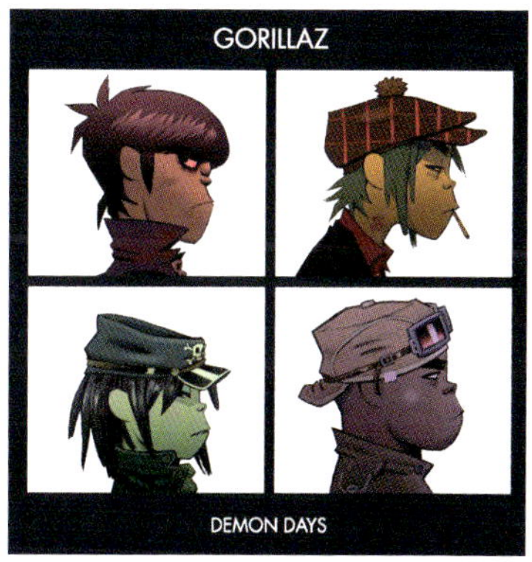

2005 · Jamie Hewlett · UK · Record cover

2005 · Experimental Jetset · NL · Poster

2005 · Experimental Jetset · NL · Poster

2008 · Experimental Jetset · NL · Poster

2007 · Experimental Jetset · NL · Poster

Experimental Jetset (1997, Amsterdam) is a Dutch graphic design studio (whose partners met at the Gerrit Rietveld Academie) with a strong focus on print work and site-specific installations. With their conceptual approach of "turning language into objects," the team quickly gained international recognition and a string of successful projects led to a major acquisition of their works by MoMA in New York in 2007. Studio members have taught at both the Rietveld and Werkplaats Typografie in the Netherlands.

Experimental Jetset (1997, Amsterdam) ist ein niederländisches Grafikdesignbüro, das sich insbesondere auf Arbeiten im Printbereit sowie mit standortspezifischen Installationen spezialisiert hat. Das Team – dessen Partner sich an der Gerrit Rietveld Academie kennenlernten – fand durch sein Arbeitskonzept, „Sprache in Objekte zu verwandeln", rasch internationale Anerkennung. Eine Reihe erfolgreicher Projekte hatte zur Folge, dass das MoMA in New York 2007 bedeutende Arbeiten des Studios erwarb. Mitglieder von Experimental Jetset haben in den Niederlanden sowohl an der Rietveld Academie als auch an der Academie Werkplaats Typografie unterrichtet.

Experimental Jetset (1997, Amsterdam) est un studio de graphisme néerlandais (ses associés se sont connus à l'académie Gerrit Rietveld) dont le travail porte principalement sur les travaux d'impression et les installations in situ. Avec leur approche conceptuelle visant à «transformer le langage en objets», l'équipe s'est rapidement fait connaître à l'échelle internationale. En 2007, une série de projets très remarqués a conduit à une acquisition substantielle de leurs œuvres par le MoMA de New York. Les membres du studio ont enseigné aux académies néerlandaises Gerrit Rietveld et Werkplaats Typografie.

»We believe that abstraction, a movement away from realism but towards reality, is the ultimate form of engagement.« Experimental Jetset, AIGA Voice Conference, 2001

2005 · Experimental Jetset · NL · Poster

2004 · Experimental Jetset · NL · Poster

2004 · Experimental Jetset · NL · Identity · Stedelijk Museum

2006

The design blog **Brand New** begins, run by Texas-based design studio UnderConsideration

The magazine design blog **magCulture** is set up in London by creative director Jeremy Leslie

2006 · Paula Scher, Julia Hoffmann, Pentagram · US · Logo · Criterion Collection

2006 · Melchior Imboden · CH · Poster

2006 · Jorge Alderete · MX · Poster

2006 · Mark Gowing · AU · Logo · Title Music and Films

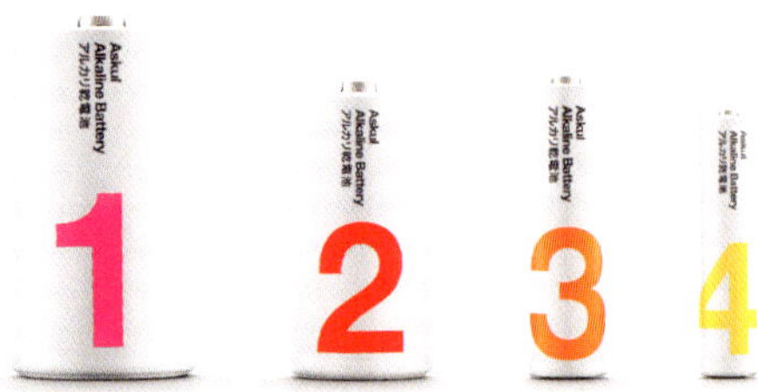

2006 · Joe Finocchiaro, Jerry Kuyper · US · Logo · Cisco

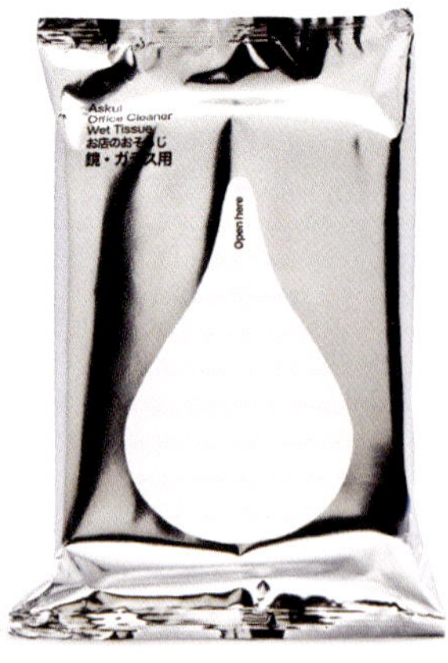

2006 · Stockholm Design Lab · SE · Packaging

2006 · Mark Gowing Studio · AU · Poster

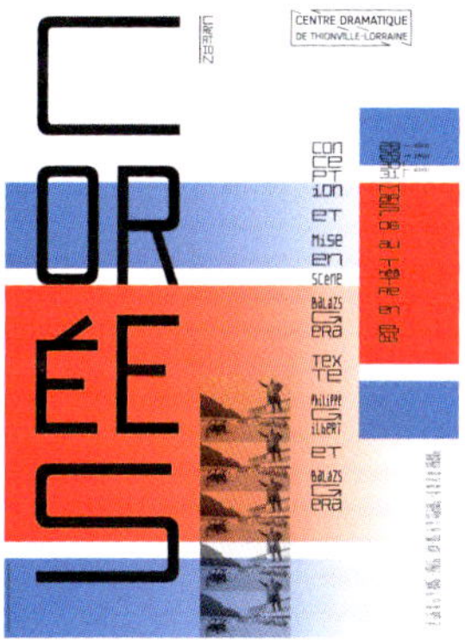

2006 · André Baldinger · FR · Poster

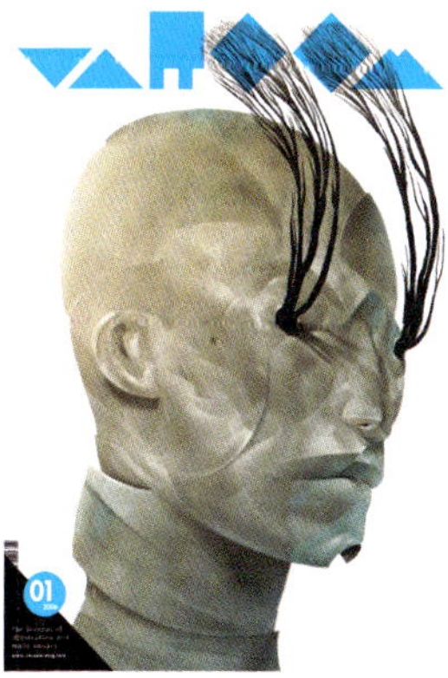

2006 · Non-Format · UK/NO · Magazine cover

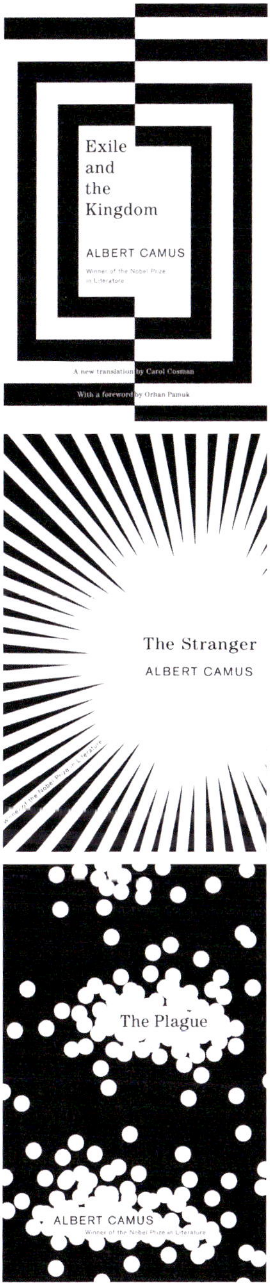

2006 · John Gall, Helen Yentus · US · Book covers

2006 · Hort · DE/US · Poster

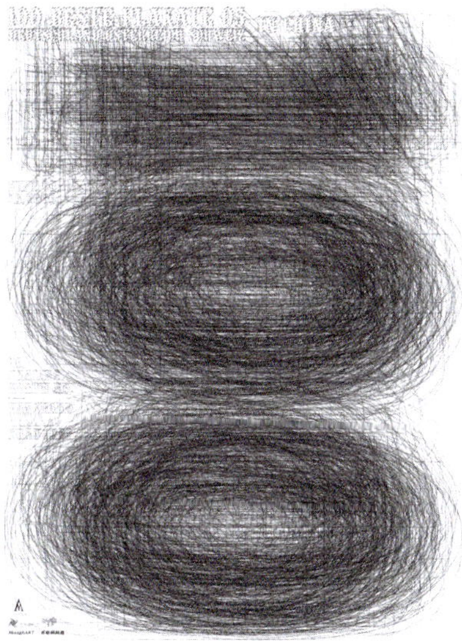

2006 · Jianping He · CN · Poster

2007

LACMA

LOS ANGELES COUNTY MUSEUM OF ART

2007 · 2x4 · US · Identity · LACMA

t'ea

2007 · Holger Jacobs, Mind Design · UK · Logo · Tea

DELTA

2007 · Lippincott · US · Logo · Delta Air Lines

Gary Hustwit's film documentary on the **Helvetica** typeface premieres

2007 · Michael Bierut, Pentagram · US · Identity · Saks Fifth Avenue

The first **European Design Awards** are held

2008 · Edmund Wee, Zann Wan, Epigram · SG · Identity · Simply Sandwich

2007 · Atlas · ES · Magazine spread

2007 · Erich Brechbühl · CH · Poster

2007 · Kyosuke Tsuji, Takashi Kamada, Romando · JP · Poster

The design blog **It's Nice That** is founded

2007 · Steve Fuller, Mark Gardner, Imaginary Forces · US · Opening titles

2007 · Marian Bantjes · CA/UK · Magazine cover

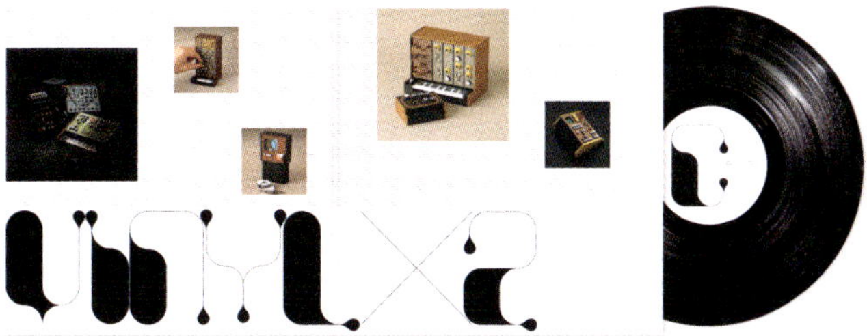

2007 · Non-Format · UK · Record cover

2008

A **Graphic Design Museum** (later renamed the Museum of the Image) opens in Breda, Netherlands

The **Replica** typeface is created by Norm

2008 · Summa, Tilman Solé, Rocío Martinavarro, Joern Oelsner · ES · Logo · Radiotelevisión Española

2008 · Andreas Uebele, Sabine Schönhaar, Büro Uebele · DE · Logo · Bree

2008 · Sol Sender · US · Logo · Obama Campaign

2008 · Tyler Brûlé · CA/UK · Editorial design

2008 · Karlssonwilker · US · Magazine cover

2008 · Neville Brody · UK · Newspaper design

2008 · Jorge Silva, Silvadesigners · PT · Poster

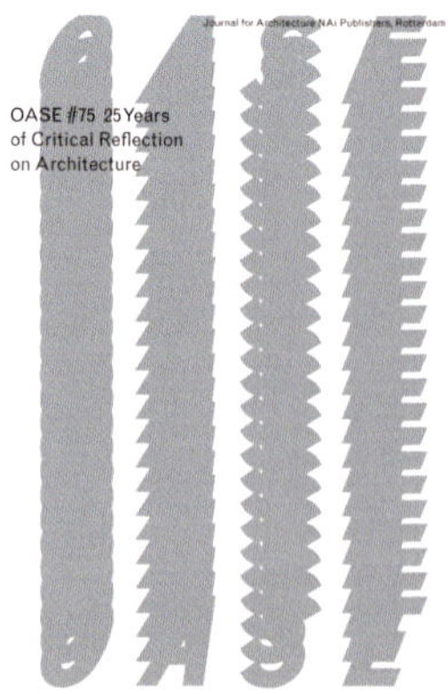

2008 · Karel Martens · NL · Magazine cover

2008 · Mehdi Saeedi · IR · Poster

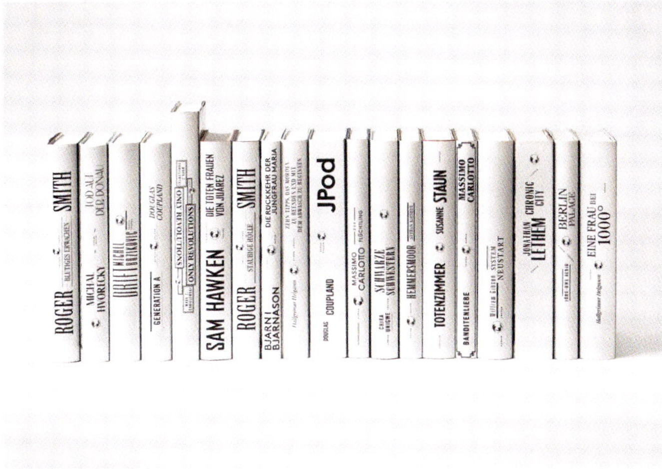

2008 · Herburg Weiland · DE · Book spines

2008 · Jianping He · CN · Poster

2008 · Oded Ezer · IL · Poster

2008 · Gavillet & Cie · CH · Poster

For many years, designing a logo meant coming up with a sign in just one color and measuring only a few centimeters across so that it would fit neatly on a ballpoint pen. At the turn of the 21st century, the advances offered by digital design technology led to purely cosmetic improvements which simply added a third dimension to existing two-dimensional logos. This development was followed by a surge of completely three-dimensional designs, which only worked if they were in color and of a specific minimum size. International corporations, such as AT&T and DC Comics, were amongst the organizations to adopt this short-lived trend. After a few years though, many firms went back to using two-dimensional logos. Designed by computer and with the help of graphic reduction, these provided clear and simple brand recognition.

Über viele Jahre galt im Logodesign der Grundsatz, dass ein Zeichen auch einfarbig und wenige Zentimeter groß – beispielsweise auf einem Kugelschreiber – funktionieren muss. Fortschreitende Möglichkeiten der digitalen Entwurfstechnik führten Anfang der 2000er-Jahre zunächst zu rein kosmetischen Aktualisierungen, die zweidimensionalen Logos nachträglich einen räumlichen Effekt gaben. Auf diese Entwicklung folgte eine Welle vollständig dreidimensionaler Entwürfe, die nur in farbiger Anwendung und in einer gewissen Mindestgröße funktionierten. International agierende Unternehmen wie AT&T oder DC Comics folgten diesem Trend, der sich jedoch nur als kurzlebige Phase herausstellte. Nach wenigen Jahren kehrten viele Firmen zu zweidimensionalen Logos zurück, die auch im digitalen Anwendungsbereich dank grafischer Reduktion für eindeutige und einfache Wiedererkennung sorgen.

Pendant bien des années, le design de logos s'est cantonné à des symboles monochromes de quelques centimètres pour par exemple tenir sur un stylo à bille. Au début des années 2000, les possibilités accrues offertes par la conception numérique ont d'abord conduit à des actualisations purement cosmétiques qui dotaient les logos en 2D d'une troisième dimension. À cette évolution a succédé une vague de projets entièrement tridimensionnels, fonctionnant exclusivement en couleurs et avec une taille minimale déterminée. Des entreprises internationales comme AT&T ou DC Comics ont suivi cette tendance passagère. Après seulement quelques années, bien des compagnies sont revenues à des logos bidimensionnels conçus par ordinateur et dont la réduction graphique assure une reconnaissance sans équivoque.

2005 · Interbrand · US · Logo · AT&T

2012 · Landor · US · Logo · DC Comics

2012 · Thjnk · DE · Logo · Unitymedia

2013 · Happy F&B · SE/UK · Logo · Thomas Cook

»In recent years, purely 3D logos have become increasingly popular. Because of their complexities of color and design, 3D logos cannot be produced in single-color versions without losing important details of the design. The old ground rules, which made it impossible to include color or too many details because of reproduction problems, no longer apply thanksto advances in printing technology.«

Jens Müller, *Logo Modernism*, 2015

2001 · Hiroshige Fukuhara, Takuya Kawagoi · JP · Logo · Sony Ericsson

2007 · Bruno Maag, Moving Brands · UK/CH · Logo · Swisscom

2010 · Kiko Farkas · BR · Logo · Brasil

2004 · Steven Garrity, Jon Hicks · UK · Logo · Firefox

2008 · Anonymous · US · Logo · Google Chrome

2009 · SDG · NO · Logo · Statoil

2007 · Anonymous · US · Logo · Silverlight

2008 · Interbrand · US · Logo · Xerox

2006 · Anonymous · SE · Logo · Malaco

2007 · Anonymous · US · Logo · Lay's

2008 · Anonymous · MY · Logo · Champions League

1996 · Irma Boom · NL · Book

2011 · Irma Boom · NL · Book

2013 · Irma Boom · NL · Book

2008 · Irma Boom · NL · Book

»Graphic design is an interesting profession when one is asked to be a participating developer on a project. Graphic design is not interesting when a designer is asked to make things on demand.«

Irma Boom, *Graphic Design for the 21st Century*, 2003

Irma Boom (1960, Lochem, Netherlands) is a world-renowned book designer based in Amsterdam. Boom's attention to detail and deep knowledge of production, typography, and composition have earned her a rare status among designers and publishers. More than 50 of her books are in the permanent collection of MoMA, and in 2001 she won the prestigious Gutenberg Prize (the youngest recipient to date); she has also won a gold medal at the Leipzig Book Fair, and the Johannes Vermeer Award in the Netherlands. Boom's clients have included Chanel, the architect Rem Koolhaas, and the Rijksmuseum in Amsterdam

Irma Boom (1960, Lochem, Niederlande) ist eine weltbekannte Buchgestalterin mit Sitz in Amsterdam. Durch die Aufmerksamkeit, die sie auf Details richtet, und durch ihr immenses Wissen bezüglich Herstellung, Typografie und Komposition genießt sie unter Gestaltern und Verlegern einen ausgezeichneten Ruf. Über fünfzig ihrer Bücher liegen in der ständigen Sammlung des MoMA. 2001 wurde Boom als bislang jüngste Preisträgerin mit dem renommierten Gutenberg-Preis ausgezeichnet. Ferner erhielt sie die Goldmedaille der Leipziger Buchmesse sowie den niederländischen Johannes Vermeer Prijs. Zu Booms Auftraggebern gehören u.a. Chanel, der Architekt Rem Koolhaas und das Rijksmuseum in Amsterdam.

Irma Boom (1960, Lochem, Pays-Bas) est une conceptrice de livres de renommée internationale installée à Amsterdam. Son sens du détail et sa connaissance approfondie de la production, de la typographie et de la composition lui ont valu un statut d'exception parmi les designers et éditeurs. Plus de 50 de ses livres figurent dans les collections permanentes du MoMA et en 2001, elle a remporté le prestigieux prix Gutenberg (elle en reste à ce jour la plus jeune lauréate). Elle a aussi remporté une médaille d'or à la Foire du livre de Leipzig, et le prix Johannes Vermeer aux Pays-Bas. Les clients de Boom comptent notamment des marques comme Chanel, l'architecte Rem Koolhaas et le Rijksmuseum à Amsterdam.

2010 · Irma Boom · NL · Book

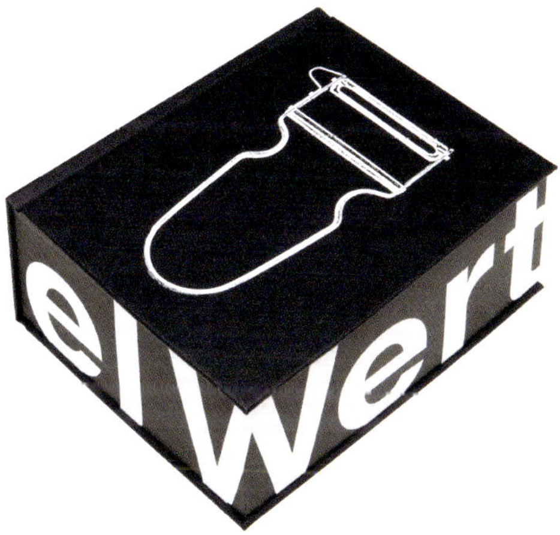

2009 · Irma Boom · NL · Book

2009

The first **Offset** design conference is held in Dublin

The **Weltformat** festival is established in Lucerne to promote poster art

2009 · Proud Creative · US · Logo · Syfy Television

2009 · Landor · US · Logo · Hertz

2009 · Jean-Pierre Ploué, Landor · FR · Logo · Citroën

2009 · Majid Abbasi · IR · Book cover

2009 · Antoine+Manuel · FR · Poster

2009 · Neil Kellerhouse, Kellerhouse Inc. · US · Poster

2009 · Designpolitie · NL · Posters

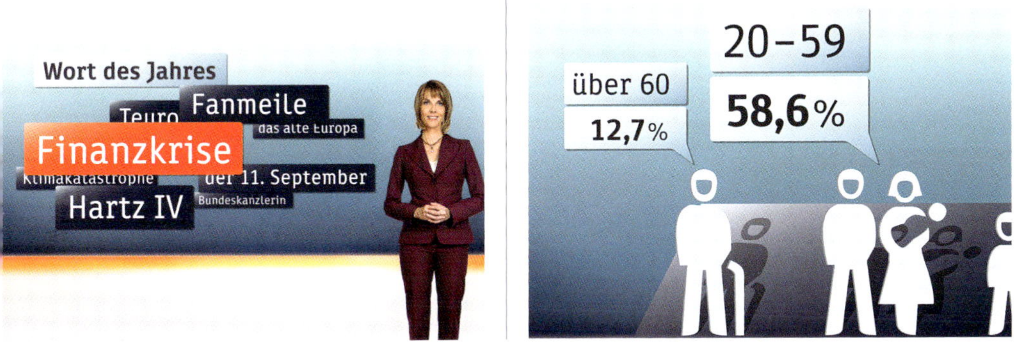

2009 · Erik Spiekermann (TY), Edenspiekermann · DE · Identity · ZDF Heute Journal

2009 · Holger Jacobs, Mind Design · UK · Identity

2009 · Daniel Trench · BR · Magazine cover

2009 · Marian Bantjes · CA · Magazine cover

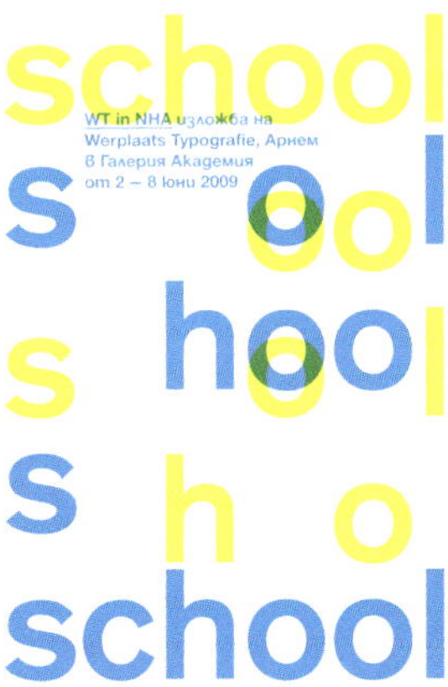

2009 · Poststudio · BG · Poster

2009 · Gavillet & Cie · CH · Poster

2016 · Louise Fili · US · Poster

2010

2016 · Les Graphiquants · FR · Poster

2014 · Jens Müller · DE · Stamp

2010 · Neil Kellerhouse (AD), Frank Ockenfels (PH), Kellerhouse Inc. · US · Poster

2014 · Hvass & Hannibal · DK · Poster

—2019

2017 · Craig & Karl, Christian Tönsmann (AD) · UK/US/DE · Magazine cover

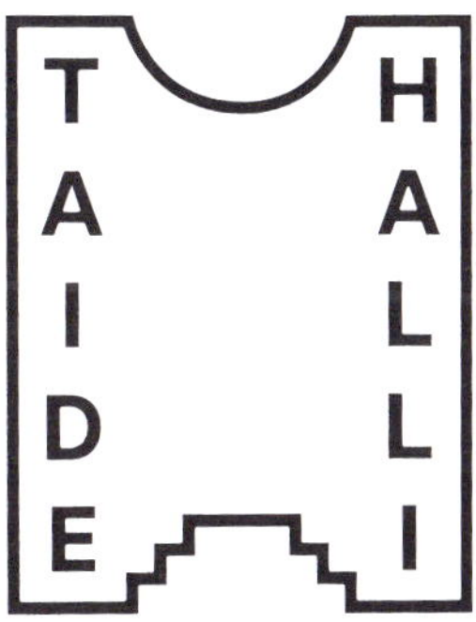

2014 · Tsto · FI · Logo · Helsinki Art Museum

The 2010s are already recognized as the age of social media, together with all the various aspects associated with it, both positive and negative. Never before has it been so easy to see such a diverse assortment of design works and to follow the creation of new styles in near-real time. Thus enabled, sophisticated designers work towards stronger positioning and an even clearer assertion of their own visual vocabulary. Sometimes, however, global networking can lead to big problems, for example, when the logo of a major sporting event in Japan looks too much like that of a provincial theater in Belgium, or the clientele of a fashion house protest vociferously when the company's trusted trademark is changed. Even so, the industry's persistent navel-gazing doesn't necessarily result in second-rate designs, and in fact in many cases it actually contributes to the stimulation of adventurous and innovative approaches. All of this makes it exciting to observe how new visual trends can, as always, develop at first at the local level, and likewise, how continuing technological advances are a firm guarantee that there will always be new designs.

Die 2010er-Jahre gelten schon heute als das Zeitalter der sozialen Medien – mit einer Reihe von positiven wie negativen Aspekten. Noch nie zuvor war es so einfach möglich, unterschiedlichste Arbeiten zu sehen und die Entstehung neuer Stilrichtungen nahezu in Echtzeit zu verfolgen. Anspruchsvolle Gestalterinnen und Gestalter zwingt dies zu einer noch stärkeren Positionierung und einem noch deutlicheren Bekenntnis zur eigenen visuellen Sprache. Manchmal führt die globale Vernetzung jedoch auch zu ganz handfesten Problemen, etwa wenn das Zeichen einer japanischen Großsportveranstaltung dem eines belgischen Provinztheaters zu ähnlich sieht oder wenn die Kunden eines Modekonzerns sich lautstark gegen die Überarbeitung des lange vertrauten Markenzeichens wehren. Die allgegenwärtige Nabelschau der Branche führt jedoch mitnichten zwingend zu zweitklassigen Entwürfen, sondern sie trägt in vielen Fällen zu gewagten und innovativen Ansätzen bei. Es ist dabei spannend zu beobachten, dass sich neuartige visuelle Tendenzen nach wie vor lokal entwickeln können. Ebenso bleibt die fortschreitende technische Entwicklung ein steter Garant für neue Gestaltung.

Les années 2010 sont déjà considérées aujourd'hui comme l'ère des médias sociaux, avec tous les aspects positifs et négatifs qui sont liés. Jamais auparavant il n'a été aussi simple de découvrir une variété de travaux et de suivre la genèse de nouvelles tendances quasiment en temps réel. Des graphistes de haut vol travaillent ainsi à un positionnement plus marqué et à une affirmation encore plus claire de leur langage visuel. Mais la mise en réseau globale soulève parfois aussi des problèmes de taille, par exemple quand le logo d'un grand événement sportif japonais ressemble trop à celui d'un théâtre de province belge, ou quand les clients d'une maison de couture s'opposent énergiquement au remaniement de leur marque de confiance. Cela dit, ce nombrilisme du secteur ne produit pas forcément que des projets de second rang et donne souvent lieu à des approches audacieuses et novatrices. Il est passionnant de voir qu'aujourd'hui comme toujours, les nouvelles tendances visuelles peuvent se développer d'abord en local, et que les progrès technologiques garantissent un éternel renouveau dans le graphisme.

The bus described as the Moscow Design Museum's "mobile exhibition hall" matching the visual identity created for the museum by the Dutch design studio Lava in 2012.

Ein Werbebus des Moscow Design Museum, gestaltet gemäß der visuellen Identität, die das niederländische Designbüro Lava 2012 für das Museum entwickelte.

Bus publicitaire du Moscow Design Museum, conforme à l'identité visuelle de ce musée, telle qu'elle a été développée en 2012 par l'agence de graphisme néerlandaise Lava.

2010

Hannes von Döhren creates the **Brandon** typeface

The independent graphic design publisher **Unit Editions** is founded by Tony Brook, Patricia Finegan, and Adrian Shaughnessy

2010 · Spin · UK · Logo · Unit Editions

2010 · David Pidgeon · AU · Logo · Museo Italiano Cultural Centre

2011 · Chermayeff & Geismar & Haviv · US · Logo · Library of Congress

2010 · Hort · DE/DK · Posters

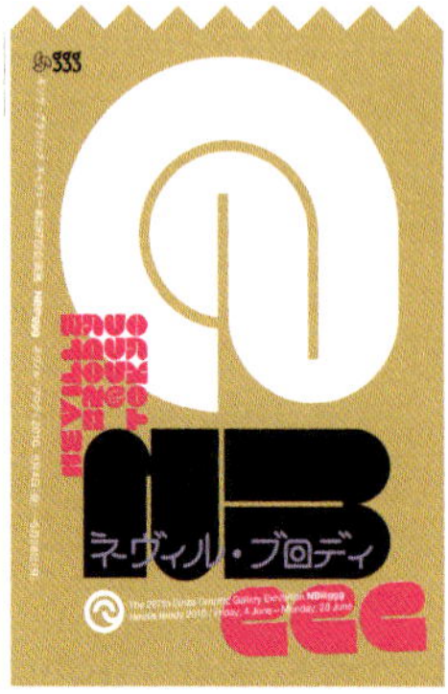

2010 · Neville Brody · UK/JP · Poster

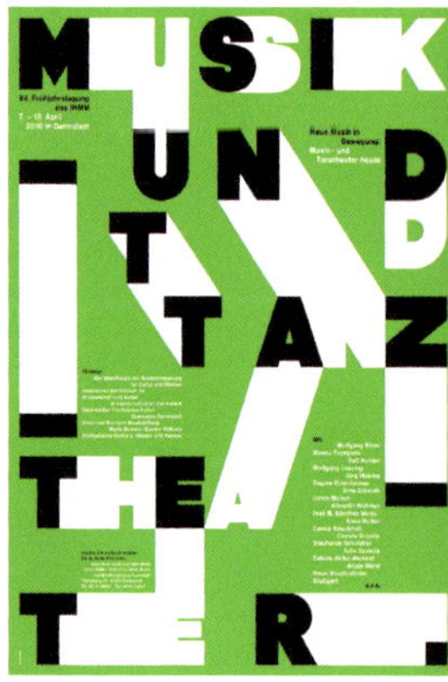

2010 · 2xGoldstein · DE · Poster

2010 · Thonik · NL · Identity · VPRO

The introduction of a new logo for the fashion brand **Gap** fails because of customers' negative reactions to it

2010 · Francesco Franchi (AD) · IT · Magazine spread, Information graphic

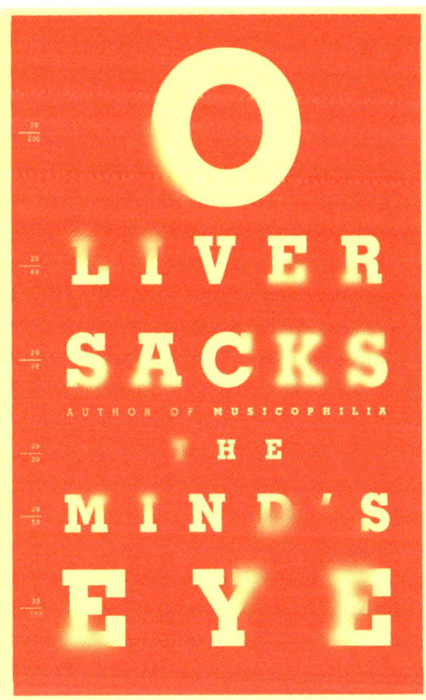

2010 · Chip Kidd · US · Book cover

2010 · Felipe Taborda, Glaucio Ayala (PH) · BR · Poster

The rise in internet use at the turn of the 21st century had a drastic effect on print media circulation, so much so that a number of experts predicted its imminent demise. By the 2010s, however, fresh opportunities offered by digital media production, and the immediacy of online sales, which functioned without the standard model for distribution, had resulted in the rise of new, non-mainstream magazines. Exciting publications, unhampered by the need to please a mass readership and hence able to make use of uncompromising design concepts, soon began to appear. The boom in such indie magazines led to the opening in several major cities of a new type of shop, a cross between a news kiosk and a bookshop, set up to sell the increasing numbers of intriguing magazines emerging around the world.

Mit dem Anstieg der Internetnutzung nach der Jahrhundertwende reduzierten sich die Auflagen von Printmedien drastisch, viele Experten prophezeiten gar deren Ende. Die neuen Möglichkeiten digitaler Medienproduktion und des Onlinevertriebs ohne klassische Vertriebsstrukturen führten spätestens ab den 2010er-Jahren jedoch auch zu einem Anstieg neuer Magazine jenseits des Mainstreams. Unabhängig von den Konventionen massentauglicher Publikationen entstanden faszinierende Hefte mit kompromisslosen Gestaltungskonzepten. Durch den Boom der Indiemagazine entstand in Großstädten sogar eine neue Gattung Shops zwischen Kiosk und Buchhandel, in denen sich immer wieder neue faszinierende Hefte aus aller Welt finden lassen.

Avec la montée en puissance d'Internet au tournant du millénaire, les tirages de la presse écrite ont radicalement chuté, à tel point que de nombreux experts prédisaient sa disparition. Dans les années 2010 néanmoins, les nouvelles possibilités offertes par la production de médias numériques et l'immédiateté de la vente en ligne en dehors des structures de distribution standard ont donné naissance à de nouveaux magazines en marge du courant dominant. D'intéressantes publications ont ainsi vu le jour à l'écart du grand public en recourant à des concepts graphiques sans concessions. Suite au boom de ces magazines indépendants, les grandes villes ont vu s'ouvrir un nouveau genre de boutiques entre le kiosque et la librairie, qui proposent un nombre croissant de revues singulières éditées dans le monde entier.

2010 · Paul Willoughby · UK · Magazine cover

2013 · Paul Willoughby · UK · Magazine cover

»The term 'independent' is constantly questioned. What does it mean? I suggest it represents a working process where creative and financial decisions are made in tandem; the vision underlying these projects supercedes short-term financial gain in favor of longer-term creative ambition.«
Jeremy Leslie, *subtraction.com*, 2016

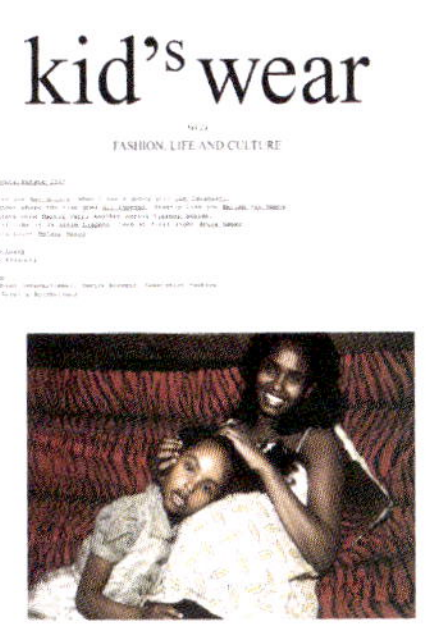

2007 · Meiré und Meiré · DE · Magazine cover

2011 · Felix Burrichter, Dylan Fracareta · US · Magazine cover

2015 · David Lane, Harri Peccinotti (PH) · UK · Magazine cover

2009 · Rob Longworth, Geoff McFetridge (ILL) · UK · Magazine cover

2011 · Brian McMullen, Walter Green, Noriko Yamaguchi · US · Magazine cover

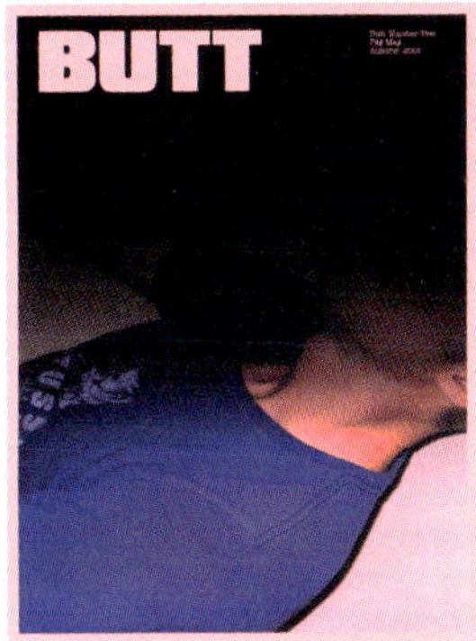

2001 · Jop van Bennekom · NL/UK · Magazine cover

2009 · Omar Sosa, Albert Folch · ES · Magazine cover

2011 · Jop van Bennekom · NL/UK · Magazine cover

2011

The exhibition **Graphic Design Worlds** is shown at the Triennale Design Museum in Milan

A new edition of **Bauhaus** magazine is launched in Germany, celebrating the legacy of the famous design school

2011 · Thelab · US · Logo · Comedy Central

2011 · Kurppa Hosk · SE · Logo · Unit Portables

2011 · Lava · NL · Logo · THNK

2011 · Experimental Jetset · NL · Poster

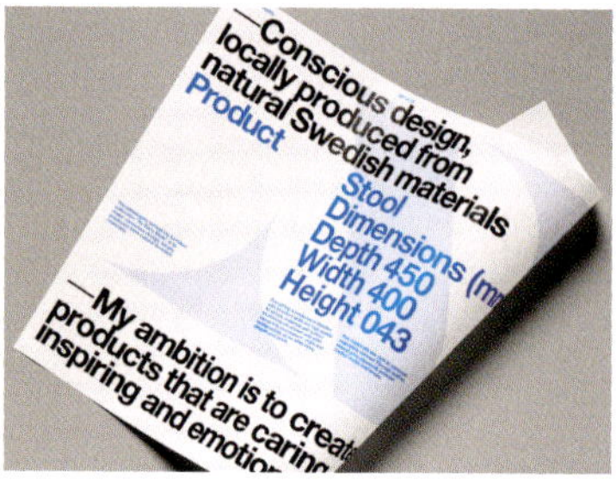

2011 · Kurppa Hosk · SE · Identity · No Early Birds

2011 · Alejandro Ros, Marcelo Setton (PH) · AR · Record cover

2011 · Elastic · US · Opening titles

The exhibition **Wim Crouwel: A Graphic Odyssey** opens at the London Design Museum

2011 · Ad Busters · US · Poster

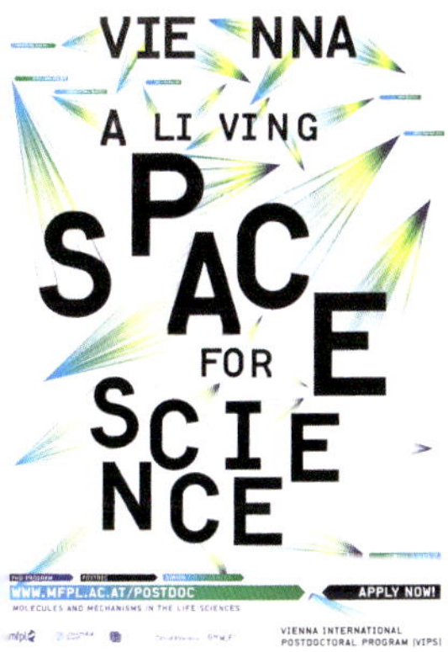

2011 · Buero Bauer · AT · Poster

2011 · Marian Bantjes · CA · Poster

2011 · Mehdi Saeedi · IR · Poster

2011 · Götz Gramlich · DE · Poster

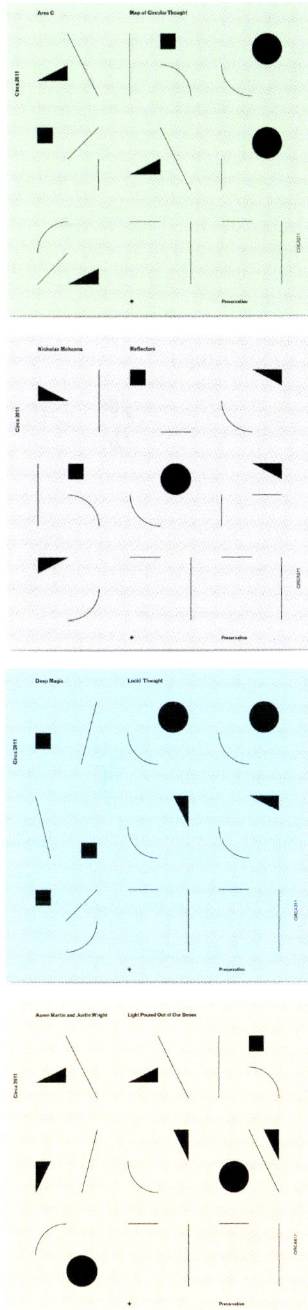

2011 · Mark Gowing · AU · Posters

The American business magazine *Businessweek* was first published in 1929, and in 2009 the media company Bloomberg acquired and totally revamped the long-established publication. The young British art director Richard Turley introduced an entirely new design concept to the renamed *Bloomberg Businessweek*, and it was above all his imaginative ideas for the front cover which gave the magazine a whole new look, earning it many "likes" on social networks.

Das erste Heft der amerikanischen Wirtschaftszeitschrift *Businessweek* erschien 1929. Der Medienkonzern Bloomberg kaufte das Traditionsblatt 2009 und überarbeitete es vollständig. Unter der Artdirection des jungen britischen Designers Richard Turley erhielt *Bloomberg Businessweek* ein neues Gestaltungskonzept. Vor allem die genialen Coverideen sorgten für eine völlig neue Wahrnehmung der Zeitschrift und für viele Likes in den sozialen Netzwerken.

La parution du premier numéro du magazine économique américain *Businessweek* remonte à 1929. Le groupe de médias Bloomberg acquit cette publication historique en 2009 et la transforma intégralement. Sous la direction artistique du jeune graphiste britannique Richard Turley, elle fut renommée *Bloomberg Businessweek* avec un concept graphique entièrement nouveau. Ce sont surtout les idées géniales des couvertures qui ont entièrement changé la perception du magazine et suscité quantité de *likes* sur les réseaux sociaux.

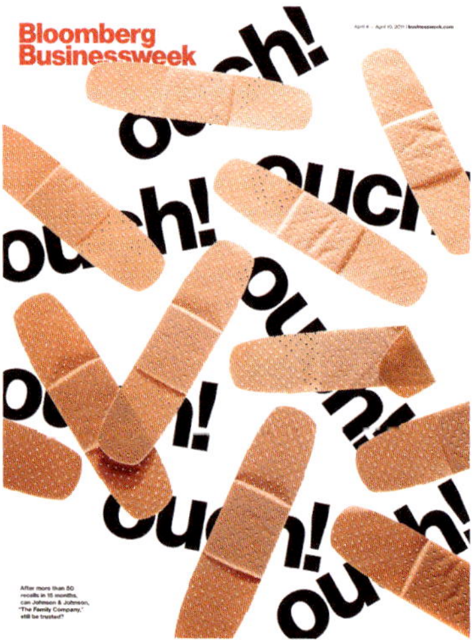

2011 · Richard Turley (AD) · UK/US · Magazine cover

2011 · Richard Turley (AD) · UK/US · Magazine cover

2013 · Richard Turley (AD) · UK/US · Magazine cover

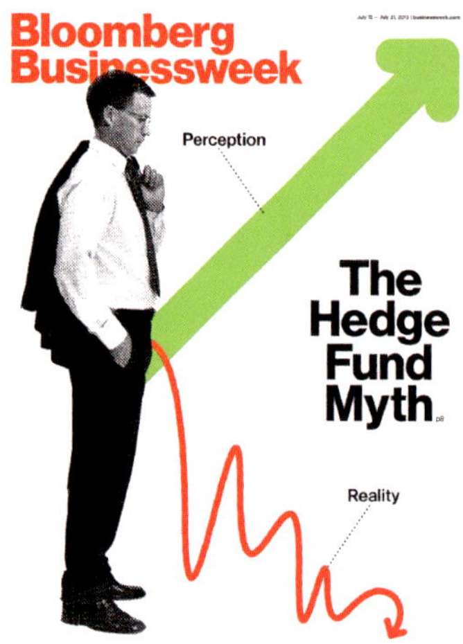

2013 · Richard Turley (AD) · UK/US · Magazine cover

»Our covers were sharable visual content. They weren't necessarily designed like that, but that's essentially what they were. At their best, the covers became the kind of thing people passed around on Thursday morning, and we put them on Twitter.« Richard Turley, *032c*, 2015

2010s · Richard Turley (AD) · UK/US · Magazine spreads

Richard Turley (1976, Bristol, England) is a creative director with a body of distinguished work in media. In 2010 he was responsible for the complete visual overhaul of *Bloomberg Businessweek*, and then went on to join MTV in 2014 as its first Senior Vice President of Visual Storytelling. With a deep understanding of both design and editorial, Turley has expanded the remit of the creative director and its influence on the way information is communicated. Having studied at art school in Liverpool and worked at *The Guardian* in London, he has become a key force in transforming traditional media in the digital era.

Richard Turley (1976, Bristol, England) zeichnet sich als Kreativdirektor insbesondere durch seine Arbeit in den Medien aus. 2010 übernahm er die vollständige Neugestaltung der Zeitschrift *Bloomberg Businessweek*, 2014 ging er als erster Senior Vice-President of Visual Storytelling zu MTV. Durch sein Verständnis für die grafische ebenso wie die redaktionelle Seite des Mediums hat Turley den Aufgabenbereich des Kreativdirektors erweitert, aber auch seinen Einfluss auf die Art und Weise, Informationen zu kommunizieren. Nach dem Besuch der Kunstakademie in Liverpool und einer Anstellung bei der Tageszeitung *The Guardian* in London ist er zu einer maßgeblichen Gestalt beim Übergang der traditionellen Medien in die digitale Ära geworden.

Richard Turley (1976, Bristol, Angleterre) est un directeur créatif qui s'est distingué par un ensemble de projets dans les médias. En 2010, il a été chargé de la refonte visuelle de *Bloomberg Businessweek*, avant de rejoindre MTV en 2014 en qualité de premier vice-président pour la narration visuelle. Doté d'une profonde connaissance du graphisme et de l'édition, Turley a élargi son champ de compétences de directeur créatif et son influence sur la manière de communiquer l'information. Après des études artistiques à Liverpool et un passage par *The Guardian*, à Londres, il est devenu un acteur clé de la transformation des médias traditionnels à l'ère du numérique.

Already in the 1920s Lucian Bernhard had developed a design concept which was the first to allow companies to adopt a flexible trademark. For one particular wholesale business he designed more than 40 logos to present the firm's across-the-board activities. Some 90 years later, other designers came up with the same idea, for clients such as the internet service provider AOL and the city of Melbourne. The various design solutions included changing configurations or colors, shapes, or even typefaces, as in the case of the German art exhibition documenta. Stefan Sagmeister created an unusually innovative concept for Casa da Música, the concert hall in Porto. Software created especially for the project analyzed a number of possible motifs for use in the design of the logo, and then helped to combine different elements to construct a distinctive symbol.

Bereits in den 1920er-Jahren entwickelte Lucian Bernhard ein Gestaltungskonzept, das erstmals ein flexibles Markenzeichen für ein Unternehmen vorsah. Für einen Großhandelsvertrieb entwickelte er über vierzig variable Logos, um die inhaltliche Bandbreite der Firma zu visualisieren. Neunzig Jahre später kamen Gestalter auf die gleiche Idee, beispielsweise für den Internetkonzern AOL oder für die australische Stadt Melbourne. Die Varianz der Lösungen reichte von wechselnden Mustern, Farben, Formen und sogar Schriften, wie bei dem Erscheinungsbild der Kunstausstellung documenta. Ein besonders innovatives Konzept entwickelte Stefan Sagmeister für das Konzerthaus Casa da Música im portugiesischen Porto. Eine eigens für dieses Projekt entwickelte Software analysierte die im Kontext des Logos verwendeten Bildmotive und generierte ein darauf abgestimmtes individuelles Zeichen.

Dès les années 1920, Lucian Bernhard élaborait un concept graphique permettant pour la première fois aux entreprises de bénéficier d'une marque flexible. C'est ainsi qu'il développa pour un grossiste plus de quarante logos à l'image des activités globales de la société. Environ 90 ans plus tard, d'autres graphistes ont eu la même idée – notamment pour le fournisseur de services Internet AOL ou la ville de Melbourne. La palette de solutions incluait des variations sur les motifs, les couleurs, les formes et les caractères, comme pour l'exposition d'art documenta en Allemagne. De son côté, Stefan Sagmeister a développé un concept particulièrement novateur pour la salle de concerts Casa da Música à Porto. Un logiciel spécialement conçu pour ce projet a analysé divers motifs possibles pour le logo et généré un symbole spécifique à partir de différents éléments.

orquestra nacional
do porto

2007 · Stefan Sagmeister · US/PT · Identity · Casa da Música

»Fifty years ago, a brand was just a single mark [...]. Now a brand has become a platform where like-minded people come together, and an experience that creates emotional attachment. Brands need to constantly adapt to their fast-changing environment in order to survive.«
Irene van Nes, *Dynamic Identities*, 2012

2009 · Wolff Olins · UK/US · Identity · AOL

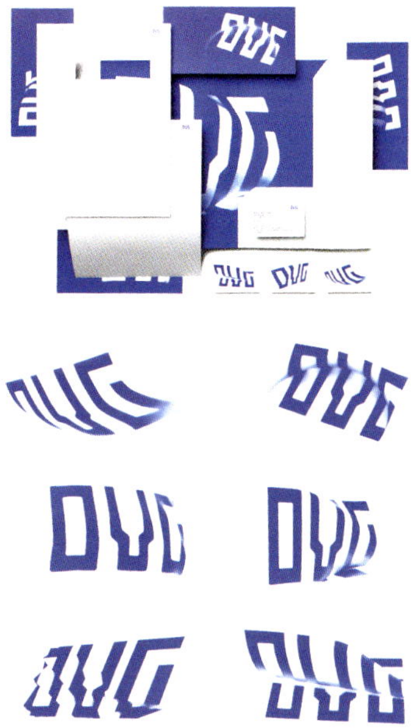

2011 · Studio Dumbar · NI · Identity · OVG

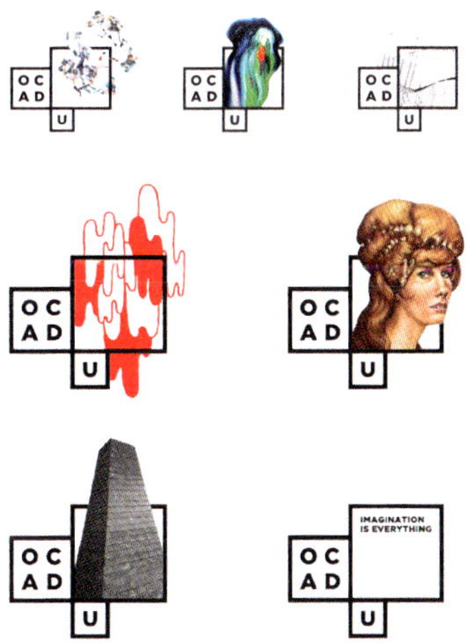

2011 · Bruce Mau Design · CA · Identity · OCAD University

2012 · Leftloft · IT/DE · Identity · documenta (13)

2014 · Designpolitie · NL · Identity · Proud

2016 · Kurppa Hosk · SE · Identity · Stockholm concert hall

2012

Stefan Sagmeister's exhibition project **The Happy Show** opens at the Chicago Institute of Contemporary Art

The exhibition **The Printed Book: A Visual History** is shown in Amsterdam

2012 · Chris Martin (ILL), Love Design · UK · Packaging

2012 · Michael Bierut, Pentagram · US · Packaging

london

2012 · Wolff Olins · UK · Logo · London 2012

2012 · Francesco Franchi (AD) · IT · Magazine spreads

Windows 8

2012 · Paula Scher, Pentagram · US · Logo · Windows 8

P A M M
Pérez Art Museum Miami

2012 · 2x4 · US · Logo · Pérez Art Museum, Miami

2012 · Ariane Spanier · DE · Poster

2012 · Oded Ezer · IL · Poster

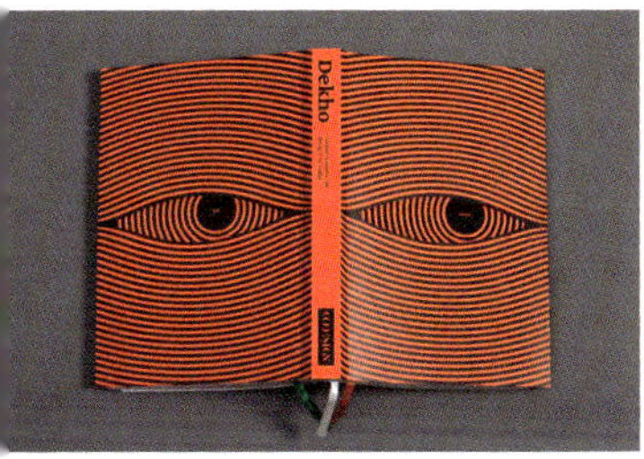

2012 · Codesign · IN · Book cover

2017 · Craig & Karl, Thomas Alberty (AD) · UK/US · Magazine cover

2012 · Louise Fili · US · Stamp

2012 · Lamm & Kirch · DE · Poster

2012 · BVD · SE · Identity · Seven Eleven

2012 · Heine/Lenz/Zizka · DE · Packaging

2013

The public service website **gov.uk** receives the Design of the Year Award from the London Design Museum

The **Systems Graphic Design** exhibition is shown in London

2013 · Michael Bierut, Pentagram · US · Logo · Mohawk Fine Papers

ARTRIO

2013 · Dupla Design · BR · Logo · Art Rio

TELEMARK

2013 · Snøhetta · NO · Logo · Telemark

2013 · Anette Lenz · DE/FR · Poster

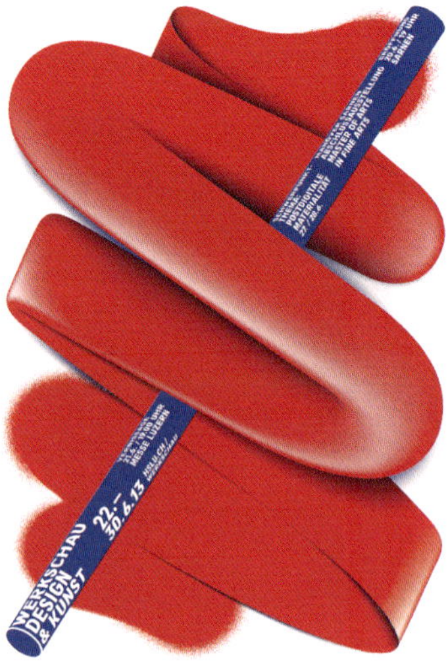

2013 · Felix Pfäffli, Studio Feixen · CH · Poster

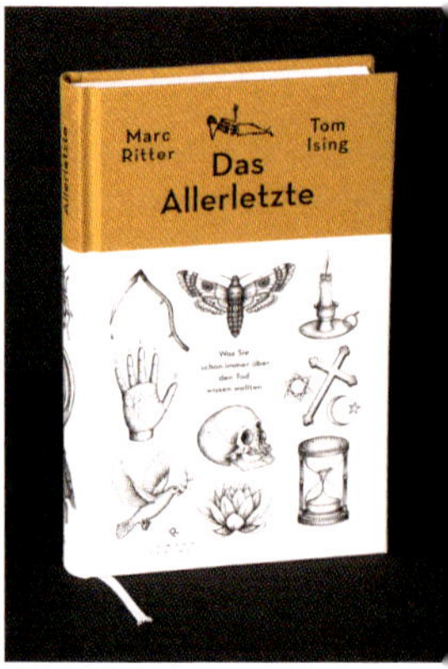

2013 · Herburg Weiland · DE · Book cover

2013 · Anna Berkenbusch · DE · Book cover

2013 · Antoine+Manuel · FR · Poster

Erik Spiekermann sets up **p98a**, an experimental letterpress workshop in Berlin

Adobe releases its design software exclusively through the **Creative Cloud**

2013 · Les Graphiquants · FR · Poster

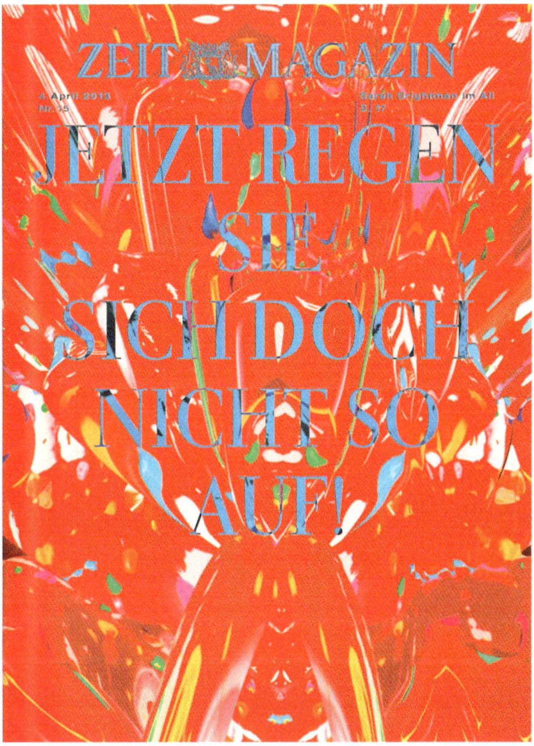

2013 · Mirko Borsche · DE · Magazine cover

2013 · Lamm & Kirch · DE · Poster

2013 · Alejandro Ros · AR · Record cover

2014

The exhibition **Century: 100 Years of Type in Design** is held at the AIGA National Design Center in New York City

The book **100 Years of Swiss Graphic Design** is published by the Museum für Gestaltung in Zurich

2014 · Holger Jacobs, Mind Design · UK · Logo · Ecelctic

2014 · Jessica Hische · US · Book cover

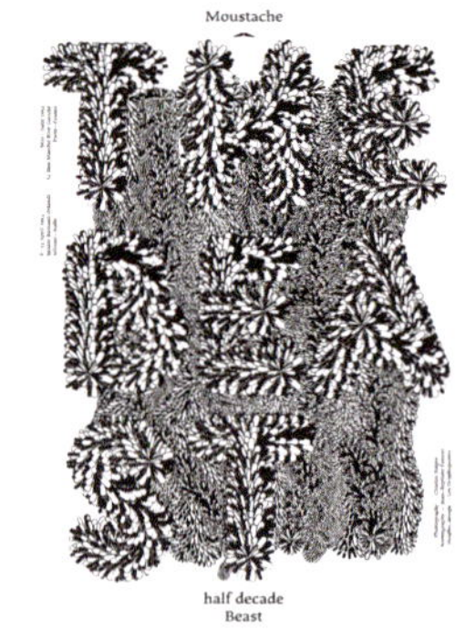

2014 · Les Graphiquants · FR · Poster

2014 · Michael Bierut, Pentagram · US · Logo · MIT Media Lab

2014 · Erich Brechbühl · CH · Poster

2014 · Ariane Spanier · DE · Magazine cover

2014 · DesignStudio · UK/US · Logo · Airbnb

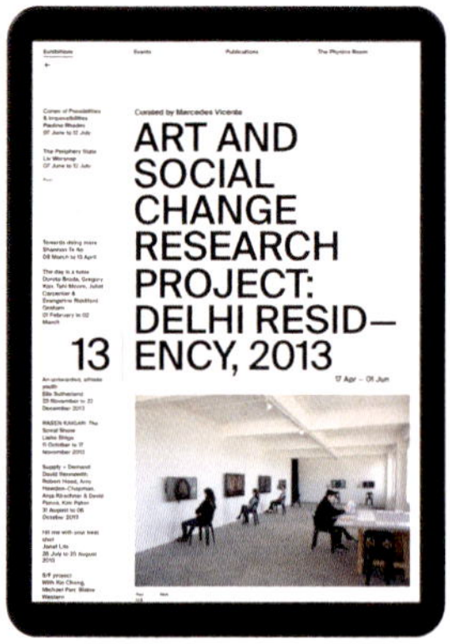

2014 · Timothy Kelleher, Matthew Arnold, Greg Brown, Sons & Co. · NZ · Website

The work of French graphic designer Philippe Apeloig is presented in **Typorama** at Les Art Décoratifs in Paris

2014 · Anagrama · MX · Identity · Amado

2014 · Eduardo Aires, White Studio · PT · Identity · Porto

2014 · Snask · SE · Brochure cover

2014 · Frédéric Vanhorenbeke, Coast · BE · Poster

2014 · Majid Abbasi · IR · Poster

2014 · StudioStudio · BE · Poster

2014 · Jorge Silva · PT · Book covers

2015

Controversy erupts concerning the new logo for the **Tokyo 2020 Olympics**, claimed by some to be plagiarism

The Zurich **Museum für Gestaltung** moves to a new space at Toni-Areal, a former dairy factory

FRANK DANDY

2015 · Kurppa Hosk · SE · Logo · Frank Dandy

VILLA NOAILLES–HYÈRES

2015 · Antoine+Manuel · FR · Logo · Villa Noailles-Hyères

Google

2015 · Google design team · US · Logo · Google

2015 · Atlas · ES · Magazine

2015 · Ermolaev Bureau · RU · Packaging

2015 · Bureau Borsche · DE · Posters

The first **Graphic Design Festival Scotland** is held in Glasgow

A Kickstarter campaign to back the reissue of the 1975 **NASA** graphics standards manual raises almost a million dollars

French design magazine **Étapes** celebrates its 20th anniversary

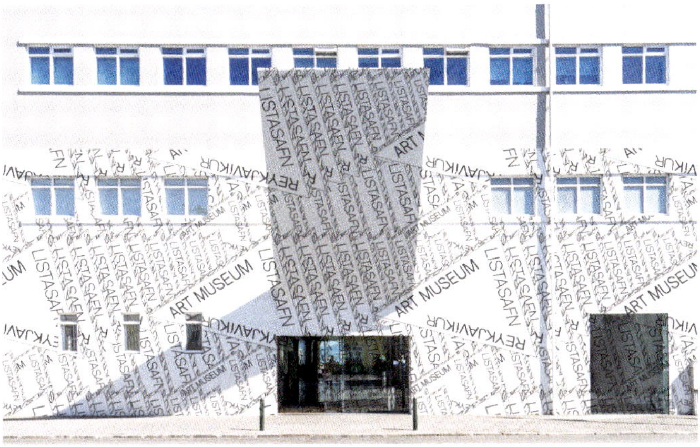

2015 · Karlssonwilker · US/IS · Identity · Reykjavik Art Museum

2015 · Studio Claus Due · DK · Poster

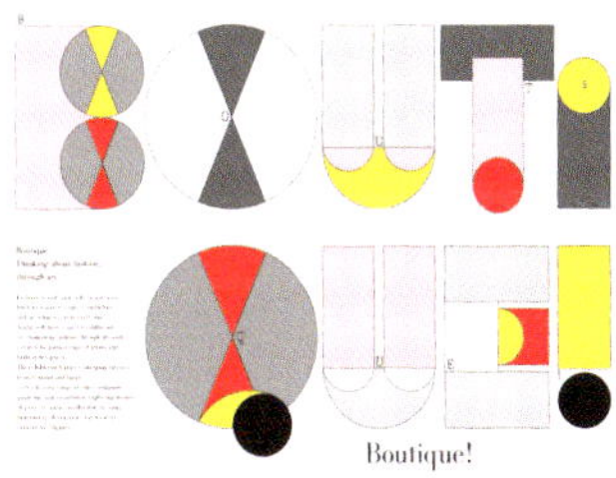

2015 · Ryosuke Uehara · JP · Poster

2015 · Ariane Spanier · DE/US · Magazine cover

2015 · Jens Müller, Optik · DE · Magazine cover

2015 · Bruce Mau Design · CA · Identity · Sonos

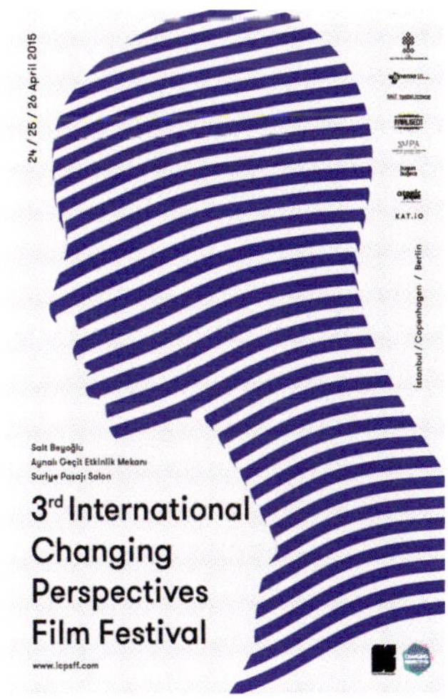

2015 · Fol · TR · Poster

2014 · Christoph Niemann · DE/US · Magazine cover

2011 · Christoph Niemann · DE/US · Magazine cover

2015 · Christoph Niemann · DE/US · Magazine cover

Christoph Niemann (1970, Waiblingen, Germany) is a designer, author, and visual artist with extensive work in editorial. His straightforward approach to vector illustration has brought Niemann plenty of commissions for magazine covers, including *The New Yorker*, *The New York Times Magazine*, and *The Atlantic*, amongst a host of others. A frequent lecturer on design and illustration, he has won several awards from the Art Directors Club, AIGA, and *American Illustration*. After living and working in New York for over a decade, Niemann moved to Berlin where his work is regularly exhibited in art galleries.

Christoph Niemann (1970, Waiblingen) ist ein Grafikdesigner, Autor und Illustrator, der insbesondere im Printbereich arbeitet. Seinen erfrischenden Umgang mit Vektorgrafik nutzten zahlreiche Magazine für ihre Coverillustrationen, unter vielen anderen *The New Yorker*, *The New York Times Magazine* und *The Atlantic*. Niemann ist ein vielfach gefragter Dozent zum Thema Design und Illustration, zudem wurde er mit Preisen vom Art Directors Club, des AIGA und vom *American Illustration* ausgezeichnet. Er lebte und arbeitete über zehn Jahre lang in New York, ehe er nach Berlin zog, wo seine Arbeiten regelmäßig in Galerien ausgestellt werden.

Christoph Niemann (1970, Waiblingen, Allemagne) est un graphiste, auteur et artiste visuel avec un vaste éventail de projets dans le domaine de l'édition. Son approche très directe de l'illustration vectorielle lui a valu une foule de commandes de couvertures de magazines, notamment pour *The New Yorker*, *The New York Times Magazine* et *The Atlantic*, parmi bien d'autres clients. Niemann donne souvent des conférences sur le design et l'illustration, et il a remporté plusieurs prix de l'Art Directors Club, de l'AIGA et d'*American Illustration*. Après avoir vécu et travaillé plus de dix ans à New York, Niemann s'est installé à Berlin, où son travail est régulièrement exposé dans des galeries d'art.

2015 · Christoph Niemann · DE/US · Magazine cover

2007 · Christoph Niemann · DE/US · Magazine cover

»We have these stock images of life in our head, and only when you start looking at real life and the imperfections do things start to become fun.« `Christoph Niemann, *itsnicethat.com*, 2015`

2003 · Christoph Niemann · DE/US · Magazine cover

2004 · Christoph Niemann · DE/US · Magazine cover

2001 · Christoph Niemann · DE/US · Magazine cover

For a number of years now, Christoph Niemann's cover designs for *The New Yorker* have demonstrated how the power of artwork can persist in an age when photography is omnipresent. Niemann not only experiments with different ideas for images but also with technology. In 2016, he produced a cover for the magazine which became an augmented reality when viewed using a smartphone app, as well as a cover that could be accessed as a 360-degree video animation to be used in conjunction with various popular virtual reality interfaces (including iPads and Google Cardboard).

Mit seinen Coverentwürfen für das Magazin *The New Yorker* beweist Christoph Niemann seit einigen Jahren, wie kraftvoll Illustration gerade in Zeiten der omnipräsenten Fotografie ist. Dabei experimentiert er nicht nur mit unterschiedlichen Bildideen, sondern auch mit der Technik. 2016 entwickelte er ein Cover, das als Augmented Reality auf dem Smartphone weiterentwickelt wird, weiter ein Cover, das auch als begehbares 360-Grad-Video für die boomenden Virtual-Reality-Brillen entwickelt wurde.

Avec ses conceptions de couvertures pour le magazine *The New Yorker*, Christoph Niemann démontre depuis quelques années toute la puissance de l'illustration, particulièrement à une époque où l'image photographique est omniprésente. Il a pour cela recours non seulement à toutes sortes d'idées graphiques, mais aussi à la technologie. En 2016, il a conçu une couverture qui devenait une réalité augmentée si on la regardait avec une application pour smartphone. Il a également créé une couverture conçue comme une animation à 360 degrés pour diverses interfaces de réalité virtuelle, dont l'iPad et le Google Cardboard.

2016 · Christoph Niemann · DE/US · Magazine cover

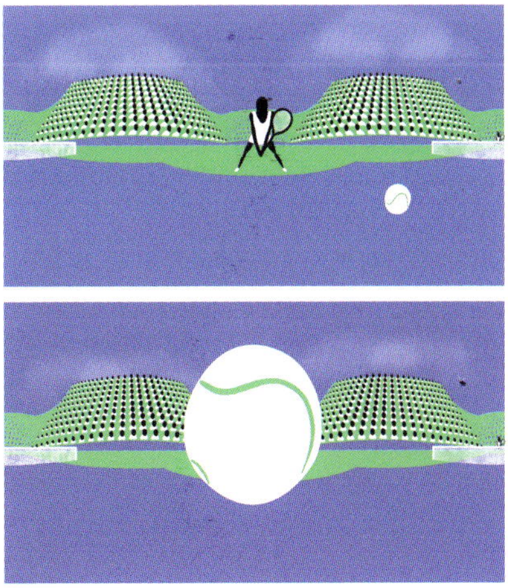

2016 · Christoph Niemann · DE/US · 360° animation

2016

ELECTRICITEITSFABRIEK

2016 · Mainstudio · NL · Logo · Electriciteitsfabriek

LENY

2016 · Studio Koniak · IL · Logo · Leny

2016 · André Baldinger, Toan Vu-Huu, Baldinger Vu-Huu · FR · Logo · CCCOD

The **London Design Museum** moves into a new space in smart new premises in Kensington

2016 · Herburg Weiland · DE · Book

2016 · StudioStudio · BE/IS · Brochure cover

2016 · Raffinerie · CH · Poster

The **International Poster Biennale of Warsaw** celebrates its 25th competition

2016 · Cyan · DE · Poster

2016 · Build · UK · Ad

2016 · Felix Pfäffli, Studio Feixen · CH · Poster

Stefan Sagmeister's film documentary **The Happy Film** premieres at New York's Tribeca Film Festival

The **Ladies, Wine & Design** salon is started by Jessica Walsh with the aim of fostering creative women

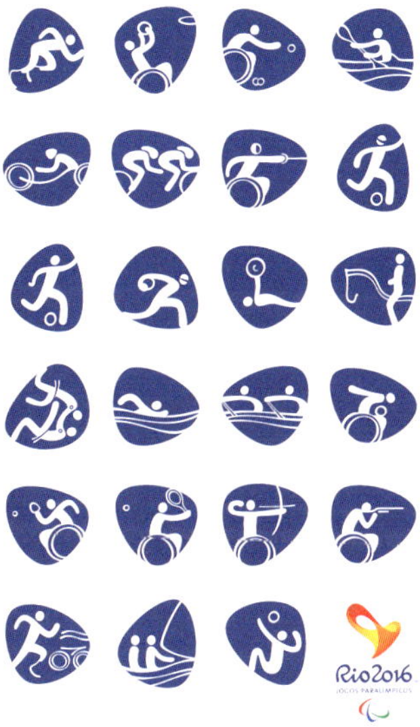

2016 · Dupla Design · BR · Identity · Rio 2016 Olympic Games

2016 · Anette Lenz · DE/FR · Poster

2016 · Irma Boom · NL · Book

2016 · Erich Brechbühl · CH · Poster

2016 · Mousegraphics · GR/CN · Packaging

2016 · Sawdust · UK/DE · Magazine cover

2016 · Thonik · NL · Identity · Dag voor de Dieren

2015 · Hey · ES · Identity · Arrels

2014 · Hey · ES · Packaging/Identity

2014 · Hey · ES · Book cover

2010 · Hey · ES · Book series

»We always start by doing research, getting to know the client and learning a few things beforehand. Then we look for a concept to meet the client's requirements and establish a powerful aesthetic.«
Verònica Fuerte, *ligature.ch*, 2012

2012 · Hey · ES/CL · Identity · Chile Film Commission

Hey

Hey (2007, Barcelona) is a design firm specializing in brand identity, editorial design, and illustration. The studio is a rare example in Spain of design work being undertaken for clients abroad, which includes Apple, Turkish Airlines, General Electric, *The Wall Street Journal*, CBS, and Penguin Random House. With a visual language based on geometry, color, and the application of direct typography, Hey have helped to bring a modern form of Spanish design to the world stage. Since 2014, they have also run their own online store.

Hey (2007, Barcelona) spezialisiert sich als Designfirma auf Brand Identity, Editorial Design und Illustration. Dem Studio ist es als einem der sehr wenigen in Spanien gelungen, einen internationalen Kreis an Auftraggebern aufzubauen, unter anderem Apple, Turkish Airlines, General Electric, *The Wall Street Journal*, CBS und Penguin Random House. Mit einer visuellen Sprache, die auf Geometrie, Farbe und direkter Typografie beruht, hat Hey dazu beigetragen, eine moderne Form des spanischen Designs international bekannt zu machen. Seit 2014 betreibt das Studio auch einen Onlineshop.

Hey (2007, Barcelone) est une firme de design spécialisée dans l'identité de marque, le design éditorial et l'illustration. C'est un des rares studios espagnols à s'être constitué une base de clients internationaux, parmi lesquels Apple, Turkish Airlines, General Electric, *The Wall Street Journal*, CBS et Penguin Random House. Basant son langage visuel sur la géométrie, la couleur et l'emploi d'une typographie directe, Hey a introduit une forme moderne du design espagnol sur la scène internationale. Depuis 2014, l'équipe gère sa propre boutique en ligne.

2016 · Hey · ES/FR · Poster

2015 · Hey · ES · Poster

2017

2017 · Interbrand Milan · IT · Logo · Juventus F.C.

2017 · Johnson Banks · UK · Logo · Mozilla

2017 · Werklig · FI · Logo · City of Helsinki

The first season of the Netflix documentary series **Abstract: The Art of Design** is aired, featuring Paula Scher, Christoph Niemann, and others

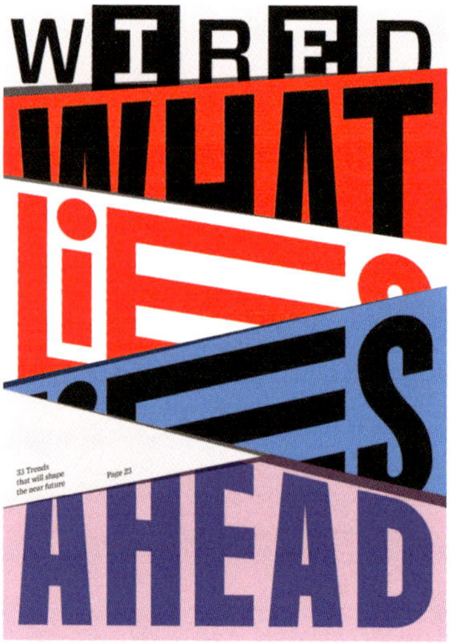

2017 · Felix Pfäffli, Studio Feixen · CH · Magazine cover

2017 · Sociedad Anónima, Mauro Bonillo (AD) · MX · Signage

2017 · Richard Turley (CD), Wieden+Kennedy · UK · Identity · Formula 1

The final printed issues of American graphic design magazines **Print** and **How** are published

2017 · Atlas · ES · Poster

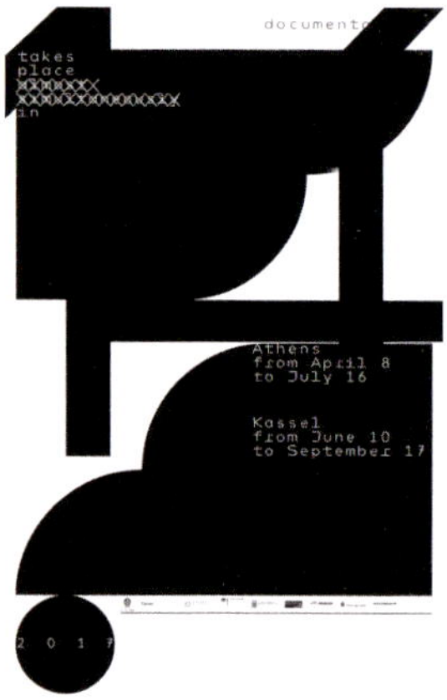

2017 · Ludovic Balland · CH · Poster

2017 · Studio Claus Due · DK · Poster

Briar Levit's film documentary **Graphic Means: A History of Graphic Design Production** is released

Pentagram partner Marina Willer's first feature film **Red Trees** premieres at the Cannes Film Festival

IBM releases the **IBM Plex** type family, designed by Mike Abbink, to be shared and used by everyone for free

2017 · Thonik · NL · Poster

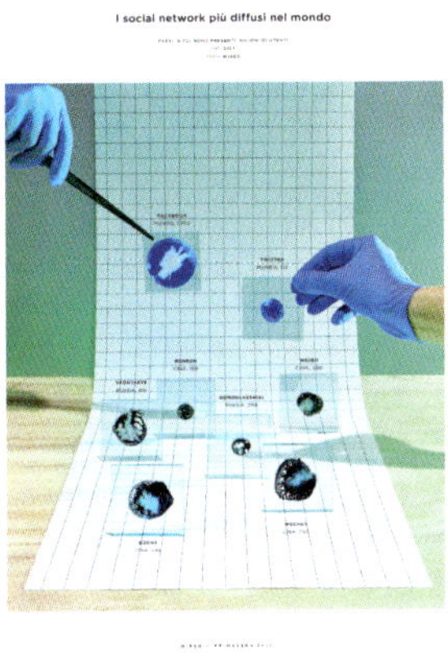

2017 · Raffinerie · CH · Poster

2017 · Götz Gramlich · DE · Packaging

2017 · La Tigre · IT · Information graphics

2017 · Milkxhake · HK · Poster

2017 · Gavillet & Cie · CH · Book

2018

The poster project **Footb-All Mix** is initiated by Felipe Taborda and Susana Machicao to celebrate the soccer World Cup in Russia

Greg Durrell's film **Design Canada** is released

2018 · Chermayeff & Geismar & Haviv · US · Logo · US Open

2018 · Koto · UK · Logo · BlaBlaCar

2018 · Vladimir Lifanov, Ilya Lazuchenkov, Egor Myznik, Denis Shlesberg, Erken Kagarov · RU · Logo · Tourism Russia

2018 · Craig & Karl, David Whitmore (AD) · US/UK · Magazine cover

2018 · Neville Brody · UK · Poster

2018 · Commission, Bureau Borsche · UK/DE · Identity · Rimowa

2018 · OCD · US · Magazine cover and spread

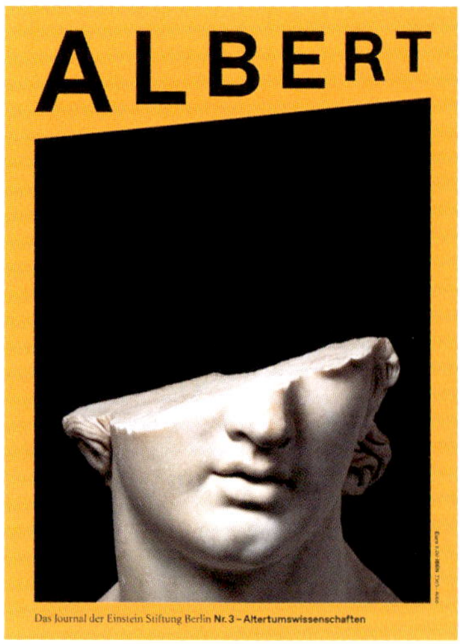

2018 · Fons Hickmann m23 · DE · Magazine cover

The exhibition **Design Studio** examines the creative design process at the Museum für Gestaltung in Zurich

2018 · Wolff Olins, Agence Zélé (signage) · UK/FR · Identity · Lafayette Anticipations

2018 · Louis Byrne · UK · Record cover

2018 · Lufthansa Design, Martin et Karczinski · DE · Identity · Lufthansa

2016 · Edel Rodriguez, P.W. Pine (AD) · CU/US · Magazine covers

2016 · Edel Rodriguez · CU/US/DE · Magazine cover

2017 · Edel Rodriguez · CU/US/DE · Magazine cover

2017 · Edel Rodriguez · CU/US/DE · Magazine cover

2017 · Edel Rodriguez · CU/US/DE · Magazine cover

2017 · Edel Rodriguez · CU/US · Magazine cover

2017 · Edel Rodriguez · CU/US/DE · Magazine cover

»My work encourages people who are a little afraid. When they see what I do, and all the stuff that comes at me, they might say, 'Wow, that guy has some guts. Maybe I should get some too.'«
`Edel Rodriquez, huffingtonpost.com, 2017`

2017 · Edel Rodriguez · CU/US/DE · Magazine cover

2017 · Edel Rodriguez · CU/US · Magazine cover

Edel Rodriguez (1971, Havana) is a Cuban-American artist and illustrator who rose to fame as a graphic designer with his political magazine covers. He studied painting at New York's Pratt Institute and received his Master's degree in 1998 from the city's Hunter College. As well as working as a freelance artist, Rodriguez has also worked as an illustrator for publishing houses and magazines, and during the 2016 U.S. election campaign he was commissioned by *Time* to design a cover depicting the presidential candidate Donald Trump. This much-admired "Meltdown" design attracted international attention and brought him many more assignments on the same subject.

Edel Rodriguez (1971, Havanna) ist ein kubanisch-amerikanischer Künstler und Illustrator, der im Bereich des Grafikdesigns mit politischen Illustrationen für Zeitschriftencover auf sich aufmerksam machte. Rodriguez studierte Malerei am Pratt Institute und erhielt seinen Master 1998 am Hunter College in New York. Neben seiner freien künstlerischen Arbeit war er parallel als Illustrator für Verlage und Zeitschriften aktiv. Im US-Wahlkampf 2016 beauftragte ihn das *Time* Magazine mit dem Entwurf eines Covers zum Präsidentschaftskandidaten Trump. Das viel beachtete „Meltdown"-Cover sorgte für internationale Aufmerksamkeit und brachte ihm zahlreiche weitere Aufträge zum Thema ein.

Edel Rodriguez (1971, La Havane) est un artiste et illustrateur cubano-américain qui s'est fait remarquer dans le domaine du graphisme par ses couvertures politiques de magazines. Il a suivi ses études de peinture à l'Institut Pratt et obtenu un master en 1998 au Hunter College à New York. À côté de son travail d'artiste indépendant, il a exercé comme illustrateur pour des maisons d'édition et des magazines. Pendant la campagne présidentielle de 2016, le magazine *Time* l'a chargé d'un projet d'illustration du candidat à la présidence Trump. La très remarquée couverture «Meltdown» a attiré l'attention internationale sur Rodriguez et lui a valu de nombreuses autres commandes sur le même thème.

2018 · Edel Rodriguez · CU/US/DE · Magazine cover

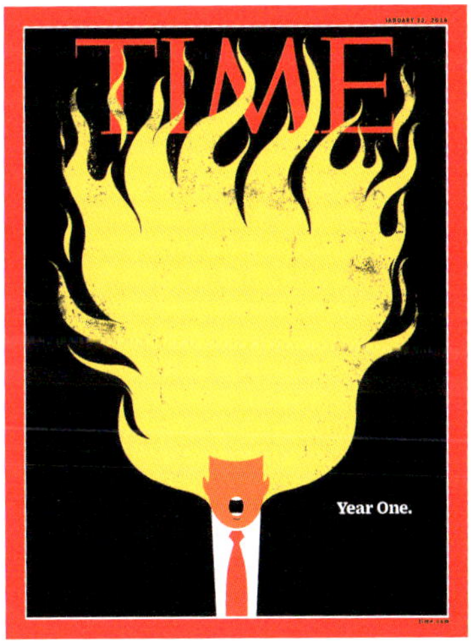

2018 · Edel Rodriguez · CU/US · Magazine cover

2019

The 100th anniversary of the **Bauhaus** is celebrated with events, publications, and exhibitions around the globe

BDG, the trade association of German graphic designers, celebrates its 100th anniversary

2019 · Snøhetta · US · Logo · Vy (Norwegian State Railways)

NAMU NATIONAL ART MUSEUM OF UKRAINE

2019 · Banda · UA · Logo · NAMU National Museum of Ukraine

Techniek Nederland

2019 · Lava · NL · Logo · Techniek Nederland

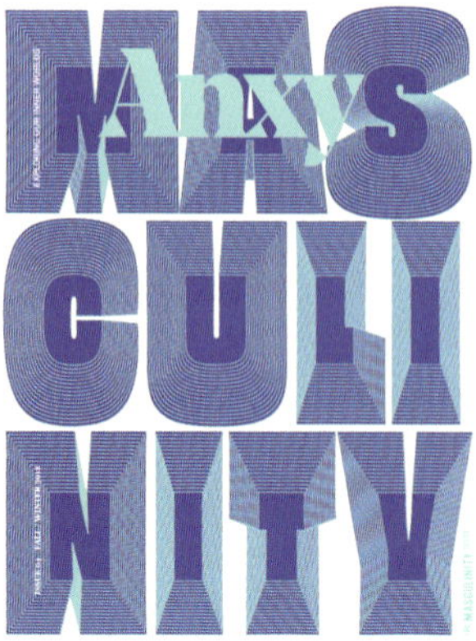

2019 · Indhira Rojas (AD), Anagraph · US · Magazine cover

2019 · Malika Favre · FR/US · Magazine cover

2019 · Neo Neo, Xavier Erni, Thuy-An Hoang · CH · Brochure cover

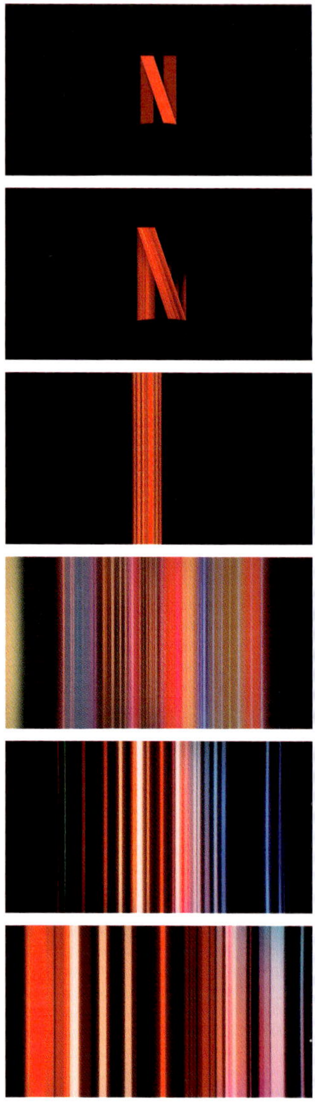

2019 · Imaginary Forces · US · Opening titles • Netflix

Researchers at Maastricht University present a system driven by **artificial intelligence** which is capable of synthesizing logo designs

The **Poster House** museum opens in New York

2019 · Serge Ricco · FR · Magazine spreads

2019 · Daniel Wiesmann · DE · Corporate design · Kieler Woche 2019

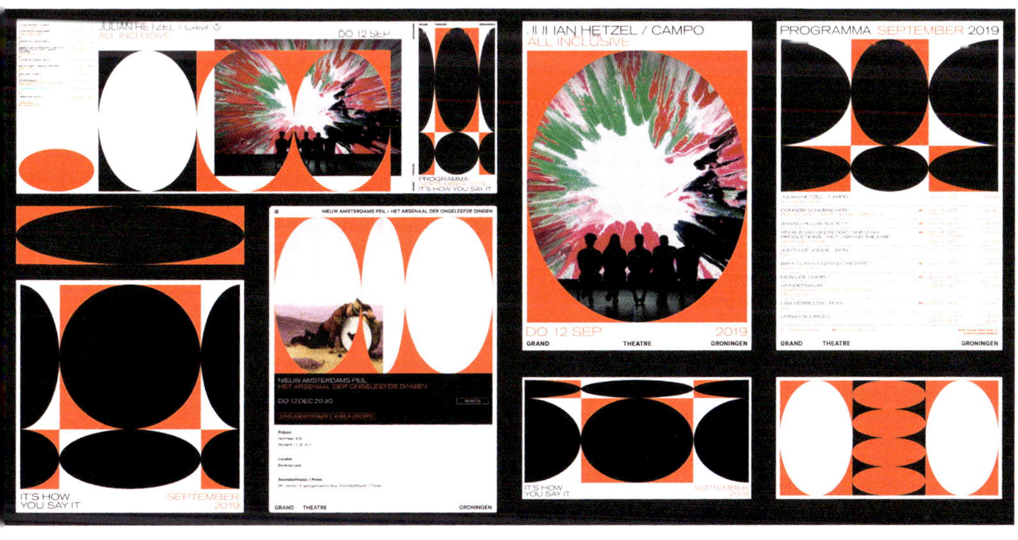

2019 · Studio Lennarts & de Bruijn · NL · Corporate design · Grand Theatre Groningen

INDEX

IMPRINT

EACH AND EVERY TASCHEN BOOK PLANTS A SEED!
Each year, we offset our annual carbon emissions with carbon credits at the Instituto Terra, a reforestation program in Minas Gerais, Brazil, founded by Lélia and Sebastião Salgado. To find out more about this ecological partnership, please check: www.taschen.com/institutoterra.
Inspiration: unlimited.
Carbon footprint: (almost) zero.

Want to see more? Visit taschen.com to view our current publications, browse our latest magazine, and subscribe to our newsletter.

Hohenzollernring 53
D-50672 Köln
www.taschen.com

Design
Jens Müller/vista
www.studiovista.de

English Translation
Isabel Varea-Riley

German Translation
Ursula Wulfekamp

French Translation
Wolf Fruhtrunk

Printed in
Bosnia-Herzegovina
ISBN 978-3-8365-8806-5

Acknowledgements
The making of this book has truly turned out to be a journey round the world and through time as well. My first thanks go to the many, many supporters of this project in all parts of the globe, who have so generously shared their knowledge and materials. When TASCHEN approached me with the idea of producing a general book on the international history of graphic design it seemed like a virtually impossible task. However, under the lead of Julius Wiedemann and in close association with his experienced team of Nora Dohrmann and Daniel Siciliano Brêtas, the concept was developed and made into a reality. My heartfelt thanks go out to these three for their never-ending passion and enthusiasm throughout the production of this book. Big thanks must also go to the translators, copyeditors, and proofreaders who have been involved in working on the text, and especially to the production team at TASCHEN. I would also like to thank my studio colleagues Andreas Magino, Friederike Spielmannleitner, and Janine Uhlke, Esther Jakob, and Valeria Sava for their long-standing hard work and support. Last but not least my very personal thanks go to my partner Katharina Sussek for her invaluable judgment and encouragement, and for continuing to bring joy and love to my life.

Jens Müller

dedicated to helmut schmid (1942–2018)
teacher, inspirer, and friend

Picture Credits

Bass, Saul © Saul Bass Estate; Bayer, Herbert © VG Bild-Kunst, Bonn 2026; Bernhard, Lucian © VG Bild-Kunst, Bonn 2026; Birkhäuser, Peter © Birkhäuser-Oeri Foundation; Brownjohn, Chermayeff & Geismar © Chermayeff & Geismar & Haviv; Byrne, Louis © courtesy of Domino Recording Co Ltd (p.499); Cassandre, A. M. © & ™. Mouron. Cassandre. Lic 2017-13-09-01 www.cassandre.fr; Distéfano, Juan Carlos © Fundación IDA/Fondo Instituto Torcuato Di Tella; Dudovich, Marcello © Olivetti S.p.A.; *Endless Summer* © Bruce Brown Films, LLC; Flora, Jim © Jim Flora Art LLC.; *Game of Thrones* © courtesy of Home Box Office; Games, Abram © Estate of Abram Games; Getty Images (p.087); Ghent University Library: Faivre, Jules Abel (p.071); Giménez, Edgardo © Fundación IDA/Fondo Instituto Torcuato Di Tella; *Harper's Bazaar* © Hearst Communication, Inc.; Hausmann, Raoul © VG Bild-Kunst, Bonn 2026; Heartfield, John © The Heartfield Community of Heirs/VG Bild-Kunst, Bonn 2026; Henrion, F. H. K. © Marion Henrion-Wesel; Him, George © Estate of George Him; Hofmann, Armin © Estate of Armin Hofmann; Horst, Horst P. © Condé Nast Collection/Getty Images; Kahn, Fritz © Kosmos/von Debschitz; Kokoschka, Oskar © Fondation Oskar Kokoschka/VG Bild-Kunst, Bonn 2026; Lamm, Lora © Museum für Gestaltung; Lewitt, Jan © Estate of Jan Le Witt; Lois, George, *Covering the 60's: George Lois, the* Esquire *Era*. New York: The Monacelli Press, 1996 © 1996 George Lois (p.304); Lustig, Alvin © Estate of Elaine Lustig Cohen; *Mad Men* © Lions Gate Television, Inc. Lionsgate/Weiner/American Movie Classics; Mucha, Alphonse © Mucha Trust 2017; Neuburg, Hans © Museum für Gestaltung; Pedroza, Gustavo, Estudio MMB © courtesy of Fundación IDA; Pintori, Giovanni © Olivetti S.p.A.; Poster Photo Archives, Posters Please, Inc., New York: anonymous (p.097) / Bonelli, J. (p.201) / Briedé, Johan (p.105) / Dlugach, Mikhail (p.144) / Havas (p.208) / Mahlau, Alfred (p.148) / Matejko, Theo (p.182) / Matter, Herbert (pp.172–173); Rodchenko, Alexander © VG Bild-Kunst, Bonn 2026; Rodrigues, Sebastião © Biblioteca Silva, Lisboa; SLUB Dresden/ Deutsche Fotothek (p.155); Smiling Sun logo © Anne Lund / © OOA Fonden, smilingsun.org (p.336); © Subafilms Ltd (p.306); © Wolfgang Stahr (profile picture, p.363); Steinweiss, Alex © Estate of Alex Steinweiss; Stenberg, Vladimir © VG Bild-Kunst, Bonn 2026; Stoecklin, Niklaus © VG Bild-Kunst, Bonn 2026; Tschichold, Jan © Estate of Jan Tschichold; Undated billboard (AAA0613) Outdoor Advertising Association of America, Inc., David M. Rubenstein Rare Book and Manuscript Library, Duke University (p.057); Viera, Mary © Isisuf, Archivio Belloli-Vieira, Milan, Italy; Wilson, Wes © Wes Wilson; Wyman, Lance © Lance Wyman.

1920s · "PUM" · AR · Poster

1960 · Kees van Roemburg · NL · Poster

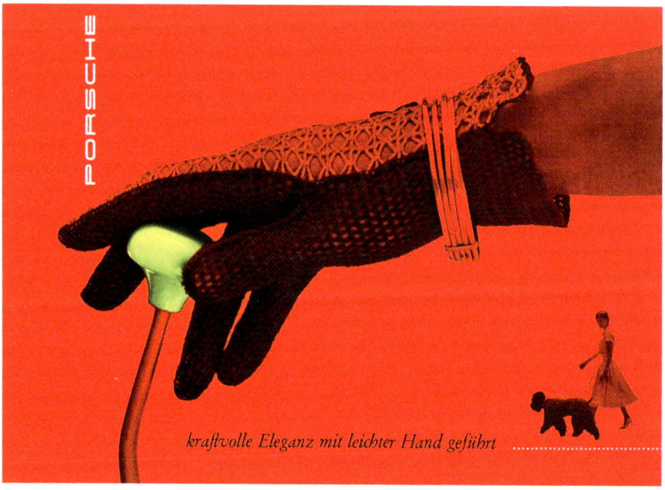

1958 · Hanns Lohrer · DE · Brochure cover

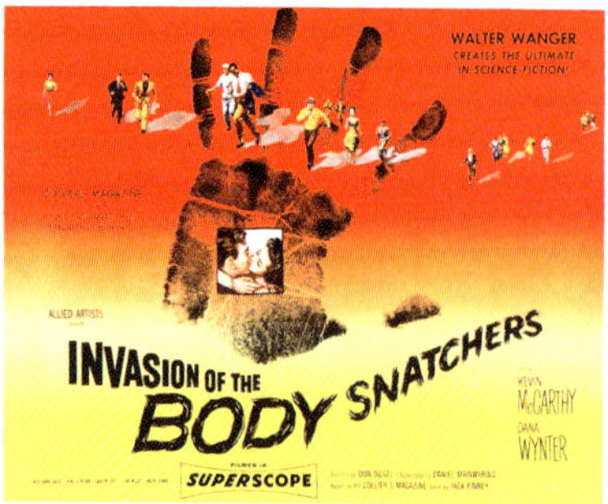

1956 · Anonymous · US · Poster

1952 · Gerd Leufert · VZ · Logo · Venezuelan Supply